"Sick of the scale being the boss of me, I needed a different voice in my head. Then I stumbled upon Wendy's 40-Day Sugar Fast, and suddenly the spiritual connection between food, my heart, and God clicked for me. I started to see food as less of a reward or a temptation and more of a means to align my heart back with God's. Food, like all of His good gifts, should always point us back to the Giver. It shouldn't accuse us or guilt us. It should simply remind us what we need to sustain us. This shift in thinking has taken me forty days and beyond. And I'm so grateful for the mental overhaul more than any pounds lost. More than anything I want to be able to say with Jesus, 'My food is to do the will of him who sent me' (John 4:34). And traveling with Wendy and the 40-Day Sugar Fast community was the beginning of that journey for me."

Lisa-Jo Baker, bestselling author of *Meet Me in the Middle,*
Never Unfriended, and *Surprised by Motherhood*

"If Wendy is leading, I want to follow. This woman is exceptionally wise with an impressive earnestness for leading people to the feet of Jesus. She is a highly respected mentor and communicator with a passion for pointing people to what matters most. Wendy is much more than a writer who can string a bunch of nice words on the page. Her words bring real results."

Jennifer Dukes Lee, author of *The Happiness Dare* and *Love Idol*

"We all want freedom. We want to break free from habits that haunt us, voices that taunt us, chains that bind us, and emotions that blind us. Wendy's onto something huge here! She speaks with depth and authority from the Word of God, and she knows that the emancipation we're all really longing for is actually a person: Jesus. *The 40-Day Sugar Fast* helps each participant experience meaningful growth and lasting peace, as it ushers them to a fresh, personal, and satisfying banquet with the One who longs to be their portion."

Gwen Smith, cofounder of Girlfriends in God and author of
I Want It All and *Broken into Beautiful*

"To fast from what we crave in order to find sustaining satisfaction in God is a message for this clamoring culture. And it's a message for me. Wendy's words are for every one of us whose reach for sugar is never enough."

Sara Hagerty, bestselling author of *Unseen*

"Each day of Wendy Speake's book *The 40-Day Sugar Fast* shifted my cravings for sweets to the sweet words of Jesus. I couldn't have broken the stronghold of sugar without Wendy's gracious and wise influence in every chapter. A life-changing book to be read over and over again!"

Amber Lia, bestselling coauthor of *Triggers* and *Parenting Scripts*

"Too many Christian women today feel trapped by sugar cravings and addiction, wondering if they'll ever break free. Through her annual 40-Day Sugar Fast, Wendy has offered thousands of women, myself included, the opportunity to taste the sweetness of Jesus and experience His bondage-breaking power in their lives. Truly, freedom and fullness are found only in Jesus's presence, and Wendy has proven herself a worthy guide year after year."

Asheritah Ciuciu, author of *Full*

"I have to share a praise report. I believe that my addiction to sugar is gone for good! I can't believe it's been two years since I last fasted with Wendy and my cravings are not back. God really changed my perspective about sugar and food during those forty days. I did this fast three years in a row, but that time there was real and lasting change! I'm reminded of how Elijah kept going back and looking for rain, and finally he saw a little cloud and then the rain!"

Amy J. Bennett, founder of Abiding Ministries and host of the podcast *Feathers*

"Wendy Speake is gifted at capturing biblical truth in profoundly relevant ways to help us discover new ways of thinking about not only sugar and our addiction to it but also the strongholds that keep us from experiencing the fullness of God's presence in our lives. If you're ready to fast from sugar so that you can feast on more of God's Word, *The 40-Day Sugar Fast* is for you."

Elisa Pulliam, biblical transformation and wellness coach at MoreToBe.com and ItIsWell.us

40-Day Sugar Fast Testimonials

"Every day for forty days, I said, *Jesus, I need You. You are enough.* That prayer changed my life."

Chanda T., CA

"I am teary just thinking of where I am now compared to forty days ago. I am twenty-nine pounds lighter, my skin and mind are clearer, and (most importantly) I am closer to my one true love, Jesus. He was so good to me during this fast. I have never been able to resist sugar before. And yet, I have not missed it. Oh how He loves me!"

Lynn K., MA

"It's been years since I've gone more than three days without chocolate. I knew this fast was something I needed to do. Chocolate made days doable. Now, I'm learning Jesus makes days doable. And livable. And abundantly full."

Kristin G., TN

"Fasting has unlocked so many doors inside my heart that were closed off for far too long. I have a long way to go with some of the things God has revealed, but for the first time, I feel equipped. I feel ready to put on the full armor, step out onto the battlefield, and fight the good fight. Thank you, Wendy."

Barbara N., MI

"Over these forty days it has been refreshing to not run to sweets every time something went wrong. Since I didn't run to sweets first, Bible verses came to mind when I needed them—at the most appropriate times, in a way I hadn't experienced before. God faithfully showed me that He has been there waiting for me to simply seek Him. I feel like this is just the beginning—I feel that God broke strongholds I've lived with for so many years."

Beth I., CA

"Day 40 of this sugar fast is not the end for me! I have hope and faith that when this is all over, because I have fed on Jesus, I will not ever revert back to my old ways."

Hannah S., Australia

"What an absolute blessing this fast has been for me. I'm sugar FREE!"

Ronda M., CA

"This sugar fast is a direct answer to prayer!"

Anne Marie L., CA

"This has been an amazing journey. The thing I'm most grateful for is that I am walking away with a more intense desire to let Jesus fill my cravings with His Word and not relying on my sweet tooth."

Kyla N., PA

"I fought God so much about my sugar, coffee, TV, and social media . . . yet I've given them up and I don't miss them because I have found true satisfaction in Him. My prayer these forty days has been, *Lord, I don't want to go back to the same person I used to be. I want to continue to know You more, daily. I need You to satisfy my soul.*"

Kris D., TX

"God has been so present these forty days. I am beyond grateful. He has been so alive in me and has taken another sin-struggle and helped me through. I could never have done this on my own. I am going to continue feasting on the Lord!"

Michelle O., MI

"I admit that I originally wanted to do the 40-Day Sugar Fast to streamline my dieting process. However, I quickly learned God had so much more in store for me. He called me to Himself in ways I've never experienced before. I get fasting now. I didn't before. I understand why God calls us to it and asks us to rid ourselves of physical desires so we can turn our hearts to Him."

Megan S., CO

"Amazing! I felt led to do the 40-Day Sugar Fast because I needed to quit sugar. Little did I know all the transformation that God had in store for me."

Ashley T., FL

"My skin is less wrinkled and broken out. My stomach has flattened a bit. But internally, I finally feel at peace. I'm not chasing all the things. And it feels so good."

Jaymie M., IL

"I came to this sugar fast specifically as a way to intercede for my family. First, I asked God to heal my two-year-old son, so that he can live without a feeding tube. Second, I needed God to redeem my marriage. Here's the praise: halfway through this fast, my son was taken off the feeding tube, and by the end of the fast, he was gaining weight. And my husband and I are in a good place together! My tummy is a little empty, but my heart is so full!"

Whitnee M., AR

THE 40-DAY

Sugar Fast

WHERE PHYSICAL DETOX MEETS
SPIRITUAL TRANSFORMATION

WENDY SPEAKE

BakerBooks

a division of Baker Publishing Group
Grand Rapids, Michigan

Published by Baker Books
a division of Baker Publishing Group
PO Box 6287, Grand Rapids, MI 49516-6287
www.bakerbooks.com

Printed in the United States of America

Library of Congress Cataloging-in-Publication Data
Names: Speake, Wendy, 1974– author.
Title: The 40-day sugar fast : where physical detox meets spiritual transformation / Wendy Speake.
Description: Grand Rapids : Baker Books, 2019.
Identifiers: LCCN 2019017286 | ISBN 9780801094576 (paperback)
Subjects: LCSH: Sugar-free diet. | Detoxification (Health) | Food—Sugar content.
Classification: LCC RM237.85 S67 2019 | DDC 613.2/8332—dc23
LC record available at https://lccn.loc.gov/2019017286

ISBN 978-1-5409-0111-8 (hardcover)

The Author is represented by the William K Jensen Literary Agency.

20   21   22   23   24   25   26   12   11   10   9   8   7   6

green press INITIATIVE

To the women who joined me online for the first sugar fast five years ago—I didn't feel equipped to lead, still you followed me as I followed Jesus. He's brought us a long way since then! Our diets have changed but our lives have changed even more. This book is dedicated to you and to the One we followed together in those first forty days.

Open your mouth and taste,
open your eyes and see—how good GOD is.
Blessed are you who run to him.

Psalm 34:8 MSG

Contents

Foreword

DO YOU LOVE ME MORE THAN SUGAR?

That thought startled me out of my reverie. What kind of a question was that?! Of course I loved Jesus. I grew up in church, surrendered my life to Him at the age of five, and have faithfully served Him ever since. I have loved Jesus as far back as I can remember.

But if you'd have to give up sugar—for the rest of your life—would you do it? This new thought threw me. Now why would I do that?

Would you choose Jesus over sugar? The questions pelted me like an unwelcome hailstorm.

This was getting out of hand. Of course I'd choose Jesus. I'd given my life to Jesus! I'd die for Him!

Then why are you running to cookies instead of running to the cross? Why do you seek solace in a pint of ice cream rather than the Prince of Peace? Why are you feasting on warm bread rolls instead of the Bread of Life?

Ouch.

My life slowly came into focus, scenes from past binges flashed before me. I slowly realized that with my mouth I confessed one thing as true, but my eating habits revealed another truth entirely.

Sugar was my savior, not Jesus.

My heart broke in two.

"What do I do?" I cried out to the empty sunroom. The sunbeams streamed through billowy curtains as despair overran my soul. My eyes fell to the paragraph I had underlined just moments before those daunting questions first came to my mind. This time I read more slowly.

> If you don't feel strong desires for the manifestation of the glory of God, it is not because you have drunk deeply and are satisfied. It is because you have nibbled so long at the table of the world. Your soul is stuffed with small things, and there is no room for the great. God did not create you for this. There is an appetite for God. And it can be awakened. I invite you to turn from the dulling effects of food and the dangers of idolatry, and to say with some simple fast: "This much, O God, I want you."[1]

This much, oh God. This much.

. . . As much as I crave my morning mocha.

. . . As much as I desire a second serving of pie.

. . . As much as I anticipate the taste of my next sugar fix.

That much? No. If I was being honest, I didn't desire God that much. But I wanted to.

"Help me want You more," I wrote in my journal that day. "Stir in me a hunger for You." That's when the Spirit began piercing my soul with His convicting questions, not to heap condemnation but to lead to inner transformation. His invitation to me was clear: a forty-day fast from sugar to break the stronghold it had become in my life and train my affection on Christ alone.

I drew in a shaky breath and agreed.

A few days into my sugar fast, withdrawal hit me hard. What had I done? What was I thinking? This was crazy! Not only had my sugar cravings intensified but a hidden part of me had surfaced that I had never seen before. I was irritable, impatient, and intent on getting my way. I snapped at anyone who so much as looked at me the wrong way.

All I could think about was sugar: donuts, milkshakes, creamer, cookies, instant oatmeal . . . even ketchup. Sugar was everywhere, and I was craving it with reckless abandon, much like a drug addict. The pull toward sweets seemed magnetic.

"I'm not going to make it," I confessed under my breath when a coworker brought cookies to share at work. "I can't do this anymore."

But God, being rich in mercy, provided just what I needed. I learned that an online friend was leading a sugar fast—oh the "coincidences" that come when we learn to trust Him!—and I immediately signed up to join her, eager for the community and accountability.

Wendy proved a trustworthy companion. Gentle yet firm, she redirected my gaze away from my momentary sacrifice to fix my eyes on the grand prize. Not skinnier thighs or a healthier thyroid, not glowing skin or grounded emotions. No. These may have occurred, but my reward was Jesus.

Jesus.

He is enough. And in fasting from the small things of this world, like sugar, we invite Him to awaken in us a hunger for Him. "He satisfies the longing soul, and the hungry soul he fills with good things" (Psalm 107:9)—yes, even with Himself.

Those forty days with Wendy taught me that I didn't really have a sugar issue after all—I had a heart issue. Jesus wants our undivided, unadulterated affection. He wants us to love Him with all our hearts, all our souls, all our minds, and all our strength (Mark 12:30). All of us. Everything. Every last molecule crying out for more of Him. And when we beg Jesus to lead us to that place of longing, He will gladly satisfy us with the very best He has to offer—Himself.

The enemy of our souls comes only to steal, kill, and destroy, and he often uses sugar addiction to cripple us spiritually, emotionally, and physically. But Jesus has overcome, and He offers us the full life found in Him alone (John 10:10).

That first fast became the battleground where I discovered the truths I share in my book *Full: Food, Jesus, and the Battle for Satisfaction.* Over the years that followed, Wendy graciously invited me to join her in leading the 40-Day Sugar Fast, and together we have seen thousands of women encounter the freedom and fullness found in Jesus when we give Him everything—even our sugar addiction.

This journey will not be easy, friends, but it is so worth it because Jesus is our satisfaction and He is our reward.

Better even than chocolate cake?

Oh, yes. Come and see.

Asheritah Ciuciu, author of *Full: Food,
Jesus, and the Battle for Satisfaction*

Before You Fast

"MY NAME IS WENDY AND I'M A SUGAR ADDICT."
Those nine little words changed the trajectory of my life when I posted them online in 2014. Innocently, I invited people on my Facebook page to join me for a 40-Day Sugar Fast. I wasn't simply having a problem with sugar, I told my friends, I was experiencing physical and emotional problems too. My sugar tooth was dictating my thoughts and my days. On top of that, constant neck pain and stomachaches plagued me. I was gaining weight, my muscles and joints were always hurting, my sleep was fitful, and my emotions were a wreck. I was grumpy, tired, and impatient with my kids and my husband. Sadly, sugar wasn't making me sweet. I didn't need any more conviction, what I needed was transformation. I needed more than another diet; I needed something deep within me to change.

The response to my online invitation was overwhelming. "Me too," they cried. "Yes!" they affirmed. "My name is Melissa . . . My name is Alexis . . . My name is John . . . My name is Jenn . . . and I'm a sugar addict." There's something about sugar that has a grip on us, and we know it. We run to sugar for our comfort and our reward. We turn to it in boredom. We depend on it when life is stressful. We crave it when we're depressed and use it as confectionary therapy. And even when life is at its best, we celebrate with cake.

We've been running to sweet snacks to get us through our days for far too long. It's become a habit. No, worse than that, it's become an *addiction*. And addiction works much like a prison. We're unable to break out of the bars and the bondage that hold us back from health and wholeness. Men and women the world over have traded their freedom—along with their health—for sugary shackles, and they're so ashamed.

If that's you, if you are feeling powerless over your addiction to sugar, if you have lost sight of God's power in your life, know that you are not beyond redemption. **Fad diets and workout routines can't set you free, but God can.** Sugar is everywhere but so is He. What would you be willing to give up in order to gain the powerful presence of God in your life? With His help you can be set free—free from your shame, free from your cravings, free from your addiction.

Fasting is merely denying yourself something temporal and ordinary in order to experience the One who is eternally extraordinary.

Join me for this forty-day journey to food freedom, faith, and the discovery that He is enough. Lay down sugar so that you might taste and see His good and satisfying sweetness in your life. Fasting is merely denying yourself something temporal and ordinary in order to experience the One who is eternally extraordinary.

What This Book Is and Is Not

Before you turn another page, let me clarify what this book is and what it is not. It isn't a scientific source recounting the evils of sugar; there are plenty of books that do that. Nor is this a diet book or a collection of recipes. While I love to cook and share some of my favorite meals with others, I am not a nutritionist. I am simply a Jesus-hungry woman who is passionate about turning hungry hearts toward the only One who can ever truly satisfy.

Are you a binge eater? A secret eater? An emotional eater? Tell the Lord all the reasons why you can't go forty days without sugar, and let Him show you that with Him it's possible (Matt. 19:26). Over the course of these next few weeks, as you stop cramming food and other fillers into the hurts and holes of your life, the power of Christ will fill each empty place with His peace. He will make you whole.

Nutritionists and diet experts encourage us to "crowd out sugar" by eating plenty of delicious and nutritious foods. I love that idea and have used the same technique in my own eating habits. However, the purpose of the 40-Day Sugar Fast isn't just physical detox; the goal is spiritual transformation. Not only will we be fasting from sugary sweets, we'll also be fasting from all the things we turn to instead of Him. The 40-Day Sugar Fast is primarily a spiritual fast, so the main way we will "crowd out sugar" is by intentionally turning to the Lord and consuming His living Word instead. We are focusing on taking in more of Him and less of the things that don't make us more like Him.

We suffer spiritually each time we reach for a sugar high rather than the Most High. Our sugar fixation stops us from fixing our eyes on Jesus, and hungering for sweet treats gets in the way of our hunger and thirst for Him. **The goal of this fast isn't that you will begin to choose healthy food options; it's that you will come to see Christ as the only option.** The more you ingest of Him, the less hungry you will be for the things you once craved. **We're fasting from sugar so that we might feast now. This is how we crowd the sugar out.**

Think of this book as a daily companion to help you do just that. Each day's reading is packed with Scripture and application so that you might feast on God's Word in lieu of the world's sweetest fare. Ingesting sugar might not make us sweet but consuming Him certainly does. Sweet and satisfied and stable. Physically, spiritually, and emotionally so.

We're fasting from sugar so that we might feast now. This is how we crowd the sugar out.

If you want His peace, love, joy, and gentleness, and you're desperate for His self-control, turn to Him. Abide with Him. He's told us clearly, "Those who remain in me, and I in them, will produce much fruit. For apart from me you can do nothing" (John 15:5 NLT).

The 40-Day Sugar Fast is for those who are sugar-dependent but long to be dependent on God. You've tried to muscle through and grab hold of self-control—and all the other fruits of God's Spirit—on your own, but it doesn't work that way. **Abide in Him, consume Him, and His fruit will consume you and transform you.**

How to Begin

Perhaps you're convinced that this fast is what you need, but you don't know where to begin or what to expect. I understand. But don't worry, it's quite simple.

Make a commitment to join me in saying no to refined sugars for forty days. No sugary snacks, baked goods, ice cream treats, sweet coffee creamers, sodas, candies, and so on. Nothing that includes refined sugar or high-fructose corn syrup. From there, the specifics are up to you. Some people choose to avoid all forms of sugar, while others use limited amounts of raw honey, maple syrup, and fresh fruit in their diets. Some keep Stevia, Erythritol, and monk fruit on hand, while others feel convicted to lay all sweeteners down during the fast. Many say no to the sneaky sugars hidden in marinades and condiments such as barbecue sauce, teriyaki sauce, and ketchup, but others don't. Plenty of people cut all simple carbs from their diet as well, along with alcohol and anything else that turns to sugar in the gut. You'll need to make some choices before you begin.

Take a day or two to pray before you fast. Ask God to show you what your fast should look like. You're not putting on a show for anyone else. Privately seek His will for your private fast. What will work best for you and your family may be different from what will work for me and my family. **Ask God to speak to you about anything in your kitchen that you're running to in a frenzied or habitual attempt to satisfy your soul's deep hunger and then give it to Him as an offering.** Maybe He will lead you to simply stop eating donuts, drinking mochas, and grabbing an afternoon Snickers bar and late night bowl of ice cream. Or perhaps He will speak to you about the alcohol in your cupboard that not only turns to sugar but can easily become a daily reward that you run to as soon as it's five o'clock somewhere.

Seek Him first before you fast. Tuck this Scripture-promise deep in your heart and frame it on your kitchen counter: "But seek first the kingdom of God and his righteousness, and all these things will be added to you" (Matt. 6:33).

Seek Him daily as you fast, filling yourself with more of Him and His righteousness, and you will likely drop pounds. But that is just a by-product of something weightier still. While your weight may decrease, your faith will increase and God's power will begin to flow in your life again. **Fasting from physical food increases one's spiritual hunger, and that's the hunger that** leads not only to a transformed body but also to a transformed life. When we empty ourselves and ask Him to fill us, He does. When we are at our weakest, His strength is most evident. When we don't know what we're doing, He does it all. When God sets us free from the strongholds in our lives, we're free to experience His strong hold.

I'm excited to journey through the next forty days with you. Let's kick this sugar fast off with a prayer, because communicating with God is what turns this physical fast into a spiritual one.

Dear Lord, nothing has worked to set me free from the compulsive way I turn to sugar when I could be turning to You. Before I even begin this fast, I know I need more of You and less of the stuff that leaves me hungry. Take all the refined sugars I'm laying down and teach me to lean into Your gentle refining. Take my life as I empty it out and fill me with Yourself. Your Word proclaims: "It is for freedom that Christ has set you free." I'm choosing to believe that's true. Set me free! In the bondage-breaking, freedom-giving, sweet, sweet name of Jesus, Amen.

Guidelines

YOU HAVE MADE A COMMITMENT to say no to all your sugary sweet treats for the next forty days. Nothing made with sugar. No soda or syrupy drinks. No ice cream, donuts, pancakes, cake, or Peanut M&M's. Nothing containing sugar or high-fructose corn syrup. Beyond that, it's between you and the Lord. Take the details of this fast to Him in prayer. Should you keep fresh fruit in your diet? How about natural sweeteners such as raw honey and maple syrup? Since breads and pastas are broken down into glucose by your body and cause an increase in blood-sugar levels, many people choose to fast from them as well. Talk it through with the Lord, and make a plan before you fast.

What You Can Eat

Before you fill your heart, you have to empty your heart of what has been filling it. The same is true in your kitchen.

This book doesn't focus on what you can eat because the goal of this fast is that you increase your devotion to God—not your devotion to sugar-free foods. Rather than substituting one treat for another, allow yourself to go hungry. Treat yourself to more of God in lieu of food. You are fasting so that you might learn to feast on Him. **Don't simply switch your obsession with sugar for a sugar-free obsession—obsess over the One who** cares more about transforming your life than transforming your diet.

I realize that you may need a little practical help as you prepare your pantry, stock your fridge, and learn to prep meals as you fast and pray. Here are some ideas to get you started.

1. *Take a moment to remove all the high-in-sugar and highly processed items in your pantry and refrigerator.* Simply bag them up and hide them from sight. Better yet, give them away. It may feel like you're throwing away money but think of it as trashing temptation.

   Don't forget your special stash of chocolate. Our favorite sweets are often the hardest to toss. Start there. Don't put them in the freezer to keep, put them in the trash to lose. It's possible that when you finish forty days of fasting from sugar, your whole outlook on what you eat and how you eat and why you eat will have changed. If you go back to the old treats on day 41, you'll find yourself right back where you started. **Toss the temptation before you're tempted.**

2. *Stock your pantry and fridge with healthy food options.* Here are some of my favorite foods to keep on hand as I fast from sugar.

   Pantry:
   Raw nuts
   Nut butters
   Unsweetened, dried fruit
   Unsweetened coconut flakes
   Chia, flax, and sunflower seeds
   Dehydrated veggie chips
   Lara or RX bars

Beef sticks and beef jerky

Oatmeal and sugar-free granola

Olive oil, avocado oil, coconut oil, and ghee

Balsamic vinegar, rice vinegar, and apple cider vinegar

Salt, pepper, herbes de Provence, and other spices to keep veggies and meats tasting good (and not the same night after night)

Fridge:

Precooked rotisserie chicken

Plenty of poultry, fish, and beef

Sandwich meat and cheese

Eggs (hard boil a few)

Seasonal vegetables (leafy green lettuce such as spinach and kale, eggplants, broccoli, asparagus, brussels sprouts, tomatoes, cauliflower, and squash)

Seasonal fruits in moderation (raspberries, strawberries, blueberries, kiwis, lemons, grapefruit, green apples, grapefruit, and watermelon)

Avocadoes

Hummus

Pesto

Sparkling water and herbal tea

3. *Take the time to do some meal planning.* I like to prep a couple of large batches of my favorite meals each week so that I'm not obsessing about food as I fast. This isn't the time to become the world's best sugar-free cook. You want to keep your focus on fasting from sugar, not

transfer your focus to sugar-free cooking. **Keep it simple so that you can see that He is simply enough.** Here are a few (simple) favorites I like to keep on hand.

> Chili and soups
>
> Taco meat to add to salads
>
> Chicken salad (which is easy to take on the go)
>
> Large egg dish for a quick high-protein breakfast or snack

Find a few of my favorite recipes at 40daysugarfast.com.

4. *Avoid using sugar substitutes.* While I keep raw honey and Stevia on hand when I need to sweeten something for a family meal, I purposefully choose not to make sugar-free desserts when I fast from sugar. I hope that you will join me. We don't want to exchange our high-calorie addictions for sugar-free options; instead, we should grow to desperately crave Jesus as the only option. Remember, this fast is yours. Take the details to the Lord and ask Him to guide and convict you as you make your plan.

5. *Choose which day you will begin and then invite your family and friends to come along.* While fasting is a very private thing, accountability increases when you invite others to come into the intimate space of your prayer closet with you. You've welcomed guests around your table and served them the sweetest food you've had to share, but this experience is sweeter still. You'll be surprised how many of your family members and friends say yes to joining you!

ADDITIONAL RESOURCES

If you would like additional books to help you meal plan or better understand what is happening with you physiologically or spiritually as you fast and pray, check out appendix B at the back of the book for a list of suggested resources.

day 1

TASTE AND SEE

> Taste and see that the LORD is good;
>   blessed is the one who takes refuge in him.
> Fear the LORD, you his holy people,
>   for those who fear him lack nothing.
> The lions may grow weak and hungry,
>   but those who seek the LORD lack no good thing.
>
> Psalm 34:8–10 NIV

WHEN I WAS A YOUNG CHILD, I was all about the sugar. I craved candy with every fiber of my being. It was sweet and it was good and it was an exciting part of my weekly routine. Every Friday after school I got two dollars for my allowance, immediately hopped on my little pink bike—the kind with the white wicker basket—and pedaled to the corner store a few blocks away. My neighborhood friend Kerry had an equally impressive sweet tooth, so I'd swing by her house first. Together we'd go fill that basket with Cherry Bombs and Lemon Drops, strawberry Nerds, peach Jelly Bellies, sour apple Jolly Ranchers, Red Vines, and Reese's Peanut Butter Cups.

Walking into that corner store each week, the bell over the door announcing our arrival, was a happy ritual for me. Just thinking about it reminds me of the scents and makes my mouth water. I can even feel the thin, soft crinkle of the brown paper bag that the elderly Japanese man who owned the store put my candy into. I also remember how generous he was with the pennies he kept in an ashtray beside the register. If my purchase was ninety-one cents, he would take a penny from the dish and put it in the register with my dollar bill and hand me back a dime. Kerry and I would step out into the bright afternoon sunlight, jump on our bikes, and ride the cracked sidewalk back to one of our houses. Oh how we loved our sugar!

On the afternoons when I didn't have a nickel to my name, I would come home from school and scour the back of the refrigerator where my mom often hid the half-emptied tub of Betty Crocker's vanilla frosting. As I sat watching *Little House on the Prairie*, one spoonful from the tub would turn to two, then three, then four, until the tub was empty.

Since both of my parents worked, I had a key dangling from a shoestring around my neck. As a latchkey kid, I had plenty of time home alone to make some unhealthy habits for myself. Don't get me wrong; I'm not blaming my parents for my sugar addiction. There are plenty of kids who learned to stash their sugar in the bottom drawer of their desks, under lined paper and a collection of heart-shaped erasers, with Mom and Dad just down the hall.

Why am I sharing this with you? Because I need to remember where I came from and how I got here. You do too. The treats we loved and the memories we have tied to them have led many of us here today. We have loved our sweets for a long time, but we are finally ready to love God more. Though our sugar has been a faithful friend to us, we are eager to forge a new friendship with a faithful God, a God who promises to make things new for us. We're ready to build new memories—memories of turning to Him when we're happy and running to Him when we're sad. We've been running to the wrong things for far too long.

Perhaps you've read the Bible, and believed the promise that God is good, but how much better it will be to actually taste and see His goodness for yourself. That's the transformation we're after. However, it is absolutely possible to read the Bible, fast and pray, feel convicted, and still choose to remain unchanged. Transformation isn't automatic—you have to put God's Word into practice.

I know because that same little girl who rode her bike to the corner store on Friday would also sit in a pew on Sunday. Here's what I've discovered: Sunday morning messages don't always influence the everyday habits of our lives. We're told that God alone can save us, that He alone can satisfy us, that we can taste and see His sweetness and ingest Him as our daily bread . . . but then we hop on our metaphorical little pink bikes and pedal our way to the store or to anything else that promises to fill our baskets, our hearts, and our lives.

It is absolutely possible to read the Bible, fast and pray, feel convicted, and still choose to remain unchanged.

What have you been running to? That's the type of question I'm learning to ask myself as the Sunday service comes to a close. As the worship team plays one more song and the congregation begins to leave, I ask myself, *Where am I pedaling off to these days? What am I running after? If all this is true, how should my life look? If Jesus truly came to set me free, why am I still running to food? If I really have been bought with a price . . . If Jesus fasted and prayed and literally fed His disciples . . . If Jesus alone can satisfy my deepest longings . . . If . . . If . . . If . . .*

If what I learn on Sunday mornings is true, it should affect everything about how I spend my days: the way I love my family, the way I hold my thoughts captive, the way I spend my money, the food I eat, the words I say, and all the details of my life. Everything that I do needs to line up with God's Word.

Psalm 34:8–10 is a passage I pray over and over when I am fasting.

> Taste and see that the LORD is good;
>> blessed is the one who takes refuge in him.
> Fear the LORD, you his holy people,
>> for those who fear him lack nothing.
> The lions may grow weak and hungry,
>> but those who seek the LORD lack no good thing. (NIV)

We are no longer children, friends. The One we worship on Sunday must remain Lord over our lives Monday through Saturday. We are mature men and women who have been invited by the Lord Himself to taste and see how good He is all week long. He has invited us to run to Him when we're tempted to run into the corner store (whether grabbing candy or a bottle of wine). We can run to Him rather than running to the recesses of our pantry. And we can run to Him and find refuge in Him when we're tempted to hide behind our phones.

The One we worship on Sunday must remain Lord over our lives Monday through Saturday.

His invitation calls us out of all our habits and immature addictions, whether we're abusing sugar or bingeing on Netflix shows and YouTube videos. God calls out to each of us, "Taste and see Me. Hide yourself in Me. Let Me be what you run to! All other beasts suffer hunger, even the lion. But not humanity. No, I have redeemed humanity for

Myself, and those who come to Me, who taste and see Me for themselves, will lack no good thing."

Dear Lord, I have a long history with sugar. You know I do. You were there as my habits were formed. But those years are behind me now. My future with You, however, stretches on forever. Please help me to make You my new habit. Help me run to You so that I might taste Your sweetness and allow You to satisfy all my needs. In Jesus's satisfying name, Amen.

day 2

RETURN TO ME

"Even now," declares the LORD, "return to me with all your heart, with fasting and weeping and mourning."

Joel 2:12 NIV

I REMEMBER THE FIRST DAY of my first 40-Day Sugar Fast. I came to it with great hope of experiencing joy in God's presence. I had three young boys and I was worn out and joyless. As I entered into that season of fasting, I quoted Psalm 16:11 expectantly: "In your presence there is fullness of joy." Yes, I was after joy and eager to be filled to overflowing. I don't think there was anything wrong with that prayer. After all, it is biblical. Scripture tells us that when we abide with God, we will bear the fruit of His joy in our lives (John 15:5). Fasting is abiding on a gut level—an *empty* gut level.

When I stopped filling my emptiness with sweet treats so that I might be filled up with God, His Spirit surprised me. Before God led me up to the high places of gladness, He took me through a valley of deep sadness. He flooded my heart with conviction, and conviction felt more like heartache than happiness. As I realized how far I'd drifted from God's presence,

I experienced a holy sort of sadness. No wonder I was hungry for joy; I'd wandered from the Joy Giver. Before I could be satisfied by His joy-inducing presence, I had to grieve over how far I'd strayed, and return to Him. "'Even now,' declares the LORD, 'return to me with all your heart, with fasting and weeping and mourning'" (Joel 2:12 NIV).

Fasting is abiding on a gut level—an empty gut level.

Here on the second day of your sugar fast, I invite you to take an honest look at where you are and where God is in relation to you. He is not a far-off God; He hasn't gone anywhere but it's possible that you have. It may be that instead of running to Him to fill you, you have been running to the pantry. Perhaps, instead of opening up your Bible, you've been opening up your smartphone and scrolling through social media. It's not sugar, but it is another filler.

What do you turn to instead of to Him? Take a few moments today to consider this question. If you find that you habitually turn to anything but Him, I urge you to deal with your wandering prayerfully and to seek Him faithfully. Weep, mourn—and return to Him for in His presence you will find the joy you've been searching for.

I'm reminded of the Christmas story and of the name Jesus was given before His birth. Matthew 1:23 proclaims the angel's message: "'Behold, the virgin shall conceive and bear a son, and they shall call his name Immanuel' (which means, God with us)." The name *Immanuel* proclaims Jesus's mission: to be with us. And, by His indwelling Holy Spirit, Jesus remains a very near and present God. Unfortunately, our free will allows us to wander from the One who promised never to wander from us. So today, we need to purpose in our hearts (and in our lifestyles too) to turn back to Him—to return.

The Old Testament is full of stories about the wayward-ness of God's people. Their unfaithfulness broke the hearts of many of the prophets and biblical leaders. Joel, Jeremiah, Isaiah, Ezra, and Nehemiah all fasted, praying that God would turn the hearts of His people back to Him.

Take a moment to read Nehemiah's prayer below.

> LORD, the God of heaven, the great and awesome God, who keeps his covenant of love with those who love him and keep his commandments, let your ear be attentive and your eyes open to hear the prayer your servant is praying before you day and night for your servants, the people of Israel. I confess the sins we Israelites, including myself and my father's family, have committed against you. We have acted very wickedly toward you. We have not obeyed the commands, decrees and laws you gave your servant Moses.
>
> Remember the instruction you gave your servant Moses, say-ing, "If you are unfaithful, I will scatter you among the nations, **but if you return to me and obey my commands, then even if your exiled people are at the farthest horizon, I will gather them** from there and bring them to the place I have chosen as a dwelling for my Name." (Neh. 1:5–9 NIV, emphasis mine)

Allow Nehemiah's prayer to inspire one of your own. Pick up a pen and write out a prayer of repentance (or lift up your voice and cry out). Ask the Lord to help you see your own wayward tendencies, and then confess them. He is faithful to forgive you and welcome you back into a restored relationship with Himself because of His Son, our very present Savior.

Throughout the Scriptures and throughout history, people have struggled to remain in God's presence. Time and again we wander away only to feel the pain of putting distance between ourselves and the Father. If that is where you find yourself today, weep and mourn and return to Him. It is my experience that once you return to the Joy Giver, joy isn't far behind.

So consider this: Is it possible that you have wandered away from God? Perhaps you know it's true, but you aren't sure what it would look like to turn from your old ways or if you even can. You've experienced conviction but don't know how to get to transformation. You know your tendency to fashion a makeshift god from sweet confectioneries but you haven't been able to stop. Pinpoint your vices and repent—turn around, pull a complete 180, and go in the opposite direction. If you've been running to all the wrong fillers in lieu of the only One who can fill you up and make you full, repent. Confess it to the Lord "with fasting and weeping and mourning." Turn and return to Him.

> *It is my experience that once you return to the Joy Giver, joy isn't far behind.*

Dear Lord, thank You for being my Father, even when I am a wayward child. I'm sorry. Your forgiveness is life! And because I've been so completely forgiven time and time again, I ask that You bind me close to Your heart and help to keep me in step with Your joy-giving Spirit. In Jesus's name, Amen.

SOME THINGS TO BE AWARE OF WHILE YOU FAST

Your body is detoxing as you fast. That physiological reality is likely intensifying your emotions as well. While I believe that fasting heightens your spiritual senses, causing conviction and repentance, I know that cutting out sugar cold turkey can cause emotions of sadness and anger to flare up as well. In the early days of your fast, you may experience what many refer to as a "sugar flu." As you go without your tasty mood enhancers, you may feel grumpy or emotional. This is normal and common when you first embark on a sugar fast. You've been dependent on sugar for far too long, and that's partly why you feel miserable without it. Let your awareness of your dependency on sugar rather than on Christ convict you of your waywardness and prompt you to turn and return to Him. And as you do, be on the lookout for joy. While sugar provides a temporary jolt of happiness, this promise is long and lasting: "Weeping may last through the night, but joy comes with the morning" (Ps. 30:5 NLT).

day 3

WHEN SUGAR WALLS CRUMBLE

As soon as the people heard the sound of the trumpet, the people shouted a great shout, and the wall fell down flat.

Joshua 6:20

SUGAR IS A STRONGHOLD for many people. Does it hold you back from the good life that God has planned for you? Perhaps over time your sweet tooth has turned into a full-fledged addiction, dictating your days, driving you from one sugary fix to the next. **Unfortunately, no sugar fix can fix you.** In fact, when you give sugar that job, you'll end up more broken than before because sugar weakens our physical bodies and clouds our minds. If only you could break free from this sweet, strangling stronghold, but you feel powerless. The walls are too thick and too wide, the habits too ingrained, the enemy too big and too strong, and you are too addicted.

However, all throughout the Scriptures, God demonstrates that He has the power to open prison gates and set captives free. Today I encourage you to shout God's victory over your life even before He helps you tear down the stronghold of sugar. Why? Because that is exactly what God instructed the Israelites to do as they marched around the strong walls of the city of Jericho. This massive stronghold was in their way, preventing them from entering God's promised land. For the walls to come tumbling down, God's people had to first shout the victory. In full obedience and faithful expectancy, they lifted up their voices to Him in praise.

Do you know the story? Did you sing the song about Joshua and the battle of Jericho when you were young? Do you know that the same power to bring down strongholds is available to you? We read in the book of Joshua, chapters 5 and 6, that Joshua was taking Israel from their wilderness wandering into the promised land. But before they could take possession of God's good promises, they had to pass through Jericho. The city walls were high and well-fortified, and the people of Israel felt hopeless.

That's when a man with a drawn sword appeared to Joshua, saying he was the commander of the Lord's army. Joshua fell down in reverence at his feet. The warrior told him to remove his sandals for he was standing on holy ground, and then the Lord spoke to Joshua, telling him exactly what he needed to do. For six days all the mighty men of war were to march around the walls of Jericho one time. Behind them the priests would follow, blowing on rams' horns. On the seventh day, however, they were to march around Jericho's walls seven times, with the priests blowing their horns continually. After the seventh time around the stronghold, the Lord commanded all the people of Israel to shout triumphantly. Then and only then, would the walls come tumbling down.

What a thrilling story! If you've never read it for yourself, please take a moment to ingest it now. It is my hope that you see that the Bible is so much more than a thrilling story; it's your story and mine. My fasting friend, just as the fortified city of Jericho was blocking the Israelites from entering the promised land, the stronghold of sugar may be holding you back from the abundant life God has planned for you. For that reason, I encourage you, amid your withdrawal symptoms and cravings, to give praise to the Lord because of what He's *about to do*. Shatter the strong hold sugar has on you and replace it with a sweet dependence on Him.

The same God who set His people free from bondage in Egypt, the same God who parted the Red Sea and led them across dry land, the same God who fed them in the wilderness and delivered them from their enemies and finally ushered them into the promised land is alive and available today.

The same God who saves also speaks! So listen.

Here are five takeaways from the crumbled walls of Jericho that can help you on your journey from slavery to freedom.

1. **Believe that this place is holy (Josh. 5:15).** If you want the Lord to do a deep soul-work in you, slip off your shoes and place the soles of your feet on holy ground. God is at work in you and you get to march, barefoot and believing, through these forty days. Plant your feet on the solid ground of faith.

2. **Ask Him to tell you His plan for you (Josh. 3–7).** God gave the Israelites specific instructions about how to take down the stronghold of Jericho. He will do the same for you if you ask Him for help with each challenge you face.

   This wasn't the only time God gave His people clear directives. He spoke to Esther as she fasted and prayed,

He spoke to Daniel as he fasted and prayed, He spoke to King Jehoshaphat as He fasted and prayed. The details of each fast were different. The circumstances of each life were different. The questions were different. And God's answers were all uniquely different. God will give specific instructions that apply to your circumstances as you fast and pray. Ask Him what His plan is for you.

3. **Listen to the Lord (Josh. 6:2).** God is not a far-off or silent being. He has given you His living and active Word, along with His living and breathing Spirit, to be in communication with his people. **The same God who saves also speaks! So listen.** Allow the Lord who spoke clearly and kindly to Joshua to speak directly to your heart. Though His Word is inspired for all, He whispers to individuals in a private and loving manner. In order to hear Him, you must get quiet and listen.

> *God, what walls do You want to bring down?* Listen.
> *What does freedom in You look like?* Listen.
> *Is there anything else that You want me to fast from?*
>   Listen.
> *How do I do this?* Listen.
> *When should I meet with You and pray each day?* Listen.
> *What's Your plan for me as I fast?* Listen.

4. **Obey (Josh. 6:8).** The old hymn says it best, "Trust and obey, for there's no other way to be happy in Jesus but to trust and obey."[1] Fasting requires obedience. And extended fasts like this one will require extended obedience. It's easy to justify changing things up a bit mid-fast in order to make it easier. I know from experience. However, when you stay committed to doing what God

has told you to do (I'm talking following God's clear leading, not legalism), God in His supernatural power enables you to bring down the strongholds in your life. Yes, even the stronghold of sugar. The people of Israel had to march for seven days before they experienced deliverance. You have committed to forty days. Keep marching in obedience.

5. **Shout the victory before the walls fall (Josh. 6:20).** This is your main charge today. Shout His praise, believing in what He *will* do before He even does it. The same God who has set captives free can set you free today. Believe Him and shout His victory over your dependence on sugar.

God, You are strong and good and faithful. I'm shouting Your praise before a single brick falls from the walls holding me in and holding me back. You are able to set me free from all addictions, to heal all hurts and get to the root of what's causing my sin and sadness. I can't stop praising You for what You have already done in my life. I am confident that You will bring down the strongholds in these present struggles. Lord, You are able and You are God. I'm blowing my horn and shouting Your name. Amen.

day 4

TRUSTING GOD
WITH THE BATTLE

Listen, King Jehoshaphat and all who live in Judah and Jerusalem! This is what the Lord says to you: "Do not be afraid or
discouraged because of this vast army. For the battle is not
yours, but God's."

2 Chronicles 20:15 NIV

THE FIRST YEAR I hosted the 40-Day Sugar Fast online I
posted a picture of an old vinyl record on our private Facebook
page and asked my friends to help me put together a playlist of
songs we could sing at the start of our fast. Hundreds of people
responded in the comment thread with links to their favorite
praise songs. We had worship music to last us forty days and
well beyond! Ever since that first year, compiling a list of worship songs has become an annual tradition at the start of each
of our community fasts because, when we sing songs of worship, we proclaim out loud that the battle belongs to the Lord.

Four days into this fast, your body may feel like it is going
through a physical battle. Perhaps you feel like the fast is your

enemy or that sugar is your enemy or that your children are your enemy or that I am your enemy. Today I want you to focus on letting go of the fight and embrace praise, trusting that God will go to battle on your behalf.

When we sing songs of worship, we proclaim out loud that the battle belongs to the Lord.

I'd like to share a story from the Bible about a man who faced a terrible battle. In 2 Chronicles 20:1–30, Jehoshaphat, king of Judah, received word that "a great multitude" was advancing against him. "Jehoshaphat was afraid and set his face to seek the LORD, and proclaimed a fast throughout all Judah. And Judah assembled to seek help from the LORD; from all the cities of Judah they came to seek the LORD" (vv. 3–4).

The first thing that strikes me about Jehoshaphat is that he was *afraid*, yet he sought God's help. Perhaps that's where you are right now: afraid of the withdrawal symptoms, afraid of laying down your addiction, afraid because you've already cheated on this fast and wonder if you should just give up, afraid of failing further . . . If so, I encourage you to take a moment to set your face toward the Lord. You've intentionally turned your eyes away from food, but have you decidedly turned your eyes to God in sugar's stead? Are you seeking His help as you fight this battle?

Read these words from Psalm 121:1–2 with me.

> I lift up my eyes to the mountains—
>> where does my help come from?
> My help comes from the LORD,
>> the Maker of heaven and earth. (NIV)

King Jehoshaphat came from the lineage of David, the man who wrote the lyrics to the psalm-song above. David penned

Psalm 121 as he hid from his enemy, King Saul. Similarly, these words from Psalm 56:3–4 came to him when he was captured by the Philistines: "When I am afraid, I put my trust in you. In God, whose word I praise, in God I trust; I shall not be afraid. What can [man] do to me?" What a picture both David and Jehoshaphat paint for us. When they were afraid, they turned to God.

You've intentionally turned your eyes away from food, but have you decidedly turned your eyes to God in sugar's stead?

Jehoshaphat, however, didn't do it alone; he asked his people to fast and pray with him. Can you imagine all the people of Judah, fasting and seeking God together? I'm reminded of this promise from Psalm 33:12: "Blessed is the nation whose God is the LORD, the people he chose for his inheritance" (NIV).

Jehoshaphat believed this and invited his people to believe it too. Together they fasted and together they prayed, and consequently God came to their aid, told them what to do, and assured them of victory.

Listen, King Jehoshaphat and all who live in Judah and Jerusalem! This is what the LORD says to you: "Do not be afraid or discouraged because of this vast army. For the battle is not yours, but God's. Tomorrow march down against them. . . . You will not have to fight this battle. Take up your positions; stand firm and see the deliverance the LORD will give you, Judah and Jerusalem. Do not be afraid; do not be discouraged. Go out to face them tomorrow, and the LORD will be with you." (2 Chron. 20:15–17 NIV)

Immediately, Jehoshaphat fell on his face and worshiped. And all the people of Judah followed him to their knees. Every one of them laid prostrate before God. That's when some of the Levites—Israel's worship leaders—stood and sang praises in a very loud voice. "As they began to sing and praise, the Lord set ambushes against the men of Ammon and Moab and Mount Seir who were invading Judah, and they were defeated" (v. 22 NIV). The priests sang, and God Himself defeated their enemies as Jehoshaphat and his men looked on.

God assured King Jehoshaphat and the Israelite people that He would deliver them, and so they celebrated their victory *before* God defeated their enemies. Yesterday we learned that God's people shouted before the walls tumbled; today we see that they sang before an army tumbled. They believed that the battle belonged to the Lord. Do you? Are you muscling through the early days of this fast on your own or are you singing your faith songs out loud, trusting that this battle belongs to Him?

God is still speaking this same message over you now with His promise: "Do not be afraid or discouraged because of the battle you face today [where food or anything else is concerned]. The battle is not yours but mine." Therefore, go out today with praise on your lips and your eyes fixed on Him.

Mighty God of angel armies, thank You for giving me the story of King Jehoshaphat to grow my faith today. When he was afraid, he knew where to turn. I have turned to other gods in my fear, my loneliness, my emptiness, and my pride, to give me courage and strength each day. But the battles of this life continue to rage, and I need You, Redeemer. Only You. I choose to set my face toward You today. As I wait to see You move, I will sing Your praises and eagerly anticipate Your deliverance. In Jesus's name, Amen.

YOUR SWEETEST NEMESIS

Speaking of going to battle, sometimes sugar feels like the enemy. Agreed? The average American eats between 150 to 170 pounds of refined sugar every year.[1] While that may seem impossible at first glance, the reality is that it's not hard to accomplish. Four sodas a day times 365 days a year amounts to nearly 150 pounds of sugar! Oftentimes during our online sugar fasts, I hear from men and women who discovered that sugary treats in general isn't their problem, their problem is Dr Pepper . . . their problem is sweet tea . . . their problem is wine . . .

Take a moment to pinpoint your "enemy." What's your sweetest nemesis?

day 5

FASTING AND FEASTING

Your words were found, and I ate them,
and your words became to me a joy
and the delight of my heart.

Jeremiah 15:16

A FEW DAYS into my last fast, I was putting dishes away when I noticed two of our family Bibles on the kitchen counter. My husband's big, blue study Bible and the slender, brown, leather-bound one I usually keep in my purse. As my stomach growled, I found myself inspired. Immediately I pulled out my prettiest cake stand and placed it on the countertop, stacking the Bibles on it. Together they looked like a multitiered cake on display. I smiled.

Over the next thirty-five days, I kept the cake stand front and center as a reminder. When I found myself bored and looking for something to nibble on, I was reminded to feast on the Word! Each time I was tempted to mindlessly grab a handful of sugar-coated something, I'd grab hold of my well-worn Bible instead. Fasting from sugar and feasting on God's words became the theme of my afternoons and evenings—any time of the day or night that my stomach growled again.

The imagery of consuming God's Word is found over and over throughout Scripture. In Ezekiel 3:3 we read that God fed the prophet Ezekiel a scroll containing His Words. God said to Ezekiel, "Son of man, eat this scroll I am giving you and fill your stomach with it." To which the prophet responded, "So I ate it, and it tasted as sweet as honey in my mouth" (NIV).

In Revelation 10:8–11, John was charged to eat the scroll that an angel handed to him. Devouring God's Word is the secret to our fasting days, the key to stopping us from consuming anything and everything else. As I mentioned in the introduction, we are crowding out sugar with the satisfying sweetness of Christ, and the main way we are doing that is by ingesting His Word.

Are you hungry to ingest the transforming and filling presence of Christ? You get to do that each time you "consume" His words. When you read John 6, for example, you eat up the story of Jesus feeding the five thousand and believe that He can fill you in miraculous ways. Then you read on and ingest the account of Him walking on water, and you're ready to jump out of the boat and follow Him too because you have tasted and seen Him for yourself.

Each time I fast from food, I rediscover that Christ truly is as sweet as honey in my mouth. Unfortunately, after some time has passed, the flavor fades and the things of this world attempt to crowd Him out again. That's why I fast for forty days *a few times each year*. It's not that I want to live a fasting life, it's that I need to live a feasting life. Each time I forget to feast, I fast in order to remember. Don't think of fasting as a magic trick. Abracadabra, once and done. Fasting may transform your diet, but it is a feasting life that will change your life.

Each time I forget to feast, I fast in order to remember.

One of the practical things I've learned during my seasons of fasting and feasting is that God's Word can be served up all day long in different sized portions. There are snack-sized portions for on-the-go encouragement, main courses when we can really sit down and feast, and desserts that are sweet reminders of just how loved we are! The first time I led this fast online, my dear friend Christy Nueman sent me a long list of Bible passages and categorized them for me this way: "Here are some wonderful *snacks* for you, Wendy," she wrote before listing her favorite verses. "Enjoy these main courses," she prefaced a list of longer, meatier passages—many of them whole chapters. And then, under the heading "Desserts," she put some of the most familiar verses that are applicable when I needed a loving reminder of God's sweet presence and faithful promises.

Practically speaking, here's how I live out this feasting life. In the morning, when I wake up early enough, I snack on a verse or two to help me fix my eyes on a truth. I don't have much time to myself since I am often rushing my kids off to school, so I enjoy my main meal of the day once I have them all settled. I read an entire chapter, sometimes multiple chapters, and then write out the verse that the Lord used most mightily to speak to me. That verse becomes a snack-sized portion I take with me everywhere I go. Oftentimes I read it in a few translations on the Bible App and then link over to other verses that flesh the lesson out further. I write down one or two of those as well. If I struggle during the day, I reach for one of the familiar verses that I've loved for years and years as a midday dessert to remind my heart how loved I am. When I get a text from a friend in need of encouragement, I reach again for those verses and send them off like a care package. Often, the people I encounter each day need exactly what I've been feasting on.

Do you see what I mean? You must remain in the Word. Five minutes of nibbling on a verse in the morning won't fill you up and fuel you through the other 1,435 minutes of the day. You need a continual feast to carry you through long fasting days. First Thessalonians 5:17 tells you to "pray without ceasing." If praying is talking to God, then reading God's Word is listening. Let's make the *conversation* a continual feast! Read and pray, then read and pray some more. Let your fasting days propel you into a feasting life!

Five minutes of nibbling on a verse in the morning won't fill you up and fuel you through the other 1,435 minutes of the day.

Keep your Bible open on your kitchen counter, my fasting friend, on a cake stand or open on top of your recipe books. Write down the verses that you read—even the ones I've included here in this book. Write them out on an index card (or a recipe card) and carry them with you to snack on. Better yet, open up the Word and read the verses I share in the context of the chapter. That's the feasting life!

Sugar offers you empty calories, but Christ's Word is sustenance. It is the meat that sticks to your ribs and turns to spiritual muscle, so that you might be strong to live out what He tells you to do.

Oh Lord, You are so good to chase me down in the midst of my addictions and afflictions. This is about so much more than sugar. Teach me to live a feasting life as I spend these next few weeks fasting and praying continually. In the redemptive name of Jesus, Amen.

day 6

ARMOR UP!

Finally, be strong in the Lord and in the strength of his might. Put on the whole armor of God, that you may be able to stand against the schemes of the devil. For we do not wrestle against flesh and blood, but against the rulers, against the authorities, against the cosmic powers over this present darkness, against the spiritual forces of evil in the heavenly places.

Ephesians 6:10–12

AS I BEGAN WRITING THIS BOOK, my computer started autocorrecting *Holy Spirit* to *Hokey Spirit*. When I shared this with one of the women who was fasting with me, she exclaimed, "Get behind me, Siri!" which made us both laugh. Of course, she was being punny, making a play on words out of Jesus's strong command, "Get behind me, Satan" (Matt. 16:23). But even as we laughed, I recognized that the devil had been working overtime in my life since I began *The 40-Day Sugar Fast*. Perhaps you've been experiencing something similar now that you're on this journey from fasting to feasting.

Satan hates you. But for the most part, he pays you no mind as long as you are entangled in sin and struggling with

shame. He likes you lethargic and ineffective. He prefers it when you struggle with migraines and emotional instability, when you are irritated with your spouse and your kids and your coworkers. He loves it when you blow up at your family or friends over a sugar-induced spike and crash. However, when you turn to Christ for His free and freeing power, Satan takes offense and goes on the offensive. He hates it when you fast and pray because he knows that each time you go to God rather than to sugar to fill your longings, the Spirit of God floods into the empty places in your heart and life. Satan hates losing ground.

When you started your forty-day fast from sugar, you may have anticipated temptation, but you may not have expected the tempter himself. The good news is that "the one who is in you is greater than the one who is in the world" (1 John 4:4 NIV). Each day, as you go to Him rather than to food, the Spirit of God gives you strength that those empty calories never could! As you turn to Him, He moves into your heart and into your home and into your neighborhood.

Each day, as you go to Him rather than to food, the Spirit of God gives you strength that those empty calories never could!

That is why as God advances, the devil advances right up into your intimate business. In fact, I don't doubt that as soon as you began fasting, you experienced at least one, if not many, of the following:

- conflict with friends
- a spike in negative self-talk
- financial challenges
- angry outbursts at your loved ones

- annoyance with your spouse
- misunderstandings with colleagues and neighbors

If so, be encouraged. Why? Because the devil is not happy that God is taking His rightful place at the center of your life. First Peter 5:8 says that the devil is prowling around like a roaring lion looking for someone to devour. When you were stuffing your face, comforting yourself with food instead of turning to the Comforter, the devil paid you no mind. Now that you're on the alert, however, Satan has been alerted!

Thankfully, God has written out exactly what you need to do in order to fight this spiritual battle and win. Ephesians 6:10–18 tells you to armor up! You're told to dress for battle every day, but I'm telling you to especially prepare as you fast and pray. Tie truth around your waist, and make it a double knot! Put on the protective breastplate of righteousness to guard your heart. Slip on your gospel-shoes and walk out your faith. Lift high your shield of faith, which is able to protect you from the devil's attacks. And wield the sword of the Spirit, which is the Word of God. Finally, put on the helmet of salvation.

While I hope that you'll meditate on all the spiritual armor at your disposal, I want to focus in on the helmet of salvation today. I believe that many, if not most, spiritual battles begin in the mind. This is especially true where addiction is concerned. That's why it is critical that you discipline your mind to think spiritually.

Years ago, I was working through a Bible study by Beth Moore. In it, Beth painted a picture with her words that has stayed with me. She asked us to imagine ourselves holding the helmet of salvation in our hands each morning, filled to the brim with the cleansing and protective blood of Christ. Then she said that when we lift it up and place it on our heads each new day, Christ's blood covers us anew—running down from the top of our heads to the bottoms of our gospel-loving feet! We're sealed from head to toe! But it all starts at the top, with our thinking. Begin each day of this fast by affirming:

> Whatever is true, whatever is noble, whatever is right, whatever is pure, whatever is lovely, whatever is admirable—if anything is excellent or praiseworthy—think about such things. (Phil. 4:8 NIV)

Here's what is true: If you have put your faith in Jesus Christ to save you, He has! And because you've been saved, God has the power to continue to save you today and tomorrow and throughout these forty days and beyond. Remember that. Remember what's true when the fiery darts fly. Your helmet of salvation is covering and protecting your mind today.

Before your feet hit the floor, remind yourself: "I've got an enemy and he wants my life today, but my life is safe in Jesus's hands." Focus your thoughts on what is true about God, even when Satan slithers in with his lies. Even when your life doesn't testify that God is good and protective and near, remind yourself that He is, has been, and will always be. Use your lips to declare, "My life and my thought life are completely bound up in Christ. He is for me. So, Satan, get behind me!" When the devil tries his best to stir up strife, speak aloud what you know to be true, and tell him to take a hike.

The same God who saved you eternally has the power to save you internally.

"I know what's true; I know who I am and whose I am . . . get out of here!" The same God who saved you eternally has the power to save you internally. Believing that truth is where the spiritual fight begins.

Place your thought life in His capable hands as you put on that helmet to guard your thinking today. He alone is able to save you from every weapon formed against you. I know it sounds allegorical, but you are in a literal battle. Satan would love nothing more than to keep you from your freedom in Christ, so armor up!

Dear Lord, thank You for keeping me in Your perfect peace when I actively fix my daily thoughts on You. Keep me steadfast and immovable, stayed and secure, believing what is true each day. Help me to prioritize putting on my armor at the start of each new day. This fast is not merely a physical detox but a spiritual battle, which is why I need You and Your full armor, Holy Spirit! In Jesus's name, Amen.

day 7

A HOLY HUNGER

Blessed are those who hunger and thirst for righteousness, for they shall be satisfied.

Matthew 5:6

AS YOUR BODY DETOXES in the weeks ahead, remember that no amount of sugar has *ever* been able to satisfy your hunger. Sugar's temporary pleasure is short-lived. Fleeting. Think about it. Even when you've just had a slice of key lime pie on a hot summer's day or a serving of apple cobbler in celebration of fall's bounty, don't you often hunger for more? I know I do, no matter the season. As I'm scraping food off of dinner plates and wrapping up leftovers to stick in the fridge, somehow I always end up eating "just one more bite." I had to go through this forty-day sugar fast three times—that's one hundred and twenty days without sugar!—before I began to understand my problem. **My issue isn't actually with sugar, or with food, but with hunger—misplaced, insatiable hunger.**

Now, it's true that there are physiological reasons why sugar is tremendously addictive. But there are deeply spiritual reasons too. Nothing convicts me of my sugar fixation quite like fasting does because when I stop running to sugar, I realize how my misplaced hunger has kept me from running to God. My hunger for sweet treats gets in the way of my hunger and thirst for Him.

Fasting from eating doesn't change our hunger, but when we exchange what we hunger for, it can change the way we eat. The only way I've learned to change my hunger is to change my mind about what I'm most hungry for.

Fasting from eating doesn't change our hunger, but when we exchange what we hunger for, it can change the way we eat.

In Christ's clear-spoken Sermon on the Mount, he said, "Blessed are those who hunger and thirst for righteousness, for they shall be satisfied" (Matt. 5:6). What does this mean in light of our insatiable appetites? If we want to live satisfied lives, we must focus on the One who is able to fill us with a reservoir of righteousness!

When we change our minds about what we're most hungry for, when we finally begin to hunger for His righteousness, our eating habits start to change, as do our lives. That's when we begin to be transformed. Here's how it works: As we feast more on the Word and less on food from the fridge, His Word transforms our minds. It changes how we think about life and God. Not only that, our bodies are also changing. Because we are eating less food, we are also losing weight and gaining more energy. I've said it before: The size of our waists will decrease as the size of our faith increases. We will become increasingly more interested in spending time with Him instead of running to the pantry or connecting with friends online. For when we start to crave the True Bread, we will be filled and fully satisfied.

It is my hope that you don't simply read a few verses and pray a few prayers and drop a few pounds during these forty days. If that's all you do, then the pounds will likely come right back, along with your insatiable appetite. Instead, I pray that you discover a different sort of hunger—a holy hunger that leads to a satisfied life.

I have a handful of friends who model this hungry, holy life. Even in busy seasons with young children and overwhelming work schedules, they take the time each morning to sit at Jesus's feet, hungry for His Word and His presence. He is their chief concern. Years ago, one of these friends told me that she has prayed a prayer inspired by Matthew 5:6 for the majority of her adult life: *Lord, help me to hunger and thirst for Your righteousness more than anything else.* Each time I go on a sugar fast, her simple Scripture-prayer comes to my mind and directs my own prayers. In the early days of your fast, I encourage you to pray it too. Exchange what can never satisfy you for the only thing that can. When we grow in our devotion to Him, we grow in our hunger for Him and His righteousness.

Exchange what can never satisfy you for the only thing that can.

> As the deer pants for streams of water,
> so my soul pants for you, my God.
> My soul thirsts for God, for the living God.
> (Ps. 42:1–2 NIV)

My fasting friend, you've got to change your mind about what it is you're most hungry for today. It's been seven days since you started your sugar fast, and you are likely still experiencing some pretty intense cravings. Allow each one to bring you to your knees. Ask God to help you exchange your sweet tooth with a new hunger for the satisfying sweetness of Christ. When you hunger most for Him, it will change your life. Your hunger for sugar will decrease, and your hunger for Him will increase. This holy hunger will transform more than your diet; it will transform your life.

Dear Lord, as the deer longs for streams of water, so I long to long for You. For You alone can satisfy thirsty souls and fill hungry hearts with that which is good. Therefore, Lord, I'm asking You to help me with Your Spirit—help me to hunger and thirst for Your righteousness more than anything else. In Jesus's name I pray, Amen.

day 8

CANDY CANES AND CRUTCHES

Behold, God is my helper;
the Lord is the upholder of my life.

Psalm 54:4

I WAS IN HIGH SCHOOL the first time I heard an atheist argue that Christians are just weak people in need of a crutch.

"Jesus," he accused, "is the crutch you lean on to get you through this life." I was only sixteen years old, but I remember thinking, *Of course He's a crutch. Praise God for sending His Son for us to lean on, with the fullness of our fallen weight, or we'd be hobbling through this crazy life alone.*

I couldn't understand why this combative boy in my geometry class was challenging my faith with that ridiculous crutch analogy. The image of Jesus holding me up, making me able-bodied and sure-footed, only strengthened my believing heart. "You're right," I conceded, "you're absolutely right. Christians need Jesus every day. However, I think we're all leaning on something. But I've come to believe that whatever we lean on in this life better have the ability to get us ready for the next life too."

"Heaven?" he asked with a sneer.

"Leaning on Jesus in this life is the only thing that will allow us to walk into His eternal kingdom when this life is over. But put heaven aside if you want. We all need something to lean on. Perhaps you're leaning on your abilities just as heavily as I'm leaning on my Savior's ability to hold me up."

God is absolutely a crutch! He's the only crutch that enables us to not only walk through the valleys on this earth but also to run full-speed ahead into the high places of eternity. Praise the Lord for his sustaining, upholding, and eternal support.

The trouble is, sometimes I forget that faithful crutch and grab other things to get me through at three o'clock in the afternoon when the stresses of life add up. It's often in the midst of real life stress that I forget to lean on the real Life Giver. For instance, when my school-age kids are melting down over math homework and my husband has just called to say that he'll be late, I sometimes grab a handful of chocolate chips. When I've been cleaning the house all day but still have three loads of laundry to fold and put away, I have been known to throw some highly sugared creamer into my afternoon cup of coffee or tea. When I've had a challenging morning at work, I often grab a leftover brownie from the night before to push me over the hump. Instead of leaning on Christ, I lean on something fleeting to boost my adrenaline and give me a surge of dopamine so that I will feel better.

It's often in the midst of real life stress that I forget to lean on the real Life Giver.

Even as I write this, what comes to mind is the image of a candy cane, which is made to look like an actual cane or, better yet, a crutch. The problem with leaning too heavily on a candy crutch is, almost immediately, it breaks and I break too, because God never intended for sugar to sustain me. Instead, God says, "Cast your burden upon the LORD and He will sustain you; He will never allow the righteous to be shaken" (Ps. 55:22 NASB).

Big burdens, daily burdens, seemingly insignificant burdens. God can handle them all when you place them in the palm of His hands. Other translations of Psalm 55:22 similarly exhort, "Cast your cares upon the Lord . . ." I like that image too. You can cast your cares on Him because He cares for you.

You can cast your cares on Him because He cares for you.

In contrast, sugar doesn't give a rip about your joy or your health, your stress or your family, your ability to bear the fruit of God's Spirit in your life or your emotional well-being. My friend Amy Bennett journeyed with me through the first couple of sugar fasts, and one day she came to a profound conclusion. She likened her sugar addiction to an abusive relationship. By the end of one of our fasting seasons, she realized that she loves sugar, but sugar doesn't love her back. Like a hurtful, unbalanced suitor, over and over again, sugar showed Amy its inability to be faithful and loving. So Amy made the hard choice to break up with sugar, once and for all.

You're only one week into your fasting, but perhaps you see yourself in Amy's story. Believe me when I say that candy crutches can't hold your weight; they only increase it. Only Christ is able to hold you up. Because Jesus sacrificed His life, He alone is able to save and sustain yours.

Nowadays when I think of the crutch analogy, I imagine a cane—not a candy cane but a shepherd's staff. Jesus was the ultimate Good Shepherd and I am the epitome of a foolish, wayward sheep. But I know my Shepherd's voice, and I can hear Him calling me back into His presence again. Jesus is the true and faithful lover and sustainer of my soul. He leaves the ninety-nine to grab me each time I wander off. Jesus picks me up and carries me back with the full weight of my burdens resting on his shoulders.

Friends, all other crutches will break under the weight of your burdens. Only Jesus can pick you up and carry you today, because He alone has the authority and power and position to carry you into an eternal life with Him. So praise God for sending His Son so that you don't need to hobble through another day alone. Because of Jesus, you can run, full-speed ahead, into this abundant and eternal life! Lean your full weight on that.

Dear Jesus, I'm leaning on You today, as I lean into Your Word. You and You alone are able to make me able-bodied. You can carry my burdens because You care for me. You are able to sustain my life because You gave Yours. No one else and nothing else was created to carry my weight. Thank you, Jesus. It is in Your name I pray, Amen.

day 9

WHEN JESUS SHARES HIS FOOD

"My food," said Jesus, "is to do the will of him who sent me to finish his work."

John 4:34 NIV

I LOVE EATING OUT with friends and family members who like to share what they order at restaurants. "You've got to try this!" they exclaim. "Hey, let me taste a bite of that," they request, fork already poised in midair. I would like to think that if Jesus were going out to dinner with me tonight, He would definitely want to share an appetizer and split a main course. Sharing is fun; however, I believe that the food Jesus ate and wants to share with us is different than we may think.

I like to imagine Jesus eating. He came to earth, fully God and fully man, which means he fully got hungry. But fish and cheese and fruits and bread weren't the things that ultimately fed Him. What enabled and empowered Jesus to keep going each day was doing the will of His Father and finishing the work God had sent Him to do.

All of food's tasty nutrients, all the energy it provides, and all the pleasure it brings pale in comparison to the satisfaction of doing God's will. That is why doing the Father's will fueled the Son.

But what exactly was the will of God that so beautifully motivated and sustained our Savior? John 6:40 tells us, "This is the will of My Father, that everyone who beholds the Son and believes in Him will have eternal life, and I Myself will raise him up on the last day" (NASB). It was God's will for Jesus to die in our place, offering us freedom in the form of forgiveness, thus securing our eternal redemption. That mission kept Jesus moving onward and upward. Like real food that gives energy to the body, our need for salvation energized our Savior. Our right to stand by His side before the Father was the driving motivation for all He did. It kept Him going.

Like real food that gives energy to the body, our need for salvation energized our Savior.

More than anything else, it is God's will that we spend our forever life with Him. His love for us is so radical that He sent His own Son to chase us down in our addictions, our compulsions, our sin, and our shame and bring us into a right relationship with Himself. The Father's will sustained the Son to carry the cross all the way up Calvary's hill. Christ was powered by the will of God! And we need to be too.

As you get more hungry for Christ, you may find yourself getting hungrier for what He hungered for. As you get to know His heart for the world, your heart for the world will be transformed to look more like His, and you will be inspired to share Him with others. Ultimately, what fueled Him will fuel you. The salvation of those you know and love and interact with each day will become a blessed burden in your belly. Like Christ, you will hunger for the salvation of the world and of your family and friends. It will become your passion, just as it was His.

We're told in Romans 8:29 that Jesus was the firstborn among us, and now it's our job to follow in His footsteps—letting the Father's purpose for Jesus's life transform our life's purpose. Isn't this what He charged us to do in the Great Commission? Before our resurrected Savior returned to the Father's side, He told His disciples—and us—to continue sharing the good news with others. He passed the baton, or passed the plate, as the case may be. It is our job now to share the news that He came to seek and to save. Let's get hungry for the salvation of the world and let that be the motivating factor in our lives today.

My oldest son is currently reading the Left Behind series for teens. He's absolutely on fire for the first time in his young life, inspired by fictional characters who are passionately sharing Christ's salvation with those who are perishing. There's an urgency to the story that most of us don't sense in our everyday lives. If we're honest, our urgency has more to do with what we will eat next and who we will eat it with and what we will wear and maybe even how we will snap a picture of it and post it to Instagram. We're motivated by what we buy and what fun activity next awaits us. We are a hungry people.

I've encouraged you before to exchange your all-consuming hunger for sweets with a new hunger: a holy hunger. Let the salvation of those who are lost fuel you. During this fast, as you begin to hunger and thirst for Christ, also let yourself hunger and thirst for opportunities to share Him with others. Offer up the food you thought you needed to eat in order to survive. Share, instead, the only thing that any of us need to truly live eternally: Christ's eternal salvation.

Let the salvation of those who are lost fuel you.

Let the will of the Father and the purpose of the Son become your food and your purpose, energizing and sustaining you through these fasting days.

The mere thought of spending forever with you sustained Jesus as He walked in sandaled feet, healing lepers and giving blind men back their sight. His love for you, dear friend, kept Him moving forward. Accept that today, if you haven't already, and let the salvation of others become your food as well.

Dear God, thank You for saving me. Help me to keep my eyes set on You as I walk out my salvation each day, looking for others to share You with. In Jesus's generous, life-giving name, Amen.

day 10

HIS PRESENCE,
OUR PRESENT

And when you fast, do not look gloomy like the hypocrites, for they disfigure their faces that their fasting may be seen by others. Truly, I say to you, they have received their reward. But when you fast, anoint your head and wash your face, that your fasting may not be seen by others but by your Father who is in secret. And your Father who sees in secret will reward you.

Matthew 6:16–18

NUMEROUS BOOKS ABOUT FASTING smack of a prosperity gospel, promising that God rains down riches on our lives when we practice this spiritual discipline. While I agree that fasting ushers us into a life of great blessing, the more I fast, the more I change my mind about what the blessing truly is.

Each year as I go through this fast I get quiet and, in the quiet, the Lord brings to mind a fresh awareness of His love. It is intimate and wonderful, and there is no greater wealth I desire more on earth or in heaven. The same is true when I pray and the same is true when I give. In Matthew 6, Jesus tells us that giving and praying and fasting are *all* to be done privately rather than publicly and that a reward awaits us when we do. Like a cord of three strands carefully woven together, we are to pray and fast and give in secret. In my own life I have found that these three spiritual disciplines go hand in hand and so does the reward. They are intimately connected with one another and with God Himself.

While we tend to think that our reward for giving is that we will receive, that our reward for serving will be that we are well taken care of, and that our reward for praying will be in the form of answered prayers, I suggest, instead, that God Himself is our reward. The presence of God is our present-reward when we join Him in giving and caring for others; the nearness of God is our near-reward when we join Him in prayer; and as we empty ourselves through fasting, we experience the reward of His fullness. This intimate partnership of knowing Him and being known by Him becomes the reward much more than any earthly treasures or pleasures ever could.

> *The presence of God is our present-reward when we join Him in giving and caring for others; the nearness of God is our near-reward when we join Him in prayer; and as we empty ourselves through fasting, we experience the reward of His fullness.*

The passage I claim and cling to as my life-verse is Psalm 73:25–26, 28: "Whom have I in heaven but you? And there is nothing on earth I desire besides you. My flesh and my heart may fail, but God is the strength of my heart and my portion forever. . . . For me it is good to be near God."

Fasting brings me near God. Praying brings me near God. Giving brings me near God. When we slow down and get down on our knees, He proves Himself faithful and answers our prayers. When we join Him in sacrificial giving, we share in His work in the world and experience His heart for others. As we talk life through with Him each day, as we would a friend, His friendship is our greatest good.

God has made it clear that when we fast—or give or pray—we're not to do it in order to be seen by others. Quite the contrary. In fact, if that is our motive, our reward is forfeited. We can't keep our eyes and our hearts fixed on Him and others at the same time. Intimacy with Him, not with this world, is our goal. **We're not looking for other people's attention as we fast and give and pray; we're after God's attention and affection. That's our reward.**

I am also desperately aware of my need for Jesus when I fast, whether it's for one day or a string of days. Going without food makes me weak, and my weakness allows me to experience His strength, which is another form of reward. When I fast and pray, He proves Himself able to exceed every need that I have. His obvious nearness astounds me. His availability blows my mind. He really is present; He really is near. And there's nothing better.

The truth of this overwhelms my heart each time I fast and pray. When I am not fasting, I tend to lose sight of Him because I am running, running, running. But when I fast, I slow down and get down, low to the ground. Fasting brings me to the feet of my Savior, humble and aware of my need. Fasting reminds me that He is my Savior still, my ever-present, saving Savior.

When we are truly aware of how desperately we need Him, we have nothing to boast about. In fact, when we are fasting, boasting about it is unthinkable because true fasting only makes us aware of our need for salvation. We lack the ability to do this life without Christ at the helm. That's what we're boasting about now, one quarter of the way through this forty-day fast. It doesn't make sense to boast about how holy we are, when only Christ is our holiness. We see this most of all when we fast. That radical realization is just one more part of the precious reward.

The reward for giving and praying and fasting is found in the giving and praying and fasting. Because fasting and praying and giving allow us to experience more of Him. And He is everything. Our reward is the

The reward for giving and praying and fasting is found in the giving and praying and fasting.

intimacy forged in prayerful conversation with the One who stitched us and knows us and sits enthroned within us and over us.

As we fast from food and feast on Him, He fills the empty places in our hearts and lives with Himself. Even now, **as we go without, He goes within.**

I used to think that when Scripture talked about our rewards, it was speaking only about eternal treasures. Matthew 6:19–21 clearly tells us that there's a mighty treasure trove of blessing awaiting us in heaven: "Do not lay up for yourselves treasures on earth, where moth and rust destroy and where thieves break in and steal, but lay up for yourselves treasures in heaven, where neither moth nor rust destroys and where thieves do not break in and steal. For where your treasure is, there your heart will be also." However, now that I've been in His company on this side of glory for nearly half a century, I know that a great portion of our reward is our relationship with Him, here and now.

When we give and when we pray and when we fast, He intimately communicates with us His astounding grace, His abounding love, and His abundant goodness. He comes near to us and speaks to us clearly, as with a friend.

Are you looking for a reward as you fast and pray? **His presence is our present. His nearness, our reward.**

Dear Lord, thank You for giving me such clear directives on how to know You and experience the riches of Your presence in this present life. While I believe that You are storing up for me a heap of blessings in Your heavenly kingdom, I thank You for the gift of You, intimately near, in my life today. You are my ultimate reward! You are my gift! You are my everything. In Jesus's name, Amen.

day 11

SHINE!

You are the light of the world. A city set on a hill cannot be hidden. Nor do people light a lamp and put it under a basket, but on a stand, and it gives light to all in the house. In the same way, let your light shine before others, so that they may see your good works and give glory to your Father who is in heaven.

Matthew 5:14–16

WHETHER YOU'RE A MAN OR A WOMAN, old or young, short or tall, single or married, with children or without, you have one overarching call on your life, and that is to shine. You are called to let your light shine for Christ, wherever you are and whatever you're doing.

While that command feels nearly impossible at times, the reality is that Jesus came to show us how to be a light in the darkness. He left the glory of the kingdom of light and came to earth to live in our midst, leaving a light-drenched path for us to follow. As He walked this earth, serving and sacrificing and loving others, He referred to Himself as the Light of the World, then He passed the torch to His followers when He said, "You are the light of the world" (Matt. 5:14).

The problem is that the light in most of us has dwindled over time.

Sure, there have been seasons when we've shined unhindered, expressive, generous, bright, and bold. Others have been drawn to us at those times because we were open and welcoming and full of hope. People are drawn to light-bright individuals like a moth to a window in the black of night.

You know it's true, perhaps, but maybe it hasn't been true for you . . . recently. Somehow, during a string of long days or a season of loneliness and disappointments, your light has flickered and grown dim and maybe it's all but dead now. You feel it; you know it. Nothing in you shines bright these days. You harp on your loved ones, count the minutes until you can go to bed, retreat into social media, and hide in the pantry. When you're with people, you spend your time complaining rather than rejoicing, spreading darkness rather than shining light.

Where did your joy-light go? How did it get switched off? There are too many reasons to count and too many shadows darkening your life and snuffing out your testimony: the worries of this world, the challenges of marriage and child rearing, financial stresses, broken hearts, broken dreams, dashed expectations, and an unhealthy lifestyle full of unhealthy habits. All these things can overwhelm you, zap your energy, and throw your emotions out of balance, hiding the light of Christ within you.

I'm reminded of a song I used to sing in Sunday school that went like this, "This little light of mine, I'm going to let it shine. This little light of mine, I'm going to let it shine, let it shine, let it shine, let it shine. Hide it under a bushel? No! I'm going to let it shine. Hide it under a bushel? No! I'm going to let it shine, let it shine, let it shine, let it shine."

While I am not here to address all the "bushels" that may be hiding your light, I do want to invite you to invite Jesus, the Light of the World, back into the dreary corners and dark recesses of your heart today. He is the Light and He promises that when you walk with Him, you'll not walk another step in darkness.

> Again Jesus spoke to them, saying, "I am the light of the world. Whoever follows me will not walk in darkness, but will have the light of life." (John 8:12)

Have you been struggling in the dark? Maybe your dearest friend has died, your marriage has ended, your health is failing, or your inner dialogue is one long monologue of self-loathing. Sin and soul-sadness thrive in the dark. But God promises that if you fetter yourself to Him and walk by His side, you will walk in His life-light. And like Moses, whose face shone with the brightness of God after he stood face-to-face in His presence for forty days (Exod. 34:35), you will start to shine again. That's what these forty days are for.

He is the Light and He promises that when you walk with Him, you'll not walk another step in darkness.

Friends, in this life we will encounter many dark trials, but we can be of good cheer—and cheer is a lot like shining—for our Savior has overcome the world and is overcoming still. His love and overcoming goodness radiates off our faces as we abide in Him. So don't go moping about as you fast, complaining about your withdrawal symptoms and all the sacrifices you're making so that God draws near. Splash some water on your face and shine. Shine amongst your family members during these forty days. Your spouse and children and neighbors and coworkers should have to shield their eyes because you're suddenly so radiant and bright. You're not only reflecting His light but it is also coming from within you now! You've got light down in your core because you're plugged into the light source.

> Let your light shine before others, so that they may see your good works and give glory to your Father who is in heaven. (Matt. 5:16)

Are you able to let your light shine before others today? If not, I encourage you to run back into the presence of the Light of the World. If you have been complaining this past week, be quiet today. Take a shower and go for a walk and speak grateful blessings over your life and the lives of those around you. Look for new ways to love and serve. If your children and your spouse have been demanding and you've responded to them with nasty words and expressions, ask the Lord to shine His love in you and through you. Let the Holy Spirit shine in your home. If you are lonely, go to the One who can fill each hollow hurt with His holy healing.

In this life we will encounter many dark trials, but we can be of good cheer . . . for our Savior has overcome the world and is overcoming still.

And if you grumble every time you walk into the breakroom at work and see a plate of cookies, turn around and take your break somewhere else. When you're able, walk back in there and shine without complaining.

You are the light of the world—so shine.

Dear Light of the World, shine in me and shine through me today as I commit to walking with You. Amen!

day 12

FOOD TRIGGERS

Search me, O God, and know my heart!
Try me and know my thoughts!
And see if there be any grievous way in me,
and lead me in the way everlasting!

Psalm 139:23–24

IN 2016, my friend Amber Lia and I were ministering online to overwhelmed moms who were struggling with anger. In our private Facebook group Amber and I shared biblical, practical parenting advice and told stories of our own challenges with our kids. One day we asked this simple question: "What are your triggers?" There was no need to define what a trigger was; these moms knew. Within an hour, hundreds of women responded: "When my kids talk back." "When they whine." "Sibling rivalry!" "Why can't they get their shoes on and get in the car?" "Naptime." "Bedtime." "Dinnertime." "My messy house." "My messy life."

Amber and I didn't try to teach those moms how to train their kids to behave better so that they wouldn't get angry. Instead we focused on our need to submit our triggered hearts to the gentle lordship of Jesus Christ—only then can our triggers lose their tight hold on our hearts. After months of addressing each trigger one at a time, Amber and I published a book, which we aptly titled *Triggers: Exchanging Parents' Angry Reactions for Gentle Biblical Responses*. I share this now to convey that I understand what it means to be triggered—triggered internally by our emotions and triggered externally by our circumstances.

Most of us have food triggers as well. **When our triggers are out of control, so is our eating.** As a matter of fact, the National Institute for Mental Health has confirmed that binge eating is the most common eating disorder in America today.[1] Even if we don't consider ourselves clinical cases, I bet we can each put a finger on a trigger or two that sets us off and causes us to eat compulsively or emotionally.

Perhaps your food trigger is your sensitive feelings, and you use food to comfort yourself each time you feel wronged or angry. Or maybe your trigger is a desperate desire to feel loved or the memory of a past hurt. Food triggers abound but we need wisdom to know which ones have mastery over us.

I often pray Psalm 139 when asking the Lord to give me spiritual vision to pinpoint my own food triggers. I ask Him to search me, acknowledging that He knows me better than I know myself. He made me and I am His—hurts, habits, and all. He isn't angry with me but loves me unconditionally. He wants to heal me from unhealthy eating, living, and thinking, so I invite Him to reveal anything that's harmful or offensive in me that He wants to make right. Humbly I ask Him to lead me in the everlasting way.

> *He made me and I am His—hurts, habits, and all.*

Have you asked Jesus to reveal to you why it is that you overindulge on sugar? He can show you what your triggers are. Maybe He'll give you eyes to see that when your children melt down at 3:00 p.m. and you're tempted to melt down too, you turn to chocolate chips rather than to Him. You open the refrigerator rather than opening the Word. Or perhaps He'll show you that when your spouse isn't showing you love and respect, you run to food to relieve the hurt. Take a moment to consider your food triggers.

While I've intentionally focused on the spiritual side of things during this fast, there is a physical side to our love for sugar as well. Physiologically, when you ingest sugar, dopamine floods your body making you feel happy and hopeful. If you struggle with sadness every day, dopamine feels like a savior. Unfortunately, the happiness quickly retreats and the mournful feelings return, spiraling you downward again. The next time you turn to food to relieve your emotional sadness, you need a larger portion to achieve the same result. After a while, the body stops releasing dopamine without the assistance of sugar (or sex or drugs or anything else you've trained your body to respond to). That is why sugar is addictive. Your body actually becomes dependent upon sugar to complete its natural function and release the feel-good chemical of dopamine. How sad.

Another physiological reason people overeat is that many foods have been synthetically engineered and genetically modified to become an addictive substance. While this might not have been the intention of engineers, it has been a direct result of modern chemical innovations. In his book *Wheat Belly*, cardiologist and author William Davis tells us that there is actually an addictive ingredient in wheat today that keeps people coming back for more. Here is how he summed it up on his blog:

> Modern wheat is an opiate. And, of course, I don't mean that wheat is an opiate in the sense that you like it so much that you

feel you are addicted. *Wheat is truly addictive.* . . . But the "high" of wheat is not like the high of heroin, morphine, or OxyContin. This opiate, while it binds to the opiate receptors of the brain, doesn't make us high. It makes us *hungry*.

This is the effect exerted by *gliadin*, the protein in wheat that was inadvertently altered by geneticists in the 1970s during efforts to increase yield. Just a few shifts in amino acids and gliadin in modern high-yield, semi-dwarf wheat became *a potent appetite stimulant.*[2]

Simply put, certain foods can make us hungrier. I'm reminded of the Lay's Potato Chips slogan that challenged, "Bet you can't eat just one!" This is what we're up against physically as we go to battle spiritually. Food, the very thing God created to satisfy our physical hunger, has been engineered to stimulate it! That's just one more reason why food triggers abound.

> *Food, the very thing God created to satisfy our physical hunger, has been engineered to stimulate it!*

Ironically, the first group of people I invited to join me for this 40-Day Sugar Fast were actually the same overwhelmed moms in the Facebook group I wrote about earlier. They immediately recognized that their emotional triggers weren't just causing them to get angry with their kids, they were pushing them to run to food to cope with their stress. And the sugar they consumed made them even more emotionally unstable than before. Those moms knew that they needed a physical detox and a spiritual fast!

One woman who joined me for that first fast was my friend Asheritah Ciuciu. A few years later she published a book entitled *Full: Food, Jesus, and the Battle for Satisfaction.* In chapter 7 of her book, Asheritah focuses solely on food triggers. She begins,

"It's useful for us to determine what our particular triggers are, and when faced with that trigger, we can make the intentional choice of whether to go to God or go to food."[3] Pinpointing your personal food triggers is one of the most practical and helpful things you can do if you want to learn to turn to Christ when triggered. Asheritah suggests keeping a running log of the times you find yourself desperate to put something into your mouth so that you can see the patterns and identify your personal food triggers. Perhaps you'll discover that you are tempted to binge only at night once the kids are finally asleep. Or maybe your triggers appear at work when you're struggling to complete a big project. Once you identify your triggers, you won't be powerless against them. You'll be able to make a plan and choose how to cope with them in a healthy way.

As you look back over the past twelve days of your fast, consider when you were most tempted to cave. Was it out of stress or sadness? Did you feel out of control in your parenting or unattractive and unloved in your most intimate relationship? Ask the Lord to search you and know you and reveal to you when you're tempted to turn to food instead of to Him. Then take it one step further and come up with a better plan. Commit to recognizing the underlying feelings and take them to the Lord. With His help, you can also build a healthier and holier habit to combat your most triggered moments.

Dear Lord, search me and know my hungry heart today. Try me and know my triggered thoughts. See if there are any unhealthy habits in my eating and my thinking and my living, and lead me in the everlasting way. I invite You, Lord, to reveal to me why it is I run to food instead of You. Teach me that You are what I need every time I'm triggered. In Jesus's name, Amen.

day 13

WEIGHT AND WORSHIP

But seek first the kingdom of God and his righteousness, and all these things will be added to you.

Matthew 6:33

THERE'S NOTHING WRONG with wanting to lose the extra weight you may be carrying around, whether the extra load comes from literal pounds or from pounds of pain. However, **for deep and lasting physical and emotional transformation to occur, you first need deep and lasting spiritual transformation.** Matthew 6:33 makes it clear: **When you turn your eyes, first and foremost, on God, everything else will fall into its rightful place.** Conversely, when you look to the scale first, it's nearly impossible to see past it to the soul.

When you're tempted to obsess about your weight, ask yourself this: Which will last forever—my spirit or my body? Of course, you know that your body will wear out and your flesh and bones will pass away. But have you considered the never-ending expansiveness of your soul? **Though God's Spirit takes up residency within you when you put your faith in Jesus, your skin isn't His eternal dwelling place—nor is it yours. It's your spirit that dwells with Him.**

Eventually we will leave our bodies and receive glorified bodies. Philippians 3:21 promises: "He will take our weak mortal bodies and change them into glorious bodies like his own, using the same power with which he will bring everything under his control" (NLT). When we get to heaven, we will see God face-to-face—our new forever face to His eternal face. But for now, He is deep within us, looking at us spirit-to-spirit. He is gazing, eyes fixed, at the eternal spirit within us, so we must turn our attention to what He's most passionate about—our spirit's rightness. One million years from now our spirits will still be with His Spirit. Oh, the thought of it!

Those of us who have walked through these forty days before have discovered that when we seek Him first—when we fast from sugar in order to feast on Him—the pounds often start falling off. When we think about the fullness of Christ in us, we stop thinking so much about filling ourselves with food. When we long for the One who truly satisfies, we tend to stop turning to momentary fillers.

Do you see where I'm going with this? The natural man turns his attention to his natural body first: his diet, his exercise, his New Year's resolution. The natural woman steps onto the scale and counts her steps. But weigh this concept carefully. What if we stop counting our steps and start walking in step with God instead? What if we run to Him before we take a run around the block?

Let me be clear. I am not saying you should forget about your physical well-being. Whether your body is oversized or under-nourished is important, and you need to take good care of it. You need cardiovascular exercise for heart health and strength training for muscle health. You need to drink plenty of water too for healthy, hydrated cells and muscles. These are all good things to do. But the starting point for your whole health does not begin with *whole foods* but with *holiness*.

Christ didn't die for your hips or your bust or your belly. He died so that your spirit would remain with Him now and forever. While your body will fail, your spirit will never wear out from age or gravity. That's why you need to spend more time considering the rightness of your spirit and the righteousness of God rather than how right or wrong you think your body is. Do you need more exercise? Perhaps. But running to Jesus has to be your number one form of cardio.

Your eternal spirit is the Holy Spirit's chief concern.

It's easy to obsess over our personal appearance, because we live in a culture obsessed with appearance. However, 1 Samuel 16:7 reminds us, "The Lord does not look at the things people look at. People look at the outward appearance, but the Lord looks at the heart" (NIV).

In order to keep our spiritual health in focus, we have to keep the Spirit in focus. We must seek Him before all else. Though the unseen Spirit of God seems elusive, He is the fullness of God in our daily lives. We need a steady diet of seeking Him and finding Him at the forefront of all we do each day. In Jeremiah 29:13, God promises us, "You will seek me and find me when you seek me with all your heart." Deuteronomy 4:29 tells us, "But if from there you seek the Lord your God, you will find him if you seek him with all your heart and with all your soul" (NIV). We're given even more assurance of His promises in 2 Chronicles 15:4, "But when they in their trouble did turn unto the Lord God of Israel, and sought him, he was found of them" (KJV).

Over and over again throughout the Scriptures God tells us that when we turn to Him, we will find Him. But the miracle gets even more miraculous! When we give the Spirit of God access to our spiritual lives, He lovingly addresses the present reality of our physical and emotional lives too. He doesn't say, "Good! You've got heaven now, that's enough"; instead, He says, "In light of our eternity together, let's deal with this present life together."

You're living two lives now: a temporary existence bound up in the flesh and an everlasting life bound up in the spirit. Much of this Christian life is learning how those two lives flow together. I have personally found that when I focus on that which is fleeting, I lose sight of that which will last. However, when my eyes are fixed on my eternal life, I have a deep sense that the Lord cares deeply about my present life too.

When you seek Him first, you can trust Him with the rest. When you seek the eternal God, you can trust Him with even the temporary struggles. Pounds and pain melt away in a red-hot relationship with the eternal Son. Seek Him spiritually, and you will see what He can do in you physically.

When our lives begin to change from the inside out, our eating habits will change from the outside in. That's why this book doesn't focus on what we can eat each day. We're seeking Him first and foremost. These daily readings are the soul food we need. The problems of this world—whether to do with weight, relationships, finances, popularity, or emotional and physical health—will pass away, but God's righteousness stretches from the past to the present and points us toward forever. Worship His righteousness today. Seek Him and find Him! Get into His righteousness and His righteousness will get into you, satisfying as nothing else can.

> *When our lives begin to change from the inside out, our eating habits will change from the outside in.*

Dear Lord, help me take this Scripture from Matthew 6:33 and hide it in my heart and believe it when I start to chase after all the other things first: "Seek first the kingdom of God and his righteousness, and all these things will be added to you." I'm trusting You with all things as I learn to seek You first. Because of Your Son and in His name, Amen.

day 14

WHAT ELSE ARE YOU CRAVING?

> For you created my inmost being;
>> you knit me together in my mother's womb.
>
> Psalm 139:13 NIV

HALFWAY THROUGH my last forty-day fast, I mindlessly opened up one of my children's apps on my phone and started playing a game. It wasn't a game I'd played before, but I was bored and it caught my eye as I waited for a load of laundry to finish tumbling in the dryer. Two hours later, I looked at the clock and saw that it was time to pick my sons up from school. I hadn't finished doing the laundry or started preparing for dinner, so I was agitated and short-tempered with the boys when I brought them home from school. Their banter and efforts to get my attention only annoyed me, and I finally retreated into the bathroom where I played yet another round of my new game!

True, I hadn't run to food to distract me—after all, I was fasting from sugar!—but I also had not turned to the Lord. I **had crammed something new into the empty places sugar**

left behind. I had consumed a new distraction and numbed my annoyance with a new medicine.

Have you found yourself doing the same? Exchanging one false filler for another? You are now two weeks into your fast; perhaps some of the other addictions that have been simmering on the back burner of your life are moving to the forefront. Or maybe you've found yourself turning to something entirely new. Either way, I want to encourage you to look beyond your sugar addiction so that you can see what else you might be running to.

Picture sugar as the doorway through which you invite the Holy Spirit to come into the private, innermost places of your life. Imagine Him now, deep within your heart, looking around and taking inventory. See Him smiling as He says, "Thanks for the sugar, but I want it all." What started as a sugar fast has the potential to be so much more. I'm praying that God will give you the eyes to see other hidden idols in your life in the days ahead. Layer after layer, as you seek God in His Word, allow Him to convict you of other stuff you may be turning to.

Scottish minister Andrew Bonar said, "Fasting is abstaining from anything that hinders prayer."[1] Not just food. *Anything.* As a matter of fact, Bonar often fasted from reading in order to spend more time with the Lord. *Reading!* His example ought to challenge us to consider what else might be hindering our intimate friendship with the Lord. If we want to experience His sustaining hand in our lives, it may be a good idea to take a season to set aside anything that might be in *our* hands. I like to say it this way: We abstain so that He might sustain. This isn't just about food. We don't just run to the pantry—we run to online games, we run to romance novels, and we run to Starbucks too.

We abstain so that He might sustain.

When we regularly run to anything or anyone else other than Christ to meet our deepest needs, we find only a temporary solution. Christ, however, is eternal. He satisfies us as nothing else can because He is intimately acquainted with each and every part of our souls. After all, He created our innermost beings. Psalm 139:13 tells us clearly, "For you created my inmost being; you knit me together in my mother's womb" (NIV). He made us and He knows us, and He knows what will truly satisfy and fill us.

> Now on the last day, the great day of the feast, Jesus stood and cried out, saying, "If anyone is thirsty, let him come to Me and drink. He who believes in Me, as the Scripture said, 'From his innermost being will flow rivers of living water.'" (John 7:37–38 NASB)

If we want our innermost places filled to overflowing, we've got to turn to God instead of food or other false fillers. In John chapter 7, *innermost being* has been translated from the Greek word *koilia*, which is often used to describe one's belly. However, it not only represents the physical cavity of the stomach but also the emotional seat, which in English we consider our heart.[2] In the above passage, Jesus describes a spiritual emptiness in the heart of humankind, not a physical hunger in one's belly. He understands it because He made us. **The One who made our core is the only One able to fill it.**

Today, as you move deeper into fasting, ask yourself: "Is there anything else that I'm running to? Is there anything else that I need to lay down? Am I turning to anything or anyone else to fill the God hole within me?"

Physicist and theologian Blaise Pascal wrote:

> What is it, then, that this desire and this inability proclaim to us, but that there was once in man a true happiness of which

there now remain to him only the mark and empty trace, which he in vain tries to fill from all his surroundings, seeking from things absent the help he does not obtain in things present? But these are all inadequate, because the infinite abyss can only be filled by an infinite and immutable object, that is to say, only by God Himself.[3]

These words from Pascal inspired the American evangelist Bill Bright to pen this famous statement: "There is a God-shaped vacuum in the heart of every man which cannot be filled by any created thing, but only by God the Creator, made known through Jesus Christ."[4] If this is true, and I believe that it is, then we should be more excited about the fruits of this fast than words can express. God is eager to rush into all the empty places we long to fill. God has the power to turn our hollow places into a hallowed place.

God has the power to turn our hollow places into a hallowed place.

First we must recognize that the Creator made us to crave Him. So often we misunderstand the hunger in our hearts, the grumbling deep inside us, and we turn to the wrong stuff. Lysa TerKeurst, author of *Made to Crave*, said it this way, "God made us to crave—to desire eagerly, want greatly, and long for Him. But Satan wants to do everything possible to replace our craving for God with something else."[5]

Let's not underestimate the devil as we fast and pray in the weeks ahead. You might have picked this book up simply to help you as you detox your body. I urge you to not only offer God the food you consume but also to offer Him everything you turn to instead of Him. Perhaps you turn to those you "like" online rather than the One who loves you to the cross and back. Perhaps you run to the store when you could be storing up treasures in heaven. What do you turn to for satisfaction each time your innermost being cries out for Jesus? Are you restless to fill the void? What you live to fill, Christ died to fill! The satisfied life is yours for the taking if you want it.

What started as a sugar fast can be so much more. What else do you need to surrender for the remainder of this fast?

Dear Lord, I know that sugar isn't the only thing I turn to when I could turn to You. Prick my heart with conviction in the days ahead as I consider what else it is that I'm running to instead of You! You made me to crave You, but I need Your help to set all my other cravings on the altar first. Humbly, Holy Spirit, I'm asking for Your help. Amen.

day 15

DIVISIVE DEVICES

My people have committed two sins:
They have forsaken me,
    the spring of living water,
and have dug their own cisterns,
    broken cisterns that cannot hold water.

Jeremiah 2:13 NIV

THERE WAS A TIME when I slept with my thin, brown Bible under my pillow. It was during one of the hardest seasons of my life—when loneliness threatened to undo me. I would go to sleep with my head literally resting upon my Bible and my heart resting there too. It was symbolic, perhaps, but all I knew was that I needed it close.

In the morning, when the sun rose, I'd reach my hand under my pillow before wiping the sleep from my eyes. My Bible was my daily bread because I was so hungry for love. I'd open it up and start reading where I had left off the night before. **Verse after verse, chapter after chapter, God's Word flooded into all the hurting places of my heart.**

I did this until my husband and I were happily married. That's when I moved my Bible from beneath my pillow to beside my bed. In the morning I would wake up, stretch, reach for my Bible, and then continue reading where I had last left off.

Ten years after we were married, I got my first smartphone. I plugged it in and charged it beside my bed, right beside my Bible. Since my phone held both my alarm clock and my Bible app, it was easy to pick up and open up. The trouble was, all the notifications from the night hours would immediately catch my eye. Before I knew it, instead of spending the early moments of my day with the Lord, I was spending them online with everyone but Him. I found myself eager to know what my friends had to say to me before I turned my attention to what God had to say to me. The temptation was both subtle and obvious.

Verse after verse, chapter after chapter, God's Word flooded into all the hurting places of my heart.

Each time I host the 40-Day Sugar Fast online, I receive hundreds of letters with confessions like this: "I know that sugar is a struggle for me, but my real addiction is to my phone." My friend, author Katie M. Reid, joined me in the fast one year. She publicly confessed her own temptation to turn to social media over and over again each day, though she longed to turn with such fervor and consistency to the Lord. She pointed out the apple on the back of most of our phones, and we all saw her point. No wonder there's a bite taken out of that apple! Just as Eve was tempted away from God's best plan for her life, we feel the pull of temptation too.

Our smartphones can keep us connected to the world, but they can't keep us connected to Christ. They can keep track of our schedules, but they can't order our priorities. They can play our praise music with a single voice command, but they cannot fill our souls with praise.

Jeremiah 2:13 is the verse I'd like you to focus on today, and the verse I try to keep at the forefront of my life. "My people have committed two sins: They have forsaken me, the spring of living water, and have dug their own cisterns, broken cisterns that cannot hold water" (NIV).

His water is both cleansing and satisfying, and those who take a long, cool drink from the well of His saving grace will never thirst again.

Jesus called Himself the living water. His water is both cleansing and satisfying, and those who take a long, cool drink from the well of His saving grace will never thirst again.

You and I both know that it is easy to forsake that well of living water and dig for ourselves other wells. Other cisterns. But they are broken and can't even hold water.

> In your distress you called and I rescued you,
> I answered you out of a thundercloud;
> I tested you at the waters of Meribah.
> Hear me, my people, and I will warn you—
> if you would only listen to me, Israel!
> You shall have no foreign god among you;
> you shall not worship any god other than me.
> I am the Lord your God,
> who brought you up out of Egypt.
> Open wide your mouth and I will fill it.
> But my people would not listen to me;
> Israel would not submit to me.
> So I gave them over to their stubborn hearts
> to follow their own devices. (Ps. 81:7–12 NIV)

Oh, what a powerful passage as the Lord reminded His people of just how faithful He had been. They cried out in their distress and He answered them. Immediately He tested them and reminded them to stay close and to continue to listen. He warned them not to go looking for foreign gods because He is the God who saved them for Himself. He offered to feed them. "Open wide your mouth," He said, "and I will fill it" (v. 10). But they turned away and would not listen and would not eat from His hand nor drink from His cup. Eventually, He gave them over to their own "devices."

Do you see the similarities between the Israelites and the people so attached to their technology today? Devices—it's what we call our smartphones and tablets, our computers and iPads. Oh how divisive they can be when they become our electronic, foreign gods, dividing us from the one true God. Sugar isn't the only idol to which we turn. This fast isn't simply about cutting out sugar; it's about abstaining from anything and everything we've learned to run to time and again.

Ask the God who redeemed you to show you what devices are dividing you from Him, and consider fasting from them during the remaining weeks of your fast. Perhaps its as simple as removing all the social media apps off of your phone or charging it in the bathroom rather than on your bedside table for the next twenty-five days. Then, once your fast is over, maybe you'll set some boundaries to keep God on the throne of your life—and everything else in its rightful place.

> *Dear Lord, I want You to be the only thing I thirst for, because You are the only One who can ever truly satisfy. All the other fillers seem to intensify my desire for more, but You alone can fill me to overflowing! Show me where I've manufactured for myself broken cisterns that can't hold water—let alone living water. In Jesus's quenching name, Amen.*

THE 40-DAY SOCIAL MEDIA FAST

If you are convicted that your phone is even more addictive than sugar, you aren't alone. Find out about the 40-Day Social Media Fast at 40daysocialmediafast.com.

day 16

COMFORT FOODS AND RETAIL THERAPY

Blessed be the God and Father of our Lord Jesus Christ, the Father of mercies and God of all comfort, who comforts us in all our affliction, so that we may be able to comfort those who are in any affliction, with the comfort with which we ourselves are comforted by God.

2 Corinthians 1:3–4

WE ARE SIXTEEN DAYS into this forty-day fast from sugar, and you may think I'm backsliding but stick with me. *There's nothing wrong with sweet treats.* Let's not forget that the promised land was flowing with honey! Dates and grapes, all full to bursting with natural sugars, hung heavy on trees and vines, with honeybees buzzing all around. Throughout the Old Testament, kings, warriors, lovers, and prophets ate honey and it revived them. What a sweet gift from God!

Honey isn't simply packed with natural sugars that provide a quick surge of energy, and it doesn't merely sweeten our tea. When applied to the skin, honey can heal wounds. When applied to the throat, it soothes pain. Few things are richer in vitamins, minerals, proteins, fatty acids, enzymes, and bioflavonoids than the sweet honey produced by the honey-making bee.

God, in His kindness, gave us honey from the comb, and He likened it to His Word because it is sweet and satisfying. It nourishes our bodies and revives us when we are in desperate need of revival. However, Proverbs 25:16 warns: "Have you found honey? Eat only what you need, that you do not have it in excess and vomit it" (NASB).

The lesson today isn't simply moderation; it's that honey isn't the promised land. It's a gift of the promise but it's not the promise in and of itself. When we think that sugar—whether natural or refined—is the promised land, we miss the promised land entirely. Likewise, when we run to food for our comfort, we miss out on the Great Comforter. "I am he who comforts you" (Isa. 51:12).

Perhaps you started fasting because of a few extra pounds, but you're recognizing that you're actually carrying around loads of pain. Maybe a parent abandoned you or your spouse betrayed you. Perhaps you were verbally, physically, or sexually abused. No matter the source of the hurt, old wounds create a lonely ache that needs a comforting touch. Some hurts leave deep, dark holes that fester, raw and aching.

Many people have learned to self-medicate their pain with food. Perhaps you run to brownies or caramels—or caramel brownies—for relief, only to find that it used to take one or two to lift you up and make you happy again, but now it takes half a pan to soothe the hurt. And even then the anesthesia doesn't last long. I know because I've done these things myself. When you turn to food for pain management, the pain is not healed but only masked for a time.

I also know plenty of people who use retail therapy as a way to make themselves feel better. But believe it or not, Target isn't the promised land either (gasp). If you run to the store when you are feeling bored or lonely, only to come out with a bag of clothes or new cosmetics, you might feel a temporary high, but it won't last. A full cart never makes a heart full. Shopping may help you feel better for the afternoon, but your credit card statements will last longer than the effects of your retail therapy. Before you know it, you will be sad or unhappy or bored again, and your wallet can't cover the cost of the ongoing pain. When you try to soothe the hurt with purchases, new pain arises. Even if you're not going into debt, you can't afford to keep purchasing this way because it's getting in the way of what you need most spiritually.

Here's the thing: Comfort food and retail therapy can never bring us anything more than temporary relief. It is only when we run to an eternal God that we find lasting comfort. Sweets and new purchases may be able to revive our hearts for the moment but only He can revive us internally and eternally. We need a true revival more than an ephemeral food or shopping high. We need the promised land of God in our lives, not just the sweet treats He's included in the bounty.

Comfort food and retail therapy can never bring us anything more than temporary relief.

Jesus came to earth to chase us down in our pain and to heal us of our diseases. He walked with the disciples and talked with them too. He went to the cross and died for all our sins. He rose again, overcoming the tyranny of sin and sadness in every desperate life. During Jesus's final days on earth, He stayed with the disciples and ministered to them. When He left to return to the Father, He gave them His Spirit with these words: "And I will pray the Father, and he shall give you another Comforter, that he may abide with you for ever" (John 14:16 KJV).

If you are sad today and have been sad for a long time, open your Bible and ingest the sweetness of John 14, which begins, "Do not let your hearts be troubled" (NIV). When you learn to run to the Comforter, He will fill you with His comfort. You will be filled to overflowing when you take your hungry-for-comfort heart to Him! Eventually, you will be so full of comfort that He will make you an ambassador of His comfort. You won't be able to stop yourself from sharing His goodness with others. His comfort won't simply fill you, it will overflow from you and fill others who are sad as well. When God comforts you, He makes you a comforter; His healing makes you a healer; and His saving makes you a walking, talking testimonial to His saving grace. **When you encounter the promised land of life in Christ, healed and whole, you become ambassadors of His promises.**

His comfort won't simply fill you, it will overflow from you and fill others who are sad as well.

Shopping doesn't satisfy. Brownies don't either. Only the great Comforter does. Commit, my friends, to staying close to the Spirit of all comfort each day of this fast, for your benefit and the benefit of others.

Dear Lord, Your kindness to me is beyond my understanding. You've filled the land with sweet and satisfying things. And yet, You are the sweetest and most satisfying of all. Teach my heart to long for You and come to You. Train my legs to run to You! For You are my promised land, my Comforter, my Healer, my Savior God. Amen.

day 17

BE QUIET AND
BE TRANSFORMED

Don't shoot off your mouth or speak before you think. Don't be
too quick to tell God what you think he wants to hear. God's in
charge, not you—the less you speak, the better.

Ecclesiastes 5:2 MSG

EUGENE PETERSON, author of the poetic Message ad-
aptation of the Bible, passed away in 2018. He brought the
antiquated language of God's Word to life for many of us. In
Matthew 17 he added descriptive details to the story of Jesus's
transfiguration in front of His close friends. The idea of Christ's
transformation captured my imagination the first time that I
read these words: "His appearance changed from the inside
out, right before their eyes. Sunlight poured from his face. His
clothes were filled with light" (Matt. 17:2 MSG). **Christ's fully-
God persona burned through the thin veil of flesh that made
Him fully man.**

Can you imagine what it must have been like for Peterson to
first describe our Savior's bright and blinding presence upon

the mountaintop with His disciples, and then to actually be the disciple looking into Jesus's transfigured face? Brilliant and blinding and beautiful!

One day you will see Jesus face-to-face as well. If you have put your faith in the Son, you will stand before Him in His kingdom of light. Jesus, who first made the earth then walked upon it, will walk right up to you. His light will shine upon you. In His bright transfigured presence, you will be transfigured too.

We're told that Jesus is the lamp of heaven, the source who lights our eternal dwelling home. "The city does not need the sun or the moon to shine on it, for the glory of God gives it light, and the Lamb is its lamp" (Rev. 21:23 NIV). That's the light that blazed through our Savior from the inside out on the mount of transfiguration. That same light has the power to transfigure us! The real miracle is that we don't have to wait to encounter Him in heaven either. The same God who was transformed on earth is willing and able to transform us on earth.

The subtitle of this book, *Where Physical Detox Meets Spiritual Transformation*, is a promise. Transformation through Christ is so much more than pressing a physical restart button. **When you stop running to food and start running to the transfigured Savior, He transforms not only your figure but your heart as well!** But food isn't the only thing that stops us from running to Him. Sometimes we're so busy running our mouths that we miss out on what He's saying and what He's doing.

Consider Peter's response to seeing Jesus talking with Elijah and Moses.

> Jesus took Peter and the brothers, James and John, and led them up a high mountain. His appearance changed from the inside out, right before their eyes. Sunlight poured from his face. His clothes were filled with light. Then they realized that Moses and Elijah were also there in deep conversation with him.

Peter broke in, "Master, this is a great moment! What would you think if I built three memorials here on the mountain—one for you, one for Moses, one for Elijah?"

While he was going on like this, babbling, a light-radiant cloud enveloped them, and sounding from deep in the cloud a voice: "This is my Son, marked by my love, focus of my delight. Listen to him." (Matt. 17:1–5 MSG)

While I'd like to think that my first response to the glory pouring from Jesus's face would be to fall prostrate, perhaps I'd do what Peter did instead. He leaped into action—interrupting Jesus and making plans to build memorials. He continued babbling until God told him to be quiet. **The Father told Peter to stop speaking and listen to His Son.**

All my talking and all my planning can get in the way of hearing God's good plan for me.

Today I'm thinking about my own need to pipe down and listen. My desire to be physically transformed can get in the way of me quietly and humbly worshiping the One who was transformed and has the power to transform me! All my plans to get to the gym and get on the scale and stay on a diet (and all my meal plans too) pale in comparison to the brilliant transforming power of God at work in my life. All my talking and all my planning can get in the way of hearing God's good plan for me.

As you fast, let me encourage you to stop talking and start listening. **Stop running your mouth and start running to Him with ears to hear.** Author Bob Sorge wrote these challenging words in his book *The Secrets of the Secret Place*: "Hearing God's voice has become the singular quest of my heart, the sole pursuit that alone satisfies the great longings of my heart."[1] You have committed to intentionally lay down for forty days that which cannot satisfy in order to experience the only One who can. His voice satisfies. Hearing Him and doing what He says is the secret that can be found only in the quiet of a listening heart.

Do you need to fast from talking for the next few weeks? I don't mean twenty-four hours a day, but maybe one holy hour each morning in order to hear the Lord whispering to your spirit. Sorge goes on to say, "I strongly advocate for a prayer life that is comprised mostly of silence. It's a great delight to talk to God, but it's even more thrilling when He talks to us. I've discovered that He has more important things to say than I do. Things don't change when I talk to God; things change when God talks to me. When I talk, nothing happens; when God talks, the universe comes into existence."[2]

Be quiet. Be listening. Be transformed.

Over the course of the next twenty-three days, spend more time quietly ingesting His transforming Word than you spend speaking words. Spend more time listening to Him than you spend talking. Hear the Father say, "This is my Son, marked by my love, focus of my delight. Listen to him" (MSG). Be quiet. Be listening. Be transformed.

Dear Lord, You are magnificent. You are beautiful and Your Words transform all who listen and receive. I want to hear from You more than I want to talk to You about my plan each day of this fast. Teach me to quiet down so that I might be satisfied by Your voice. I can only imagine what it will be like to stand transformed before Your light-drenched countenance in Your eternal kingdom of light! Until that day, Lord, slowly but surely transform me into Your likeness. I'll be quietly trusting You with the process. In Jesus's name, Amen.

day 18

STUMBLING BLOCKS AND DYNAMITE

If your right eye causes you to stumble, gouge it out and throw it away. It is better for you to lose one part of your body than for your whole body to be thrown into hell. And if your right hand causes you to stumble, cut it off and throw it away. It is better for you to lose one part of your body than for your whole body to go into hell.

Matthew 5:29–30 NIV

YOU ARE NEARLY HALFWAY through your fast. Perhaps the nasty withdrawal migraines you were experiencing are gone and have been replaced with increased energy and more stable emotions. I hope so. However, I don't want you to rest on the laurels of what you've received so far. You may have lost a few pounds, but there's so much more to be gained! Gaining more often requires losing more, and now I'm not talking about pounds at all. If there are other things in your life standing between you and God, today's the day to cast them down.

In Matthew 5:30, Jesus says, "If your right hand causes you to stumble, cut it off and throw it away. It is better for you to lose one part of your body than for your whole body to go into hell" (NIV). One of the problems with familiar Bible passages like this one is that you can read them quickly and move on unchanged. However, the subtitle of this book promises spiritual transformation, which means change has to occur. If there is anything in your life that is causing you to stumble in your journey to be with God and like God, today is the day you stop tripping over it. You've given Him your sugar, and that's no small thing; you've considered your smartphone and other devices; you've surrendered your credit card and your constant go-go-going; but perhaps there is something else that's standing in the way and keeping you from feasting on Him.

Not all stumbling blocks are idols. Some things simply trip us up because we like them a little too much and our attention is pulled off course.

Not all stumbling blocks are idols. Some things simply trip us up because we like them a little too much and our attention is pulled off course. With a little conviction, however, we're back on track with healthy boundaries again. While not everything that causes us to stumble is an idol, idols can bring us down faster than anything else.

Years ago I learned to recognize an idol in my life by answering this one simple question: Would taking away _____ devastate me? Would having to give up Instagram wreck my life? Would foregoing dessert make me an emotional basket case? Would laying down my hobby for a season feel like laying down my life forever? Could I give up hosting annual family gatherings during the holidays and let my sister-in-law do it? Could I say no to a nightly glass or two of wine without panic attacks?

Could I leave my volunteer position at the church or the humane society or my child's school without losing my sense of identity? If the answer is "No, I could not do that without extreme emotional stress," then I know that I have discovered an idol—a massive blockade standing between me and God.

Consider your hobbies, the things you spend your time and money doing. While there is nothing inherently wrong with having a hobby, when your passions and pleasures become preeminent, taking up your first priority spot, you've got it backward. And walking backward is a lot like stumbling blindly in the dark.

Turn around and walk right today. Your hobbies are part of your life, but they are not your whole life. Those who hide in their garages and craft rooms or run to the gym as a form of escapism know what I'm talking about. If your hobbies become your everything, you'll stumble and fall.

The Lord has made all things, and none of them on their own are necessarily bad. I'm reminded of 1 Corinthians 10:23: "'I have the right to do anything,' you say—but not everything is beneficial. 'I have the right to do anything'—but not everything is constructive" (NIV). When your love for anything other than Him gets too big, it blocks your path. That's no good. Like a boulder in the road, your affection for other things stops you from getting through to His affection.

> For I am convinced that neither death nor life, neither angels nor demons, neither the present nor the future, nor any powers, neither height nor depth, nor anything else in all creation, will be able to separate us from the love of God that is in Christ Jesus our Lord. (Rom. 8:38–39 NIV)

God's Word is true: Nothing can separate us from His love—not even our stumbling blocks. However, our stumbling blocks can keep us from *experiencing* His love.

Have you ever been on a road trip, driving through a rugged landscape, weaving up and around mountains, bypassing boulders? Suddenly, the road bends again and you see that you're about to go straight through one of the largest mountains of all. It would be impassable except for the fact that, years ago, men with dynamite blasted through granite, shaping a tunnel clear through to the other side.

God's Word is true: Nothing can separate us from His love—not even our stumbling blocks.

Don't you know that God is dynamite—both as an adjective and a noun! He is dynamite in His awesomeness and in His ability to blow up every obstacle in our way! Those barriers, though often formed by our own two hands, can hold us back from the God who wants the fullness of our affection and attention. Our dynamite God is capable of being the dynamite that blows up each idol—each stumbling block—that separates us from Him today.

God made you for Himself. He's dynamite! Ask Him to speak clearly to your heart about any other hidden and harmful things holding you back from Him—then let Him blast through those stumbling blocks so that you might experience His loving nearness.

Dear Lord, I want to want You most of all, but I stumble over all the other things I want more. Good things, little things, big things. I am willing to cut them off and cast them down, but I need Your help. Speak to my heart today. Give me the eyes to see what idols I have made for myself, and then give me the courage to lay them at Your explosive feet. In Jesus's most powerful name I pray, Amen.

day 19

HAVE A SOBER MIND

Be alert and of sober mind. Your enemy the devil prowls around like a roaring lion looking for someone to devour.

1 Peter 5:8 NIV

OVER THE YEARS when I have asked people if they struggle with food addiction, I always receive a resounding yes. I get a similar response when I ask if they are addicted to social media or to shopping or to streaming shows and movies. When I suggest that they give up these things during our forty-day fast, I get a hallelujah chorus of Amens.

However, any time I suggest that they consider giving up alcohol, people get quiet. Real quiet. And those who don't get quiet get loud. Real loud. Defensively they exclaim, "I am not under the law, but under grace. There's nothing wrong with having a drink." They're referencing Romans 6:14: "For sin shall no longer be your master, because you are not under the law, but under grace" (NIV). But if we can't give something up for forty days, sin may still be our master.

Nobody ever tells me that this sugar fast feels legalistic, but as soon as I suggest we lay down our drinks for forty days, people accuse me of legalism.

Why? Though I agree that we are under grace to drink, why is it that we are so quick to protect our freedom to do so? What is it about alcohol that makes us protest at the thought of giving it up for forty days (or twenty-one days, if today is the day you choose to add it to the list of things you've already surrendered)?

In yesterday's reading I mentioned that the quickest way to recognize an idol in your life is to notice your response when it is taken away. If it trips you up, you've likely stumbled upon a stumbling block. **If you are convinced that you cannot forego alcohol for a few weeks, then I am convinced there's nothing you need to do more.** Matthew 19:26 makes it clear that this is impossible on your own, "but with God all things are possible." Laying down your nightly bottle of beer, glass of wine, or bourbon on the rocks may not seem possible, but with God's help it is.

This isn't about the law, friends; this continues to be a story of God's grace in our lives. This isn't a rule holding us back from fun in an attempt to be super spiritual. God gives us permission to eat and drink, but He also calls us to be on the alert and to be sober-minded. We have an enemy who loves when we are tangled up in anything that distracts us and dulls our senses. "Be alert and of sober mind," God charges us. "Your enemy the devil prowls around like a roaring lion looking for someone to devour" (1 Pet. 5:8 NIV).

It's impossible to have a sober mind when you aren't sober. Alcohol, like food and sex and getting lost online for hours, can numb our pain and dull our senses. However, more than the other addictions we've considered, alcohol dulls our senses most of all. God wants us sober because He loves us. He wants us sober as a precautionary measure, because He knows we have an enemy who is prowling around, hoping to find us distracted and, even better, a little inebriated too.

Even if we put all the spiritual stuff aside for just a moment, you probably shouldn't be drinking alcohol if you want to get the full benefit of this forty-day fast, since the sugar content is incredibly high in nearly all alcoholic beverages. Consider these facts about alcohol:

- The calories in alcohol are empty, meaning they provide no nutritional value.
- Alcohol throws off your blood sugar, interfering with your body's natural ability to regulate glucose.
- Nightly drinks disrupt other regulating hormones like insulin and glucagon.
- Even a little beer or wine can throw off the delicate balance of bacteria in your belly.[1]

There's plenty of science available to back up why it's good to fast from alcohol—whether for a season or forever—but you are still under grace to enjoy a drink if you want to. My question is, why do you want to? Or better yet, do you *want* a drink or do you *need* a drink? If you need a drink, if you need anything other than Christ to get you through each long, hard day, then I urge you to lay it down. As you abstain, you will learn that He sustains!

Nothing heightens our physical and spiritual alertness like fasting. Conversely, nothing tampers with our physical and spiritual alertness quite like alcohol. At least that is the case for me. When I fast and pray, my ears are open to hear, my eyes are open to see, and my spirit is open to discern the things of God. I'm as sober as sober can be.

> *Nothing heightens our physical and spiritual alertness like fasting.*

God is calling you to take a sobering look at your soul's sobriety today. Are you alert? Take an honest inventory of all the ways you self-medicate and self-soothe. Don't hold anything back by clinging to your freedom in Christ as an excuse to keep doing as you please. **If the mere thought of giving up your wine causes you to whine, you might have found an idol in your life.**

Heavenly Father, You are all about freedom and flavor and fun! You're not a killjoy, standing over me with a rulebook, waiting for me to fail. I already have, time and time again. But You paid for those sins already. May my forgiven life today testify to the fact that I am truly free! And if I'm free, than I'm free to set down any and all addictions on the altar of this fast! Thank you, Jesus. In Your name, Amen.

day 20

THE WORLD'S GOODS AREN'T AS GOOD

Don't love the world's ways. Don't love the world's goods. Love of the world squeezes out love for the Father. Practically everything that goes on in the world—wanting your own way, wanting everything for yourself, wanting to appear important—has nothing to do with the Father. It just isolates you from him. The world and all its wanting, wanting, wanting is on the way out—but whoever does what God wants is set for eternity.

1 John 2:15–17 MSG

THE GOAL OF THIS FAST has been to crowd out sugar by ingesting more of God, but today we're getting honest about the things that crowd Him out. Halfway through our forty-day fast, I want you to ask yourself this question: Are the things of the world squeezing out my love for the Father? Or is my love for the Father crowding out my love for the world? You only have a limited amount of love to spend each day. How are you spending yours?

Oftentimes my husband and I look at our bank account balance with fresh eyes. After we've paid all the bills and put some money in a savings fund, we only have a certain sum left for extras. One of us suggests a new couch and the other a trip somewhere special. We consider the needs of our missionary friends who we know and love, and Christmas always seems to be right around the corner. The reality is that we have a limited amount of money, and we can't afford it all. The same is true with our affection. If we spend our energy loving things, we'll come to God spent. Flat broke and bankrupt.

These past few days we've assessed the idols in our lives—those things that we pour all our time, money, and energy into. Preeminent in our lives, they take first place in our thoughts and in our spending and in our hearts. We wake up and get out of bed in order to chase down the world's best stuff, but the world will never satisfy us because we weren't made for this world! Each day, we're seeing with new eyes that the world and the things of this world can't cut it. Not only do the world's goods not satisfy us but they also hold us back from the only One who can. That's why I'm thinking about today's verse, and how the Message translates it: "The world and all its wanting, wanting, wanting is on the way out—but whoever does what God wants is set for eternity" (1 John 2:17).

I've already talked about how the body is temporary but the soul is eternal. French Christian mystic Pierre Teilhard de Chardin put it this way: "We are not human beings having a spiritual experience. We are spiritual beings, having a human experience."[1] Don't you feel it? You are not a temporal being who can be satisfied by temporary pleasures. You are an eternal being, with a deep, insatiable hunger for eternal pleasures. Try as you might, you can't spend your life with a foot in both worlds.

The English Standard Version translates 1 John 2:15–17 this way:

> Do not love the world or the things in the world. If anyone loves the world, the love of the Father is not in him. For all that is in the world—the desires of the flesh and the desires of the

eyes and pride of life—is not from the Father but is from the world. And the world is passing away along with its desires, but whoever does the will of God abides forever.

Dear friend, don't look to debate God on this one. Of course He made this earth as a good and fertile gift, from the mango and the mandarin orange to the white cliffs of Dover and the Austrian Alps. Even children are a gift from above, coming down to us from the Father who wove them together, stitch by stitch, and placed them in our homes and our hearts. God isn't telling us to hate all the good things He made in this world. He just doesn't want us to love them more than Him, worshiping things such as food and money and clothes and fame. This world, sweet as He made it, is not our final destination. It is as brief as a breath and we're just passing through. How would our lives change if our perspective changed?

God doesn't want us to abhor the things He's made here in this world, but He doesn't want us to lust after it all, take pride in it, or allow it to steal our attention or our affection either. Our passion for the gift should never rob our passion for the Giver. Our devotion to this world shouldn't distract us from the only One worthy of our devotion. That should give us great pause!

Our passion for the gift should never rob our passion for the Giver.

Throughout Scripture God likens our waywardness to adultery. That resonates with me when I pick up my phone to scroll through social media before I've taken the time to sit with Him in His Word. I know it's true when I'm tempted to buy more stuff but haven't invested my money or time in the eternal things that God values, such as orphan care and other mercy ministries. I sense it in my spirit each time I'm under stress and long for a drink instead of inviting the Holy Spirit to help me cope. I can't run in both directions at once. It's a matter of economics. If I turn to this world to get me through, I will be turning away from the One who can. It's also a matter of adultery. Adultery is the act of leaving one love for a relationship with another. This world is that other. God isn't shaming us, and I'm not trying to shame us either. But perhaps the reality of our wayward tendencies today might awake in us a *distaste* for the way we love and depend upon this world's goods just a little more than we should.

What in this world are you wanting, wanting, wanting? Are you obsessed with being thin, desired, and affirmed? Are you driven by the academic and athletic success of your children, the pride of your life? Do you spend hours on Instagram, watching home improvement shows, flipping through magazines lusting over every kitchen island and every pool overlooking Napa Valley at sunset? All those things are temporary, but you're living an eternal life now! Today is simply part of the first act in a forever musical where the eternal chorus sings, "Holy, holy, holy, is the Lord God Almighty, who was and is and is to come" (Rev. 4:8).

> *Today is simply part of the first act in a forever musical where the eternal chorus sings, "Holy, holy, holy, is the Lord God Almighty, who was and is and is to come" (Rev. 4:8).*

The Message translation speaks of our love for the world squeezing out our love for the Father. However, we're fasting now so we've turned the table. We're squeezing out the temporary pleasures of this world so that we might feast on Him forever. We're not just crowding out sugar; we're crowding out anything that has tried to crowd out our love for the Father.

Dear Lord, I want my heart to be fully devoted to You—not to this world or the things in it. Forgive me. I'm sorry it is taking me so long. Continue to show me how to love You more, because You've loved me so faithfully, and Your love never ends. Speak to me during these next twenty days. Let me hear You and see You and know You as I intentionally pull away from the things of this world and set my gaze upon eternity. In Jesus's unending name, Amen.

YOU'RE HALFWAY THROUGH

Congratulations! You've taken out sugar and perhaps some other things that have held you back from the Lord's power and presence in your life. That's the whole goal of this fast. You may have thought it was about sugar, but it's really about Jesus! More of Him, crowding out everything else. Remember, the whole point of a spiritual fast is abstaining from that which is temporary and ordinary in order to experience the One who is eternally extraordinary.

day 21

BOREDOM CAN BE
A TRIGGER TOO

Lazy people sleep soundly,
but idleness leaves them hungry.
Proverbs 19:15 NLT

WE GRAZE ON FOOD ALL DAY, misreading boredom
for hunger. And while hunger is a physical emptiness, boredom feels empty as well and we tend to get the two confused.
Perhaps, we think, *if I fill my belly, then I will feel better.* Except
overeating makes us sleepy and sleepiness makes us idle and
idleness makes us more bored and boredom makes us even
more hungry. It's a sad, lethargic cycle, and we can't break out
of it because we don't have the energy.

The New American Standard Bible translation of Proverbs
19:15 says that an idle person will "suffer hunger." *Suffering.* I
know that feeling. When I'm idle, I suffer from a false sense of
hunger—a painful urgency to fill the empty space within me,
which leads me to scour the pantry to pass the time. My favorite
translation of Proverbs 19:15 comes from the New International

Version: "Laziness brings on deep sleep, and the shiftless go hungry." *Shiftless* means lacking direction or bored and aimless. Floating here and there, without purpose, willpower, or energy— like a boat without a rudder. Can you pinpoint times in your day when you feel aimless or shiftless and mistake those feelings for hunger? Do you snack or even binge because you're bored?

The irony is that, in our boredom, too much food can end up making us sleepy. Think of Thanksgiving Day. Our family members doze on the couch after polishing off three plates of turkey, sweet potatoes, and stuffing. When we overeat, our digestive tracts get overworked. We're flooded with insulin and sero- tonin, which makes us drowsy. Instead of giving us energy, our digestive systems have to break down too much of the wrong food, wearing us out and lulling us to sleep. Our fatigue slows us down until we sit down, tired and bored again. As I said, it's a sad, lethargic cycle. Eventually we commit to waking up, so we turn to a hefty dose of sugar or a caffeinated beverage (or, better yet, a highly sugared *and* caffeinated drink).

Coffee and sweets combat our daily doldrums. When we in- gest sugar and caffeine, our adrenal glands respond to the wake- up call like they would respond to stress—by releasing cortisol to calm us down. It's ironic. We're tired so we drink caffeine to wake us up, which triggers our bodies to release a chemical to calm us back down. We're up and down and all around, bored and stressed and eating and sleeping and drinking coffee so that we can wake up and do it all over again. Unfortunately, our adrenal glands counter each pick-me-up with another calming dose of cortisol. We're on a chemical teeter-totter and more exhausted than before!

One hand over the other, one brownie followed by more sweet tea and another cuppa joe—our adrenal glands are con- stantly pumping until they are so worn out they simply stop working. Depression sets in, driving us to greater exhaustion than before, and we can't cope with simple stressors without the help of cortisol. Eventually our adrenal glands aren't able to function, so we can't function. They're fatigued, so we're fatigued. They break down, so we break down. In their exhaustion they've fallen asleep, and so have we.

However, just after God tells us that the idle person will suffer hunger, He calls us to wake up once and for all. "Do not love sleep, or you will become poor; open your eyes, and you will be satisfied with food" (Prov. 20:13 NASB). Of course, this isn't merely about waking up and working hard and holding down a job so that you won't be poor. The word *poor* doesn't merely describe your financial situation; spiritual poverty is possible too—and it looks shiftless, idle, and bored. You find yourself spiritually bankrupt when you stop going to work in your faith life. That's what this wake-up call is all about. Don't fall back asleep! Wake up and go to work spiritually. Open your eyes and be satisfied with good spirit-building instead of sleep-inducing food! Friends, forget about the sugar so that you might feast on the sustaining food of Christ!

You find yourself spiritually bankrupt when you stop going to work in your faith life.

"Come to Me," God invites. "Seek Me," He implores. Stop mindlessly eating when you're bored. It is time to wake up from your slumber and actively feast on His presence. Unlike sodas and candy, He'll give you the energy you need to keep going long term—to keep running the race He has marked out for you. Hebrews 12 is the shot that rings out signifying the start of that race.

> Therefore, since we are surrounded by such a great cloud of witnesses, let us throw off everything that hinders and the sin

that so easily entangles. And let us run with perseverance the race marked out for us, fixing our eyes on Jesus, the pioneer and perfecter of faith. For the joy set before him he endured the cross, scorning its shame, and sat down at the right hand of the throne of God. Consider him who endured such opposition from sinners, so that you will not grow weary and lose heart. (Heb. 12:1–3 NIV)

Wake up! Be alert! Throw off the sin that's entangled you and run. **Open your eyes and fix them on Jesus, because He's run this race before you, and He's in your midst, running it with you now.** Don't let yourself go shiftless again. God is setting the pace. If anyone knows temptation and opposition, it's Jesus. He knows everything that causes you to grow weary and lose heart, so stay alert and stay engaged and run with Him!

Jesus, thank You for never running away from me, though I doze off from time to time. I want to wake up and run with endurance the course You've set before me. I want to be aware of the race I'm in and stay alert and strong. I know that what I'm eating isn't helping me keep up with You. Use this season of fasting to heal my body and rouse my spirit. Heal my adrenal glands and anything else that needs Your touch today. I don't want to suffer hunger another day. In the energizing name of Jesus, Amen.

day 22

SPIRITUAL AND MENTAL CLARITY

And your ears shall hear a word behind you, saying, "This is the way, walk in it," when you turn to the right or when you turn to the left.

Isaiah 30:21

I WASN'T RAISED in a fasting family or a fasting church. This idea of fasting was completely foreign to me. And yet, one day, the Lord called me to it with such clarity I couldn't resist the urge to go without food for the day.

In 1992, I was a freshman at Emerson College in Boston, Massachusetts. I was having a hard time finding other Christians at my school, so I began visiting other local colleges' campus meetings. After a while, the leaders there challenged me to start something on my own. Did I mention that I hadn't found any other Christians at my school? That's when I decided to host a Bible study for non-Christians in my dorm room. I wasn't sure who would come or what exactly I would say, but it felt like an act of obedience. The morning of the first study, I looked outside to see the Harvard rowing team gliding over the Charles River, just outside my window. Energized and alert, their eyes were set before them, their muscles tense with a synchronized purpose. I was just waking up for the day and I lacked the mental and spiritual clarity I needed for the task at hand. It was then that I decided to fast and pray, hoping that God would speak clearly to me in the hours leading up to the gathering.

The spiritual practice of fasting felt strange to me. I didn't know what exactly I was hoping to accomplish by giving up food and praying, but the direct result was clarity. It was as though God reached out, pulled off my blinders, and gave me a fresh vision for the job before me. By six o'clock that night I knew exactly how to welcome the students who showed up for the study and what I needed to share with them. It was just a simple one-day fast, but clarity came immediately.

Now here you are, twenty-two days without sugar, and I'm guessing you're likely experiencing spiritual clarity as well. How exciting! Maybe you've received revelation regarding how to serve a family in your neighborhood, a new position you're considering at work, a move across the country to be closer to loved ones, a story you've been inspired to write as a legacy to your grandchildren, a fresh way to communicate love to your spouse, or a school-district change for your children. Suddenly you have clear insight from above: "This is the way, walk in it."

While it's exciting to receive a strike of lightning-bolt clarity about something, more often the clarity that comes from fasting feels like daily insight and alertness. Slowly but surely we begin to discern what deserves a yes and what deserves a no. When we fast from sugar and feast on Scripture, we receive spiritual clarity and understanding for the path before us. Of course we do. God promises that His Word is a lamp to our feet and a light to our path—and that lamplight gives us clarity.

But there's more! I have heard my fasting friends testify that during these forty days they have not only experienced spiritual clarity but mental clarity as well. Could it be that our minds work better without sugar? Could it be that we're sleeping better so our waking hours are more wakeful? Could this fast have both physiological and spiritual benefits?

When we fast from sugar and feast on Scripture, we receive spiritual clarity and understanding for the path before us.

Just last night, I was at a dinner party and talking with a group of friends who were all trying the latest diet craze that had them eating completely sugar-free for the first time in their lives. All three went on and on about how mentally alert they felt. "It's like I'm coming out of a fog," one said. I smiled because I knew that she was. They were all coming out from under a sugar cloud, and you are too.

Sugar and other false fillers dim our vision, but clarity is available to us when we exercise our spirits and our wills: fasting and praying, spending time in God's Word, and practicing self-control when it comes to what we eat and drink and the amount of sleep we get.

We want to hear from the Lord about which way we are to walk, and we long to clearly see His will in our daily lives. But for that to happen, we must not only ingest His Word but also consume brain food.

I've said from the start that I wouldn't be focusing on food during this fast. I know how easy it is to transfer one's obsession with unhealthy foods to an obsession with healthy alternatives. Many spiritually starving people spend their days focused solely on healthy meal planning and a workout regimen. We're not fasting from sugary food in order to fixate on healthy eating; the whole point is to fix our eyes on Jesus. He's the One who whispers instructions on where we should walk and what we should do. He's the Son who burns away the cloud cover and brings light and understanding into our days.

And so it is with caution that I encourage you to consider eating foods that are good for your brain and that help your mind work well: fish and poultry, eggs, nuts, coconuts, avocadoes, blueberries, tomatoes, broccoli, spinach, kale, and water—plenty of water. Make yourself a batch of fresh pesto or hummus to dip your veggies in this afternoon. Both are rich in Omega-3 Fatty Acids that help the brain and the body function with clarity and endurance.[1] Of course, a steady diet of God's Word is the best thing you can ingest for a clear and energizing sense of purpose each day.

We're not fasting from sugary food in order to fixate on healthy eating; the whole point is to fix our eyes on Jesus.

Again and again I remind you to feast as you fast. Let's do that now. Feast on God's Word as you pray this prayer for clarity in the days ahead.

Oh, Father in heaven, open my eyes as I open Your Word, that I may behold wonderful things from Your law. Open my ears as I open my heart to hear from You. Give me a spirit of wisdom and of revelation as I fast and pray. I humbly ask for Your clear, kind leading. In Jesus's clarifying name, Amen.

day 23

HUNGER PANGS

> O God, you are my God;
>> I earnestly search for you.
> My soul thirsts for you;
>> my whole body longs for you
> in this parched and weary land
>> where there is no water.
>
> Psalm 63:1 NLT

MOST OF US aren't very good at going hungry. We're even worse at staying hungry for long periods of time. That may be why many people transition from fasting to dieting about halfway through this forty-day fast.

Here's how it happens: You're through the ugly detox stage. Physically you feel pretty good and spiritually you're closer to God than you have been in a long time, maybe ever. Wonderful! You've discovered healthier meal options and have found a rhythm to eating sugar-free. You're not so hungry anymore, not the way you were at the beginning. Your energy is up and your thinking is clear, so you've clearly gotten everything out of this fast that you're going to get. Or so you think. You're on cruise control now.

I've seen it time and again and experienced it myself. Perhaps the biggest way to slip from fasting to dieting mid-fast is learning to fill up on sugar-free foods. However, the goal in these pages and throughout these days isn't to simply detox from sugar and transfer your focus to sugar-free recipes; it's to thirst for God as though you're wasting away in a dry and parched land, to long for Him and grow in your love relationship with Him.

You are missing the point entirely if you have found a way to fast without experiencing hunger. Hunger pangs are a holy tool, reminding us that we are fasting, why we are fasting, and whom we want to be most hungry for. I love how author Bill Gaultiere said it here: "In other words, let your hunger pangs become like church bells calling you to prayer. Whenever you're hungry for food say to yourself something like, 'Jesus, you are my sweetness and sustenance. Your name is like honey on my lips. Your words are the manna that I hunger for.'"[1]

When you replace your sugary treats for sugar-free foods, you will likely lose weight and experience other health benefits. But don't you want more than that? I do! If you want a changed life, you must do more than just change your diet. Eating sugar-free may *enhance* your life, but only the Lord Himself can *transform* it. Instead, renounce sugar and replace it with a sweet and constant dependence on Christ, the Bread of Life, your sustenance. When you do that, your life will begin to change.

> *Eating sugar-free may* **enhance** *your life, but only the Lord Himself can* **transform** *it.*

It takes longer than twenty-three days to be transformed, and it requires a measure of pain—hunger pain—which is why I want you to consider how you might increase your physical hunger as a means of unleashing your spiritual hunger. Your body is getting used to functioning without sugar, which is why you may be thinking you are ready for a transition. If you want to transition, go deeper rather than pulling back. Press into Christ rather than into some mere diet. **Lay down your refined sugars in exchange for His sweet refining. It's time to crank up the heat in the crucible of this fast.**

How might you increase your physical hunger so that you can experience greater spiritual hunger? Some people find that eliminating other foods, such as bread and pasta, is an easy way to crank up the intensity of this fast. Others choose to give up breakfast completely. By waiting to eat until after you've had a significant time with the Lord each day, you get the intense benefits of a traditional fast each morning. Some days that means you might have breakfast around midmorning, but other days it may not be until noon. This practice of turning to the Lord before turning to food will certainly turn up the heat on your fast.

Allowing yourself to go physically hungry enables your heart to grow spiritually hungry.

You'll be reminded by every empty-belly growl that you're fasting from sugar in order to feast on Him. Allowing yourself to go physically hungry enables your heart to grow spiritually hungry. God promises that when all else fails, He is our portion. Skip a meal or take other foods out of your diet for the rest of this fast. See for yourself how physical hunger ignites a deeper hunger for the One who can satisfy.

> My flesh and my heart may fail,
> but God is the strength of my heart and my portion
> forever. (Ps. 73:26)

I recognize how countercultural and counterintuitive it is to let yourself go hungry, but **when you push through the discomfort, you'll experience a deeper comfort than any comfort food could ever provide.** Take some time now to get quiet. Consider how much you have eaten today. Is it possible that you've simply transitioned into a sugar-free diet? Is your belly constantly full of sugar-free foods, or is it clanging like a church bell, calling you to prayer? Press into the hunger pangs as you press on through these fasting days.

In Psalm 63:8, the psalmist cries, "My soul clings to you." I have found that fasting intensifies my soul's desperation for God, causing me to cling to Him in a way I don't naturally do when I'm filled with the things of this world. What might you give up in order to intensify your soul's desperate need for God? For when you seek Him desperately, you will find Him abundantly, exceedingly, and more than you ever hoped or imagined.

Don't be afraid to get hungry; be afraid of a life that never hungers for God.

Dear Lord, I don't want to get less hungry as I fast but more hungry! Intensify my hunger for You. Use each empty-belly growl to remind me that I want You most of all. When I long for sweet refined sugars, teach me to lean into Your sweet refining. Twenty-three days into this forty-day fast, I want to want You more today than I did on day 1. Help me, Lord, to have the courage to go without, so that I might go with You! Amen.

day 24

HEALING PAST HURTS

Come to me, all you who are weary and burdened, and I will give you rest.

Matthew 11:28 NIV

I KEEP A FILE ON MY COMPUTER that is full of the testimonies people have sent me over the years as we've fasted together in community. I regularly receive messages like this one:

> During our fast, I developed a genuine self-love. As a survivor of childhood sexual abuse, I've struggled most of my life feeling like damaged goods. In the past, I've used food to cope and have made a huge mess of my health. Unfortunately, it's not just ruined my health, but made me miserable mentally and emotionally too! I am finally experiencing freedom from my addictions and from the negative self-talk that used to drive me to food. I am finally starting to experience the love of Jesus in my life and I am learning to completely surrender to him.

If you have been emotionally, physically, verbally, or sexually abused by a parent or a family member, a significant other or a spouse, or anyone else in this fallen world, I am so sorry.

Truly. Even as I write these words I feel compelled to stop and pray for you. (If you haven't been abused, would you join me in praying for the men and women reading this book who have been torn apart by the sins of others?)

Dear Lord, before we go on with today's reading and apply Your Word to our lives, I ask that You speak truth and love to those who have been abused and are now holding this book, eager for healing. You made them and You know them. You're not finished with them yet. I humbly ask that they would open their hearts to Your healing today. Fill them up with your adoration. I pray that they grow to adore themselves because You adored them first. Gently change their thinking and their feeling and their living, so they might become healed and whole. In Jesus's redeeming name, I pray, Amen.

Dear reader, let me give it to you straight. You are loved beyond measure and created for the explicit purpose of a safe and saving love relationship with your Creator. He made you and adores you because you are His. It is my sincere prayer that the Lord will fill you with the blessed assurance that He sees you, cares for you, and longs to redeem your hurting soul. Redeeming broken things is what He is all about. It's what He came to earth to do. He came to redeem you!

The One who knit you together in your mother's womb sent His Son to chase you down and heal you.

The One who knit you together in your mother's womb sent His Son to chase you down and heal you. Through faith you can experience Him reknitting the unraveled pieces of your life. Psalm 51:10 promises that God will make your innermost being completely new if you ask Him to. "Create in me a clean heart, O God, and renew a steadfast spirit within me" (NIV). What's more? Miracle of miracles, the reknitting doesn't happen just once. It's not a once-and-done fix. The Holy Spirit lives in you, perfecting you, healing you, and transforming you little by little as you journey toward Christlikeness and toward Christ Himself.

God didn't choose for you to be abused, but He chooses each day to redeem the abuse. He didn't want you to be hurt, but He can heal your hurt. He didn't want your mind warped by the hurtful words of others, but He can speak new words over you until you start hearing His Words rather than the words that wounded you in the past. He can and He does do all this and more when you surrender to Him as your redeemer, remaker, renewer, reknitter. All you have to do is respond to His loving invitation in Matthew 11:28, "Come to me, all you who are weary and burdened, and I will give you rest" (NIV).

He can heal any life that's been torn apart; He can fill any hole and make it whole. If you have been hurt by others and you now run to food for comfort, I know that you've found food lacking because I have too. It's not what food was made for. It's not food's job to mend you and speak truth into the lies you hear. It's God's job to comfort and fill you. He is the Great Comforter, and I'm praying that He brings you tremendous comfort and healing today and in the days ahead.

When we fast and pray, the Lord clearly and graciously shows us our soul-sadness and sin-struggles. He speaks to our hearts, tenderly and clearly, about where we've been hurt in the past and how it has caused us to behave in the present. **I've come to discover that food can be like noise, keeping us from hearing. When we set food down for a season, however, we turn the sound down and are finally able to hear the revelation of God speaking truth over our lives.**

Today I invite you to directly ask the Lord if you're running to sugar because you're running from past or present pain. It's a hard question, but one that our good God can lovingly answer. There are so many reasons why you may habitually turn to sugar. This powerful poem by Rebecca K. Reynolds lists many reasons you may run to sugar instead of the Savior.

> Sugar because I'm tired—
> because there's simply too much to do
> and no way to do it.
>
> Sugar because it's fast—
> and I need 30 more minutes
> of strength.
>
> Sugar because I'm lonely—
> because something sweet
> tastes like
> human touch feels.
>
> Sugar because it's cheap—
> one buck instead of five.
>
> Sugar because I didn't plan—
> didn't take time to prep
> to stand against the current.
>
> Sugar because I'm sad—
> about so many things,
> and for two seconds I can forget.
>
> Sugar because I don't want to move—
> and sugar sits here with me.
>
> Sugar because I'm scared—
> of what might pull me
> if I were fit.

Sugar because I'm so angry—
I don't care what happens.

Sugar because I'm ashamed—
of how far I've let it go already.

Sugar because I'm addicted—
caught in a drunken cycle
of lows and highs.

Sugar because she loved by sugar—
when she wanted to give me comfort,
and I remember.

Sugar because I haven't learned to value—
what is simple and beautiful.

Sugar because I don't trust—
that manna will appear again in the morning.

Sugar because I don't believe—
I will ever adjust.

Sugar because those first three days—
are war.

Sugar because tomorrow—
tomorrow—
tomorrow I'll start.

Sugar because I never can see—
that every single today
is the first day
of the rest of a better life.[1]

Has God shown you something new during this fast? Has He helped you understand your complicated story and some of the age-old reasons why you turn to sugar in lieu of Him? Has He revealed where some of your wounds came from? Perhaps the ones that cause you to run to food as a source of comfort? If so, you now know one of your triggers. Knowledge is power.

Each time you are triggered to heal the hurt with sugar, choose to respond instead by going to the One who can heal your hurt with His love. Self-medicating your pain with food keeps you from the Great Physician.

Self-medicating your pain with food keeps you from the Great Physician.

If past abuse has left you feeling unlovable, and you've learned to hide the pain behind pounds, bring those age-old hurts to the altar, and lay them there beside your sugar. Remember that giving up sugar was simply the door through which you invited the Holy Spirit deeper into your life. Now that He's up close, pressing against your hurting heart, invite Him to reknit those tattered places deep inside.

Lord Jesus, do what You are so good at doing. Knit me together again on the inside—reknit me, and renew me, and make me whole again. Fill my aching places with Your holy comfort. As I learn to rest in Your nearness, Lord, transform my thought life. Reknit my thoughts about myself. Not only does my self-loathing hurt me but it hurts You too. Teach me to love myself because You love me. Give me the eyes to see how loved I am. Fill my mind with understanding. Teach me what it means to be fearfully and wonderfully made. Though people have unmade me with their abuse, Lord, You have the authority to remake me. Mend me, Lord, and let me know the joy of being whole and wholly chosen! In Jesus's name, Amen.

day 25

GOD CARES ABOUT
THE DETAILS

So we fasted and sought our God concerning this matter, and
He listened to our entreaty.

Ezra 8:23 NASB

A FEW YEARS AGO I fasted from sugar as I worked on an
intense writing project with a tight deadline. I'm a slow writer,
so I needed clarity and focus and, perhaps, a miracle. While
God answered that prayer, giving me inspiration in spades and
allowing my fingers to fly over the keyboard with Scriptures and
application, He was busy making improvements in my personal
life as well. Though many of my hours each day were spent
writing, my mind kept returning to my kids during their school
days. Various needs for each one kept coming to my heart, so,
as I fasted and wrote, I prayed for my children.

**Oftentimes we come to a fast looking for one benefit, but
the Lord decides to benefit us in other ways as well.** That's
what He did as I fasted. He gave me what I asked for, then ad-
dressed details that I had not invited Him into. During those

days of writing and fasting, I prayed for my children and saw very specific strongholds fall away from their young lives. Grief over sin, forgiveness in broken relationships, breakthroughs amid learning challenges . . . the details.

Oftentimes we come to a fast looking for one benefit, but the Lord decides to benefit us in other ways as well.

Similarly, we came to God twenty-five days ago with a specific prayer request, asking that He do that one thing well. From that humble place, in that dependent state, we have heard from Him that sugar isn't the only thing He wants to talk to us about. In His kindness, He took us beyond what we hoped or imagined.

One by one, He has begun to reveal new details about our lives that He wants to deal with. He's getting in our personal business now, asking us to give up more things: coffee, late-night television, and online shopping too. One detail at a time, He's peeling back the layers of our lives like an onion. And just as peeling the layers of an onion can cause tears, so can peeling back the layers of our lives, revealing details that need God's attention. Sometimes we don't know we need Him until the other needs are peeled back revealing more. But these are good tears because they are a result of learning that God cares about all our issues—from the big and the ugly to the private and unseen.

He is sovereign over the details of our lives. Some details are overwhelming in size, such as our addictions, while others are small, such as our hidden thought lives. Marital struggles or a child's diagnosis, financial pressure and choices at work, a parent's failing health, and a possible school change for one of the kids rise to the top as God peels back layer after layer. So many details.

I'm reminded of Ezra the scribe who, after God's people were exiled to Babylon, was commissioned by King Artaxerxes to return the survivors to Jerusalem along with all the silver and gold that had been taken from the treasuries of the house of God. As Ezra prepared for the journey across the desert with the small remnant of Israelites traveling with him, he was suddenly overcome with concern for their safety.

> Then I proclaimed a fast there at the river of Ahava, that we might humble ourselves before our God to seek from Him a safe journey for us, our little ones, and all our possessions. For I was ashamed to request from the king troops and horsemen to protect us from the enemy on the way, because we had said to the king, "The hand of our God is favorably disposed to all those who seek Him, but His power and His anger are against all those who forsake Him." So we fasted and sought our God concerning this *matter*, and He listened to our entreaty. (Ezra 8:21–23 NASB, emphasis added)

Ezra brought his concern before the Lord because he knew that the details of our lives *matter* to God! What matters to us matters to Him when what matters to us is aligned with His will.

What matters to us matters to Him when what matters to us is aligned with His will.

What details concern you today? What matters deeply to you right now? Is it your work, your family, the health of a loved one, the bills that keep coming, or a specific decision that must be made this week? I have a couple of those concerns myself, but I don't want to make these decisions without God's wisdom and direction.

During the first half of this fast we focused on getting our hearts right with God, but by now God has dealt lovingly with your heart. Today you get to turn your heart and your full attention to the details that concern you. Ask the Lord to go with you and grant you wisdom and safety too. Not just for you but also for those journeying with you—your family and friends and neighbors. Take some time today to sit quietly before Him, at the foot of the throne, where He now dwells securely.

I suspect that in the past the stress caused by the details of your life caused you to run to food or some other form of consumption. But you've taken care of that now; God is God in your life. Today is the day that you take the details of your life to Him—not to sugar, not to wine, not to the gym or the scale or the mall. The only God who reigns in the heavens holds your life in the expansive palm of His hand, and He cares about all that concerns you today. **What matters to you matters to Him because you matter to Him.**

Dear Lord, You are so overwhelmingly big. I can't wrap my mind around Your vastness, Your enormous majesty, and Your complete rule over the galaxies. And yet, gentle Savior, in the person of Your divine Spirit, You also reside in the smallest space of my heart. You are in me, intimately acquainted with all that concerns me today. How kind of You to care for me as You do. Thank You, Lord. Thank You. In Jesus's name, Amen.

day 26

AS FOR ME AND
MY HOUSE . . .

But if serving the LORD seems undesirable to you, then choose
for yourselves this day whom you will serve, whether the gods
your ancestors served beyond the Euphrates, or the gods of the
Amorites, in whose land you are living. But as for me and my
household, we will serve the LORD.

Joshua 24:15 NIV

MANY CHRISTIANS display Joshua 24:15 on their walls and
above their mantels. Others quote it at weddings or baby dedi-
cations. Today I'd like for you to take this common Christian
saying and make it the foundation of how you live your transformed life beyond this fast.

In case you are unfamiliar with the story of Joshua, here is
a bit of background. Joshua took Moses's place as Israel ended
their forty years of wandering in the desert. Joshua was charged
with the task of leading the people of Israel into the promised land. With Joshua at the front line, the men of Israel took
the land, killed and captured the inhabitants, and settled into
their inheritance. At the end of Joshua's life, he challenged the

people to follow God and obey His commands. Joshua knew they struggled with sin and idolatry; he knew they were tempted to worship the old gods that their ancestors had worshiped, along with the gods of the people who lived in Canaan before them; but Joshua also knew that he wasn't going to live much longer, so he passionately charged them to persevere in their faith. "Throw away the gods your ancestors worshiped" he begged, "and serve the Lord" (v. 14 NIV).

When faced with a challenge that seemed overwhelming and impossible, the Israelites had a pattern of giving in to fear rather than faith. They reached for their old familiar household gods rather than the unseen, powerful, one true God. That's why Joshua delivered this charge to the next generation: "Choose for yourselves this day whom you will serve," and in the next breath, he declared, "As for me and my house, we will serve the Lord" (v. 15).

Today I want to ask you the same question. Standing on the precipice overlooking your life beyond this fast, choose for yourself—whom will you serve? The one true God or the gods who preside over present culture, who tell you to follow your appetite? Whom will you serve? And not only that but whom will your household serve? This isn't just for moms and dads and grandmas and grandpas; it's for those of you who are stepping out of your parents' home and into a home of your own for the first time. To whom will you dedicate your home and dedicate your life?

Standing on the precipice overlooking your life beyond this fast, choose for yourself—whom will you serve?

Each of us began this fast keenly aware of our sugar addiction, of our fixation on food, with the hope that it would fix us. But today we are going to turn our gaze from ourselves and our own needs to the needs of our households—to our sons and daughters, fathers and mothers, sisters and brothers, grandmas and grandpas, aunts and uncles, and to our future sons and daughters and grandchildren. Remember, we're not simply after a transformed diet but a transformed life that has the potential of transforming generations!

One of the Ten Commandments warns us that if we worship false gods, God will revisit that sin upon the next few generations (Exod. 20:5). However, if we love Him and keep His commands, He will show love to a thousand generations! Our commitment to love and obey the Lord is the most practical way that we can lead future generations to do the same! Our faith has the power to lead our future families to faith.

Our commitment to love and obey the Lord is the most practical way that we can lead future generations to do the same!

One of my favorite Bible stories that references fasting can be found in Mark 9. Here's the gist of the story: A father brought his demon-possessed son to the disciples, hoping that they would save his child from a demon's dangerous hold. After many unsuccessful attempts to call the demon out of the boy, the disciples were baffled and the father desperate. That's when Jesus walked up and asked, "What's going on?"

The father stepped up and cried:

> "Teacher, I brought my son to you, for he has a spirit that makes him mute. And whenever it seizes him, it throws him down, and he foams and grinds his teeth and becomes rigid. So I asked your disciples to cast it out, and they were not able." And he answered them, "O faithless generation, how long am I to be with you? How long am I to bear with you? Bring him to me." And they brought the boy to him. And when the spirit saw him,

immediately it convulsed the boy, and he fell on the ground and rolled about, foaming at the mouth. And Jesus asked his father, "How long has this been happening to him?" And he said, "From childhood. And it has often cast him into fire and into water, to destroy him. But if you can do anything, have compassion on us and help us." And Jesus said to him, "'If you can'! All things are possible for one who believes." Immediately the father of the child cried out and said, "I believe; help my unbelief!" And when Jesus saw that a crowd came running together, he rebuked the unclean spirit, saying to it, "You mute and deaf spirit, I command you, come out of him and never enter him again." And after crying out and convulsing him terribly, it came out, and the boy was like a corpse, so that most of them said, "He is dead." But Jesus took him by the hand and lifted him up, and he arose. And when he had entered the house, his disciples asked him privately, "Why could we not cast it out?" And he said to them, "This kind cannot be driven out by anything but prayer." (Mark 9:17–29)

The King James Version translates Jesus's response this way: "This kind can come forth by nothing, but by prayer and fasting" (v. 29). I've read many commentaries about the possible reasons most translations leave out the reference to fasting but, rather than diving into a debate about which translation is most accurate, I want to point out the role of the father's faith in this story. In verse 22, the father desperately pleaded, "If you can do anything, have compassion on us and help us." I love to consider the gentle tone of Jesus's voice as he responded, "'If you can'! All things are possible for one who believes." To which the father exclaimed, "I believe; help my unbelief!" (vv. 23–24).

Perhaps you are a parent who desperately wants to intercede for your family, but your faith feels weak. What a lesson for you to take into your home today. Do you believe? Perhaps you do, but there's still unbelief bound up in your questioning heart.

In another Gospel account of the same story, Jesus's disciple Matthew tells us that, when asked why the disciples weren't able to cast out the demon, Jesus responded, "Truly I tell you, if you have faith as small as a mustard seed, you can say to this mountain, 'Move from here to there,' and it will move. Nothing will be impossible for you" (Matt. 17:20 NIV).

Moms and dads, grandmas and grandpas, sisters and brothers, aunts and uncles, and those of you just starting to make a home on your own, choose faith. Even with faith the size of a mustard seed, you will see the Lord do tremendous things on behalf of your loved ones as you fast and pray!

Choose today whom you will serve. I know what I choose: "As for me and my house, we will serve the Lord."

Dear Lord, my household and I choose You! Over any other filler, we choose You! Before any other god, we choose You! Give me the courage to lead my family to You as I follow You by faith. I do believe; but help my unbelief! Increase my faith as I lead my family members to You. What a privilege to know You and make You known to those in my home. In Jesus's name, Amen.

day *27*

THE KIND OF FASTING GOD WANTS

This is the kind of fasting I want:
Free those who are wrongly imprisoned;
    lighten the burden of those who work
        for you.
Let the oppressed go free,
    and remove the chains that bind people.
Share your food with the hungry,
    and give shelter to the homeless.
Give clothes to those who need them,
    and do not hide from relatives who need
        your help.

Then your salvation will come like the dawn,
    and your wounds will quickly heal.
Your godliness will lead you forward,
    and the glory of the LORD will protect you
        from behind.
Then when you call, the LORD will answer.
    "Yes, I am here," he will quickly reply.

Isaiah 58:6–9 NLT

YESTERDAY WE TRANSITIONED from fasting and praying for ourselves to praying for our loved ones. Today God is calling us to look out beyond our homes, into the world.

In Isaiah 58 we read that God's people were frustrated because, despite having fasted and prayed, God seemed far away. They were eager for Him to come near to them and were frustrated that He hadn't noticed all that they were doing to seek Him. So God told them the reason they weren't finding Him was that they were going about fasting in the wrong way. "Is this the kind of fast I have chosen, only a day for people to humble themselves? Is it only for bowing one's head like a reed and for lying in sackcloth and ashes?" (v. 5 NIV). In other words, self-focused people can't garner the attention of an others-focused God!

Self-focused people can't garner the attention of an others-focused God!

Before we spend another day fasting and praying, I think we need to ask ourselves a key question: Am I fasting the right way?

The majority of people who fast do so for their own benefit. They want to hear from the Lord. They want spiritual discernment, clarity, healing, and protection. Just as the Israelites wanted to enter the promised land, we want to enter into God's promised good for our lives. Because it's hard to follow Him in such a noisy and busy world, we fast in order to pull away from the distractions. Fasting helps us hear Him clearly. That's the simple reason for fasting; it's biblical. However, as Isaiah 58 demonstrates, it's still possible to fast incorrectly.

We must be careful. Fasting isn't a magic trick. God is not a puppet whose generous strings we're pulling. **Fasting isn't a formula to get what we want but a humble invitation for God to do what He wants in our lives.** When we misuse the practice of fasting, we end up as confused as the Israelites, grumbling, "Why have we fasted? . . . Why have we humbled ourselves and you have not noticed?" (Isa. 58:3 NIV).

If you are struggling, feeling that God is not hearing you or coming to your rescue even though you've been doing this religious thing so faithfully for twenty-seven days, listen carefully.

Israel asked this question:

> "Why have we fasted," they say,
>> "and you have not seen it?
> Why have we humbled ourselves,
>> and you have not noticed?"

And God answered them:

> "Yet on the day of your fasting, you do as you please
>> and exploit all your workers.
> Your fasting ends in quarreling and strife,
>> and in striking each other with wicked fists.
> You cannot fast as you do today
>> and expect your voice to be heard on high.
> Is this the kind of fast I have chosen,
>> only a day for people to humble themselves?
> Is it only for bowing one's head like a reed
>> and for lying in sackcloth and ashes?
> Is that what you call a fast,
>> a day acceptable to the LORD?" (Isa. 58:3–5 NIV)

Isaiah 58 begins with God declaring to His people loudly, like a trumpet blast, that they have been rebellious. Israel was disappointed with God, and God was disappointed with them. He basically said, "You're fasting all wrong! You think I'm happy to see you bowing and praying and focused entirely on the fasting? No! I want to see you spend your fasting days praying to me, so that you start to look like me. If that's the case, you won't be so tired and self-focused. Instead you'll be energized with a holy purpose. You're coming to me wanting something for yourself, but when you spend time with me, my top two commands will start to make sense to you: Love me with all your heart, and then love others as much as you love yourself. You're fasting all wrong because you can't get past your love of self."

Here's the lesson, friends: **We need to turn our hearts away from self-focused fasting to others-focused fasting.** Let's fast with a focus on the needs of the world. This is the heart of fasting: that we consider the heart of God.

Perhaps, as we learn to fast in this way, we will begin to see God move not only in the world but also in our own lives. Don't get me wrong. This isn't another string for us to pull on a marionette-like master. We're not changing our focus from us to others so that we can get what we've been after all along. However, when we focus on what God wants us to focus on—others—our own lives will be blessed. Take another look at Isaiah 58:6–9. It says that when we fast according to God's will, our salvation will come like the dawn, and our wounds will quickly heal. Our godliness will lead us forward, and the glory of the Lord will protect us from behind. Then when we call, the Lord will answer.

Our call is to live generously, because we are received generously.

This is not a works-based faith I'm speaking of. This generous faith-life pours out from the abundant overflow of God's kindness to us and through us! Our call is to live generously, because we are received generously. When we live and fast this way, the blessing becomes ours.

If you are missing the blessings of this life, perhaps it's because you are not doing this life properly. James 2:26 challenges that "faith without works is dead" (NASB). Stop worrying so much about what you're not eating and start feeding those in need. When you care for others as Jesus did, that's when the full joy of your salvation comes and your wounds are healed.

Oh, Lord, my God, Your love for the world amazes me. While I am coming to You with needs of my own, help me today to slow down and love those whom You love, to care for those whom You care for, to intercede for those in need around me today. Help me to catch a vision of serving others before myself, not so that my own needs are met but because You've told me to love others as I love myself. That's how I want to live during these fasting days and into all my days. Because love for others is at the center of Your heart, I want it to be at the center of mine as well. In Jesus's name, Amen.

day 28

FEED MY SHEEP

He said to him the third time, "Simon, son of John, do you love me?" Peter was grieved because he said to him the third time, "Do you love me?" and he said to him, "Lord, you know everything; you know that I love you." Jesus said to him, "Feed my sheep."

John 21:17

WRAPPING UP yesterday's lesson was hard for me. There was still so much to say. I pray, however, that yesterday's words were enough to help you transfer your fasting focus from self-seeking to others-serving.

It's not my job to tell you who to love and serve as you fast and pray, but I do want to encourage you to be still and ask God to tell you. When I have done this myself during past sugar fasts, God has led me to partner with certain ministries who are meeting the needs of oppressed people, giving them clothes and food and visiting them in their distress. What is He asking you to do? Is He calling you to take the money you are saving from that daily latte and weekly pint of ice cream and give it to a ministry caring for the homeless people in your town? Is

He calling you to support a missions organization that is digging wells for those in need of fresh water? Ask Him to show you who needs your heart and your help, your friendship and your funds.

Others will know we are Christians by our love for them. **Our strongest testimony as Christ followers in the world is how we love the world.** It is because He loved us that we love Him and because He so generously loved us that we are able to love others generously. I mentioned yesterday that our natural tendency is to love ourselves most of all, but God commands us to love Him first and foremost, others second, and ourselves last. Fasting is a time of denying ourselves so that we might grow beyond ourselves. The temptation, however, is to live self-focused lives because God focuses His love on us, but God couldn't be clearer about His desire: I love you; you love others.

Fasting is a time of denying ourselves so that we might grow beyond ourselves.

Jesus had to restate this idea to His headstrong disciple Peter three times in a row. After Jesus asked Peter, "Do you love me?" for the third time, Peter was hurt. He replied, "You know that I love you." Jesus's reply was simple. "Feed my sheep" (John 21:17).

If you love God and want to experience the miracle of a love relationship with Him in your daily life, join Him in His loving care for others. Love whom He loves, feed His sheep, and tend to His lambs and, in turn, He will feed you all that you've been hungering for and more.

> Beloved, let us love one another, for love is from God, and whoever loves has been born of God and knows God. Anyone who does not love does not know God, because God is love. In this the love of God was made manifest among us, that God sent his only Son into the world, so that we might live through him. In

this is love, not that we have loved God but that he loved us and sent his Son to be the propitiation for our sins. Beloved, if God so loved us, we also ought to love one another. (1 John 4:7–11)

When you are focused on loving the world and meeting its needs, God fills you up with His love and amazing power. Let me show you what I mean.

In January 2017, I asked those who were fasting with me to consider giving the money they were not spending on sweets to a ministry. They liked the idea and we decided to collectively support a Christian organization that was hosting an outreach program to help pregnant, impoverished women in the slums of Uganda. Together our fasting community covered the cost of an outreach to five hundred women. Our support helped to provide them with food, water, the message of the gospel, and a birthing kit, which they could take to the ministry's local birthing center to deliver their babies in a safe and sanitized environment.

Five hundred women signed up to attend the outreach event, but eight hundred pregnant women came instead. With only enough supplies for five hundred, the ministry staff started praying for God to multiply the food and medical supplies. The pastors of the local ministry began calling the names of all the women who had come, and one by one they came up to receive their kits. Amazingly, the pile did not diminish. All eight hundred women received their supplies and their meals, and many also received Christ as their Savior that day. In the end, one hundred and fifteen kits remained on the table, and an additional outreach to a new community was planned.

It was a bona fide miracle, just like the loaves and fish blessed by Jesus Himself. It was as miraculous as the widow's oil that Elisha blessed. This miracle from Jesus not only blessed hundreds of moms on the other side of the world but also our fasting community as well.

Do you want to experience the supernatural power of the God who parted the seas and set His people free from bondage in Egypt? Do you want to know the miracle-working power of a Savior who gives sight to the blind and raises the dead to life again? He is alive and well and working throughout the world. Join Him by feeding His sheep! Each time you're tempted to overfeed yourself, stop and pray, *God, whom would You have me feed today? I don't need more.*

> *He is alive and well and working throughout the world. Join Him by feeding His sheep!*

Many of us overeat because we're bored with our self-focused lives. Let's choose instead to turn our attention to those who are physically hungry, and let that grow in us a spiritual hunger like nothing we've ever known before!

Dear wonder-working Savior, I do love You. Help me to take my eyes off myself and put them on those who are hungry and in need throughout the world, throughout my city, and even in my close circle of friends and family. Holy Spirit, inspire me and show me whom I am to love today. Show me how to love as I fast and pray for the benefit of others. In Jesus's loving name, Amen.

SHARE GOD'S LOVE WITH OTHERS

During this time of fasting, let me encourage you to choose a practical way that you might generously share the love of God with those in need. This fast isn't about you, it's about Christ in you—and ultimately He wants to love others through you. Don't worry about your own needs right now. **Trust God to take care of you as you make yourself available to care for others.**

Tally up the money you're saving from cutting out sugar and send it to a ministry that's sharing the Good News throughout the world. Sponsor a child through an organization like Compassion International.[1] Spend some of your fasting days serving with a local ministry. Or, if you would like to join me in giving to The Lulu Tree,[2] you can find out more at 40daysugarfast.com.

Fasting is a common religious practice, but remember that "religion that God our Father accepts as pure and faultless is this: to look after orphans and widows in their distress" (James 1:27 NIV). **You can share the Good News with others by sharing your love and resources.** Make giving an important part of your fasting these next eleven days.

day 29

DITTO

In the same way, the Spirit helps us in our weakness. We do not know what we ought to pray for, but the Spirit himself intercedes for us through wordless groans. And he who searches our hearts knows the mind of the Spirit, because the Spirit intercedes for God's people in accordance with the will of God.

Romans 8:26–27 NIV

DURING THE PAST FEW DAYS I have been talking about how God wants to use you to help meet the needs of others, but today it's my joy to remind you that your needs aren't going unrecognized by the Father. Romans 8:26–27 promises that the Spirit is interceding for us, and then just a few verses later, we're told, "Christ Jesus is He who died, yes, rather who was raised, who is at the right hand of God, who also intercedes for us" (v. 34 NASB). Both God's Son and His Spirit are speaking directly to the Father on our behalf today. Amazing! What's more? Their prayers for us are in complete harmony with God's perfect will for our lives.

Recently I have taken to praying a simple faith-filled prayer: *Ditto.* In other words, I bow my head and agree with whatever it is that Jesus and the Spirit of God are praying on my behalf. I throw out a hearty, "What He said," followed by an "Amen."

Marriage is hard, parenting is hard, life in this fallen world is just plain hard and, at times, I simply don't know how to pray—for myself or others. That's when I remember that "the Spirit himself intercedes for us through wordless groans" (Rom. 8:26 NIV). I imagine the Son leaning over the armrest of His father's throne, talking quietly to Him about what concerns me and my loved ones today.

Psalm 138:8 says, "The LORD will accomplish what concerns me" (NASB). Though I can't get my mind around all that is on my heart today, Jesus knows, He cares, and He is working it out. Though I don't know how to pray or what to pray, He does—in perfect alignment with the Father's sovereign and loving will for my life. Oh, what peace that affords me when the winds blow hard and the waves crash over me! The Son, who calmed the seas with a word, is speaking a word on my behalf into the Father's ear.

The Son, who calmed the seas with a word, is speaking a word on my behalf into the Father's ear.

While you came to this fast wanting to get a handle on sugar and to break its hold on you, I imagine you have other deep concerns on your mind today—needs that you might not even be able to articulate right now.

Perhaps you're in desperate need of saving in a relationship, one that has put you in physical or emotional pain. Maybe you've wandered so far from God in an area of your life, you can't imagine breaking away from where you are and coming back to Him. How do you wrap a prayer around such heartache? Maybe it's your child or your spouse who has wandered away from both God and your family, and the heart pain is so immense that it's left you groaning or even mute. Let me remind you that the God who is able to save you, can save you completely.

> Therefore he is able to save completely those who come to God through him, because he always lives to intercede for them. (Heb. 7:25 NIV)

Jesus died so that you could live with the Father eternally. Now Jesus lives to bring you to the Father prayerfully. Praise Him for His continued care and add your Amen to His continued prayers on your behalf. Agree with His good will for your life, and rest, for nothing is too difficult for Him. Nothing that concerns you today is too big for God. If you are tempted to disagree, remember Genesis 18:14, where the Lord asked Abraham this rhetorical question: "Is anything too difficult for the LORD? At the appointed time I will return to you, at this time next year, and Sarah will have a son" (NASB). Though odds and age were stacked against Abraham and his wife, God miraculously enabled them to conceive. Centuries later, Jesus looked into the eyes of His disciples and said, "With man this is impossible, but with God all things are possible" (Matt. 19:26).

Jesus died so that you could live with the Father eternally. Now Jesus lives to bring you to the Father prayerfully.

Even back before God revealed Himself to Abraham, Job confessed, "I know that You can do all things, and that no purpose of Yours can be thwarted" (42:2 NASB). Isn't that why we humble ourselves to pray this simple prayer? *Ditto.* Because we desire God's purpose above and beyond our own. Jesus and the Holy Spirit are interceding for us. What a relief!

Dear Father, You are on the throne and over all, and Your Spirit and Your Son are with You, interceding for me today. I humbly bow my head and lift my grateful Amen. Thank You for being so intimately acquainted with all that concerns my heart today. By the power of the Holy Spirit and in the name of Jesus, Amen.

day 30

AT THE TABLE WITH JESUS

He brought me to the banqueting house, and his banner over me was love.

Song of Solomon 2:4

WHEN I WAS A CHILD, I sang a simple chorus in Sunday school that was based on the verse above. The song filled my imagination with thoughts of family, belonging, and good food too. I imagined that every meal in heaven would be like Thanksgiving, with God at the head of the table. I liked to think about what heavenly desserts would be like, and I wondered how many people could fit at the table with us.

Those of you who also love good food and fellowship will understand my affection for Song of Solomon 2:4. Though other Scriptures have added to my growing understanding of heaven, I continue to love the thought of God intimately preparing a place for me, one that includes a banquet hall, a table, and good food. Above that long, inclusive table hangs one large, sweeping sign proclaiming God's love. For me, however, simply having a seat at that table is sign enough that I am loved.

The first chapter of Song of Solomon gives us another picture of God's intimate love for us. We're told: "The king has brought me into his chambers" (1:4). A castle's chambers are the innermost rooms where the family dwells, and I like to think that God invites us into the most intimate parts of *His* house. That's where we belong. That's the home that He's prepared for us, not a brand-new mansion just down the street for each new convert, as I always imagined, but a room in God's own family home.

During the writing of this book, my husband and I took our first trip to Israel. On the banks of the Sea of Galilee, in the village of Capernaum, we stood beside the ruins of an ancient Jewish home. Its outer walls were long and made of stones, forming one massive square. Inside the home were smaller rooms. Looking carefully, we could clearly see how the home had originally been divided into four large living spaces, and then subdivided each time a child or a grandchild took a wife and started a family of their own. They didn't build a new house when new additions to the family arrived; they prepared a new place within the family house. In the same way, we've all been invited into God's household through faith. And Christ, the firstborn of many brothers and sisters, went into His Father's house ahead of us to prepare places for us to dwell with Him. Dividing His inheritance, Christ made a place for each one of us in those innermost chambers, and He set a seat at His table too.

This idea of living with God in His home changes everything for me as I consider the family table He invites us to. In a family there's always someone in the kitchen. If there's bread to be made, might Christ and I be making it together then breaking it together? And if we're preparing a family meal together, won't we talk intimately as family members do? Why else is

He so passionate about sharing his innermost chambers with me? Suddenly the banqueting table represents so much more. My imagination is more alive than ever; I hear the sound of laughter and storytelling rising in our forever-home with its many, many, many rooms.

If Christ died to save me for an eternity with Him, I imagine He wants to spend it intimately with me. Why wouldn't He want me to enjoy that sweet intimacy now as well? If I am going to enjoy face-to-face conversations with my Savior each day in eternity, what should my prayer life look like today? It's a good question to ask when we're fasting and praying. Fasting makes me quiet and gives me ears to hear. It intensifies my desire to talk with the One I'll be dining with one day.

> *If Christ died to save me for an eternity with Him, I imagine He wants to spend it intimately with me.*

Will there be a large banquet table in heaven? I imagine so! Will there by an immense house with many rooms? I hope so! What will it be like to sit around the table with the Father and the Holy Spirit and the Son? I can only imagine. But I'll tell you this: I'm not going to wait to start enjoying it. I'm committed to enjoying His fellowship right now!

Use these fasting days to talk intimately with the One who intimately invites you into His family and into His home. Pray your way through these fasting days. **What's fasting without prayer? Why, I think it's merely going hungry.** Here's my question to you: Have you been enjoying His nearness during this fast? This isn't merely a physical detox; it's an opportunity to draw nearer to One with whom you will spend eternity. Don't wait for heaven to talk intimately with the Father and the Son. You're family now.

Dear Jesus, thank You for coming to earth and calling me to faith and making a way for me to come back to the Father. You generously gave Your life on earth, rose again, then went on ahead to prepare Your heavenly home for me to join You there. I'm so excited to be with You one day—to talk with You and laugh with You and share meals with You around that banquet table. Yes, that thought alone testifies to the fact that I am loved! I love You too and am so thankful that I can prayerfully talk with You right now! Amen.

day 31

PRAYING FOR HEALING

If my people who are called by my name humble themselves,
and pray and seek my face and turn from their wicked ways,
then I will hear from heaven and will forgive their sin and heal
their land.

2 Chronicles 7:14

A FEW YEARS AGO, I received a letter from a woman
letting me know that during our sugar fast she received her
hearing back. Though she had been deaf for a decade, she was
now suddenly and miraculously able to hear again. Scriptures
and Bible stories flooded my mind: Stories where the blind were
given sight and the paralyzed were invited to stand. Stories of
women and men, young and old, who were raised from sickness and death and given a new lease on life. I remembered the
story of the ten lepers whom Jesus healed and how only one of
them ran back to thank Him. With that thought swirling in my
head, I kneeled down and praised God for healing this woman
so miraculously.

Despite having been privy to this bona fide miracle, when
the next online sugar fast rolled around the following year,

I was nervous about encouraging people to ask the Lord for healing. I had lost my boldness. *What if God doesn't show up in miraculous ways?* I wondered. *What then?* While I believed that He was still able to heal any and every disease or disorder, I also knew that He doesn't always choose to do it in our way, in our time, or sometimes at all.

Around that time, I ran into the missions pastor at my church. I hadn't seen him for half a year since he'd been moving back and forth between home and the hospital, battling cancer for six strenuous months. I thought of him regularly, and each time he came to mind, I asked God to heal him. When I spotted him in the church lobby that Sunday morning, I practically ran to him. I was eager to hear how he was doing and how the Lord was answering my prayers. "I've been praying for you," I said.

Pastor Dave smiled. He was thinner than he had been the last time I saw him; his lips were dry, and his eyes wet. "I'll tell you how I have learned to pray recently," he offered instead of a prognosis. Then he leaned down, as though sharing a secret with a child. I knew in that moment that I was the student and he was the teacher, so I listened hard. My pastor went on, "I've learned to ask the Lord for whatever sort of healing He wants for me. I simply pray, *Lord, You know I have cancer and that I would like for You to heal me, but I want You to know that I'll take whatever healing You want for me. I'm hoping for my body but perhaps You want to heal my thinking or my speaking or my relationships. Heal whatever You want to heal in me today.*" With that, Pastor Dave smiled, turned, and walked slowly into the sanctuary.

His prayer made sense to me and lifted the weighty expectation that God's healing needs to be in accordance with our will. I went home and invited my fasting community to ask God to heal them during our forty days of fasting. *Lord,* we prayed individually, *You know I have this particular illness and You know all about that relationship that needs healing too. But I want You to heal me however You want to heal me. Heal my cells and heal my thinking and heal my spending and heal my family relationships too. Bring them all into submission with Your will for my life these forty days! In Jesus's name, Amen.*

After that year's fast was over, I received half a dozen letters about marriages that had been miraculously restored and children who had been miraculously healed of illnesses. I don't know if these healings were in response to specific prayers, or simply the result of a loving and sovereign God responding to the cries of those who, by faith, asked Him for whatever healing He wanted for them. When you believe in the goodness of a sovereign God—and the sovereignty of a good God—your faith in Him transcends the specifics of your prayer requests. Your desire for the Healer precedes all desire for the healing. I'm often reminded, when I am praying for specific issues, that the woman whose hearing was restored had likely not been fasting and praying for her hearing to be restored. That was her prayer long ago. She was simply fasting from sugar so that she might feast on the Healer, and His good plan for her was to open her ears.

When you believe in the goodness of a sovereign God— and the sovereignty of a good God— your faith in Him transcends the specifics of your prayer requests.

Should we pray specifically? Yes. Absolutely. Jesus said that we don't have because we don't ask. He told us that we can, by faith, point to a mountain and tell it to move and it will move! Sickness is a mountain, an unfaithful and unrepentant spouse is a mountain, a child who has gone astray is a mountain, an ailing parent's dementia is a mountain, scoliosis is a mountain, cancer is a mountain. We have been given the authority of the One who made the mountains to command them to move, but we also know that our prayers won't thwart the good purposes of a good God!

Today I invite you to pray specifically, boldly believing God will answer according to His good and overarching will.

While our focus these forty days is on the supernatural work that happens in our spiritual lives as we fast, I have come to see that physical healing often takes place when people cut out refined sugars. Inflammation in joints and muscles and common aches and pains often miraculously disappear when we fast from sugar. Headaches, acne, insomnia, restless legs syndrome, and diabetes do too. I often receive testimonials of emotional and psychological healing as well. Anxiety, depression, and debilitating fear diminish when sodas, candy, and highly sugared treats are laid at the feet of the Great Physician.

Fasting is going without that which you thought you needed in order to experience the power and presence of the One you need most of all.

If ever there is a time to pray for healing, I believe it is while one is fasting. Your body is primed and ready for a healing touch. Fasting is going without that which you thought you needed in order to experience the power and presence of the One you need most of all. Let Him heal you. With a hungry heart and a growling belly, boldly approach the throne of grace, trusting in the resurrecting power of the Great Physician and His ability to miraculously heal what most needs healing today.

Thank You, God, for knowing me. You are well aware of all that concerns me medically and relationally today. I invite You, Lord, to heal me—whatever that means to You. You know just what I need and I trust You. For my good and for Your glory I ask all of this in the name of Jesus Christ, Amen.

day 32

WAKE UP!

Rise up, you women who are at ease, hear my voice;
  you complacent daughters, give ear to my speech.
In little more than a year
  you will shudder, you complacent women;
for the grape harvest fails,
  the fruit harvest will not come.
Tremble, you women who are at ease,
  shudder, you complacent ones;
strip, and make yourselves bare,
  and tie sackcloth around your waist

Isaiah 32:9–11

WITH A LITTLE OVER A WEEK LEFT to fast and pray, you must not rest on the laurels of what God has already done. The walls that He brought down in the early days of this fast were but outer walls. All that He's said and done was just the groundwork for that which He's about to do in you. He is inside the gates now, closer than ever, but parts of you are still walled off, hidden in an inner room somewhere. The days that remain are crucial because it is often in the final days of a fast that

God tears down your most intimate defenses. The early days of your fast focused on the outer walls of your physical detox, but these last days secure your spiritual transformation. If you grow complacent now, the private and mostly unseen walls will remain standing and secure, and they will continue to separate you from the faith and freedom you most desire.

Don't let complacency hold you back from taking the final blows that can bring down the most stubborn walls. Don't lose the red-hot fire that set you on course thirty-two days ago. Stay the course. If you find that you're fasting out of habit today, don't give in these last few days. Recommit. Don't be lazy; be vigilant! Don't fast out of habit, as though fasting is merely a physical exercise of your will. Remember what God has already done and get hungry to see Him do more!

Remember what God has already done and get hungry to see Him do more!

The fire that you felt at the start of this fast must not cool or you'll enter your post-fast life lukewarm. While you may think that lukewarm is better than how you were before this journey began, don't be fooled. Scripture tells us that lukewarm is never okay.

I love the letters God inspired the apostle John to write to the early Christian churches, recorded for us in the book of Revelation. If we are humble enough, we can admit the same tendencies toward complacency in our lives today. To the church in Laodicea, God said: "I know your deeds, that you are neither cold nor hot; I wish that you were cold or hot. So because you are lukewarm, and neither hot nor cold, I will spit you out of My mouth" (Rev. 3:15–16 NASB).

Even if we have put our faith in Christ and are part of His church, we can still fall asleep in our faith. Even if we sit our bodies down in a pew on Sundays, our hearts can still be complacent most hours of every day. Fasting friends, don't fall asleep during the final days of this fast. Wake up! Let's swing open wide the innermost doors of our hearts and pray, *Jesus, I want more! I want to hear You! I want to get lit up and red hot and fired up. I've grown satisfied with being unsatisfied, and I don't want to live that way any longer.*

Revelation isn't the only place in Scripture where God expresses displeasure about spiritual complacency. He also spoke words of warning through the prophet Zephaniah: "At that time I will search Jerusalem with lamps, and I will punish the men who are complacent . . ." (1:12). Let me ask you, are you still hiding parts of your life in the dark? Because a time is coming not only in Jerusalem but throughout the whole earth, when the Son of God will shine His light into the dark recesses of every heart and in every home the world over! I cannot say what that punishment will be, in light of God's grace to those who have believed, but I have no doubt that Jesus wants more for us than a sleepy faith that rests on the laurels of "I believe."

If we believe Jesus is the Son of God who came to set us free from sin and shame and an eternity separated from the Father, then our faith lives should be red hot! We have been redeemed at a cost so high only the blood of our Savior could cover it all. English evangelist Leonard Ravenhill asked this pointed question: "Are the things you are living for worth Christ dying for?"[1] That's the wake-up question. If we truly believe we have been bought with the precious blood of God's own Son, how can we remain lukewarm? The Father will spit from his mouth a faith that is tepid.

Oh friends, there is only one week of fasting left, and I don't want you to miss out! If this fast was only about muscling the willpower to forego sugar, nothing's going to change in your

life come day 41. However, if your faith gets hot—really hot—
then the impurities in your life are going to rise to the surface.
Sugar addiction and every other sin tendency will come to the
top and the Lord will sweep it off, like a refiner removing the
dross from precious metal. You are precious to the Lord! So
precious that He gave His Son so that you might live! What
are you living for? How are you living? Are you shining for the
Lord, or are parts of you still in the dark, walled off behind an
inner door somewhere?

At the end of God's letter to the church of Laodicea, He
said:

> Behold, I stand at the door and knock; if anyone hears My voice
> and opens the door, I will come in to him and will dine with
> him, and he with Me. He who overcomes, I will grant to him
> to sit down with Me on My throne, as I also overcame and sat
> down with My Father on His throne. He who has an ear, let him
> hear what the Spirit says to the churches. (Rev. 3:20–22 NASB)

We often take this passage out of context for non-Christians,
but these words are an invitation, a knocking on the door of
the church, a letter to believers. **Don't become complacent;
open the innermost door of your heart and let Jesus have
full access to your life!**

*Dear Lord, I don't want to fool myself and believe that I have
gotten everything out of this fast. If I'm still fasting, then I'm
still praying, and if I'm still praying, then You're still listening. I want to listen too. Speak to me, Lord. Speak to me about
anything and everything that remains between us. I want those
final walls demolished, so that You might go deeper in me than
ever before. In Jesus's refining name, Amen.*

day 33

BRICK BY BRICK

The wise woman builds her house,
But the foolish tears it down with her own hands.

Proverbs 14:1 NASB

ON THE THIRD DAY OF OUR FAST, I told you to expect the Lord to bring down some nasty strongholds in your life—with sugar chief among them. Since then, the beloved Sunday school hymn about Joshua and Jericho and walls tumbling down has been playing on loop in my mind. This morning, as I opened up the Bible to the book of Proverbs, my eyes fell upon a warning: "Like a city whose walls are broken through is a person who lacks self-control" (Prov. 25:28 NIV). *Oh my!* I thought, *I want some walls to fall, but not as a result of my own foolish, undisciplined life.* In that moment I realized a simple fact: Walls are going to fall either way, but which walls and by whose hands they come down is entirely up to me.

There are bad walls—we've called them strongholds—but there are good walls too. Our job is to yield to the good structures that the Lord has protectively placed around us, as we continually invite Him to bring down the strongholds that have held us back from His promises and from His promised land. So often, we tear down the wrong walls, the walls that God lovingly erected to safeguard us within.

Looking back over my life, I see the walls He hemmed me in with: commands and instructions about everything from sexual purity and honoring my parents to not gossiping. Even today I see Him attempting to build a safeguard around me, telling me through His Word to not give in to envy. When I remain within these good walls, my life is good. But it takes ongoing submission to God's will over my will each day for me to stay planted in Him.

Our job is to yield to the good structures that the Lord has protectively placed around us.

All throughout the Scriptures God instructs us about how to pray and how to rest and how to serve and how to eat and how to live. Our natural tendency, of course, is to choose which of His instructions we will submit to, which of His walls we will allow to remain. For the most part, we do what we want and follow our own passions. Brick by brick, we choose which walls stay up and which come down. We choose who we will date, what we will look at online, if we will be generous with our time and resources, which thoughts we will take captive and which ones will hold us captive, how much we will drink, if we will read our Bible, and if we will spend more money than we make. With one hand over the other, we tear down the protective structures God has placed around us and eventually the walls come tumbling down.

What does this have to do with our forty-day sugar fast? We're denying ourselves what we hunger for as a means to submit our appetites to God. In the same way, we must deny our impulses to build the life that we want over the life that Christ died to give us. The bending of our wills concerning what we eat is an exercise in submission as much as it is in self-control. More so, in fact, for submission is ultimately about God-control. God controlling our lives, God controlling our compulsions, God controlling our tongues, God controlling the placement of each wall that holds us in or holds us back.

The more I think about the various walls that need to come down in my life, the more I sense God calling me to consider the good walls I've torn down and the ones I've constructed in their stead. Some of the strongest, saddest walls that have held me back from God's plans for my life weren't erected by a figurative Jericho but by my own two hands. **Choices I made over time turned into habits that turned into strongholds.** Even what we eat, over time, can become a wall if we're not careful. Our choices become barriers that hold us back from health, wholeness, and freedom.

Whether we understand His boundaries or not, agree with them or not, or want them or not, they are for our protection. Psalm 16 sings this truth over us: "Lord, you alone are my portion and my cup; you make my lot secure. The boundary lines have fallen for me in pleasant places; surely I have a delightful inheritance" (vv. 5–6 NIV).

God doesn't simply rebuild broken walls; He resurrects broken lives.

Today consider which walls you've foolishly torn down. Which of God's instructions that work like a protective structure have you demolished? Repent of the life you've built outside of those boundaries. God is faithful to restore what you've torn down. God doesn't simply rebuild broken walls; He resurrects broken lives. "I will build you up again, and you, Virgin Israel, will be rebuilt. Again you will take up your timbrels and go out to dance with the joyful" (Jer. 31:4 NIV).

Submit to His rebuilding!

God Almighty, Your Word is the structure I want to abide within. I am sorry I've lived undisciplined, tearing down what You've created in lieu of what I want. Today I choose to want what You want for me. Rebuild my life upon the firm rock of my salvation, Jesus Christ. Hide me within Your protective walls so that I might shout from its ramparts just how pleasant it is to dwell in the land You've given me. Thank You for Your ongoing, rebuilding grace. Because of Jesus, Amen.

ONE WEEK TO GO!

With one week of fasting left, it's time to start considering if a sugar-free lifestyle beyond these forty days would be good for you. Do you feel physically healthier, mentally clearer, emotionally more stable, and spiritually stronger? Are you less irritated with your loved ones and hungrier for the Word? **Once the stronghold of sugar comes tumblin' down, a sugar-free structure may help to keep you safe and free.**

Recently my pastor was talking about the structures God puts in our lives to keep us safe. He likened God's laws to the bars that hold you in on a roller coaster ride. That protective structure isn't intended to get in the way of having fun but, instead, to make it possible to have fun! Likewise, structuring the way you eat doesn't have to stop you from enjoying food. A protective safety structure might actually hold you in securely and free you up to enjoy all aspects of your life more fully!

You don't need to make the decision today, but give it some thought as you fast and pray.

day 34

REMEMBER!

When the disciples reached the other side, they had forgotten to bring any bread. Jesus said to them, "Watch and beware of the leaven of the Pharisees and Sadducees." And they began discussing it among themselves, saying, "We brought no bread." But Jesus, aware of this, said, "O you of little faith, why are you discussing among yourselves the fact that you have no bread? Do you not yet perceive? Do you not remember the five loaves for the five thousand, and how many baskets you gathered? Or the seven loaves for the four thousand, and how many baskets you gathered?"

Matthew 16:5–10

YOU STILL HAVE ONE WEEK LEFT to fast and pray, but today's Scripture is making me think of day 41. **When this fast is over, will you remember how God filled you to overflowing as you spent time with Him? Or will He need to keep working miracles on your behalf to keep your attention?**

At the beginning of Matthew 16, Jesus had just arrived on the other side of the Sea of Galilee after feeding four thousand men. As soon as He stepped off the boat, He was approached by a group of Pharisees and Sadducees bent on testing Him. They asked Him to show them a sign to prove that He was the Son of God, the Messiah. Of course, Jesus wasn't after followers who needed proof of His deity; He wanted (and still wants) faithful followers who believe through faith and not visual evidence. Jesus responded to their request with this: "An evil and adulterous generation seeks after a sign; and a sign will not be given it, except the sign of Jonah" (Matt. 16:4 NASB). Only after His death and resurrection would it become clear that Jesus was referring here to His own resurrection. Jonah was swallowed up in a watery grave for three days and then spit out on the shore. Jesus was in the grave for three days before God resurrected Him. Jesus knew that even after He gave the ultimate sign of His deity, His resurrection, the religious leaders would still not believe, so He walked away from them and got back into the boat with His disciples.

Can you imagine Jesus in that moment? He left the Pharisees and Sadducees and their faithless request for miracles, and was sitting with his followers who had just watched Him feed thousands of people with a few fish and a couple loaves of bread. Unfortunately, His disciples had already forgotten that miracle and were grumbling that they had forgotten to bring bread with them. That's when Jesus said, "O you of little faith, why are you discussing among yourselves the fact that you have no bread? Do you not yet perceive? Do you not remember the five loaves for the five thousand, and how many baskets you gathered? Or the seven loaves for the four thousand, and how many baskets you gathered?" (Matt. 16:8–10). Even Jesus's closest companions required sign after sign for their faith to remain engaged.

As we draw near the end of this fast, purpose in your heart to remember the faithful way God has provided for you. When you remember God's past faithfulness, you are more prone to stay faithful to Him. If He's revealed His faithful love to you these forty days, revel in it! Don't simply move on with the hope of living different. Continue living each day with Him and you will live differently. Keep on going.

When you remember God's past faithfulness, you are more prone to stay faithful to Him.

In the passage that began today's reading, the disciples exclaimed that they had forgotten to pack bread for their journey. It makes me laugh. Jesus wanted to take His friends deeper, teaching them more about Himself and the Father's love, but they were stuck on yesterday's lesson. They didn't remember what God had done to sustain them in the past.

Likewise, at the end of their forty years of wandering in the desert, Moses cautioned the children of Israel to remember the Lord's provision to them during their time in the desert. God provided food in the form of manna so that they did not go physically hungry. Moses's warning to the Israelites concluded with this reminder: "Man does not live by bread alone, but man lives by every word that comes from the mouth of the LORD" (Deut. 8:3).

Isn't that what you've been learning too—that it isn't food that ultimately sustains you but God and His Word? Your body may be learning that it feels healthier physically when you're not eating sugar, but your spirit is learning to feast on God and on every word that comes from His mouth. He's faithfully filled you with His Spirit and provided you with everything you need during this fast and beyond. **He has proven Himself faithful; now you must remain faithful.**

Don't forget the way God miraculously fed you from His own table as you fasted from the sweetest treats this world has to offer.

Let's purpose in our hearts to remember the lessons He has already taught us these past few weeks so that He might teach us new and wonderful things about Himself. Psalm 119:18 invites us to pray, "Open my eyes that I may see wonderful things in your law" (NIV). God is eager to open our spiritual eyes to new, mind-blowing realizations about life with our Savior. He bids us, "Call to me and I will answer you and tell you great and unsearchable things you do not know" (Jer. 33:3 NIV).

He has proven Himself faithful; now you must remain faithful.

There is so much more life to be had when you walk with Christ each day. Make it your goal to remember what He's already revealed so that you might be ready for more.

Holy Spirit, help me to remember what I've learned so that I don't have to go back and relearn these same lessons again and again. I'm eager to learn more from You now. Open my eyes and allow me to see wonderful new things in Your law, and open my ears so that You can tell me all the unsearchable things that I do not yet know. And when I forget, for I will forget sometimes, gently remind me again. In Jesus's patient name, Amen.

day 35

ONCE YOU'RE FREE, YOU'RE FREE TO SHARE

While they were worshiping the Lord and fasting, the Holy Spirit said, "Set apart for me Barnabas and Saul for the work to which I have called them."

Acts 13:2

GOD OPENS YOUR SPIRITUAL EARS when you fast. That is why, as I wrote this guide to accompany your fast, I asked Him to speak clearly to you. The Bible is filled with stories of people receiving a clear word from the Holy Spirit as they fasted and prayed.

Perhaps as you have been worshiping the Lord these past few weeks, the Spirit of God has spoken directly to you. Maybe you've heard Him speak about something in your life that needs to be *set aside* for a specific work that God has called you to do. Maybe He's calling you to fill a volunteer position in the church or maybe He's calling you to step down from a commitment you've made. Or it could be that He's whispered "stay" as you've fasted and prayed with open hands and a broken marriage. Sometimes He calls you to say yes and other times He calls you to say no, which is why you need to carefully listen for His still small voice.

Whether He's calling you to host an outreach event in your neighborhood (perhaps an Easter egg hunt or a Sunday brunch) or to be more present and available to your children and spouse (putting down your phone at the table and opening the Word together), God is passionate about the redemptive work in the lives of His people. I don't know the particulars of what God's Holy Spirit is saying to you, but I have to believe He is speaking, because that's what He does. I said it early on, but I'll say it again: The same God who saves also speaks. God speaks to us intimately because we are intimately His.

God speaks to us intimately because we are intimately His.

He has good plans for our lives and good works for us to do. Ephesians 2:10 tells us, "For we are his workmanship, created in Christ Jesus for good works, which God prepared beforehand, that we should walk in them." If God lovingly fashioned us for good works, preparing us for them and them for us, then He is kind enough to help us find those specific good works. He is not an elusive God, nor a far-off God, but a clear-speaking and present God who gives us the guidance of His Spirit and the illuminating light of His Word.

Still, sometimes I feel completely in the dark about what God would like me to do. One prayer I pray regularly, especially as I fast and ask the Lord for clarity, is this: *God, I'm not very smart, but I have a "here I am, send me" heart. So You've got to make it clear, Lord. You've just got to! Tell me what You want me to do and I'll do it. But please, please don't make it hard for me to understand because my heart's desire is to do Your will. In Jesus's clarifying name, Amen.*

Today, as you worship the Lord with fasting and prayer, invite Him to speak with you clearly, as with a friend. Ask Him what He is calling you to do. Now that your fast is drawing to a close, you're being freshly commissioned to do His work. After all, He didn't send just Saul and Barnabas out to do the work of the gospel; He has sent us all out. Before Christ ascended into heaven, He commissioned all believers to go and tell the world about Him: "Go therefore and make disciples of all nations, baptizing them in the name of the Father and of the Son and of the Holy Spirit" (Matt. 28:19). **Those who have experienced the bondage-breaking power of God are called to share the source of such power with those still held captive.** Every person who believes in Jesus has been charged with the clear command to go and preach the good news of salvation and freedom through Christ.

Sugar has lost its seat on the throne of your life, and Christ is securely seated there now. It's time to get going. **Your Savior King has good works for you to do and good news for you to proclaim. That is your mission and your commission.** God has an assignment for you to do. Your job now is to pray about the details of that assignment.

Once you have been called to faith, you're called to share your faith, which often looks like simply sharing your life. Early on, the disciples had to leave their homes and go to the far reaches of the world. There are still missionaries going to the unreached corners of the globe today, but you can also be called to reach those right where you are. When you share the details of your saved and redeemed life with those in your midst, you're sharing a beautiful picture of redemption.

Christ has set you free, which sets you free to share Him!

The Lord has delivered you from sugar shackles, and you're no longer running to false fillers in your life. You are a transformed, living, breathing testimony of what God can do. **Christ has set you free, which sets you free to share Him!** If you have friends and family members, neighbors and work colleagues who are still held captive by addiction and unbelief, you have at least one clear calling on your life today: share your faith by sharing your transformed life with them. Share your faith out loud, right where you are today.

God, I'm not very smart, but I have a "here I am, send me" heart. So You've got to make it clear, Lord. You've just got to! Tell me what You want me to do and I'll do it. But please, please don't make it hard for me to understand because my heart's desire is to do Your will. In Jesus's clarifying name, Amen.

day 36

TWO MASTERS

No one can serve two masters. Either you will hate the one and love the other, or you will be devoted to the one and despise the other. You cannot serve both God and money.

Matthew 6:24 NIV

WE HAVE A HARD TIME fixing our eyes on Jesus when we're fixated on food, running to the pantry when we could be running after Him. We simply can't run in two different directions at the same time. When we spend our lives pursuing one thing, it often means we're choosing to run away from something or someone else. The Message translates Matthew 6:24 this way, "You can't worship two gods at once. Loving one god, you'll end up hating the other. Adoration of one feeds contempt for the other. You can't worship God and Money both."

Likely, you picked up this book and began to fast and pray because you were convicted that sugar had an unhealthy hold on you. Not only was it ruining your health but it had moved from a physical stronghold to a spiritual one. Sugar had become master and you had become slave.

Sometimes I feel like Esau. In Genesis 25, this biblical figure was so hungry that he sold his birthright for a bowl of lentil stew and some bread. It sounds crazy that Esau allowed hunger to hold so much power over his life that it dictated his future, but I know I've let my appetite make decisions for me in the past. I don't know about a bowl of lentil stew, but I know I've traded God's best for me in exchange for a bowl of . . . ice cream with extra hot fudge.

God's Word is clear: You can't serve two masters at once! If sugar has made you its slave, perhaps it's time to tell sugar to take a hike. Christ came to set you free from all the other masters, leaving Himself as the one true and trustworthy guardian of your life. When something other than Christ has mastery over your life, it's easy to forget the Master.

When something other than Christ has mastery over your life, it's easy to forget the Master.

Perhaps it's not sugar that has a firm grip on you. Maybe it's money. The accumulation of money, the spending of money, the perception of having money—it dictates the car you drive, the friends you have over for dinner, the neighborhood you live in, the clothes you wear, the things you talk about in line at the grocery store, and the pictures you share online. Making money rules your thought life; spending money even more so. Maybe it's to the point that you can't go to Target to pick up a tube of toothpaste and a box of Ziploc baggies without spending fifty dollars on everything else that catches your eye. When you're ruled by something other than the Spirit, you are unruly, undisciplined, and out of control. You lack the spiritual fruit of self-control—in your eating, your spending, and your time online.

Or perhaps your master is your phone. It bosses you around each time it rings and you come running. It buzzes and you get an extra shot of dopamine, making your heart soar. You get a notification that someone liked what you said on social media, so you forget and forego the flesh-and-blood people right in front of you, the ones that God has charged you with loving (not merely liking).

You can't serve two masters. It's time to make a clear-cut choice.

> If you decide for God, living a life of God-worship, it follows that you don't fuss about what's on the table at mealtimes or whether the clothes in your closet are in fashion. There is far more to your life than the food you put in your stomach, more to your outer appearance than the clothes you hang on your body. Look at the birds, free and unfettered, not tied down to a job description, careless in the care of God. And you count far more to him than birds. (Matt. 6:25–26 MSG)

Where are you spending your life—your hours and your calories and your heart-affection?

This isn't to say that anything you do apart from spending time in prayer and reading the Bible is wrong. No, not at all! But you have to look back to the greatest commandment of all: "You shall love the LORD your God with all your heart and with all your soul and with all your might" (Deut. 6:5). When you love Him first and foremost, you invest your attention and affection in a high-yielding fund. The account increases and compounds so that you might enjoy all the other gifts that your master has blessed you with as well. But when you spend your affection and attention on the other masters who tempt you, you come to the true Master bankrupt—broke and broken. This isn't the first time you've heard me say this.

Jesus is the only master that gives freedom to those who are bound to Him.

Jesus is the only master that gives freedom to those who are bound to Him. Being a slave to anything else simply leaves you tangled up.

Master Jesus, You are the one and only good God. Be master of my heart and master of my days. Master over my eating and my spending. I come to You, fully submitted to Your lordship over my life, because You alone are Lord. There is none beside You. With the ongoing help of Your Spirit, I refuse to let any false masters boss me around again. I'm convicted and convinced that You're the only master who loves me, who leads me, who laid down His life for me. Only You, Master Jesus! Thank You and Amen.

day 37

KEEP KNOCKING,
KEEP ASKING

Ask and keep on asking and it will be given to you; seek and keep
on seeking and you will find; knock and keep on knocking and
the door will be opened to you.

Matthew 7:7 AMP

SOMETIMES MEN AND WOMEN who fast with me come
to the end of their forty days and cry out, "Where are the miracles? Where is the gentle whisper? And why do I still want
to lick all the frosting off of all the cupcakes in all the world?"

I love how the Amplified translation of the Bible explains
exactly how we are to ask for and seek the Lord: persistently
persistent. Over and over again we are to ask God to set us free,
to speak to our hearts, to convict and transform us. Tirelessly,
we are to pray for those we know and love. Though we grow
weary of crying out and calling out, this is how we are to ask
for healing from the Great Physician and good blessings from
the Giver of all good gifts. Over and over and over again. "Ask
and keep on asking and it will be given to you; seek *and* keep on

seeking and you will find; knock *and* keep on knocking and the door will be opened to you" (Matt. 7:7 AMP, emphasis added). God hasn't invited us to a one-and-done type of conversation. He's inviting us to a "pray without ceasing" (1 Thess. 5:17) sort of dialogue. An eternal back and forth. If there are things that you hoped to hear and receive from the Lord during this fast but haven't yet, keep asking. Keep knocking. Keep seeking.

Jesus was so committed to teaching us this persistently persistent method of prayer, He illustrated it in a parable. The parable of the persistent widow, found in Luke 18:1–8, paints a picture of a woman who pleaded for help before a judge who didn't fear God or care about the needs of others. Over and over again, day in and day out, the widow returned to the judge, begging for his help. Eventually the selfish judge agreed to help her, not because he loved her but because he loved his own peace and quiet.

Perhaps you've heard the term "the squeaky wheel gets the grease." The judge wanted the widow to stop squeaking, to stop pestering him. How much more will the eternal Judge, the Father of our Lord Jesus Christ, respond to your persistent prayers, for He loves you beyond measure.

One of my earliest memories as a new mom took place late one night as I nursed my infant son in the rocking chair beside his crib. In the dimly lit nursery, I opened up my Bible and turned to Matthew 7. "Ask and it will be given to you," I read, "seek and you will find; knock and the door will be opened to you. For everyone who asks receives; the one who seeks finds; and to the one who knocks, the door will be opened" (vv. 7–8 NIV). Though I was familiar with the passage, the words that followed felt brand-new in light of the baby in my arms. I continued reading. "Which of you, if your son asks for bread, will give him a stone? Or if he asks for a fish, will give him a snake?

If you, then, though you are evil, know how to give good gifts to your children, how much more will your Father in heaven give good gifts to those who ask him!" (Matt. 7:9–11 NIV). Though I still love that baby who is now a teenager, I realize I am more like the unjust judge in the parable than I am like our generous God. I want to be generous, but selfish motives often taint my responses, even to my kids. God the Father, however, is untainted. He responds to our every prayer with pure love.

God is not like us. His love transcends selfishness and surpasses the nursing mother's tender adoration. Because His ear is inclined toward us perpetually, we can pray persistently. He doesn't grow weary of our sin-struggles the way we grow weary of our own children's challenges. The way we grow weary when they toddle to us morning, noon, and night with the same questions. God never gives up or gives in to selfishness and pride. He loves it when we come to Him as both Father and Judge.

> *Because His ear is inclined toward us perpetually, we can pray persistently.*

If you have prayed and sought the Lord as you fasted only to hear radio silence on the other end of the line, here are three things you could try.

1. **Ask God to inspire your prayers.** Ask Him to give you clarity in what to pray. Sometimes I ask God, *Lord, show me what You're doing in my life (or in my children's lives or my spouse's life) so that I might prayerfully and purposefully join You there.* Asking God what to pray may seem backward, but it has brought a beautiful order to my prayer life. God is your kind and generous Father; He longs to give you every good gift, so ask Him what He has in store for you. Perhaps, here in these last few

days, you will find yourself praying an entirely different sort of prayer. If He puts something new on your heart, obey and pray.

2. **Pray like a squeaky wheel.** Morning and noon and nighttime too, talk to the Lord about your needs and the needs of others. Remind Him of the prayers He inspired you to pray, and confess your trust in Him out loud, again and again. And when you are tempted to doubt that He's listening or that He will answer your requests, remind Him of His Word, *God, You've told me, "You do not have because you do not ask"* (James 4:2 NIV). *Well, here I am asking.* Then set the alarm on your phone to remind you to pray it again tomorrow.

3. **Trust God for the timing and don't stop asking.** It is possible that your prayers on a certain matter may not be answered for some time yet. If that is the case, but you feel the Spirit prompting you that you are praying in accordance with God's will, don't stop praying. Just because you're drawing near to the end of your fast doesn't mean you've laid down your final Amen. It's possible that this prayer will be an anthem prayer, something you pray for a very long time. Asking God to heal your marriage, asking Him to pursue your prodigal child and bring him or her home to faith again, asking God for physical healing and emotional healing too . . . the Lord deals with some of these prayers over time, so don't stop bringing your concerns before Him.

> *Just because you're drawing near to the end of your fast doesn't mean you've laid down your final Amen.*

As Matthew 7:7 instructs, continue to "ask *and* keep on asking . . . seek *and* keep on seeking . . . knock *and* keep on knocking" (AMP). The door will be opened to you if it's the door God knows is best. Just ask and keep on asking. Because His ear is inclined toward us perpetually, we can pray persistently.

Heavenly Father, thank You for never giving up. Thank You for being a good, gift-giving dad. Thank You for giving me the strength to keep praying and keep trusting and keep clinging to Your goodness. In Jesus's enduring and endurance-strengthening name, Amen.

day 38

GETTING DOWN
TO THE ROOT

Blessed is the one
    who does not walk in step with the wicked
or stand in the way that sinners take
    or sit in the company of mockers,
but whose delight is in the law of the Lord,
    and who meditates on his law day and night.
That person is like a tree planted by streams of
    water,
    which yields its fruit in season
and whose leaf does not wither—
    whatever they do prospers.

Not so the wicked!
    They are like chaff
    that the wind blows away.

Psalm 1:1–4 NIV

THIS PAST MONTH, my youngest son has been learning about the water cycle in his science class. One interesting way that water is syphoned up from the ground is with the help of trees. Transpiration is the process by which root systems drink up groundwater, carry the water up the trunk, through the branches, and finally out to the green leaves where the moisture exits the plant in the form of water vapor. Warm air lifts the water vapor up into the sky until the temperatures cool and water droplets form around tiny dust particles. Millions of minuscule drops gather together to create a cloud. When the cloud gets heavy enough, water drops in the form of precipitation, nourishing the earth once again.

Oftentimes I look around at the natural world and am overcome by the reality of a creative Creator who so lovingly provides all we need. Good, pure, life-giving water. Yet sometimes I choose to drink from the wrong source, gulping down polluted lies that lead to a polluted life.

Psalm 1 has been one of my favorite Bible passages for most of my life. I love the imagery of a flourishing tree that starts down at the root system. It is both poetic and practical, beautiful and biological. Just like a tree, when the roots of our lives reach down deep and tap into a healthy water source, we thrive and bear fruit, season after season. But not any old water will do.

If you want a flourishing life, you must abide beside nourishing streams. Similarly, if you want to bear the fruit of God's Spirit in your thought life, your thoughts must be rooted in His Word. If you want your work life and your eating life and your home life to bear the right kind of fruit, you must be firmly planted by the right kind of water. Before you can embrace a healthy life, expecting health to extend its branches out beyond these forty days, you must consider where you have been rooted all these years. Addictions

> *If you want a flourishing life, you must abide beside nourishing streams.*

don't spring up by accident, you know. Addictions grow on the branches of lives that are rooted beside the wrong water source.

Earlier we talked about some of our food triggers, those age-old habits and hurts that cause us to run to food or drink for comfort or reward. Of course, to plant our lives beside life-giving streams, we must first uproot them from the rancid flow of lies we've believed in the past. **Just as truth nourishes healthy lives, lies feed unhealthy lives.**

Take a moment to pinpoint the lies from which your roots have been drinking. Perhaps you've been overweight since early childhood, and you drink these words daily: "Nothing I do has ever changed my weight or my eating. Nothing ever will." If you are planted beside this lie, you've got to yank it out by the root and replant your life beside what is scripturally true: "God's Word says that He makes all things new. I am loved by the Lord who came to set prisoners free and heal those who are sick. I am ready for God to do a new thing in my life because He told me that He can and that He will!"

"Overeating makes me happy" is another familiar lie. Pull it out by the root and replant your life beside this truth instead: "The joy of the Lord is my strength. With Him I am overcome with joy. I don't want a dopamine-induced happiness that a sugar high brings. I want the satisfied joy that the Most High offers to those who are planted in His Word and in His presence."

If you have believed the lie that you are unloved and unlovable, pull it out and plant this in your heart: "I am eternally and abundantly loved."

Maybe the lies you've believed are now lies that you act upon. "I deserve a bowl of ice cream after a long day with the kids." "I deserve a candy bar from the checkout lane at the grocery store." "I deserve a win after a day of losses at work." Here's the truth you need to ingest today: You don't deserve anything. You can have it if you want it, but it's not your just desserts. As a matter of fact, when you live this reward-centered life, playing tit for tat with mochas and wine, your "reward" will end up feeling more like a curse.

I'm reminded of the lesson we learned on day 10: **God is our reward.** That's the truth we need to abide by. When we turn to our next sugar high instead of the Most High, we don't get lifted high. We end up feeling lower than before because, after a sugar high comes a sugar crash—and that's no reward at all. **When we turn to sugar-substitutes for our reward, we end up both physically and spiritually malnourished.**

You're coming to the end of these forty days of fasting from sugar, but I want to encourage you to fast from lies for the rest of your life. Uproot yourself from a negative inner dialogue, then plant yourself beside true waters. The way to plant yourself in the truth is to plant the truth in yourself. Combat the lies you hear with nourishing truth straight from the Bible. That's what Jesus did. When He was tempted by the devil during His forty-day fast in the wilderness, He fought back by speaking truth. Here's how it began:

The way to plant yourself in the truth is to plant the truth in yourself.

> Then Jesus was led up by the Spirit into the wilderness to be tempted by the devil. And after fasting forty days and forty nights, he was hungry. And the tempter came and said to him, "If you are the Son of God, command these stones to become loaves of bread." But he answered, "It is written,
>
> > 'Man shall not live by bread alone,
> > but by every word that comes from the mouth of
> > God.'" (Matt. 4:1–4)

When you are firmly planted beside true waters, nourished by and meditating on God's Word, what you read becomes what you speak. What you take in flows out. It's the living water cycle!

Forty days of truth won't be enough to sustain you for life. This must become a lifestyle now. Whether you pick up a candy bar on day 41 or continue living a sugar-free life, continue feasting on the Bible! Ingest God's Word because that's where God has invested His transforming power!

Oh Lord, thank You for Your Word. Increase in me a hunger for it, because it brings nourishment to my life. As I meditate upon its truth, establish my roots so that I might drink deeply and bear Your fruit in my life. In Jesus's fruitful name, I pray, Amen.

day 39

GOD WANTS YOUR LIFE, NOT YOUR SUGAR

Therefore, I urge you, brothers and sisters, in view of God's mercy, to offer your bodies as a living sacrifice, holy and pleasing to God—this is your true and proper worship. Do not conform to the pattern of this world, but be transformed by the renewing of your mind. Then you will be able to test and approve what God's will is—his good, pleasing and perfect will.

Romans 12:1–2 NIV

THIS FAST WAS NEVER about the sugar. Remember, our sugar cravings were simply the doorway through which we invited the Holy Spirit into our hungry lives. Once He came in, He looked around, smiled, nodded, and said, "Thanks for the sugar, but I want it all."

God doesn't want your sugar; He wants your life. A physical detox isn't going to leave you changed. Forty days in the Word won't outweigh the other 325 you spend chasing the world this year. There's more to it than that. If all you did during your fast was surrender your sugar on the altar before the Lord, then you misunderstood the whole point. **God doesn't want a temporary sugar sacrifice; He wants a forever living sacrifice.**

Hudson Taylor, a missionary from the nineteenth century, once said, "Christ is either Lord of all, or He is not Lord at all."[1] We can't invite the Lord to inhabit our lives like a dwelling place, then ask Him to stay out of the small room at the end of the hall.

> *God doesn't want your sugar; He wants your life.*

He must be the sovereign ruler over our whole metaphorical home. That's why we keep coming back to consider if there's any "room" we need to surrender to His lordship in order to make more room for Him. Even now, in a humble, eleventh-hour attempt to invite the Lord to be Lord of all, let's read the passage above once more, considering a few key phrases.

In view of God's mercy. Don't skim over these four little words that appear near the beginning of Romans 12. In light of God's mercy—mercy simply means that He withholds His judgment so that we might know His grace—how should we live? In light of all He's done to rescue and redeem us, how can we help but love Him back? I'm not talking about just a little love; I'm talking about all our love. Not only has He given us each new day but He's also granted us an eternity of days in His kingdom of light. In light of that, we should respond with our whole selves. **We should give Him access to our whole lives because He saved our whole lives!**

Holy and pleasing to God—this is your true and proper worship. God is speaking directly to Christ followers here. He is saying: "Since I made you holy, live holy. Since I made you pleasing, be pleasing. This holy and pleasing life is how you worship Me. Your holy and pleasing life is an offering of thanks back to Me." Every moment of every day, with our lives set upon the altar, this is how we worship.

Do not conform to the pattern of this world. We know the temptation to conform to the world, rather than conform to the Word. With only two days left in our fast, we need to be sure to heed this warning or we'll end up right back where we started. Though we've experienced both physical and spiritual breakthroughs, the world is eager to get us back in its clutches and tangled in old, familiar sins. That's why we need to throw off anything and everything that hinders us as we transition into life beyond the fast.

> Therefore, since we are surrounded by such a great cloud of witnesses, let us throw off everything that hinders and the sin that so easily entangles. And let us run with perseverance the race marked out for us. (Heb. 12:1 NIV)

You're enlisted in God's service now. Second Timothy 2:4 says, "No soldier in active service entangles himself in the affairs of everyday life, so that he may please the one who enlisted him as a soldier" (NASB). Don't get tied up with the affairs of everyday life again. Whether you choose to remain sugar-free or not, you must continue to live free!

Transition out of this fast carefully, so that you don't find yourself running back to sugar instead of God. **If you give the devil a foothold, sugar may become a stronghold again.** Test and approve God's will for your life carefully.

If you aren't sure what God's will for you is beyond this fast, keep spending time with Him. Stay in His Word and pray. Focus your thinking on God's will, and He will transform your thinking to match His will. If you let Him, God will renew your mind so that you might clearly understand His will—His good, pleasing, and perfect will. You've simply got to stay close to Him. All of you placed on the altar before Him. I love how the Message implores us:

So here's what I want you to do, God helping you: Take your everyday, ordinary life—your sleeping, eating, going-to-work, and walking-around life—and place it before God as an offering. Embracing what God does for you is the best thing you can do for him. Don't become so well-adjusted to your culture that you fit into it without even thinking. Instead, fix your attention on God. You'll be changed from the inside out. Readily recognize what he wants from you, and quickly respond to it. Unlike the culture around you, always dragging you down to its level of immaturity, God brings the best out of you, develops well-formed maturity in you. (Rom. 12:1–2)

That's what this fast has been about all about. Staying close to Jesus! **He never wanted your sugar, it's you He's been after all along.**

Dear Lord, You can have it all. You can have my waking and my sleeping, my holidays and my ordinary days too. You can have my weekdays and my weekends, my daytime and my nighttime. You can have my thinking and my feeling too. Take my sugar and take my life. You, God, can have it all! Amen.

NEARING THE END

As you near the end of your fast, let me encourage you to see the end as a beginning. This intimate fasting friendship doesn't have to be reserved for times when you need a spiritual breakthrough. Now that you know how tangible, how present, how very wonderfully near God is, make fasting a regular part of your relationship with Him.

After five years of doing these forty-day sugar fasts, I decided to try a new type of fasting. Today I fast during the morning hours Monday through Friday and break my fast at noon. My time in the

Word has never been more applicable; my time in prayer, never more conversational; and my sensitivity to the promptings of the Spirit, never more exciting.

Instead of setting aside a season to fast, choose seasons *not* **to fast.** Take breaks from the intimate practice of fasting in order to spend more time enjoying the things of this world—rather than the other way around. When friends are in town or the holidays are upon us or you're traveling, fast from fasting. As you near the end of these forty days, consider the benefits of this fast and how you might continue to enjoy the feasting life!

day 40

LIVE LIKE IT'S TRUE!

Satisfy us in the morning with your unfailing love,
that we may sing for joy and be glad all our days.

Psalm 90:14 NIV

LONG-TERM HUNGER can leave a long and lasting mark on
a person. My grandparents, who were raised during the Great
Depression, never wasted food or money. They always took
their leftovers home from restaurants. Grandma kept an account of every grocery item she bought. After she died, I came
across a pile of spiral notebooks that listed every purchase,
every box of powdered milk and each five-cent stick of gum.
She used each tea bag multiple times and taught me to do the
same. Growing up hungry marked the way she shopped, cooked,
ate, saved, and lived.

Growing up hungry left a mark on me as well, only mine was
a different kind of hunger. For the first twenty-five years of my
life, I experienced an emotional hunger that drove me to food
and the approval of others. That's how old I was when I finally
came across the verse above and committed it to memory. I
decided that bondage-breaking day to pray Psalm 90:14 every

morning, believing that Christ was the only One who was able to satiate my hungry heart. I told Him that I was willing to cry out morning after morning, but He had to do the filling. After all, He made my heart; He knew every crack and crevice, every hurt and every hole.

I had come to a point in my life, and perhaps you have too, where no person or purchase, not even a half-baked pan of brownies, could fill me up. I was at the end of trying because I'd tried it all. After twenty-five years, I gave God complete access to my hungry heart, much more of me than I had given Him before. I prayed, *Lord, satisfy me with your unfailing love this morning so that I may sing for joy and be glad all day long.*

While I was eager for an instant filling that would keep me supernaturally satiated until bedtime, it was more complicated than that. As I said, long-term hunger leaves its mark. So I made a choice to believe that God had, indeed, faithfully filled me that morning, instantaneously and supernaturally, whether I felt it or not. I had to learn to live satisfied. I was accustomed to feeling hungry and running to food. I needed to learn to live differently, because my life was now different. This new awareness of having been made full had to reshape my thinking, one believing moment at a time.

Throughout those early days especially, when loneliness or insecurities threatened me, I had to recognize the lies and actively decide that they were false. "I'm not hungry, I'm full," I'd say to myself. "I'm not insecure; I am completely secure as a child of the One who filled me up this morning. I'm full, and I'm glad I'm full." My inner dialogue throughout the day worked to keep me in step with God's answered prayer every morning.

The key to living a full life beyond this fast is actively reminding yourself that you have been filled. Choose to believe that God has filled you, and then live like it's true! Believe that you are full, and you will live a full life. Keep believing it and keep walking it out each day.

So often, at the end of these forty days, I hear this question: "How do I stop myself from falling right back into my sugar addiction again?" My answer is simply, "Keep in step with what is true, and keep in step with the Spirit!" **As you step beyond this fast, remember the truth of God's filling, or you will run to false fillers again.**

Believe that you are full, and you will live a full life.

Today I want to serve up one final helping of Scripture. Read slowly, savoring one of our final meals together. As you read, look for specific instructions to help you stay the course in the days ahead.

> It is for freedom that Christ has set us free. Stand firm, then, and do not let yourselves be burdened again by a yoke of slavery. . . .
>
> So I say, walk by the Spirit, and you will not gratify the desires of the flesh. For the flesh desires what is contrary to the Spirit, and the Spirit what is contrary to the flesh. They are in conflict with each other, so that you are not to do whatever you want. But if you are led by the Spirit, you are not under the law.
>
> The acts of the flesh are obvious: sexual immorality, impurity and debauchery; idolatry and witchcraft; hatred, discord, jealousy, fits of rage, selfish ambition, dissensions, factions and envy; drunkenness, orgies, and the like. I warn you, as I did before, that those who live like this will not inherit the kingdom of God.
>
> But the fruit of the Spirit is love, joy, peace, forbearance, kindness, goodness, faithfulness, gentleness and self-control. Against such things there is no law. Those who belong to Christ Jesus have crucified the flesh with its passions and desires. Since we live by the Spirit, let us keep in step with the Spirit. (Gal. 5:1, 16–25 NIV)

My fasting friends, it is for a life of freedom that Christ set you free. The Spirit of God, which you have been consuming, is calling you to stand against the pull of the flesh. Follow His lead and stand firm by His side. Stay the course, whether He leads you to remain sugar-free or not.

Stay close to God and you won't go running after false gods again.

Stay close to God and you won't go running after false gods again. Fill your life with the Spirit, and you won't indulge the flesh. Live each day in the truth of Psalm 90:14: God has filled you with Himself.

It is true that a long life of hunger leaves an impression, but a satisfied life leaves a lasting mark too. Live like it's true!

Dear Lord, let this fast leave a lasting mark on me. You have satisfied me with Yourself, and I am full. Help me, Holy Spirit, to keep in step with the knowledge of my satisfied, Spirit-filled life, so that I do not turn again to the temporary fillers that deaden my hunger for You. Keep me hungry, Lord, so that I might daily know that You have made me full. Thank You for these forty days. In Jesus's name, Amen.

WELL DONE!

Congratulations on reaching the end of the 40-Day Sugar Fast! I have one more chapter for you to gobble up tomorrow, because I don't want you to stop feasting just because you're done fasting. Don't forget to celebrate by heading over to 40daysugarfast.com. Find the video entitled "Life beyond the fast," where I offer encouragement on how to remain free, even if you don't remain sugar-free! Then click over to the testimonials page where you can leave me a note. I'd love to hear from you!

day 41

HE'S NOT DONE
WITH YOU YET

Like newborn babies, crave pure spiritual milk, so that by it you
may grow up in your salvation, now that you have tasted that
the Lord is good.

1 Peter 2:2–3 NIV

SURPRISE! You thought you were done, but you're never
really done! You've officially completed your forty-day fast,
but now you have some choices to make about the life laid
out before you. How will you live it? Whatever you feed regularly will grow throughout your life. Feed your belly, and it
will grow. Feed the spirit, and it will grow. Feed your earthly
cravings, and they will grow. But feed your spiritual cravings
every day, and they will grow abundantly, exceedingly more
than forty days can capture. What will you feed on today and
tomorrow and the next day and the next? Will you run back to
the things that tempted you in the past or will you continue
to chase hard after God? You get to make a new plan because
this is a new life. The slate is clean and your palate is too.

Your body is strong and healthy and your mind is alert. How will you live? The choice is yours.

The One who brought down each stronghold in your life is inviting you to continue enjoying His strong hold.

The same God who brought down the figurative walls of Jericho in your life, the walls that held you back, is calling you to grow up and enter into the life that He has prepared for you. The One who brought down each stronghold in your life is inviting you to continue enjoying His strong hold.

"Like newborn babies, crave pure spiritual milk, so that by it you may grow up in your salvation" (1 Pet. 2:2 NIV). **The God who called you to salvation is charging you now to grow up and continue working out your salvation.**

> Therefore, my dear friends, as you have always obeyed—not only in my presence, but now much more in my absence—continue to work out your salvation with fear and trembling. (Phil. 2:12 NIV)

You don't need me to lead you another day! You've got the Word of God at your fingertips and the Holy Spirit camped within you. No, you don't need me. You've tasted freedom in Him, and you know that He is enough for you. This transition reminds me of King Josiah and the children of Israel, and how Josiah helped God's people hear the Word of the Lord. Once they committed to obeying God's Word as a nation, the king brought down all the high places that the previous generations had erected to false gods. The Israelites followed their leader, and an entire people turned their faces to the Lord together. However, after Josiah died, a new king took the throne and eventually the people turned back to their sinful ways. Up went their idols and before long they found themselves in bondage once again.

In a way, I took the role of Josiah these last forty days, inviting you to tear down the false idols by denying the false fillers in your life. Today I'm leaving you to continue on without me. My job here is through. That's why I'm urging you to commit to following the true King in the days to come. You don't need this guide. Christ Himself has left you with a guide, His Holy Spirit, and a light to illuminate your path, His Holy Word.

I have led you through your personal exodus from sugar captivity into the promised land of health and wholeness. Now you must go on without me. Keep walking it out, one step at a time, one hard day at a time, one tempting meal at a time, one applicable passage of Scripture at a time. Each time you're tempted to run to the pantry, run to Jesus. Run to Jesus when you believe that only a glass of wine can help you cope. Turn to His holy face, rather than turning to Facebook.

What God is offering you now is a complete makeover, a forever transformation! That's why you must continue to grow up and mature in your faith. **God's not done with you yet.** Now that those sugar shackles have fallen from your wrists, press on in your freedom and work it out 365 days of the year. Don't stop.

God's not done with you yet.

"For I am confident of this very thing, that He who began a good work in you will perfect it until the day of Christ Jesus" (Phil. 1:6 NASB). Praise God for His ongoing commitment to you, but hear this: Since He is committed to you, you must also be committed to you! Of course, God should be your first priority, but you need to value yourself because He values you. You must value your freedom, both externally and internally, presently and forevermore, for it was bought with the precious blood of Christ.

On day 41, the best way to value your life is by consuming more and more of that good-for-you spiritual milk! You're craving it now . . . keep craving it.

Break the fast if you wish, but don't stop feasting. The feasting life is the sweetest life!

Dear Lord, I want to live free. I do not want to get tangled up in old sins again. Holy Spirit, abide in me as I abide in You, so that I might bear the fruit of self-control in my life. I know that's an important part of not getting entangled again. Thank You for filling my belly and filling my mind and filling my life with pure spiritual milk these past forty-one days. I am committed to following You on day 42 and day 43 and day 44 and day 45 . . . because You have set me free! Thank You. Amen.

APPENDIX A

LIFE BEYOND THE FAST

YOU ARE FREE! Now the choice is yours if you want to remain sugar-free. God's Word says that everything is permissible, but not everything is beneficial. Perhaps you've found that refined sugar simply isn't good for you. You lost weight and found energy and clarity. Your joint pain and bellyaches are gone, and your sleep is better than it has been for decades. Your relationships are better too, because you're not riding a sugar coaster up and down each afternoon. Just because you *can* eat sugar doesn't mean that you *should*.

Here are five practical ideas for how to limit your sugar year-round so that you can feel physically healthy, emotionally stable, and spiritually alert.

1. **Make your sugar fast a sugar-free lifestyle.** Perhaps you want to go sugar-free forever, but you also want to be able to cheat every now and then. Here's the trick: Instead of taking a break from your highly sugared life, think of those "cheats" as little breaks from a sugar-free lifestyle. Live sugar-free but don't be afraid to fast from

your sugar fast every now and again. Do you see how it's practically the same thing—just backwards? Instead of taking breaks from sugar to detox, live clean and clear and free from sugar most of the time, then take breaks when there's a special occasion that includes a special treat.

2. **Never eat alone.** My most unhealthy eating choices have taken place when I've been alone. A few years ago I made the choice to only eat special treats in the company of family and friends. (And it's usually been for family and friends and fun events that I've made a batch of lemon bars or a cheesecake!) Even when I take the baked goods out of the oven and cut them up to place upon a platter, I don't nibble on crumbled edges until I'm with my loved ones. It's one way I love myself. I'm keeping in step with the Spirit as I practice self-control. (If you struggle with drinking alcohol daily, this is a good boundary for you too. Never drink alone. Never eat alone.)

3. **Give your leftovers away!** If you follow the second guideline, then this one should be easy! Package up any leftover cookies and cake and send them home as a gift to your loved ones. If you're baking for your little family, put leftovers in the freezer or walk a plate of cookies over to a neighbor.

4. **Discover wonderful sugar-free treats.** During the fast, I warned you not to exchange one obsession for another; however, if you want to make this low-sugar lifestyle manageable year-round, now's a good time to discover some sweet treats that are sugar-free. For a list of my favorite sugar-free recipes, visit 40daysugar fast.com.

5. **Join me again next year.** Finally, make the 40-Day
   Sugar Fast an annual event, and invite your family and
   friends to join you. You can link up with me every January at 40daysugarfast.com. Even when I'm actively
   living sugar-free, this annual fast works like a charm,
   reminding me to hunger and thirst for the satisfying
   sweetness of my Savior once again!

APPENDIX B

ADDITIONAL RESOURCES

THIS BOOK DOESN'T FOCUS on what is happening physiologically as you fast. I don't list the scientific reasons why you're addicted to sugar, and I don't offer sugar-free solutions. My single purpose is to lead you straight into the satisfying presence of the sweet Savior Himself. He's the missing ingredient, and the recipe to living the full life.

If, however, you would like to understand what is happening in your body as you detox, more information about why we crave sugar so intensely, and what that has to do with your spiritual life, here are a few of my favorite resources.

- *The Case Against Sugar* by Gary Taubes is a convincing look at both the addictive and destructive qualities of sugar. This is a great resource for those who are struggling with diabetes. Likewise, *Suicide by Sugar* by Nancy Appleton and G. N. Jacobs links our sugar intake to even more of our nation's health epidemics, from dementia to obesity to cancer.

- *Full: Food, Jesus, and the Battle For Satisfaction* by Asheritah Ciuciu offers an honest look at food fixation while pointing readers to the only One who can satisfy. And Asheritah's book *Bible and Breakfast: 31 Mornings with Jesus* couples sugar-free breakfast recipes with a short, easy-to-consume morning Bible study. *Bible and Breakfast* would be a wonderful resource to use during the transition into post-fast life.

- *Made to Crave: Satisfying Your Deepest Desire with God, Not Food* by Lysa TerKeurst reminds us that God created us to crave Him. This book serves as a reminder that, too often, our cravings are misplaced and misunderstood.

- *The Whole30: The 30-Day Guide to Total Health and Food Freedom* by Melissa and Dallas Hartwig is more than a recipe book; it's a movement! Hundreds of thousands of people have followed her plan to experience radical physical and emotional benefits while eating whole foods.

- *The 21-Day Sugar Detox: Bust Sugar and Carb Cravings Naturally* by Diane Sanfilippo is another whole foods–based eating plan that works to reset the body with new, healthier, sugar-free habits.

Acknowledgments

Matt Brunner—Thank you for supporting me in both prayerful and practical ways each time I lead this fast online. Balancing loving you and the boys as I love on others (via books) isn't easy. I am so grateful for your willingness to share God's love by sharing your time with me.

Bill Jensen—Your partnership, wisdom, and affirmation are gifts to me. Matt and I both appreciate you so much.

Rebekah Guzman, Mark Rice, Wendy Wetzel, and the rest of the brilliant Baker team—You caught the vision and joined me in this sugar-free adventure! I pray that the Lord does exceedingly, abundantly more than all you hope or imagine with this book.

Liz Heaney—I prayed for an editor who would challenge me to be a better writer. Thank you for being God's answer to that prayer.

Alle McCloskey—For all the years you supported me online and behind the scenes, thank you.

Caleb Peavey and the Unmutable team—I'm so grateful that Baker said yes to bringing you on board *The 40-Day Sugar Fast* team. Thank you for enabling me to serve so many men and women around the world.

Asheritah Ciuciu—You've been my partner in this nearly from the start. How kind of the Lord to give us one another.

Angie Mosteller, Kelli Stuart, Bethany Hockenbury, Amber Rogers, and Michelle Sit—Your availability to read all the words and pray all the prayers never ceases to amaze me. Your serving me allows me to serve others better.

Christy Nueman, Jennifer McClure, Amy J. Bennett, Katie M. Reid, Monica Swanson, Alexis MacPhee, Christie Thomas, Amber Lia, Christin Slade, Kasia Gilbert, Becky Keife, Elisa Pullium, Sarah Leach, Sarah Bragg, Jane Manka, Julie Kieras, and so many others—Thank you for partnering with me over the years. I could not have done these annual online fasts without a team of hungry-for-Jesus women!

Notes

Foreword

1. John Piper, *A Hunger for God: Desiring God through Fasting and Prayer* (Wheaton: Crossway Books, 1997), 23.

Day 3 When Sugar Walls Crumble

1. John H. Sammis, "Trust and Obey," 1887.

Day 4 Trusting God with the Battle

1. Jennifer Regan, "Not So Sweet–The Average American Consumes 150-170 Pounds Of Sugar Each Year," *BambooCore*, https://Bamboocorefitness.com/not-so-sweet-the-average-american-consumes-150-170-pounds-of-sugar-each-year/.

Day 12 Food Triggers

1. "Eating Disorders," *National Institute of Mental Health*, https://www.nimh.nih.gov/health/topics/eating-disorders/index.shtml.
2. Dr. William Davis, "Wheat is an Opiate," *WheatBelly Blog*, April 17, 2012, https://www.wheatbellyblog.com/2012/04/wheat-is-an-opiate/.
3. Asheritah Ciuciu, *Full: Food, Jesus, and the Battle for Satisfaction* (Chicago: Moody Publishers, 2017), 140.

Day 14 What Else Are You Craving?

1. "Andrew Bonar Quotes," *Christian Quotes*, accessed January 18, 2019, https://www.christianquotes.info/quotes-by-author/andrew-bonar-quotes/.
2. The translation and corresponding information came from *BibleHub*, accessed May 31, 2019, https://biblehub.com/greek/2836.htm.
3. Blaise Pascal, *Pensées VII* (425)1670, Blaise Pascal, Pensées.
4. William Bright, *Jesus and the Intellectual* (San Bernardino, CA: Campus Crusade for Christ International, 1968).
5. Lysa TerKeurst, *Made to Crave Devotional: 60 Days to Craving God, Not Food* (Grand Rapids: Thomas Nelson, 2011), 39.

Day 17 Be Quiet and Be Transformed

1. Bob Sorge, *Secrets of the Secret Place* (Kansas City, MO: Oasis House, 2001), 11.
2. Sorge, *Secrets of the Secret Place*, 11.

Day 19 Have a Sober Mind

1. "The Alcohol Manifesto," *Whole9*, https://www.whole9life.com/2012/09/the-alcohol-manifesto.

Day 20 The World's Goods Aren't as Good

1. "Pierre Teilhard de Chardin Quotes," *BrainyQuote*, accessed January 18, 2019, https://www.brainyquote.com/authors/pierre_teilhard_de_chardi.

Day 22 Spiritual and Mental Clarity

1. Dennis Lee and Daniel Lee Kulick, "Omega-3 Fatty Acids Benefits, Uses, and List of Foods," *MedicineNet*, October 2, 2017, https://www.medicinenet.com/omega-3_fatty_acids/article.htm#what_are_omega-3_fatty_acids.

Day 23 Hunger Pangs

1. Bill Gaultiere, "Hungry Heart Scriptures," *Soul Shepherding*, July 23, 2006, https://www.soulshepherding.org/hungry-heart-scriptures.

Day 24 Healing Past Hurts

1. Rebecca K. Reynolds, "Sugar because I'm tired," Facebook, January 19, 2019, https:/www.facebook.com/permalink.php?story_fbid=2315071788725433&id=1619110878321531.

Day 28 Feed My Sheep

1. To learn more about sponsoring a child through Compassion International, visit https://www.compassion.com.
2. To learn more about supporting The LuLuTree, visit https://www.thelulutree.com/partner.

Day 32 Wake Up!

1. "Leonard Ravenhill Quotes," *GoodReads*, accessed January 18, 2019, https://www.goodreads.com/quotes/8298551.

Day 39 God Wants Your Life, Not Your Sugar

1. "27 Hudson Taylor Quotes," *Christian Quotes*, accessed March 14, 2019, https://www.christianquotes.info/quotes-by-author/hudson-taylor-quotes/#axzz5iARcOUIb.

Wendy Speake is a trained actress and heartfelt Bible teacher. During her career in Hollywood she longed to tell stories that point audiences to the Savior. Today she does just that: writing books and speaking at events where every Bible story and personal story leads people right into the presence of God.

Wendy lives in Southern California with her husband, Matt, and their three sons. She writes regularly about motherhood and leads Bible studies at WendySpeake.com. She is the coauthor of the popular parenting books *Triggers*, *Parenting Scripts*, and *Life Creative*.

CONNECT WITH

Wendy

Discover more from Wendy at

WENDYSPEAKE.COM

or find her on Facebook or Instagram today.

Connect with
BakerBooks
Relevant. Intelligent. Engaging.

Sign up for announcements about
new and upcoming titles at

BakerBooks.com/SignUp

@ReadBakerBooks

The Kabbalist At Work

previously published as

The Work of the Kabbalist

By the same author:

Adam and the Kabbalistic Trees
A Kabbalistic Universe
The Way of Kabbalah
Introduction to the World of Kabbalah
Kabbalah and Exodus
School of the Soul
Psychology and Kabbalah
The Kabbalistic Tree of Life
Kabbalah and Astrology
The Anointed–a *Kabbalistic novel*
The Anatomy of Fate
The Path of a Kabbalist
A Kabbalistic View of History

By Other Publishers:

Kabbalah—The Divine Plan (*HarperCollins*)
Kabbalah, Tradition of Hidden Knowledge (*Thames & Hudson*)
Astrology, The Celestial Mirror (*Thames & Hudson*)
As Above So Below (*Stuart & Watkins*)

The Kabbalist At Work

previously published as

The Work of the Kabbalist

Z'ev ben Shimon Halevi

Kabbalah
Society

Bet El Trust
Registered Charity No. 288712

www.kabbalahsociety.org
E-mail: books@kabbalahsociety.org

First published in 1984 by Gateway Books
Revised Edition in 2008 by Kabbalah Society
Copyright © Z'ev ben Shimon Halevi 1984, 2008

A CIP catalogue record for this book
is available from the British Library.

ISBN: 978-1-909171-13-8

Printed and bound by Lightning Source UK Ltd., Milton Keynes

Design by Tree of Life Publishing
www.treeoflifepublishing.co.uk

For
Moses Cordovero

FIGURE 1—THE KABBALIST AT WORK
*Here a master, standing amid the four elements, Nature and the works of humanity,
connects with the Solar system, the angels, archangels and the World of the
Divine Name. This is the aim of Kabbalah, so that both the inner and outer
realms are united to make the microcosm and macrocosm one. This is why
Kabbalah is sometimes called the Work of Unification. Such an ability requires
long and deep training. The purpose is to aid God to behold God. (Halevi, 20th
century.)*

Contents

viii

Illustrations

Preface

To be acquainted with Kabbalah is one matter but to do its Work quite another. Many who begin to walk the path soon tire or turn away when the novelty has gone and some even double back after great progress when they see there is nothing for them. Only those who do the Work for its own sake are initiated. Only the individual who wants to make manifest what Kabbalah reveals can be an initiate. This process is nothing less than to integrate the body, soul and spirit and so become a finer instrument whereby the inner and outer worlds can come into communion. Each time this is done, the Divine is known by Adam upon the Earth. By such a labour of love, the Universe comes increasingly into focus as a reflection of the Absolute. When the human image of the Divine realises upon whom it gazes then God perceives God and the cycle is complete. To assist the Holy One in this aim is the Work of the Kabbalist.

Winter 5742.

FIGURE 2—JACOB'S DREAM
This vision occurs while Jacob is asleep. This means he is having a psychic experience and not a mystical or spiritual illumination. Even so, he is being shown the Ladder of Ascension and Descent between the lower and higher Worlds. The angels or 'Messengers' going up and down are human and represent advanced souls coming down to aid incarnate humanity or returning home to Heaven. Those teachers are called, in Kabbalah, the maggidim *who have climbed the Jacob's Ladder of development.* (Hayley's book on Milton, 18th century.)

Introduction

The kabbalistic method is the practical art of entering into and participating in the Higher Worlds. Whether it be by action, devotion or contemplation, its aim is always to serve God and aid in the great Work of Unification. This work is the perfection of mankind so that Adam, the image of the Divine, may realise that the exterior and interior universe is the reflection of God beholding God.

Prior to this penultimate state of being, before total union with the Absolute, the Universe and mankind have to pass through many stages. According to one view the human race as a whole is less than half-way in its development. Indeed, history and the events of the past century indicate that the vast majority of human souls on the Earth are somewhere between childhood and youth. After two global wars the possibility of a third remains quite real, as the so-called advanced nations still act like adolescent gangs over territory while the rest squabble amongst themselves for the marbles of power and wealth. Fortunately, there has always been a proportion of the human race that is more mature, even as there is a minority of childish souls in every society that is still primitive in its outlook. This evolved spearhead of mankind occurs all over the world and at every point in history. It may be seen embodied in Messianic figures, great prophets and teachers or in traditions of high spiritual development. Its indirect influence may be witnessed in the living religions of mankind and in periods of advanced culture when the creative impulse of cosmic influx has been merged into a moment of flowering in a society to produce a civilisation such as early Islam or ancient China. These great epochs, like the period of the cathedral master builders in the Middle Ages, could not have arisen without the presence of people who not only knew about the upper worlds but also had the ability to draw down their substance and power and focus it upon the activities of the Earth. Like other spiritual traditions, this is the Work of Kabbalah. However, before such a task can be undertaken by an individual, group or school there is a whole process of training and understanding of what is involved. This must be so or the operation of unifying will become no more than a magical exercise concerned with personal inflation and private interests which are the very opposite to the aim of the Work of Unification, as Kabbalah is sometimes called.

Kabbalah is one of many traditions involved with such activities. If we look at its ancient line it will be seen that Kabbalah, although it was not always known by this name, was practised in many of the great cultural centres of the Middle East and the West. It was to be found in pre-exile Israel, Babylon, Hellenistic Egypt and in Roman-occupied Judea. It was present in Islamic Mesopotamia before it transferred to Provence and Spain in the Middle Ages, and was practised in Flanders and Bohemia as well as in Poland, Italy and Elizabethan England where Shakespeare, no doubt, knew secret Jews then living in London. Kabbalah was studied in 17th century Holland and in 18th century Germany as well as Victorian England, although the system practised by this time was several removes from the Jewish line that had continued on in Eastern Europe and Western Asia.

As may be realised, mere contact with the theory of a spiritual tradition is not enough to transform an individual, let alone a society. Action has to be taken in accordance with the sequence of the four levels of existence. To will, conceive, form and carry out a spiritual project, or transmit a cosmic influence, requires not only a comprehension of esoteric principles but the skill to implement them. This book endeavours to set out the process of acquiring such knowledge and the techniques of how to use it for different purposes and at various levels. It will draw upon traditional material designed to meet contemporary conditions because Kabbalah has always adapted itself to the present. If this had not been so, the line would have died long ago in ancient Israel instead of still being alive and practised all around the world in forms appropriate to each period and place. And so we begin with the Eternal and translate it into our own time.

It is right that a man should aspire to be
like his creator, for by this he will enter
into the likeness and image of the
supernal Adam.
Moses Cordovero, 16th Century

16

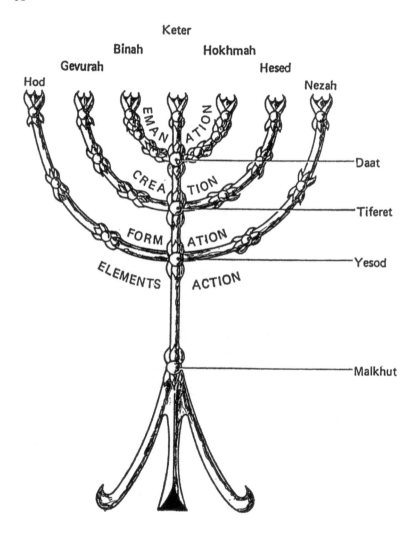

FIGURE 3—MODEL

The seven-branched candlestick, the design of which was given to Moses on Mount Sinai, is the symbol of the Tree of Life. It was to be made of pure gold, signifying Divinity. The seven cups and the nodal points make up ten key principles while the 22 other decorations refer to what will become the Paths. The two wings define the active and passive aspects of Existence with the central column as the axis of equilibrium. This sacred object, kept in the sanctuary of the Tabernacle and, later, the Temple, clearly indicates an esoteric body of knowledge only known to the priests and elders of the House of Israel. (Halevi, 20th century.)

1. Origin of the Work

The root of all practical kabbalistic work goes back to the source of everything that exists. Indeed, the whole process of coming into being, carrying out one's destiny and returning to that point of origin is the essence of the Work of Unification. Everything begins with the Most High Name of God: I AM THAT I AM. This Holy appellation is associated with the Crown of Crowns at the head of the Great Ladder of Jacob which describes, in its four interlocking worlds, all the levels of existence from its highest manifestation of pure consciousness to the lowest and densest concretion of matter.

The Divine Name I AM THAT I AM was given to Moses as he stood before the Burning Bush upon the Holy Mountain. It was in answer to his question (Exodus III.13) as to what should he say to the Children of Israel when they asked who had sent him. *EHYEH ASHER EHYEH* was the reply and then, '*EHYEH shelachan: alaychem*' — 'I AM has sent me unto you'. This was followed by the better-known Divine Name YAHVEH which came to be the title by which the Holy One was to be remembered and honoured in the exoteric tradition. Here we have the differentiation between aspects of Divinity as it enters into manifestation and multiplicity.

If one contemplates the first Name that was given, and its significance, then an awesome depth of meaning is revealed for it speaks of what was, that which is and that which shall be. This is a statement of intent as well as a cycle of being. When associated with the Crown of Crowns, I AM THAT I AM sets out the Absolute's Will with succinct precision, as God calls forth existence from the midst of non-existence. In the utterance of *EHYEH*, the hidden Holiness appears as manifest Divinity. This is symbolised in Kabbalah as Light emerging out of the darkness of a void. However, the process does not stop there, in that Divinity extends itself in order, as said, to behold Itself in reflection. Thus the Divine proceeds into *ASHER* or THAT before resolving into *EHYEH* or I AM again. Here is the plan for all existence. Everything to come into manifestation is contained in this Name of Names.

The implication of this gives us a key to why the universe and its

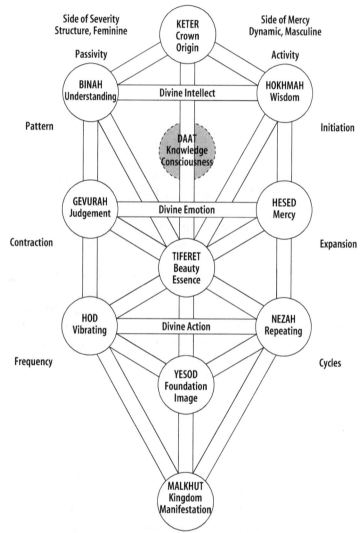

FIGURE 4—METAPHYSICS

The philosophical aspect of Kabbalah is concerned with how the sefirot or numbers and, here, the paths in between, interact. In this scheme there are the Hebrew names and their translations together with their functions. These are some of the many aspects the sefirot represent. Also to be noted are the three pillars and levels within what is known as the Tree of Life and the 22 paths which are related to the Hebrew alphabet. They vary according to different annotations, the non-sefirah of Daat was seen as the hidden connection with the higher realm beyond. The whole scheme is sometimes seen as a fiery man, Adam Kadmon. (Halevi, 20th century.)

inhabitants exist, in that everything held between the poles of unity above and multiplicity below is part of a great process of realisation. This process will be terminated when the mirror of the macrocosm reflects the name I AM back as a fully conscious image to its Divine origin. Such a moment can only happen when everything in existence has reached its full capacity of self-realisation. This will take the complete round of a great *Shemittah,* or cosmic cycle, in which all creatures will evolve through experience into knowledge of Divinity.

According to tradition, each being calls out 'I AM THAT I AM' as it comes forth into and departs from existence. Between these two instants of self-realisation lies the long loop of destiny. Some beings shorten their time out of total union with the Divine by working consciously upon themselves. This does not exempt them from the particular task for which they were called, created, formed and made but indeed obligates and equips them all the more to assist in the Work of Unification. Spiritual traditions are designed to help such people because to overcome the forces of nature, rise above fatal patterns, avoid the tricks of tempters and tactfully move among the angels on the ascent of Jacob's Ladder is no easy matter. Kabbalah is one of many disciplines concerned with spiritual evolution. Its system and methods are designed to help those who wish consciously to return to the Light and serve the Holy One. However, before access to the Upper Worlds is allowed, a series of trials has to be undergone because it is necessary to find out whether a person is fit to take up a place in the Work. Many people wish to climb Jacob's Ladder in order to escape the lessons of the lower worlds and not a few seek the path of higher knowledge for glamour and power.

The point when the descent into matter turns back up towards the Light is a crucial period. So too is the stage when a second descent occurs in order to impart to those below what has been received. All this requires delicate monitoring by spiritual mentors until ultimately one relates directly to the highest of Names and resonates Its sound in one's life on Earth. When this operation is brought to perfection, I AM THAT I AM becomes fully manifest in the microcosm of the individual. This conscious reflection of the image of God back to its point of origin meets and completes the Divine intention to behold Itself and precipitates the fourth and final journey home to the Holy One. Before this ultimate state can occur, however, much has to be gone through. An ordered first ascent begins with training which starts in this tradition with the outline of the theory of existence, the background of the four journeys of body, soul, spirit and Divinity.

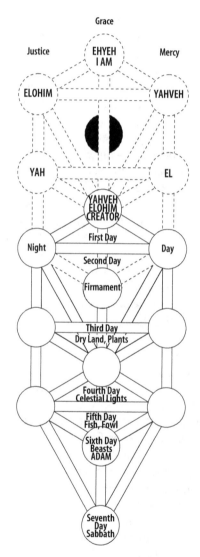

Grace

Justice　**Mercy**

EHYEH
I AM

ELOHIM　YAHVEH

YAH　EL

YAHVEH
ELOHIM
CREATOR

Night　Day

First Day

Second Day

Firmament

Third Day
Dry Land, Plants

Fourth Day
Celestial Lights

Fifth Day
Fish, Fowl

Sixth Day
Beasts
ADAM

Seventh
Day
Sabbath

FIGURE 5—CREATION

*Here a second World emerges from the Divine realm defined by the Holy Names.
At the place of the Creator, the first separation occurs as potential becomes
actual at the appearance of light (or Fire) on the First Day. This is followed by
the firmament of Air; then Water and Earth which will form the basis of the four
elements. Life is represented by plants; then comes the ordering of the cosmos
and the creation of its various inhabitants. The birds of the air (or spirits) are the
archangels; the fish of the sea are the angels while the beasts of the field are the
earthly animals. Finally comes a second, spiritual, Adam. (Halevi, 20th century.)*

2. Ladder and Descent

According to tradition, existence emerged out of a void that had been willed in the midst of the Absolute. Within this space, in the middle of nothingness, a series of Divine Lights, some say sounds, caused the manifestation of the Ten Sefirot or radiant attributes of God. These numbers, vessels or instruments, as they have been variously described, were ordered into a pattern of Laws that would govern the universe while still retaining a simple unity. Some Kabbalists have seen the sefirot as a downward-growing tree with its roots in negative existence, as the void is sometimes called, while others see the configuration of sefirot as a great Man—Adam Kadmon, the primordial human being from whom the whole of Mankind everywhere in the universe has descended.

Tradition further states that each person contains a spark of this original Adam deep within and that the pursuit of completion, arising from the sense of separation that everyone feels, is the impulse of this spark seeking to return and become one with Adam Kadmon who is the perfection of human possibility. We are, in effect, atoms of this great Image of God and contain in miniature the qualities and attributes of our ultimate ancestor and descendant because, at some point in the distant future, we shall be united as evolved atoms, to become cells of the organs and limbs of this Divine Being who lives in that Eternal and unchanging realm of Light.

Now it is because Adam Kadmon exists in this most pristine of Worlds that God brings forth the necessity for movement. In the eternal World of Emanation there is no time for it contains past, present and future and, therefore, there is no flow of development because everything just is. We are told, however, that it is not God's intention to call forth a being to mirror the Divine that cannot exercise its attributes and free will for it is these very qualities that make Adam quite different from all other creatures who were to come into existence in the three lower and separate worlds to be called forth, created, formed and made later. Adam Kadmon, at this point, is entirely innocent. Experience begins with the first seven Days of Creation that initiate

22

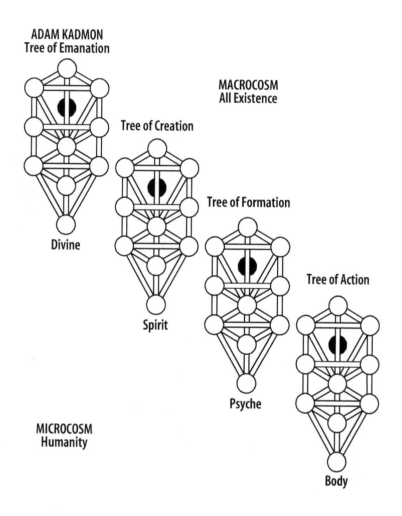

ADAM KADMON
Tree of Emanation

MACROCOSM
All Existence

Tree of Creation

Tree of Formation

Divine

Tree of Action

Spirit

Psyche

MICROCOSM
Humanity

Body

FIGURE 6—FOUR WORLDS
In this, four quite distinct realities are set out. They are presented as universes and the levels within a human being. While they are separate, they interact as the lower part of one World relates to the upper section of the reality below. All are subject to the same sefirotic laws although within their own domain. However, the lowest World of matter and nature is influenced by all the Worlds above; thus Divinity can be seen in a stone and all the Worlds in a human being who has realised his own full potential. (Halevi, 20th century.)

the process that will only finish at the End of Days, when everything in the universe is drawn back up and merges into the body, soul and spirit of a now-mature Adam Kadmon again.

The difference between the Adam of Innocence and the Adam of Experience is the reason for the four journeys down and up the ladder of Worlds. But first let us briefly set up the terrain of these descents and ascents. Out of the radiant World of Azilut or Emanation emerges Creation. Here the realm of Spirit divides into seven levels or halls with many chambers to each side filled with wondrous forces and beings, some good and some bad for with the separation from perfection came imperfection and its deviations. Genesis opens its text with the Creative world. Only the oral tradition, touched upon in the rabbinic and Kabbalistic tradition, speaks about what happened before Creation. After the Heavenly World of Beriah came the World of Yezirah or Formation, known as the Garden of Eden in the Bible. This became the World of the Chariot below that of the Throne in which sat the Divine Man of the vision of Ezekiel. The realm of Formation, as the name suggests, is concerned with the ever-changing configuration of forces flowing out of the Creative World under the direction of the Divine Will emanating from Azilut. The lowest World of Action and elements, or energy and matter, is the one with which we are most familiar. Its mineral, vegetable, animal and human levels echo the four levels in the physical universe. Kabbalistic work consists of becoming acquainted with all the Worlds and working in and with them, so as to assist in Adam Kadmon's education.

Tradition goes on to say that, as atoms of Adam Kadmon, we descend into the lower Worlds in order that Adam may know what it is to walk upon the Earth, experience all the pleasures and pains of the flesh, explore the realm of the psyche and the World of Angels before returning with our cup of experience to the Kingdom of the Spirit. From there we carry out our destiny, that is, our contribution to Adam Kadmon. The *Zohar*, the great classic of Kabbalistic literature, describes how each of us is called before the Almighty, prior to being sent down into the lower Worlds, and how we all decline to go, preferring Eden to the Earth. But go we must and so we pass out of Paradise and into the flesh; because this is what we were called forth, created, formed and made for, so that Adam Kadmon might experience every level.

Thus the cycle unfolds. First we are separated from that sublime state of union with the Divine by entering into the World of Creation where we are given the dynamic of a spirit for a vehicle. This enables us to traverse time and space, so that we may view the universe from one end to the other. However, tradition says, the spiritual power we are endowed with overlays the Light that is at our centre. Fortunately, it is not enough to dim the memory of whence we come. After this, we are brought down by the archangels into the World of Formation where the angels responsible for such things enclothe us in a form that corresponds to our particular soul, which is determined by the course of that destiny given to us when we come before the Throne of Heaven. Here we reside in what is called the Treasure House of Souls until it is time to descend to the Earth and appear in the natural World encased in matter. This process ends the first journey of which we remember but little, except as young children, or as flashes in rare moments of reflection or recognition as we begin the second journey up through the Worlds, back towards the great Light of which we are a spark encompassed by body, psyche and spirit. This situation is at the root of our sense of isolation and separateness. It is also the impulse behind the yearning to go home and be one with our Creator.

FIGURE 7 (Right)—JACOB'S LADDER
Here all the Worlds are locked together to make a fifth, vertical, Tree of Life running up and down the centre. This is called the Kav of consciousness that stretches between the two I AMs which hold Existence together. This is also seen in the nine rungs that mark stages of SELF-realisation as God beholds God in a mutual reflection at the top and bottom of the Ladder. The word THAT in between those two Holy Names is the Mirror of Existence. (Halevi, 20th century.)

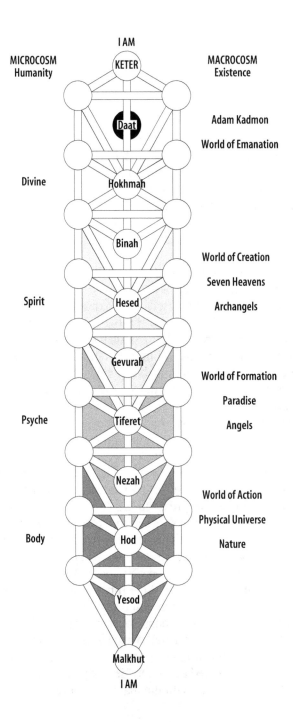

3. General Evolution

The process of evolution, like all sequences of development, follows the pattern of the sefirotic Tree. This accords with the Law that every complete World, level, organism or situation is modelled upon the Divine principles of Emanation. For those not familiar with this, the sefirotic Tree is the schematic arrangement of the Holy attributes according to the prime set of laws that govern existence. These, briefly, are as follows.

The Crown of the Tree, called Keter, represents the origin and unity of the whole. It is the place of the Will while the two sefirot immediately below and to the right and left are Hokhmah, or Wisdom and Binah, or Understanding. These head the two outer columns of Mercy and Severity which represent the expansive and contractive poles that may also be seen as masculine and feminine, or energy and form, respectively. The universe is balanced between these positive and negative pillars on the fulcrum of the central column of Grace or Equilibrium. Here we have the laws of unity, duality and triplicity.

The non-sefirah of Daat or Knowledge, which is the child of the supernal trinity above, is also called the Abyss. This is because it is the access and exit point into manifest existence of that which lies above. It is the space through which higher influences can have direct contact with the seven sefirot of Construction (as they are known) below and the place where anything beneath may contact that which is above. The two sefirot of Hesed (or Mercy) and Gevurah (or Judgement) represent the emotional poles, as against the intellectual functions of the two side sefirot above, while the two sefirot of Nezah (or Eternity) and Hod (or Reverberation) below perform as the sefirot of action. Thus, we have the three functional side pairs of the Divine mind, heart and action saddling a central column of will, knowledge and three lower levels of consciousness represented by Tiferet (or Beauty) which is the pivotal overseer of the scheme; Yesod, the Foundation, which acts as the surveyor of details and Malkhut, which is sometimes considered as the Divine Body in that it has, at this lowest point, the most contact with the material worlds.

The paths and triads that are generated by this arrangement are based upon a definite sequence that flows from the Crown to the top of the right hand column and across to the left and then on down in a primary zig-zag line before reaching the bottom. The process of ascent is in reverse up the track of this Lightning Flash, as it is traditionally called. There are many other details such as letters ascribed to the twenty-two paths and names to the triads but in this book we shall refer only to those relevant to our subject. The less-informed student should consult earlier books for a detailed account of the Tree and Jacob's Ladder.*

As we have seen, the process of evolution or return to the Light, as against that of creation or descent into matter, follows the path of the Lightning Flash but in reverse. Thus, taking the macrocosmic aspect first, the planet Earth, having emerged out of the finest of the atomic and molecular levels of existence, has become a dense and substantial ball of elemental matter. This sphere is composed of a metallic core with a mineral coat of rock. Above this floats a liquid sea and a gaseous mantle surrounded by a flamelike belt of subtle radiation that extends far out into space. Here we have the base of the four elements. Moreover, if we take metal and mineral as the upper and lower Earth elements, the same interpenetrating principle is seen between the land, the oceans, the clouds and radiation as the watery, airy and fiery elements merge into one another. This is the Malkhut (or Kingdom) of the physical world.

The next stage is the level of the vegetable kingdom, that is of organic life, as against the inorganic consciousness of the elements. This vitality relates to the sefirot of Yesod (or Foundation), Hod and Nezah comprising the triad which holds the Yesodic level of moment-by-moment consciousness in a rhythmic interaction of cycle and reverberation. Nezah (or Eternity) means to repeat endlessly while the root of the Hebrew word Hod, sometimes translated as Glory, is 'to resound'. Thus, this triad contains the repetition and vibration which maintain and yet allow fluctuations to occur, that is, the characteristic of the vegetable world in its daily and seasonal round. Such a process is quite different from the higher animal triad of Hod, Nezah and Tiferet which perceives and acts with a greater degree of consciousness because of the connection with the Seat of Solomon at the centre of the Tree. Here we have responsive will, mobility, relationship and all the instincts of the herd.

Tree of Life (Introduction); *Adam and the Kabbalistic Trees* (Man); *A Kabbalistic Universe* (Macrocosm).

28

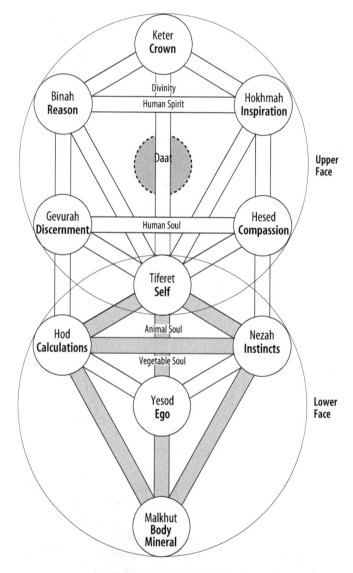

FIGURE 8—OUTLINE

Here the levels within a human being are shown in the terms of the Tree. At the lowest level it is the domain of Nature which provides a physical vehicle so that a person can exist in the Earthly dimension. This is given at the moment of conception and contains all the experience and skills of millions of years of organic evolution. The soul is the essence of the psyche of the individual while the spiritual aspect relates to the transpersonal dimension of the World of Creation. At the top is the connection with the Divine Realm. (Halevi, 20th century.)

The human parallel of this is that while mankind contains the elemental, vegetable and animal levels, it has the capacity to develop further. However, as noted earlier, the majority of the human race is still centred in the Yesod or ego level of consciousness and this makes it come under the laws of the vegetable kingdom, that is, it is principally preoccupied with having an elemental place to live with enough water, air and light so that the next generation can be propagated and fed until mature enough to flower, be fertilised and bear the following generation before withering and dying itself. This fact is not a judgement but a simple observation of how life is for most people. There are also the animal members of the human species. These are the dominators of history. They can range from Attila the Hun to the dictatorial foreman on the shop floor; or the overbearing headmistress to the pop star and politician. Their chief characteristic is to be ruler of a group of people, be it an international corporation or a village sewing circle.

At the level of the individual, where personal development begins, the process starts to take one out of the domain of these lower triads as contact with Tiferet, or the place of the Self, is made. This is where our study begins because it is the entrance to the Way and the area where kabbalistic Work is carried out. However, before this can be done certain requirements have to be met.

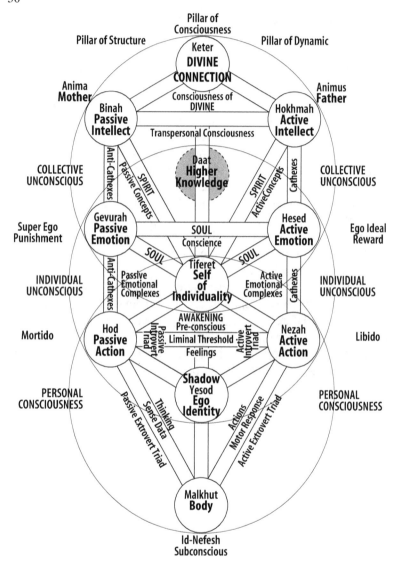

FIGURE 9—PSYCHE IN DETAIL
The Tree of the mind is the World in which a human being has direct access to all the Worlds. What is below in the body and above in the spiritual and Divine realms is beyond the horizon for the unevolved psyche. This Tree is the one from which we can learn most because it allows consciousness to explore the workings of the sefirot, paths and triads. These give a clue to how the other realities operate. This is where the Work of the Kabbalist begins with the maxim 'Know thyself' according to the principle of 'As above, so below'. (Halevi, 20th century.)

4. Individual Development

To be an individual requires many qualities. A person has to be able to support him or herself, that is manage the elemental problems of life like finding a tolerable place in which to live, with, for example, a good climate and stable economic and social conditions. This should allow him or her to earn a living and maintain a contact with the ordinary world that many seekers of the path try to avoid. In Kabbalah this ordinary life contact is vital or there is no possibility of earthing whatever may be drawn down from the higher worlds. Such individuals must also be able to feed and clothe themselves by their own labour and have the capacity to relate to their society in a balanced way, seeing it objectively whatever its current state of reaction, revolution or equilibrium. This is how conditions are at the moment as Creation unfolds. This requires a vision over and above so-called informed opinion which is often no more than pragmatism or propaganda to be disregarded, as most egocentric views are, with changing conditions. The individual must be aware of Eternal laws, even if they are only dimly perceived. This is what marks out the individual and gives that objectivity to the Work.

Such people are usually regarded as odd by their peers and, indeed, often remain isolated for years until they make contact with others like themselves when the time is ripe. This can only occur when the tests of courage and integrity have been passed and they make a committed shift, from the vegetable state of consciousness which is preoccupied with survival, through the animal level concerned with ambition, to that place which wants more than just to live comfortably or be top dog in whatever field of activity is being practised. To recognise that vegetable existence ends in death and that an animal-based reputation is a fragile bubble is to open the question as to what is ephemeral and what is Eternal.

When a person reaches this place of the soul many things become possible. In some cases such a moment of truth is too much. Some people cannot face the notion of their own physical extinction or the loss of, in their own estimation, their hard-won position. They back away and try to drown their realisation in greater or lesser activity. Many succeed, only to be repeatedly disappointed by having too much of this or desperate because they have too little of that. Either way they find no satisfaction until the day they die—or even beyond. For those who face such a moment of realisation, which may come in flashes rather than a great illumination, the opportunity offers the chance to enter the upper Worlds and so glimpse a higher form of existence. Such experiences come by Grace from above and can change a whole attitude of life. Again, such insights into another reality can cause a person to back away, if they have not the balance and the stamina to hold the Gift of Heaven. This is why, traditionally, Kabbalists have to have a degree of maturity and stability.

In kabbalistic terms, the individual who has reached this far has a measure of command over the elements of Malkhut, recognises the ego level of the Yesodic consciousness, suspects that the cleverness of Hod is not real thinking and knows the power of Nezahian passion is not emotion. At such a point people often recognise their imbalance and seek to solve the apparent problem that they are not like everyone else, in that no one seems to be bothered by the things that disturb them. Often they will look at this or that therapy, method of meditation or spiritual training. Most of these will be found to be superficial, incomplete and sometimes even sinister. Occasionally, a discipline will offer some promise, only to become disappointing because it does not go beyond a certain point or is not the right way for the aspirant. These are all preparations in discrimination set on the path to the particular tradition that is correct for that individual.

When the time is ripe the individual, often at a point of despair, meets someone to whom he can relate. It may be at a lecture or on a train; it could be at a party or even at home when someone who has a certain inner quality suddenly speaks quite out of character about the things of which he wishes to know. Such a connection may be made with an ancient line, such as the Sufis, or with a group that is only a generation old. If it is a true manifestation of the Spirit on Earth, it will have a distinct integrity about it. This is the hallmark of a real working group. Such a quality will reveal its Way in its dealings with the individual. It will apply no force or persuasion. Indeed, such groups rarely issue an invitation but merely leave the door open for the individual to enter if he or she chooses.

When that threshold is passed then the situation changes radically, often altering the life of the person beyond recognition. This is why no one is lured or pressured into a school of esoteric study. They must enter because they wish to, despite the hazards and the labour of the inner ascent. As one Kabbalist said, 'One cannot begin this Work lightly for there is no turning back, except with great peril'.

The journey from this moment on is taken in many stages. At first there is the probationary period where there are only a few obligations. Then comes the initiation which is the real beginning, long after the honeymoon period is over. From here on the Work is primarily upon the person himself as he acquires the theory of the tradition and does its practices. Later, group work is done as the individual learns to merge into a disciplined association with others on the Path. Later still, individuals become aware not only of other groups but the school of which they are part as their development takes them up through the various inner levels to contact the upper regions of the spiritual company of mankind.

On reaching a certain point of ascent in this or some future life, the privilege of just receiving is ended and the third major phase of imparting begins. Here is the third journey of re-descent or obligation of service. This not only means assisting those above and helping those below but also direct involvement in the Work of Unification, as Kabbalah is sometimes called, so as to bring the inner and outer Worlds and the upper and lower levels of existence together in consciousness. As can be appreciated, this view is totally different from that of the mundane universe that science presents. In these higher dimensions, time and space are quite beyond most people although Grace-given glimpses are seen in moments of illumination. In a kabbalistic group which has techniques to raise the level of those present, it is possible to experience and even perceive Higher Worlds and their interplay of energy and substance at will; but this requires special knowledge and skill.

The training in the application of such techniques is one of the tasks of Kabbalah. What follows is only a fraction of the repertoire used. However, it is hoped that this little might convey something of what is involved and give guidelines to anyone who can make use of what is written about individual and group techniques. The fourth journey and ultimate ascent occurs when an individual's destiny is complete and the incarnated spark of Divinity returns to its origin. Such a process is quite different from all other work because it means entering the world of Emanation and passing through the Abyss into total union with the Godhead. No one has seen the face of God and returned and so we are without a report on this final phase of realisation.

For those still standing on Jacob's Ladder, let us continue to examine the general situation and principles behind individual and group work, so as to put them in a setting. Here it must be repeated that what is described is one particular form of Kabbalah. It should not be taken as the sole approach for while the essence of the Teaching remains the same its manifestations change according to inner and outer conditions.

5. *Different Worlds*

Nearly all kabbalistic work is based upon the model of the sefirotic Tree or Jacob's Ladder. This is because, in order to be effective, any operation must not only conform to the structure of the universe but resonate with the various levels of energy inherent in it. If an enterprise is not related to the laws of Existence it simply will not follow the desired course and so obtain its objective; an aircraft cannot fly if its wings are not the right shape, no matter how powerful its engine may be. The correct relationship between form and force has to be set up. It is the same with kabbalistic work where the dynamic and the configuration of an operation have to be taken into account.

The difficulty with esoteric operations is that, unlike the elemental principles of aerodynamics and metallurgy, the Worlds in which they are set cannot be directly observed or measured. The marvels of modem technology are possible because the theory and practice of science has reached a point where the qualities, properties and characteristics of physical energy and matter are well understood. This has taken several thousand years to accomplish. For example, the principle of the steam engine was known in ancient Alexandria but never put to practical use because there was not sufficient practical knowledge of other techniques to build complex machines. Ironically, in the case of esoteric knowledge it was the reverse; more was known in ancient Egypt about magic or the art of psychic manipulation than is known today.

Since very early times it has been known that certain actions, when applied at a particular time and in a special way, generated specific effects, either in the state of an individual or within a given situation. So-called primitive shamans could cause rain to fall at will and some of the early sorcerers perceived and conversed with nature spirits after altering their perception by drugs or ritual. In later and more refined societies, priests contacted the lower angelic powers that were drawn to temples dedicated to them. They even negotiated favours in exchange for worship. The priests who acted as communicators between the gods and human beings amassed, over many centuries,

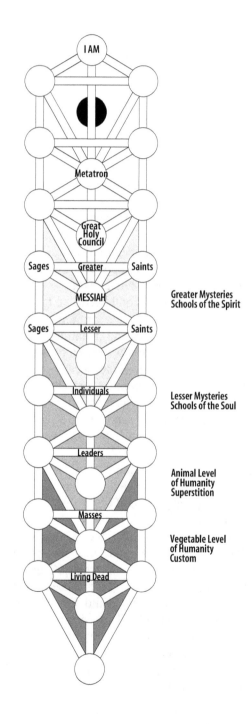

I AM

Metatron

Great Holy Council

Sages | Greater | Saints

MESSIAH

Sages | Lesser | Saints

Individuals

Leaders

Masses

Living Dead

Greater Mysteries
Schools of the Spirit

Lesser Mysteries
Schools of the Soul

Animal Level
of Humanity
Superstition

Vegetable Level
of Humanity
Custom

much empirical knowledge about the ebb and flow of natural forces, the influence of the heavens and the characteristics of the intelligences that lived in the unseen realms close to the Earth level. Some traditions built up elaborate schemes based upon observation of the hierarchy of powers and the relationship between levels and different forces at work within one stratum. The cosmologies of the ancient worlds are full of such systems and, although there are many differences between cultures, there are quite recognisable common denominators in their various pantheons of gods. The warlike qualities of the planet Mars appear, for example, in many cultures, as do the image and attributes of Mother Nature.

Besides the body of collected knowledge, there is the innermost part of any spiritual teaching that has been acquired by revelation or illumination. This is the result of the interior work of a group or of individuals who have actually changed their normal state of consciousness and risen up out of sense perception and ordinary psychological appreciation of the world to enter the supernatural realms. By definition, supernatural means above nature; and so it is, in that the group or person perceives the Higher World and its inhabitants directly. Such an experience is likely to shake the individual psyche profoundly and so generally there is a period of training under discipline for aspirants before they are allowed such experiences. We find this the pattern of both ancient and modern esoteric schools.

In the Bible the Egyptians were considered masters of many such techniques and, indeed, the training of a priest was long and complex. There were also master magicians like Balaam who not only had skill in prophecy but the power to bless or curse, within certain limits. However, there is also a level beyond which skill in the magical arts of subtle manipulation cannot be effective. The contest between Moses and the Egyptian priests, with his rod-snake swallowing up all the Egyptian snakes, is a symbol of the miraculous being superior to

FIGURE 10 (Left)—HUMAN SITUATION
Kabbalah subscribes to the notion of reincarnation. Over many centuries and lives, depending on the developmental work done, each individual finds their level in this scale. The older and wiser souls are to be seen in the upper section while the young, immature and evil people cycle around the bottom. The Living Dead relate to both stupid and intelligent persons who destroy their possibilities for growth for this life. If they persist they become crystallised, like human minerals, in contrast to those who are ascending with the aid of the Mystery schools. (Halevi, 20th century.)

the magical. In terms of Kabbalah, this indicates how the spiritual power of the Creative World of Beriah can contain and override the psychological constructions of the World of Yeziratic Forms.

From time to time in history there has appeared in the world a person or a school of the highest order which has imparted what had been received either from an incarnate master or even higher intelligence. Although usually in the guise of a great religious teacher or prophet who spoke about such matters obliquely, such esoteric teachings are often only given to a select circle of prepared people who could make good use of them at that point in time to forward the development of mankind. We see this in the hidden knowledge behind Islam, Buddhism and Christianity. Kabbalah is the esoteric teaching of Judaism. Such a body of knowledge is always based on material that has been revealed orally, rather than those things that have been written down in books, because it cannot be communicated in any other way. Although books can outline the principles, such knowledge can only be taught when there is a rising up from below to the place of inner comprehension. This takes place in that zone between Heaven and Earth where the soul hovers between the body and the spirit.

Thus we begin to see how the inner and the outer worlds are intimately related in kabbalistic work. The microcosm of a human being, because it is designed on the same principles as the macrocosm of the universe, is the instrument by which one can consciously enter the greater Worlds. This means, however, that the cosmic realms not only greatly affect but are, in proportion, influenced by a person sensitive to them. The man who is concerned only with his job will not be directly touched by or modify planetary situations, nor will the woman who just sees her own family; while individuals who have begun to resonate with the cosmos will be affected to such a degree that they will respond to the tensions between the planets. Simultaneously, their reaction can alter the terrestrial and celestial balance to a greater or lesser degree, depending on their level. For example, such persons might suddenly change their role in society and alter its values, as Buddha did, or just do something unconventional like turn down a top job which, in the long run, proves to be a killer and do something more useful. This is one of the reasons why transformation occurs in people when they begin spiritual work. They begin to live under the selective law of individual fate and not the general laws of social and mass behaviour.

The advantages and disadvantages of kabbalistic work now begin to become apparent. To gain access to the Higher Worlds and acquire knowledge of how to work in them requires great responsibility; for there are the dangers of excess, inability, temptation, inflation and many other hazards unknown to mortals who do not seek the door to immortality. However, once the commitment is made and the training is initiated, the student begins to become involved in a vast cosmic game into which one is introduced by degrees. The second stage of kabbalistic induction is to apply metaphysical theory to a known reality and so we shall continue with a brief account of the lower part of Jacob's Ladder which involves the natural and psychological Worlds. If the principles at work at these levels can be perceived, then the reality of the other worlds may come a little closer. With the practice of the exercises later they may actually be experienced. This, to many people's surprise, often confirms what they already knew but had somehow forgotten on being born; which leads us on to the first stage of study, that is, to become familiar with the different Worlds of our body and psyche, and how they interact, as set out in the diagram.

6. Different Bodies

Tradition tells us that Adam is made in the image of the Divine and that all human beings are constructed in the image of Adam. Therefore, each individual has will, intellect, emotion and action as part of their nature. We are told, moreover, that the Adams of Emanation and Creation are androgynous, that is both male and female. This is to say that the Divine Man and the Adam of the Spirit are integrated to a greater degree than the lower manifestations of humanity which are separated out into Adam and Eve at the level of the psyche and physically divided into two sexes by the body. This increasing division and sub-division is the result of the multiplicity of laws as one moves down and away from the perfection of the Divine World. Thus, by the time we incarnate on the Earth, we have acquired four distinct bodies, one for each World, which act as vehicles for consciousness and work at their own levels.

The first vehicle is the physical body which is composed of four sub-levels of mechanical, chemical, electronic and consciousness. These are held by the mineral, vegetable and animal life principles between the pillars of energy and matter. At the Tiferet of the Tree of the body is the central nervous system that watches, like the Self of the psychological Tree, over the adjacent sefirot, triads and paths that flow into and out of its sphere of influence. As will be seen in the body diagram, there are many sub-divisions within the Tree and an infinite number of finer sub divisions down to the frontier of the physical world where the particles of matter and the impulses of energy are interchangeable. From the point of view of Kabbalah, the study of the

FIGURE 11 (Right)—BODY AND PSYCHE
Because we have some knowledge of the body, we can see some parallels with the mind. A sick soul will undoubtedly affect the metabolism, making one manic or depressive in extreme cases, while the autonomic system gives some insight into the way the ego works. Both are conditional reflexes, one by Nature, the other through upbringing. The central nervous system is like the Self; it is partly unconscious and conscious, having a degree of control over the body and the mind. Much can be learned from studying how different realities relate. (Halevi, 20th century.)

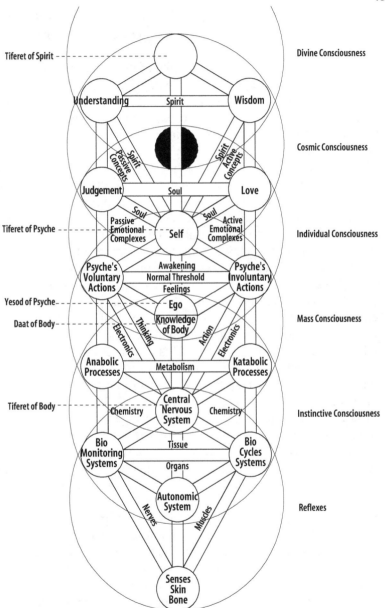

body can be very useful because it enables one to see the same processes at work as in the psyche or the spiritual Tree but at a coarser level of reality.

In Figure 11 we can see how the Tree of the psyche interpenetrates the body so that the upper half of the physical world percolates and influences the lower portion of the psyche and *vice versa*. This is directly observable in everyday life and should be remembered as an important principle when considering or working at the points of interchange between the Higher Worlds.

The psyche, like the body, is divided between consciousness and function. That is, the central column carries different degrees of awareness while the side pillars and triads perform as balances of action, emotion and intellect. In the early part of a Kabbalist's training this division must be clearly established. You are not your actions, emotions, or intellect; they are the manifestations of consciousness like, as traditional Kabbalah says, the arms and legs. Consciousness means 'to know'. However, when a person is only conscious of his body, his knowledge extends just to the orbit of influence of his central nervous system. Likewise, someone who lives primarily in the ego is indeed egocentric. This is the normal condition of most people and, as the diagram shows, their radius of consciousness is confined to routine thoughts, feelings and actions with an occasional contact with the Self when the repertoire of mental reflexes cannot cope with a new situation.

Under average life conditions, a crisis can generate a direct contact with the higher and deeper aspect of the Self but it usually fades, once the crisis is passed, as the Watcher in oneself again becomes part of the unconscious, only being able to influence indirectly in dreams, moods or flashes of truth. The Kabbalist seeks consciously to establish a permanent connection with the Tiferet of his psyche and expand his self-knowledge into the triads of emotional complexes and concepts, as well as extend it up the central column and so enter the realm of the soul and the world of the Spirit. This is done by constant observation of actions, emotions and intellect. By this is meant to perceive impartially the way those functions operate and to seek to correct and perfect their performance so as to become a balanced instrument for kabbalistic work; for a major defect in the psyche can not only mar an operation but expose some psychological malfunction to enormous stress with dire results.

The study of the soul is not something that can be easily written about. Indeed, it is perfectly correct to repeat that Kabbalah cannot be transmitted by a book but only through the intimate relationship between student and instructor. However, one has to begin somewhere which is why Kabbalists have written manuals on inner work over the centuries despite the fact that only a shadow of what is involved can be conveyed.

The soul, when set out on the Tree of the psyche, looks quite simple in its nature but, if one observes its connections to everything around it, it will be seen to occupy a crucial position. It is the bridge and the barrier between the upper and lower worlds in the individual. It has access to all the ideas and emotional memories of that person which colour and pressure the material passing through the soul, whether it is being given by Grace from above or being received externally from below. The soul is the place where all the individual experiences are processed in the light of conscience which is the synthesis of the three sefirot of Judgement, Mercy and Beauty which can also be seen as the sefirah of Truth. The soul is the gateway into the Spirit which, it will be noted, matches the lower face, as it is called, of the World of Creation in the same way as the lower psyche interpenetrates the upper face of the body Tree.

The realm of the Spirit begins at the place of the Self which simultaneously contains the Crown of the body Tree and the central sefirah of the psyche. Thus, we have three levels of reality concentrated in one place. In kabbalistic work this is the initial access point to the higher Worlds and the first of the seven great halls of Heaven. However, before these can be entered the seven lesser halls have to be passed through, although occasionally one is allowed a glimpse of the celestial chambers. There are those who have broken into these vast cosmic palaces by means of drugs but they tend to get a very distorted view of them because of their own psychological imperfections and impurities. This is often enough to frighten them away from any real possibility of a proper and balanced entry into the Kingdom of Heaven. Preparation in Kabbalah is a long and slow process for this reason as the sights and sounds of the upper Worlds are extremely disturbing if one is ungrounded, unstable and ill-prepared; that is, one's physical and psychological bodies are not in a healthy condition or are ill-matched.

In order to be able to enter the upper Worlds safely, one should have these lower organisms healed and trained by an experienced instructor within the context of a group which is part of a larger school in direct contact with those concerned with the spiritual life of humanity. Therefore, let us now look at such a group, so as to see how and why it is organised as it is.*

*For greater detail of body, psyche and spirit see the author's *Adam and the Kabbalistic Trees* (Kabbalah Society).

7. School

In this outline of the setting of Kabbalistic work we will follow the sequence of the Tree to show the anatomy of a school. While the source of the line must come from the Crown with its contact with the lowest sefirah of the Divine World, the Work begins at the bottom, at the Malkhut or Kingdom of a Tree that corresponds to the Yeziratic World or the psychological Tree.

The Malkhut of a group is the place where they meet. This can be a room or a house. Such meetings should be daily or weekly; any less frequent use will not build up an energy field and no subtle charge will remain in the place while the group is absent. Over the months and years the *Bet Midrash* or House of Study will become saturated with the dynamic and substance drawn down from the Higher Worlds through the being of the group. People entering such a place for the first time often sense a clear strong presence in the atmosphere. Such a quality is to be noted in any place where sacred work is done. This is because the energy and matter of a higher order has permeated, then saturated, the physical fabric of the building to form a reservoir and transform the elemental aspect of the school to put it on a level above that of an ordinary building.

The ideal place should provide enough room for the rituals, devotions and contemplation of the group, that is for group enactments, meditations and discussion. It can be a space in which little decoration is to be seen, so that whatever is done is projected in an abstracted form by imagination, or it may be physically laid out according to a definite plan, ranging from a simple altar table and chairs to a room full of Kabbalistic images to evoke a heightened state as soon as one enters the chamber. The particular formula used will depend upon the particular line of the tradition, the type of instructor in charge and the kind of students who are drawn to that way of working.

The members of a Kabbalah group may vary enormously. In the orthodox tradition they will nearly always be mature men who have studied the Torah in its original Hebrew and are familiar with the rabbinical commentaries of the Talmud. However, times change and

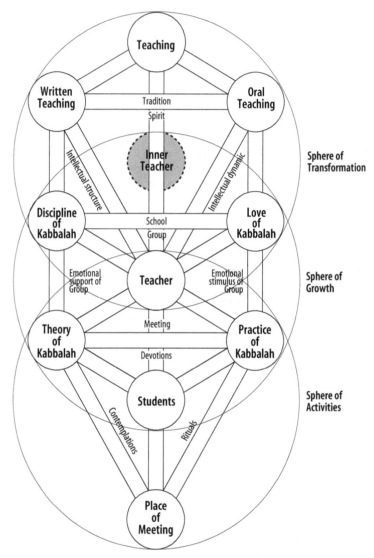

FIGURE 12—ESOTERIC SCHOOL
Every organisation is based upon the principles of the Tree. If it is not, it never matures or works as a successful system. Here, a school of the soul is shown in all its aspects. The key is the teacher or tutor who acts as the Self or Tiferet of the operation. He or she should have experience of a living esoteric tradition so as to check and balance the school's work, like the captain of a ship. Some schools are inclined to the Way of Action, others to that of Devotion or Contemplation. To enter the level of a group requires commitment, otherwise meetings become a lifeless cyclic routine. (Halevi, 20th century.)

so does Kabbalah. Kabbalists no longer live, as many religious Jews do, in a ghetto of orthodoxy. This is not to say that the old ways do not have value but that, in order to continue the living tradition, Kabbalah moves, as it has always done, with the needs of each generation. Thus, in our Western emancipated society we might find groups composed of women as well as men, who may not read or speak Hebrew and who, indeed, may not even be Jewish but who nevertheless wish to work in the Way of Kabbalah. In this manner the biblical injunction 'to be a Light unto the Nations' is fulfilled.

After the entry into such a group, the initial training is to study the theory of Kabbalah and to do the routine practices given out by the instructor. These will include becoming familiar with the Tree and carrying out such operations as perhaps meditating three times a day. Weekly exercises will be of a progressive nature, in that each topic to be considered or acted upon is held for that week in the forefront of consciousness and reported upon to the group at the next meeting. An example of this is to examine one's habits and see how they stop any possibility of self-knowledge. Out of this will come an exercise for dealing with a useless tendency and observing how another habit will compensate for it. This is a continuous process of discipline in the pursuit of making one's inner Tree balanced. On a larger scale, the subject being examined may extend over a whole term of three months to draw out, for example, the implications of the workings of fate and how our lives are governed by gentle but quite compulsive trends. This study may lead into a year's project of learning about the laws of destiny and why so many opportunities to find real fulfilment of our potential are lost or missed in life.

The exercises of rituals, devotion and contemplation are the three methods of the sphere of action on the Tree of the group while the triad of awakening is where the meeting takes place. It is here that the group gathers before the instructor who occupies the place of the Teacher at the Tiferet centre of the Tree. This Seat of Solomon may be filled by a senior group member who does no more than perform as the chairperson from which standard instructions are given out, if he or she has no personal experience, or a gifted teacher with an inner connection to the tradition. The latter is rare because to work with someone directly in contact with the higher levels means that the group has reached a relatively advanced state itself. Generally groups are run by people who have enough knowledge to be able to act as the Elder or *Zakan* of the group.

The heart of the group lies in the triad of the soul, between the sefirot of Tiferet or Truth, Gevurah or Discipline and Hesed or Love. In a junior group not all the people taking part in the meetings will necessarily be members of the group. They can be visitors, probationary students or people passing through. At a more subtle level the people present may, at any time, enter or leave the state of inner contact with the soul of the group. This can include the leader of the group when the attention wanders or ego intervenes, as in the case of a power trip. Such things do happen. The senior or inner group may have only a few members at any one time or it can, for a moment of Grace, include all who are present, even the stranger who has just been invited to observe. Such visitors, of course, are carefully selected because, by the nature of the Work, not every person who wants to know about Kabbalah is a suitable candidate.

The school to which the group belongs may or may not be discernible to most of its members. However, those who have begun to move into a condition of interior development, with its implications and responsibilities, will slowly become aware of other spiritual lines. This contact may be direct, in that they meet other students through their leader's connection with other fraternal instructors, or they may detect intuitively during the meetings the scale of a wider scope that involves other 'Companions of the Light' working at the same level. The association with other groups may be intimate or distant; they can be in close proximity within the same city or oceans away, for beyond a certain level distance does not matter when the group's work is with the higher Worlds where time and space are quite different.

A cohesive collection of groups constitutes a school. This sometimes has an obvious guiding teacher or group of senior people who see the overview and direct its particular aim. Here it must be said that while there is a spiritual hierarchy it is not always apparent. The real core of a school, for example, may sometimes be hidden in amongst the tutors or students, so that only someone of perception can identify it. A school is an organism dedicated to certain objectives. These might be perpetuation of knowledge, revival of religion, esoteric science, art or social questions. A school can be a loose association of groups or a tightly woven organisation with a physical headquarters. On the other hand, it might not have any home on Earth and even be located somewhere else in time. As said, at these levels ordinary laws and logic do not apply.

A tradition is the sum total of all the lines, schools, groups and individuals involved in that way of operation. The root of this tradition, in our case, goes back to Kabbalah which is represented by many hundreds of schools down the ages. Most of these are Jewish but some are Christian and occult in form. However, all have their origin in the knowledge that lies behind the Bible that was revealed to Solomon, given to Moses and passed on to Abraham by Melchizedek. Beyond this point, it becomes the pure Teaching as handed down from the first fully realised man, called Enoch, whose name means the 'Initiated'. He became Metatron, the great Instructor of Mankind. At this level we perceive the source of the various roots of spirituality running through human history which have become the great esoteric traditions of the world.

The initial training of Kabbalah is to help raise the individual to a place where he or she can work harmoniously with a group which has a greater capacity to receive higher knowledge, in the early stages, than any one person. This operating in concert enhances the group's capability within the larger context of its school which, in turn, is related to the wider field of the tradition. The tradition is a stem which carries the various schools like blossoms. Such blooms, if pollinated by the Spirit, will turn into fruits that may feed many over hundreds of years. We see this pattern in the Hassidic and monastic movements. Like fruit, these spiritual impulses decay and then fall. The seed they scatter is then sown into the ground for the next phase of general development. Fructifying these seeds is one of the main tasks of a tradition, so that each generation has the spiritual capability to take up the work.*

The training of individuals is also an important function of esoteric schools for it is through them that a group can become a finer vessel. Greater receptivity to what can be received from above and imparted to below not only means in the present but also applies to what can be drawn from the past and transmitted into the future. Thus the group is a crucial vehicle in *Avodah*, the Hebrew word for work and worship. However, before becoming a member of such an assembly various prerequisites have to be met.

*For greater detail see the author's *School of the Soul* (Kabbalah Society).

50

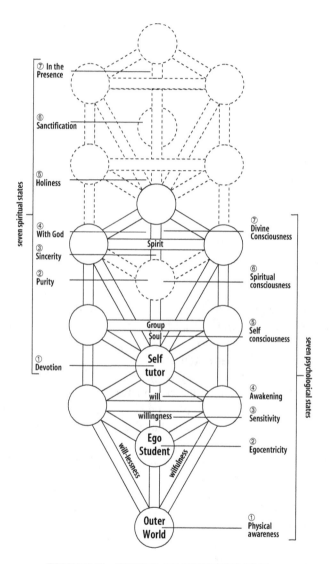

FIGURE 13—STAGES OF DEVELOPMENT

Here the seven levels of the psyche lead up to what are known as the seven Upper Halls of Heaven. This can only occur when a great deal of work has been done to balance and refine the mind. If the spiritual realm were entered before this process is well under way, the pressure of cosmic force would cause a psychotic episode as the Self became inflated or exploded. An example is when people take psychedelic drugs and are burnt out as the untrained mind and brain are blasted by spiritual power. One must proceed with great care when climbing Jacob's Ladder. (Halevi, 20th century.)

8. Prerequisites

Following the sequence of the Tree upwards, the first thing that is required of the Kabbalist is that he or she is relatively prepared to be wherever and whenever they are wanted. This means they must place the Work as a top priority in their lives. Moreover, they should be free of problems that could influence their commitment. These include personal as well as practical pressures that might corrupt as well as retard flexibility. To add to this reliability a high level of external stability and internal integrity is vital, so that the person is not only well-rooted in ordinary life but able to be effective and, indeed, influential if need be. Professional or even social status is irrelevant provided the motive is to be of service. A kabbalistic lawyer, businessman or craftswoman whose work is respected is more useful in the world than a holy hippy or transcendental tramp. Kabbalah is not the way of those who withdraw from life. This is the contact with Malkhut.

Awareness of Yesod and its strengths and weaknesses is crucial in the Work. To know one's projections upon oneself, others and situations is to recognise the ego's power to transmit or block what is coming from deep within the psyche. To observe and have command over the processes of action, thinking and feeling that fluctuate within the ego is to be able to use rather than be used by them. This requires the capacity to rise above the opposing tendencies of wilfulness coming from the right side of the Tree and will-lessness from the left. To be able to lift consciousness, at will, out of the purely Yesodic personal into the triad of awakening is to achieve mastery over the four lower halls of the psyche and come under the will of either the Self (or Tiferet) or the direction of one's teacher, if one cannot maintain the state on one's own. This is another reason why a group is important in the early stages. The support of others as well as one's instructor is a great aid in the initial steps of the Work before we develop the important prerequisite of willingness, without which nothing can be done.

Underlying all the foregoing is the issue of commitment. Many people come in contact with spiritual work out of curiosity. Fortunately, Kabbalah is a deep and complex subject and soon bores or frightens the curious away. Some are attracted to it out of need. This may be a purely psychological attraction. If so, then a crisis will occur in which the person is confronted with the possible loss of identity as his individuality is diminished in relation to the scale of spiritual work. An encounter with the cosmic level of existence reduces one's self-importance, from either negative or positive inflation to its true place, and this often turns people away from Kabbalah. To give up all one has, including vanity or suffering, and become as a child is not easy. However, if the need is a spiritual one, then the deep yearning is fulfilled by the surrender of one's will to the Work and then the Divine. Ultimately, the latter is the only commitment.

Upon entering the triad of the soul, a series of tests is initiated. Here contact with good and evil is to be expected. Power is given to one to see how it is handled and temptation in many subtle forms is encountered. Values that you think you hold may be challenged inwardly, or in external situations, in order to make sure that you are as reliable in the invisible as well as the practical world. The fact that only you may know that you are being immoral about something small, like stealing paper clips, is an illusion because by this time one has the unseen supervisor of the soul which monitors all activities to see if one is up to the work that may be given at some time. Real responsibility cannot be handed to someone with a split psyche and morality. If it were given to a gifted but corrupt person, the Teaching could be distorted. Such people spread much delusion amongst those whose souls they have been given to instruct. These tests are applied over many years as the Kabbalist progresses up the Tree. It has to be, so as to be sure that the quality of the Work remains pure. That is why many good individuals in spiritual work seem to have such difficult lives. These trials, however, are not just to seek out weaknesses but to strengthen the being of the person so that they may become better and finer vessels in which to receive the Light flowing down from on high.

When a person has reached the place of soul through diligent inner and outer effort, they establish the possibility of a permanent link with the third level of the Self. The first two levels are the Crown of the physical and the Tiferet of the psychological organism. Often an initiation ceremony into the Malkhut of the Spiritual world marks the entry into the first of the Seven Halls of Heaven. Such a ceremony may be a public acknowledgement or an essentially private moment of recognition. Schools may differ in how they indicate transformation. However, whatever the form is, the most important factor is that from that point on the person, while still in obedience to the instructions of his senior or directly under the Will of God, is now fully responsible for his actions. This is the coming of age in the Work. Here begins spiritual adulthood, although there are still six further stages to go before reaching the seventh Heaven. Thus while you have access to the higher realms and will be given powers and knowledge that cannot be learnt, even from others, you still have the choice of free will and may deviate for many reasons, ranging from a moment of pettiness to allying oneself with Lucifer himself. Indeed, this demonic son of God will now constantly approach the Kabbalist from every angle as he climbs higher in order to test the various stages of Devotion, Purity and Sincerity before reaching the level in the fourth Heaven of being in the presence of God. Even then, the middle path up through the Halls of Holiness and Sanctification to the place before the Abyss that lies in front of the Divine Face will not be without its testing for Satan, in Hebrew, means the Tester.

However, before you reach these exalted regions much has to be done, for the aim of the Work is not just to realise yourself alone. To be more explicit, the second and third journeys of acquiring experience and imparting go on simultaneously. It is not just a question of getting to the top then coming down again before finally returning home. It is a process of ascent while simultaneously passing on, to the levels immediately below, material that is still fresh in experience. This gives an insight into why there is a spiritual hierarchy. The great spiritual leader is concerned, like a general, with the grand strategy of humanity. Such beings have an over-view of things which less developed people cannot hope to grasp, such as the life span of a civilisation. Moses came into this class. Senior commanders, such as great masters like Baal Shem Tov, would be involved with specific epochs and places like the Hassidic movement in Eastern Europe whilst sages, like Cordovero who founded a particular school, would be concerned with specific lines of transmission. Lesser saints would supervise groups or be responsible for watching over individual people. Those who are being spoken about may be incarnate or discarnate, depending on the needs of the situation. In some cases, a great personage may be born just to initiate one impulse, like Isaac the Blind whose life's work altered the direction of Kabbalah, whilst others may return regularly in order to instruct those close to them. Of these we read little although they may recall past lives and reveal who they were to their immediate circle.

All these prerequisites are necessary if the Work is to be carried out well. If there is a major defect in the individual or the group, it will never function correctly. Indeed, any attempt to harness the influx of the Higher Worlds under improper conditions will only precipitate a breakdown in the individual and a break-up of the group. Even Lucifer cannot work without some order and the demonic tendency to chaos merely implements laws that disintegrate and disperse the accumulated energy and form back to their primary elements. Having examined the development of the individual in relation to the group, let us now look in greater detail at the aim of the kabbalistic Work.

9. Aim

The aim of kabbalistic Work is to act as the conscious agent of transformation between the upper and lower Worlds. That is to say, the raising of energy, matter and awareness from the ordinary level to a higher state and the bringing down and transmission of power, substance and consciousness from the realms of soul, spirit and Divinity, so that the natural World may experience Paradise, Heaven and the presence of God on Earth.

While the aim is not uncommon to all religious traditions, its implementation is often beyond the capability of most individuals and institutions. This is either because there is no understanding of what is required or because over time the existing methods have become corrupt and can no longer act as sacred vehicles for interaction between the Worlds. To live a devout life, to study, and even to perform religious practices may eventually lead to this capability. As the lives of many good people have demonstrated, this is possible without esoteric instruction and methods but the process is very long and not guaranteed in one lifetime. Moreover, the rituals of synagogue, church and mosque cannot always be relied on to bring about such transformations although, when the conditions are right and everyone is in a particularly harmonious state, even the most simple or elaborate service can generate a remarkable atmosphere; but this is rare. Thus, for some, the conventional approach is not enough because however pious a congregation may be, it is often too cluttered with rigid customs and attitudes to facilitate any flow or unification between the Worlds.

When you consider the ordinary ego state of most people during a religious service, with its rare moments of higher consciousness, and then set them up against the many hours spent dreaming by day and night each year, then it is clear that there is only a small percentage of real spirituality in people's lives. Such a minute amount of lift can only have a limited effect on raising the general consciousness of the human race. Something more potent has to take on the task and this is where the esoteric schools within the orthodox (and sometimes not so orthodox) traditions have to accept the responsibility. More than one great teacher has said that if there were only a few more thousand spiritually advanced people in the world, the course of history would be changed. War and crime would diminish and then vanish and many economic and social injustices would be corrected if the human race could begin to perceive (unconsciously at first) its familyhood. This state has been touched at the high points of civilisation when the balance of the Creative forces has been in equilibrium or there has been enough true spirituality to generate a moral conscience in that society. The Buddhist Emperor Asoka's India was such a case. Alas, this condition has usually only lasted, at the most, over the one generation that was sensitive enough to provide the spiritual fulcrum. The focusing of this Heavenly pivot in the world is the first general aim of the Work. As one rabbi remarked, 'The righteous are the foundation of the World'.

It will be appreciated that a great deal of preparation has to be done before such changes can be brought about. Centuries of labour often bearing no obvious fruit must pass before even the groundwork can be laid. Many Kabbalists, Sufis and Christian mystics have never seen the effects of their labour. Most of the Kabbalists of Medieval Provence and Catalonia probably had no idea of the impact that their new formulation of the esoteric tradition was to have on Judaism, Christianity and occultism, although it might be suspected that the masters foresaw what they were doing when they sought to solve the conflict between faith and reason that was confronting their time. The task of today is in no way different. We work to help what the Chinese mystics called 'the removal of the Capital'. This is the continual progression of the Holy Council through time, at the head of which is what the Moslems call the *Katub*, or Axis of the Age, whom Kabbalists call the *Messiah* or Anointed One.

Little is known or can be said about such a person, except that whoever occupies this position, at any moment in history, is the most highly evolved human being present on Earth. This makes that person the Crown of humanity and therefore its most direct connection between incarnate mankind and God. Below this is a hierarchy of spiritual individuals who hold their place in a pyramid of rank according to their development and destiny. The upper part of this celestial company is small but well integrated, as might be expected, whereas the lower levels are more fluid, with the lowest members entering and departing as they attain different states of consciousness ranging from flashes of enlightenment to routine glimpses during meditation or group work. The purpose of the training to be described is how to reach and experience the bottom sections of this pyramid and so bring the lower and upper Worlds into fusion both in the individual and in general life.

The methods by which this is accomplished vary from one century to the next and from one country to another. Some things that were valid at the time of Abraham are no longer relevant to later generations, although the principles and objectives are the same. Hence it was decreed, after the destruction of the Temple by the Romans, that animal sacrifice should cease and the power of the priests be curtailed. Likewise, as the tradition evolved, so various techniques were discarded and new ones brought in. Contrary to orthodox belief, many of the practices now in use are relatively recent or have been borrowed from other spiritual traditions because they were more efficacious. For example, the Christian rosary was adapted from the Moslems during the Crusades; and when the devout Jew declares the Thirteen Principles of Faith he is also concurring in its author's use of the Greek philosophical method.

Most kabbalistic techniques of work are based on principles contained within the metaphysical scheme of the tradition. This system is an amalgam of ancient Jewish teaching, Babylonian and Persian cosmology and many other influences such as the Gnostics and Sufis. The strongest outside factor is neo-Platonism which had a profound impact on the Jews of Medieval Spain. Many of its concepts were adopted by the Kabbalists of Gerona to bring about the system we use today. All these external adaptations, however, do not detract from the essential teaching of the tradition which goes back to the first and most Holy Name of God.

58

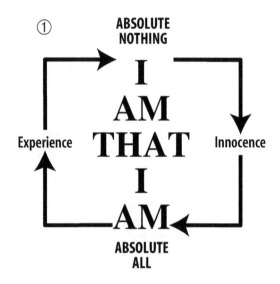

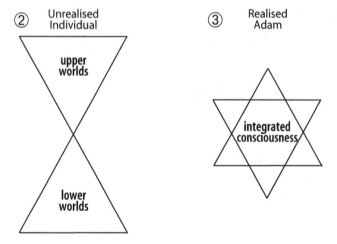

FIGURE 14—MANIFESTATION
Here consciousness emerges from ABSOLUTE NOTHING in the first word of the
Holy Name. It then goes on to become in the second, be fully manifest in the
middle and then in consciousness return to be one with ABSOLUTE ALL, having
passed from innocence to experience of ITSELF. The two lower diagrams
symbolise the upper and lower Worlds meeting in a focus of human consciousness
and their union in a perfected Adam. (Halevi, 20th century.)

10. Vehicle

The first principle of practical work in Kabbalah is the manifestation of the Divine saying I AM THAT I AM. This Name must always be present in operations because it contains the essence of everything done *Ba Ha Shem*, that is, 'In the Name'. The reason, as said, is that it sets out the cycle of coming out of nothingness into something through the focus of the word 'THAT' and then its return, after experiencing all that exists in 'THAT' which leads the manifest consciousness back to its Source from whence it came.

In the first diagram of Figure 14 we see the process laid out as a descent and ascent with 'THAT' at its pivot. The second figure shows how the midpoint is like the focus of a lens which reduces the light of consciousness from above into a spot of nothingness in the midst of existence while simultaneously focussing the reflected light from below into the same void that contains everything, before each beam opens out and passes on in the downward and upward flow of light. This focal point is the position of Adam in a state of innocence; while the third figure, of the integrated star composed of the now unified upper and lower triangles, represents the Adam of experience and completion. Here the individual and the universe merge as the Image of God.

Mankind is at the place of intersection which is midway between Heaven and Earth. Thus, we are the only creatures capable of experiencing both upper and lower Worlds simultaneously. Tradition tells us that the angelic beings cannot walk the Earth, eat or propagate; neither can the creatures of the elemental and natural World consciously enter into the Heavens and participate directly in the celestial activities. Only human beings can do this, for they alone possess the higher vehicles of individual soul and spirit as well as a physical body which can bridge the Worlds. However, to be able to do this requires either a high degree of evolution in the organisation and refinement of the physical, psychological and spiritual bodies or a system of techniques whereby those who have not reached a sufficient level of development to enter, at will, into the upper Worlds may ride on

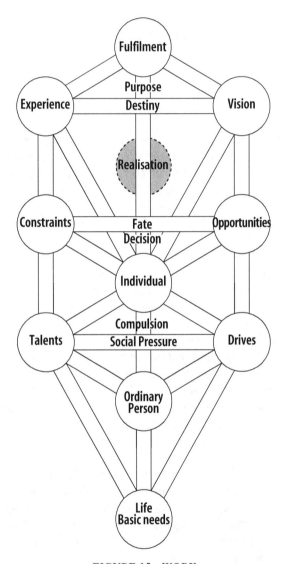

FIGURE 15—WORK

The lowest of the four kabbalistic Worlds is that of Action. Here are all the conditions needed to evolve. Life is like a gymnasium of the body, soul and spirit where the maximum progress can be made. In this Tree are the principles to be noted if one is to develop. One needs to meet the needs of ordinary life in order to become an individual who is master of his fate. Over many lives, experience builds up, vision comes, and the realisation of one's full potential, destiny and fulfilment is possible. This requires great effort but is well worth it. (Halevi, 20th century.)

especially constructed vehicles of ritual, devotion and contemplation. These vehicles of ascent were called in ancient times the technique of *Merkabah* or chariot riding which was the old name of Kabbalah.

As might be expected, the techniques were usually designed on the basis of the sefirot. This is the second principle. Thus, any exercise is modelled on the dynamics and structure of the Tree, that is, it will contain the major laws of the aim of unity, the interaction of the three pillars and the flow between the upper and lower faces of the Tree. It will also include the principles of the four levels of action, emotion, intellect and will and the corresponding stages of consciousness in the body—Malkhut, ego—Yesod, self—Tiferet, spiritual knowledge—Daat and contact with the Divine at Keter. Some operations may be limited to one or two levels but the others always have to be present, even if they are not being considered, or the exercise will not work.

In this particular exposition we are going to look at a blend of ancient and modern techniques. Traditional methods such as juggling with the Hebrew letters or praying and contemplating in the orthodox manner have been written about in the *Way of Kabbalah** and by other authors in detail, so we will not repeat these modes but speak about the ones that have been developed since medieval times or have not been described until now. This is permissible because many esoteric secrets that have been kept discreetly for centuries are now being disclosed in order to meet the needs of our time. With the prospect of a global holocaust, those responsible for the spiritual welfare of mankind have indicated that the Work must be intensified so as to offset the tendency towards conflict and disintegration. This is why one can now buy, in any esoteric bookshop, material for which many seekers over the ages have made hazardous outer and inner journeys. It is also the reason why books like this are being written. The current generation of Kabbalists needs to be informed and trained more quickly than perhaps any other over the ages.

When it is realised that a kabbalistic operation has to be carried out, be it for an individual or for the widest possible purpose, then the technique appropriate must be carefully selected. In some cases, there may already be one in existence in the repertoire of the group. This could be a very ancient form that has been handed down, such as certain prayers and rituals, or it might be a ceremony that was constructed in the recent past. If the situation cannot be met by what

---

Way of Kabbalah, published by Samuel Weiser, York Beach, ME and Kabbalah Society.

is already to hand then something is either modified to suit the occasion or a totally new technique is designed. Traditional schools, by definition, tend to rely on old methods but in time the power of these fades, as each age has its own peculiar balance of forces. Thus, while the sacrifice of the scapegoat was efficacious in Second Temple Jerusalem, it is not appropriate in twenty-first century New York (which is not to say that there are not always some people who might consider it as being still valid).

To design and construct a vehicle to meet the moment is a very subtle art which requires more than just a theoretical understanding of kabbalistic principles. It needs a certain experience of the different levels involved and a deep understanding of the nature of the sefirot. Many people believe that by reading and talking about the Tree they know what it is; however, time and maturity reveal again and again that what they had thought they knew was not only a fraction of the truth but often a distorted image of the reality. A common example of this is the statement made by many who have recently mastered the theory of the Tree, that it is quite a rigid system. After some years most students remark that the reverse is in fact true. Indeed, that is why it is called the Tree of Life. Thus, when it comes to designing an exercise, all aspects of the Tree have to be taken into account because the forces focused during the operation are very powerful and can easily be miscalculated by the inexperienced. Therefore, one must proceed with prudence.

Following the model of the Tree, every kabbalistic operation must embody the same general principles. It should have a Malkhutian base, so as to earth any energy and ground the participants, and a stable Yesod or foundation in which the ordinary ego mind can be held securely by a pattern of actions, thoughts and feelings. It should have a clear Hodian programme of instructions and a good internal and external communication system, as well as a strong Nezahian input of vitality and rhythm or there will be no power in the flywheel of momentum. The triad of awakening must be activated or the whole operation will just be mechanical. The place of the Self should be on maximum alert as the watcher and supervisor while the side triads of the emotional and intellectual complexes are held in balance, so that there is no personal interference or opportunity for demonic intrusion. The soul triad must be as receptive as possible to whatever comes down from the great triad of the Spirit and last, but not least, a profound awareness of the Divine Presence, symbolised by Keter the

Crown, must never be forgotten as one remembers that everything is done *Ba Ha Shem*, in the Holy Name.

Having laid out the general plan of an operation, let us examine some techniques, beginning with Malkhut at the base of the Tree.

11. Elements

The training of a Kabbalist uses various techniques for each stage and level. First there are those concerned with self-discovery, both inward and outward, and then the methods by which the student becomes aware of different dimensions of time and space. These are related to one's own life, the scope of the group and the scale of the Tradition. The aspirant will be shown, by various means, the interior connections he has between different parts of himself as well as his relationship and function within the group and the tradition. Thus, he comes in contact with the individual, historic and cosmic aspects of the Work in which he will serve.

The process of instruction begins with the individual. The first step is to get to know the body which is the Malkhutian vehicle for the psyche and Spirit. If the student remains unaware of the body's structure, dynamics and several levels of intelligence, then not only will much be lost by not seeing the analogue and resonance with the higher Worlds but its powerful influence on the psyche may not be detected and, if necessary, controlled. To know the body does not mean that one must be as intimately familiar with its anatomy as a medical student but to be acquainted with the general principles upon which it is based and how it works. This requires a rudimentary understanding of physiology, so that one can distinguish between different levels of work within the body.

From the kabbalistic view the body can be said to contain four basic levels. The first and densest is that of solids, which would include any structure that supported, carried or operated according to mechanical laws, that is the skeleton, certain organs and muscles. The next would be of fluids which encompass blood, sweat, urine or anything that flows through the organism. The element of air is seen in all the gases present in the blood, organs, and cavities of the body, besides that passing in and out of the lungs. Fire would be the principle behind all the heat and light generated in the tissue which is radiated by the body.

In order to become aware of this elemental division, the student sits or stands in a relaxed position and focuses the senses on these

Malkhutian levels. Beginning with Earth, he senses the weight and mineral composition of the body, how it hangs upon the carefully designed structure of bones which are held in position by connective tissue and the balance and counter-balance of the muscles. The student would then observe how the body moves with great subtlety and precision through every movement in a flow of positions that are held in a momentary equilibrium. This is the mechanical aspect of the body. Next the attention is shifted to the Watery element. This is done by a blend of sense and imagination. Thus, the fluid-saturated tissue and organs are perceived as they hold and guide the slowly percolating fluids from their intake at the mouth to their exit in excretion and sweat. It will be noted how the body has quite distinct views about its mass and fluid content, whether it wishes to take on more or lose some. This gives an insight into the vegetable mind and its effect both on the body and the psyche. By the same principle in reverse, we perceive how the will can influence the state of the metabolism by, for example, excessive drink or fasting.

The level of Air is then examined by controlling the breath and observing the reaction of the body as various quantities are absorbed and penetrate the tissue. It should also be noted that the atmospheric balance in and about the body is crucial to its well-being and how a shift of consciousness can extract fresh air from a stuffy room. This demonstrates how there are levels within levels, in that a rarer dimension lies within the heavier aspect of the atmosphere that can be tapped and used. The principle of coarse and fine levels of an element is represented by the three intermediate elemental combinations of mud, vapour and flame, which is the earthly counterpart of Fire.

The element of Fire is examined by becoming conscious not only of the heat but of the radiance that is emitted by the body. This can be detected by very close observation and an attunement to the subtlest level of the physical world. Some people, either by gift or by diligent practice, can glimpse or see the field of light that hovers just above the skin and others, of a more sensitive nature or of greater development, can actually perceive the various lines of the aura as they shimmer around a person. In the early stage of this exercise the aura can be detected by the palm of the hand which registers the different sheaths of bodily radiation as gentle pressure fields set at various distances.

The purpose of this exercise is to acquaint the student with the manifestation of the four Worlds in their most physical form. If the experience is developed, then much insight can be gained into the nature of the higher Worlds and their relationship to one another. For example, the principle of inter-penetration of body and psyche can be clearly observed in the watery aroma of sweat or breath which reflects the psyche's condition in the metabolism. In this way the three lower elements can be related to physical, emotional and intellectual states with Fire representing consciousness. Thus solidity is usually concerned with practicality whilst fluidity is associated with moods. As regards gaseousness, people often speak of their minds being foggy or clear and anyone who has seen a corpse knows that the light of consciousness has departed from it in that it emits no heat and the eye has no radiance.

This exercise in bodily awareness may be taken even further in that the consciousness of the student can be made to penetrate and observe the work of various areas of the interior anatomy, ascertain their performance and so learn much about his own psyche by elemental analogy. For example, much insight could be gained about the feeling triad of the psyche if you could perceive the flow of the circulation and its patterns and characteristics, of which heartache and sluggishness are examples. Likewise, a great deal could be gathered by being acquainted with the working of the autonomic nervous system which corresponds to the Yesod of the body and, therefore, relates to the ego and its habitual reflexes. Everyone knows about the beating of the heart and intake of breath in moments of crisis; but how many people are aware of the less spectacular shifts within the central nervous system that relate to the Self? If we noted the habitual tightening throat or the ever-cramped shoulder, we might register that we had a malfunctioning psyche long before disease set in in the body.

Perhaps one of the most important lessons to be gained from this Malkhutian study is that the body has a definite mind of its own. It protests if it is pushed and resists any threat to it by its owner, such as excessive strain, as well as to any outside assault. Over a period of time the will of the body can be trained; but this is not easy as it relies on ancient instinctive processes, such as sleep, as well as recently acquired habits. Conscious experience of the body brings one into direct contact with its intelligence. This can be an encounter of confrontation or co-operation, depending on the objective of the student. For example, sometimes habits have to be broken because they misuse or waste valuable energy. Occasionally, the body has to be coerced into a hyper-effort in order to accomplish something on a higher level. Fasting or working overtime, or performing much quicker or slower actions than the usual rhythm—or even breaking rhythm—can be means of attaining certain inner states. These, like rapid breathing for a short period, must always be used intelligently because, whilst the body has enormous resources, it does have limits and its capability, if not its will, may be broken. The yoga freak and damaged junky illustrate such excesses.

The foregoing exercises may be varied in many ways. Their prime purpose, however, is not only to make the Kabbalist aware of the elemental levels at work within the body but also to root the Work in the Earth, so that the student can return to *terra firma* any time he or she feels out of depth after entering the higher realms. This retrieval method is as vital as an astronaut's ability to abort his mission, because an ungrounded mystic can get into serious trouble if he is not in touch with physical reality. Indeed, one should always terminate a kabbalistic operation by becoming conscious of the body. Symbolically stamping the feet is a good way to establish contact with Malkhut again after an exercise.

The next chapter takes us up the Tree to teach us how to use Yesod and its power of imagery as a tool.

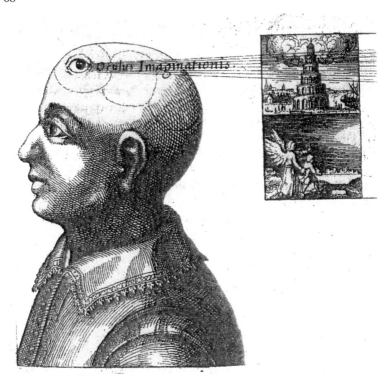

FIGURE 16—IMAGINATION

Human beings have the capacity to review the past, observe the present and speculate about its influence on the future. They can, moreover, enter into the microscopic and telescopic dimensions beyond what the eye can see. It can also invent, create or become enmeshed in delusion. The inner eye can visualise, in symbolic form, what the higher Worlds are like as well as work out, through metaphysics, how principles operate. Indeed, there is no end to what imagination can do except behold the Absolute. And yet this is the very instrument that God uses to behold God in the reflection of Existence. (Robert Fludd, 17th century.)

12. Imagination

Yesod or the Foundation of the Tree in a human being relates to the ego or the ordinary consciousness. This includes not only the awareness of the external world and the body's state, in the form of sensual impression, but the capacity to perceive what is not perceptible to the senses by means of imagination. This is because the non-sefirah of Daat or Knowledge lies behind Yesod when two Worlds, or Trees, are related to each other. Thus, the Yesod of the psyche overlays the Daat of the body and the Daat of the psyche underlies the Yesod of the World of the Spirit. By studying the nature of the relationship between Daat and Yesod in the lower Worlds, it is possible to become acquainted with how the same combination might operate in the higher Worlds and levels of being.

Taking the level of ego, the one to which we have most access, we can see how, for example, the Yesod of the psyche can know about events going on in the body. Contrary to general belief, we do not perceive the body directly but through the agency of the central nervous system, that is the Malkhut of the psyche, which is the simultaneous Tiferet of the body. The lower part of the physical Tree, composed of the electronic, chemical, tissue, organic and mechanical levels, are out of direct cognisance of the psyche. It is only by the medium of the etheric field, which joins the upper face of the body to the lower face of the psyche and the sefirot that make up these two faces, that we experience our bodies. The way this occurs is unconsciously via the functions of the side sefirot of psycho-biological processes and consciously through the sefirot of the central column. The latter are made up of three levels. The bottommost is a general awareness of the body's condition which only comes into prominence during a crisis, such as a toothache, when the autonomic system passes the problem on to the central nervous system, whilst the topmost of the place of the self comes to the fore when a moment of self-consciousness is present, again perhaps because of a crisis. Between these two conditions is the ordinary awareness of the ego which is informed, in detail, about the body's condition by the physical Daat in the form of a sense-based image. This capacity to produce readable images is useful to the Kabbalist because it gives the facility to explore the Worlds above and beneath the normal range of sensual and psychological perception with knowledge and skill, if applied.

The reason for this is that the Daat-Yesod combination is a door between Worlds through which consciousness can come down or go up. Thus, it is possible not only to look into the most minute recesses of one's own physical organism but also to penetrate, through imagination, the most remote corners of the psyche and even cast into symbolic forms material coming through the Daat of the psyche from the realm of Spirit. This is why the practice of the art of imagination and guided imagery is part of a Kabbalist's training. Some people regard this as a relatively new idea; but if they read the books of Enoch, apocalyptic literature and the methods of the rabbis in the Second Temple period, they will recognise the technique as quite ancient.

To demonstrate and practise the use of applied imagery as a means of viewing different levels and evoking their properties we will use a simple exercise, based on the four elements and levels found in the physical body, so as to show how a Kabbalist can extend the vision of consciousness beyond its usual range. This exercise should be done under the direction of an experienced guide.

First the student lies down on the floor and arranges himself like a human landscape with mountains and valleys composed of his body and limbs. After making himself comfortable he freezes into a deep rigidity and imagines that he is an island surrounded by the sea of the floor. He does not move but observes how, after a time, tensions set in and his body wants to move. He does not adjust his limbs because he is now made of solid rock and can only shift gradually to ease any discomfort. By doing this he perceives his body on the scale of a real island and this enlarges his appreciation of time so that he senses the passing of years instead of minutes. As the moments elongate he imagines the coming and going of the seasons and the expansion and contraction of the rocky strata within the body. He notes an unacceptable stiffness in one limb and suddenly there is an earthquake as the muscles of this human mountain go into spasm. The island shudders several times before the new configuration of the posture emerges. As the student becomes increasingly cold or hot, he observes the mineral intelligence within his body react in its slow motion as bones strain and grind within the pressures of the situation. Perhaps for a moment the student understands what it is like to be a landscape and recognises that it, too, has movement and life in accordance with its mineral perception of time and space.

The next exercise is to experience water and the vegetable world. In this the student begins by rolling himself into a ball. This is a cell in the primordial ocean. At first you imagine the vast watery depths below and above as the powerful currents carry the cell along in a flow. Whilst holding this in the imagination you note all the watery processes within, observing closely the vegetable principle at work as it grows, feeds and dies throughout our lives. You see hair and skin as leaves and bark and blood as sap. You note the intelligence of the organs and how they select and reject material from the fluids passing through them. You begin to open out as the limbs become roots and branches that wave about in the watery space enclosing us. You flower into an elegant pattern and wait to be fertilised. You conceive and gestate fruit and give birth to other vegetables that grope with a dim consciousness towards the earth below and the air and light above. Maybe for an instant you enter the cellular world of plants and recognise that many of your motivations come from this kingdom, that the seeking of a home, a mate and children is not an animal or human drive but derives from the primeval intelligence of that first cell which emerged in the primordial waters to bridge the evolutionary gap between inorganic and organic consciousness.

The third exercise is to imagine we are standing alone or with others upon a great plain. Above, a vast ocean of air moves in a state of mild breeze whilst we crawl or walk on the ground and feed. Acting out this situation with our arms as wings, we mingle with our own kind, ignoring all other creatures except those that we fear might eat us and those we eat. Circling round our flock, we avoid enemies and associate with friends, pecking those who are lower in the order to keep our place. We court and are challenged to a fight by a rival but, before we compete for favours, there is a cry of alarm which all take up. Raising our wings-arms, we all fly up and away in panic before following our leader who is, at this moment, the strongest member of our company. We climb up on the wind to gain a safe vantage point from which to view everything below. The danger having gone we begin to enjoy ourselves, 'following my leader' about the room-sky. Our leader sweeps and turns, swoops and climbs in a complex set of manoeuvres that have taken the flock millions of years to perfect. The air is our calm friend today although tomorrow it may drive us earthwards in a storm. We descend on its gusts and streams to land once more upon our feeding ground. From this enactment we can perceive the animal in us and recognise the powerful forces that operate upon society, and our own unconscious depths, to prevent people from becoming individuals. We also glimpse something about the nature of the element air and its higher counterpart, the Spirit.

The last exercise is to experience fire or consciousness. This may be done by becoming a human being, which is not an easy matter. Let the student take up the posture of Rodin's statue *The Thinker* who sits pondering with his chin in his hand. Let him remain outwardly quite still and consider what he has learnt from the three previous exercises. Let the mind contemplate the implication of the evolutionary processes still at work within. Let the heart feel the difference in the levels and the body sense their operation, even at this moment of reflection. Allow the beam of consciousness to extend backwards in time to experience not only what has just been seen but the historic epochs of mineral, vegetable and animal phases of dominance before man came upon the Earth. Then allow the aim of consciousness to reverse and project into the future and the possibilities that lie before mankind, including the choice of its own destruction. Perhaps some illumination will reveal an insight or prophecy about yourself or the human race. In that moment you may experience what it is to be beyond the realm of nature and in touch with the Light of Eternity. This is a human being's capacity.

13. Preparation

Drawing together the exercises involving the body, that is the Malkhut of the psychological Tree, let us synchronise them into a kabbalistic practice. The body of a human being is modelled upon Adam Kadmon who is, in turn, an image of the Divine. Therefore, an individual's body is a reflection of the sefirotic pattern of the Tree of Life. As such it can be used as an instrument to receive and impart what comes down into the Malkhut of the psyche from the Spirit and beyond. Indeed, the body is the last stage in any kabbalistic process and if whatever is flowing down does not reach the body, the operation is incomplete.

Taking the body as a Tree in itself, we can teach it, and ourselves, to become aware of its resonance with Adam Kadmon, consciously relating its matter, energy and consciousness to the structure and dynamics of the Tree. The first part of this exercise is to stand upright in the attention position and become aware of the body as a whole. Having perceived it as a unity in which everything contained within its field is working in unison, we then begin to separate out the various aspects in sequence. We begin by swaying the body gently from side to side in order to observe the two pillars. We note their relationship and how, in most of us, the right side is more powerful and active whilst the left is more gentle and passive. This is seen in cutting a slice of bread, in which the left hand steadies whilst the right actively works. Having seen this, we will observe that our consciousness is centred on a line that runs from our crown, through the middle of our brain, throat and heart, to our pubis and feet. If we ignore this axis we are unbalanced in more ways than one. In work or rest, the body and psyche always seek equilibrium. This is the central column.

Having established the three pillars you then divide the body horizontally at the level of the solar plexus, thus separating the upper and lower faces from each other. You then observe the four elements or levels; Earth and Water, which correspond to the legs and gut, and Air and Fire which may be seen as related to the lungs and brain. Using the experience gained in your training exercise, you may begin to sense more keenly the meaning of these levels within our bodies. This is perceived if we allow the attention to rise slowly from the feet to the crown of the head whilst taking in the various levels and pillars to be found in the body. This exercise will not only enhance the idea of your physiology being an image of the Tree but will prepare it for any kabbalistic operation that you might be about to do. This preliminary action is vital, for the body's will and intelligence, as already noted, can interfere with any deep process if it is not asked to co-operate or at least be quiescent.

Taking body consciousness to a yet more refined level, you may now begin to place the sefirot upon it. Beginning with Malkhut you can imagine this to be centred around the feet in contact with the earth. Here you are not using the interpenetrating scheme but the simple scheme of one Tree. The sefirah of Yesod is traditionally placed on the genitals, from which the ego derives its power and identity in the way it presents itself. The two sefirot of action, Hod and Nezah, are usually related to the hips where they function as the active and passive connections with the lower part of the body whilst Tiferet, the centre of the Tree, lies over the solar plexus, the pivot of the body. The two sefirot of Gevurah and Hesed relate to the heart and are set out on either side of that organ. They are sometimes seen as the two chambers of the lungs where the blood changes from venous to arterial, that is the intermingling of Water and Air. The non-sefirah, Daat, is traditionally placed over the throat but the face, with its organs of sense perception and expression, may be included as they illustrate the inflowing and outflowing of knowledge in the eyes, ears, nose and mouth. These organs are themselves expressions of the four elements in that the eyes are related to light, the nose and ears to air, the tongue to water and the rest of the body to touch, that is earth. Binah and Hokhmah, the sefirot of Understanding and Wisdom, are related to the two hemispheres of the brain whilst Keter is seen as a Crown set upon the head.

While many people know this kabbalistic scheme, there are few who have actually experienced what it means. As one teacher remarked, 'Some think that to know the name of anything is to comprehend it'. In Kabbalah this is very apparent by the lack of real understanding of, for example, Hod and Nezah; many expositions dismiss these two vital sefirot with a vague sentence or two. No! One is not a Kabbalist because one can read the texts in the original Hebrew. Indeed, mere learning invariably distorts simple principles by the complication of numerous cross-references. Nothing can make up for direct experience of the sefirot in action or personal entry into even the lowest of the heavenly Halls. No amount of scholarship can match the moment when one passes through the dark glass of Daat and into the next World. However, before we get to this stage there has to be much preparation. This involves bringing theory and practice together so as to generate the right conditions for something to happen. So far, we have seen how an individual makes his body ready. Now comes a procedure which many Kabbalists follow in order to bring their body, soul and spirit into closer relationship.

Before beginning whatever has to be done, the Kabbalist stands to, and in, attention with his arms by his side. He then leads his consciousness up from Malkhut at the feet through Yesod to the pelvic cavity that lies within the triads composed by Yesod, Hod, Nezah and Tiferet. As he says the names of the sefirot in sequence, he then climbs up the 'lightning flash' to focus upon Tiferet before moving up into the chest cavity that contains Gevurah and Hesed where he pauses for breath. From here he rises to Daat and silently speaks this name before proceeding, as he raises his hands, to the sefirot of the brain and the crown, so completing the sequence. By this time, the hands should be well to each side and above the head with the palms up, although some Kabbalists, like the Sufis, face the left one down so as to impart what is received. The body is now fully alert and co-ordinated with the psyche and spirit at the ready for the next stage of any operation.

14. Ritual

Having set out our first series of exercises based upon the Malkhut of the body and the imaginative faculty of Yesod, let us proceed by examining some more related to the three triads centred on the ego. Here we see how the principles of the Tree generate the form and dynamic of an operation. However, whilst the level of the Tree involved remains the same, the way it is explored and developed can be varied, giving rise to many possibilities. These variations of a principle are related to whatever is the aim of the project. The great beauty of Kabbalah is that every generation can design its own method according to the need of the time and the place although, if one examines the texts of different epochs with the Tree in mind, one can discern the same essential principles, despite the vast difference in form, language and culture. Thus we find that the design of the Tabernacle in the Sinai desert is echoed in the Temple in Jerusalem, in the layout of the church and mosque, as well as in the Freemason's Lodge and the occultist's sanctuary.

Taking the great lower triad bounded by Malkhut, Hod and Nezah, which contains three small triads centred at Yesod, we shall describe three methods of sensitising the processes of action, thinking and feeling which are associated with them. The triad of action is made up of Malkhut, that is the body, Yesod, the ego, and Nezah which is the sefirah behind the instinctive and psychological involuntary processes. By this is meant all those rhythms and routines of the psyche and body that form the patterns of everyday life, like dressing automatically, remembering multiplication tables or anything that does not require any thinking through. Let us suppose that we wish to perform a simple ritual which is the working mode of this triad. Its aim, in this case, is to alert the triad and make the student aware of its qualities.

The first thing is to formulate the objective. This we have done. We now set out the process into a sequence, so as to build up and focus the attention and so charge the situation. Thus, there has to be a preparation stage, an initiation of the operation, a development of the impulse, a climax and a resolution before coming back to earth with,

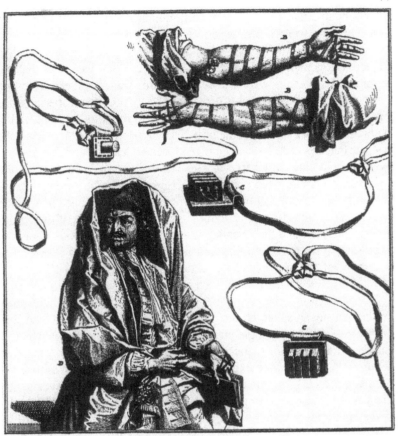

FIGURE 17—THE WAY OF ACTION
*Here a devout Jew of the 18th century puts on what are called Tefillin. These are
sacred objects that are bound ritualistically to the head and close to the heart.
The boxes contain verses from the Torah, the sacred Teaching. The straps are
wound seven times around the arm and hand to make the Hebrew letter Shin
which is the symbol of the Divine Name, SHADDAI or ALMIGHTY. Every tradition
has its rituals but Kabbalists can add their own so as to experience a creative freshness, as some familiar routines can lose their ability to awaken the soul to their
inner meaning. (17th century engraving on Jewish customs.)*

we hope, an advanced degree of comprehension and experience. Here is a rising up through the four levels and a return to equilibrium.

Having decided what is to be done, all the physical factors are then gathered together and arranged in an order that has a kabbalistic significance in relation to what we wish to do. This may mean arranging a room or a corner in such a way that it not only becomes a special space but also, by its particular set-up, will become a structure that will aid the Kabbalist to hold and direct the principles invoked. Thus, there has to be a space that has been specially created for the operation and one or more objects in it that will serve as the limiting factors and axis of the operation to contain and direct the energy of the ritual. An example of this may be a room that faces East which has a table-altar upon which stand two candlesticks. The significance of the East is self-evident to Jews, Christians and Sun-worshippers alike, as the solar point of arising is an archetypal direction. The altar is likewise symbolic as the field of attention with its two candlesticks representing the two pillars. The space between represents the third unseen presence of consciousness and will.

The student now begins to prepare himself. At first he ablutes, that is, he washes his hands and face and makes his body clean and comfortable. Some people might carry this to its extreme when a major ritual is about to be performed. In this case a bath is often required. With a minor exercise the symbolic ritual of washing the hands and face may suffice. Again, fresh clothes or ritual vestments are usually put on in a major enterprise. This is done to inform the body and lower psyche that something special is about to be performed. It also helps to evoke the body's awareness and obedience to the will that must not be distracted. If you are a Jew, then a *tallit* or prayer shawl and *yarmulke* cap is sufficient for a ritual garment. If not then anything, from a hat only used on such occasions to an elaborate and specially designed robe, may be put on to indicate that a kabbalistic operation is to be performed. Such vestments should not be worn on any other occasion or they will lose whatever sacred power they may acquire during such rituals and so become debased in substance. When such objects are used out of context they can be used by the perverse for quite a different purpose, although at high spiritual cost.

The act of putting the garment on should be a ritual in itself. It must be done with full consciousness of what it represents. In the Bible the priestly vestments relate to the three levels of the psyche, spirit and Divinity. One composite robe with the appropriate symbols can suffice. When this is done and the student is aware that he is about to leave the state of ordinary consciousness, then he proceeds to the place of ritual where, with others or alone, the operation is begun. This may be with a period of silence in which the awareness is extended, as set out in the chapter on *Elements*, throughout the body, as consciousness of the mineral, vegetable and animal levels draw the being into a heightened sense of physical unity. This is held until the ego is in equilibrium and the body consents to become quiescent as the field of consciousness is opened.

As the hands of the Kabbalist are raised to receive whatever might be given, so an invocation is uttered. This might consist of a single prayer of praise or petition or a complex progression of words that take the person up the Tree from Malkhut to Keter. The effect of this is usually quite striking because, by setting up a physical and psychological vessel, there begins the collection of what is called 'the Dew of Heaven' that is continually falling from the Higher Worlds. This is the spiritual mannah that nourishes the human race, although only a small proportion are sensitive enough to be conscious of it without special techniques. The accumulation of this celestial substance usually raises the Kabbalist further by its conversion into psychic energy. This, however, can only occur in those who have developed enough of their inner capability to be able to convert the celestial influx passing down. To do this requires much practice and experience—but one must begin somewhere.

Having reached a point of contact through the Tiferet of the self, the ritual may then proceed on to its particular objective. In this case it is not to receive and transmit higher influences but to request, if it be Divine Will, that you may learn more about the nature of ritual. At such a moment a match might be struck high overhead and its flame brought down to light the candles. It must be said 'might' for this is only one way of representing a principle. During this act of ignition you may realise how out of Nothingness came Light, the symbol of Divine Will and the highest World Emanation. As the flame is lowered the words, 'Thy will be done' should be said, in this case to remind the Kabbalist that nothing may be carried out without the Holy One's permission or the operation is no more than an act of magic or human manipulation of subtle powers. This is crucial because later the inexperienced may find that, like the sorcerer's apprentice, they cannot handle the forces released and panic. This can have dire consequences on the unbalanced and should not be attempted without a tutor.

On lighting each candle, bearing in mind which represents what pillar, the ritual may then be taken further in exercises to develop the art of conscious action with a sacred purpose. Orthodox and ancient forms of this mode are to be found in synagogue and church ritual. However, special rituals may be made up by the Kabbalist so as to meet an individual need or a specific objective, such as healing. This, however, requires much knowledge and we are not yet at this point. Therefore, let us confine ourselves just to studying the principles of ritual. Having completed the exercise in preparation, the process is then reversed. After a period of silence in which consciousness is stretched to its limit to mark the summit of the operation, the Kabbalist then gives thanks for whatever has been received. After the hands have been lowered and the verbal descent of the Tree is complete, the candles may then be blown out with the words, 'Holy! Holy! Holy! art Thou Lord of Hosts; Thy Glory fills all the Worlds.'

After a pause you then stamp the feet to earth and disrobe, so bringing the body and psyche back into the mundane condition, while still retaining an awareness of the Higher Worlds for as long as possible. Over the years the effects of such operations will cease to fade, as everything the Kabbalist does in life will become a sacred ritual. As one student noted, 'I learnt much about Kabbalah from my teacher by just watching him practise his profession.' This is the method of ritual in daily life which is the practical way of the Work.

15. Contemplation

The technique of contemplation applies to the triad formed by Malkhut, Yesod and Hod. This combination is found on the passive side of the Tree and so one would expect it to be reflective rather than active. This is reinforced by the fact that the sefirot of the body and ego are matched by Hod which is concerned with the collection and communication of information within the body and the psyche. To learn about the nature of this functional triad the following exercise can be used.

After making the preliminary preparations to indicate to the body and psyche that a kabbalistic exercise is about to take place, the student sits down in silence before a table prepared with paper, pens, compass, ruler and inks. The student then makes a prayer, asking to be shown insights into the question being posed. Let us assume that the question is 'What is the nature of the four ego types?' That is, those sub-triads that surround the ego and connect with Malkhut and Tiferet. Having made the petition the process of contemplation begins.

The first part of the exercise is to set up a frame of reference, like the ritual but this time in the abstract. Thus, you carefully lay out the sheet of paper and square its base line to the table with its long axis aligned to the solar plexus, that is Tiferet. Then you proceed to draw with the ruler the line of the central column of the Tree. Taking the compass and inserting it into the middle of the line, a circle is then drawn. This process is repeated above and below with the pivot of each circle placed where the middle circle's circumference bisects the axis line. This will give the three interpenetrating circles that mark out the positions of the sefirot. Thus, the Crown comes where the upper circle bisects the axis line at the top, whilst Daat is located at its pivot. Tiferet is the central circle's pivot point with Yesod at the place where the lower curve of the inner circle bisects the axis. This is the pivot of the lower circle. Malkhut comes where the lower curve of this circle touches the bottommost point on the central line. The side sefirot are marked out by the three points of intersection made up by the circles on either side. To complete the geometry of the Tree, lines are ruled

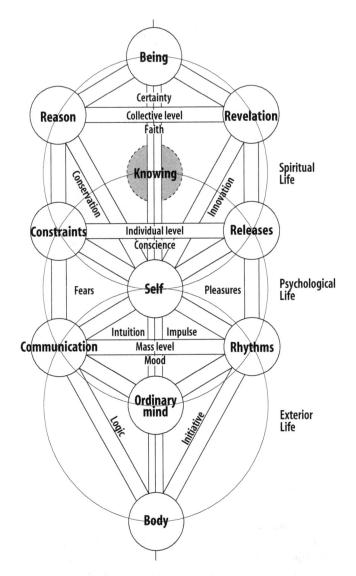

FIGURE 18—WAY OF CONTEMPLATION
Here the geometry of the Tree can lead to a profound understanding of its structure and dynamics. This enables the contemplator to understand how the Tree works and how levels affect each other. For example, the Self has access to the body, mind and spirit. If one is not conscious of all these dimensions simultaneously then the Self is not complete. A person, for example, may be spiritually oriented but not really in touch with his mind or body. If the Self is unaware of the wholeness of life it cannot develop. (Halevi, 20th century.)

between the relative sefirot and the pillars. Out of this, all the triads should emerge. The sefirot are then indicated by small circles and the paths made thicker by doubling the guidelines.

To draw the Tree and the sefirot is a contemplative act. It connects one with the geometry of its structure, so that one begins to perceive during its construction the form and dynamic that compose it. To use another person's Tree or study it from a book is not enough. One has personally to enter into contact with the Tree and participate in its extraordinary, beautiful symmetry. Here, we experience the meaning of Truth being Beauty and Beauty being Truth as we, by our contemplative action, resonate with the Divine principles contained within it. In some kabbalistic groups, to draw one's own Tree and then one's own Jacob's Ladder of the four Worlds is considered an initiation in itself because it is done as a formal ritual to indicate a commitment to the Work. To have one's own Tree in sight at home or work is to be ever aware of the Way of Kabbalah, in the same manner as a cross or a calligraph of the Name of Allah on the wall is a reminder to a Christian or to a Moslem.

Having drawn up the Tree, coloured inks are now applied to separate out the various levels. Following the guidelines in the Book of Exodus we leave the triad Keter, Hokhmah and Binah white, as the colour of pure light, but paint the great triad of Binah, Hokhmah and Tiferet blue to represent the Spirit. The side triads from Hokhmah and Binah down to Hod and Nezah, including Gevurah and Hesed, centred on Tiferet, are coloured purple with a lighter shade to indicate the triad of the soul. The triads of the lower face of the Tree can be coloured in red of various hues with a purple-red in the triad of awakening. Here, we have the colour of flesh and blood separated from the blue of the heavens by purple, the blend of the two. This exercise should generate much thought about the different triads.

Having completed the frame of reference, we now turn to the question and begin to contemplate the nature of the four ego triads by using the Tree. In this our triad of thinking is led, by conscious will, to dwell upon the diagram. Now the thinking triad works not only automatically but with extraordinary skill. It will draw upon facts and observations made over many years and apply them to the problem. In the Watcher of the Self, you can observe the analysis at work. For example, the triad will deduce, from the layout of the four ego triads, that the lower two, connected with Malkhut, will be concerned with the outside world and the body while the two upper triads will relate, through their connection to Tiferet, with more introspective matters (in contrast to the thinking mind being used) because they are partially divided by the line of ordinary consciousness stretched between Hod and Nezah. This reveals that these two inner triads are often only perceived as thoughts and feelings which rise occasionally to the surface of consciousness like fish. It will also be noted that, by their association with the side pillars, the left-hand triads must be passive whilst their complements are active. This leads the thinking triad to conclude that it itself must be an outward reflecting process that takes the facts it can perceive and systematically processes them while the upper left-hand components of Hod, Tiferet and Yesod must work by intuition, that is, its logic is not so discernible or reliable because it is overlaid by the feelings and the normally dormant awakening triad.

Now the same process of analysis can be applied upon the other side to conclude that the lower right triad, like its double of physical action, is inclined to take the initiative psychologically whilst its upper counterpart can unconsciously manipulate a situation from beyond the threshold of the liminal line between Hod and Nezah. An example of this is when someone creates tension by silently building up a pressure of anxiety or anger. Likewise, the mechanics of how the four triads must gain or lose ascendancy from mood to mood may be discerned, as well as the fact that a triad of a given moment must have its counterbalance. Thus a powerful intuition, in the top left, will precipitate a strong reflex in the lower right so that practical action will want to check out a hunch or intuition. Many discoveries and conclusions can come by the technique of contemplation. For instance, speculation on the effects of these triads on health or inner growth can be explored by analogy, and projections of the same processes at work in the deep psyche can throw light on the same four triads of the Spiritual Tree. In this way a theoretical understanding of the way that various parts of the Tree operate is enhanced.

It will be clear that all this is but a part of a total working method. However, like ritual, contemplation on its own is limited. Action and thinking must be balanced and, if you look at our diagram, you will see that they are complemented by the third triad of feeling which, in its central and inner position, reconciles the lower outer two. This gives us a clue to its nature and function which we shall explore in the next chapter. Meanwhile, let us conclude our exercise of the thinking triad by considering what contemplation is. If you examine the Tree, you will see that above the thinking triad are the sefirot of Hod,

Gevurah and Binah with their adjacent triads of intuition, emotion and concepts. Being on the passive pillar they are supportive by nature, so that you can see how the cleverness of Hod, the discernment of Gevurah and the reasoning of Binah might act as an unconscious background to the process of contemplation and help formulate its conclusions. In this way, what is being contemplated is considered at many levels. Superficial and lateral thought occurs when only the thinking triad is being used. This is because the triad on its own is no more than a brilliant instrument. It is seen, at its worst, in the clever fool who believes that logic is all. However, the operation is to train one to become aware of the higher and deeper levels of experience and so we move on to examine the techniques of devotion which belong to the triad of feeling, which completes the ego-centred great triangle of the lower face of the Tree.

86

שְׁמַע יִשְׂרָאֵל יְהֹוָה אֱלֹהֵינוּ יְהֹוָה | אֶחָד :

בָּרוּךְ שֵׁם כְּבוֹד מַלְכוּתוֹ לְעוֹלָם וָעֶד :

וְאָהַבְתָּ אֵת יְהֹוָה אֱלֹהֶיךָ בְּכָל־לְבָבְךָ וּבְכָל־נַפְשְׁךָ
וּבְכָל־מְאֹדֶךָ : וְהָיוּ הַדְּבָרִים הָאֵלֶּה אֲשֶׁר אָנֹכִי מְצַוְּךָ
הַיּוֹם עַל־לְבָבֶךָ : וְשִׁנַּנְתָּם לְבָנֶיךָ וְדִבַּרְתָּ בָּם בְּשִׁבְתְּךָ
בְּבֵיתֶךָ וּבְלֶכְתְּךָ בַדֶּרֶךְ וּבְשָׁכְבְּךָ וּבְקוּמֶךָ : וּקְשַׁרְתָּם
לְאוֹת עַל־יָדֶךָ וְהָיוּ לְטֹטָפֹת בֵּין עֵינֶיךָ : וּכְתַבְתָּם
עַל־מְזֻזוֹת בֵּיתֶךָ וּבִשְׁעָרֶיךָ :

Hear, O Israel: the Lord our God, the Lord is One.

Blessed be his name, whose glorious kingdom is for
ever and ever.

And thou shalt love the Lord thy God with all thine
heart, and with all thy soul, and with all thy might.
And these words, which I command thee this day, shall
be upon thine heart: and thou shalt teach them
diligently unto thy children, and shalt talk of them
when thou sittest in thine house, and when thou walkest
by the way, and when thou liest down, and when thou
risest up. And thou shalt bind them for a sign upon
thine hand, and they shall be for frontlets between thine
eyes. And thou shalt write them upon the door posts
of thy house, and upon thy gates.

FIGURE 19—WAY OF DEVOTION
*The Shema is the most important Jewish prayer and is said on every appropriate
occasion. Its message is quite clear and gives direction on how to be devoted to
God. There are others that a Kabbalist can use, such as repeating the Names of
God, praising or petitioning the Holy ONE. A very powerful meditation is to say
I AM THAT I AM while observing one's inner and outer life. If we fully know of
WHOM we speak, we might be shown who we really are and what we are meant
to do. (Jewish prayer book, 19th century.)*

16. Devotion

The feeling triad is situated between Nezah, Hod and Yesod so it has no direct connection with Malkhut and the body. However, there is a process of resonance between it and the corresponding triad of the body which relates to the organs. In this way, the feelings are often associated with the heart, the stomach and the intestines. In the same way, the triad of action is manifested in the corresponding triad of the muscles and the thinking function in the triad of nerves. None of these correspondences are direct communications but what are called referred connections. This is particularly true of the feelings and is the reason we feel stomach cramp or heartache in difficult situations.

The capacity for such a response is due to the fact that the feeling triad is in contact with both pillars and therefore can become active or passive. Moreover, its connection with the ego makes it particularly susceptible to the loading of events that stimulate this or that response. Under ordinary conditions, the usual pattern is that the feelings are influenced either by what is being projected in from the outside world through the ego or what unconscious influences are at play from within the psyche. In kabbalistic training the process is reversed, in that the sensitivity of this triad is used to conscious advantage so that it can receive and transmit, by way of the feeling triad, whatever is thought to be useful in a given situation. For example, by conscious projection through this triad a tense confrontation can be eased and a way through to a resolution be made. 'Blessed are the Peacemakers', said one great Kabbalist. This requires, however, a high degree of consciousness being combined with training that can apply the principles we are examining.

As we have seen, there are various levels of will. There is the body's considerable volition and the wilfulness and will-lessness of the side pillars. These can be controlled either by a conscious intention coming from the self of a person, the direction of an instructor or by the application of discipline based on the rules of the tradition such as 'Thou shalt not bear false witness.' The state of willingness, associated with the feeling triad, has to be cultivated by practice in accordance with the theory that the Self comes to the aid of an individual open to its direction. In this way there is a constant watch over the inclinations of the Yesodic ego to command according to its limited comprehension. This we will come to later. If the situation of willingness can be maintained, then many things become possible.

The first thing to occur is that the struggle between the three triads of thinking, action and feeling stops for as long as willingness is sustained. This means that no energy is wasted and that, on the contrary, it is conserved. As a result there is an accumulation of power that is not usually experienced or available in the *Katnut* or lesser state of consciousness. Moreover, the body becomes less tense and increasingly alert to external events, while inwardly a greater sensitivity to what is happening in the psyche is acquired. In order to reach this state, various exercises to develop the feeling triad can be devised.

A simple example is to sit in a chair and remain there in silence for half an hour. After a while the body will begin to be bored. It will want to move, cough or get something to eat or smoke. It will create aches and pains and will even invent strange sensations in order to get some action going. If one simply allows all this to go on but is obedient to the idea of becoming willing, the conflict is minimised. After a period of time the body will stage a crisis, like wanting to go to the toilet, but if this is met with quiet acceptance then the demands will subside. Such a moment must, of course, be subject to common sense. Do not force the body beyond its proper limit. Such an exercise should be carried out over several weeks, so that in time the body will accept considerable periods of physical stillness without complaint.

Another example of getting to know and command the feeling triad is to observe its patterns. It will be noticed in daily experience that the feelings have a general cycle. In the morning one often feels this way, at midday after lunch usually that and, in the evening, yet another set of feelings. If these habits are not enacted (and this includes the bad feelings too) then the day will seem to be different. Here we discover that, contrary to popular belief, most of our feelings run like clockwork and are not so prone to change after all. An example of this is that we always feel the same pleasure or apprehension when we come into a particular place and meet certain people. Indeed, some individuals we know always arouse deep dislike without fail, even though nothing has been said or done by them to us. The kabbalistic student is trained to observe thoughts, actions and feelings all the time, so as to realise how he or she is at the mercy of their habitual dominance. The great lower triad that contains these three sub-triads centred on the ego is, for most people, just like a psychological computer with a set of triggers which are continually repeating a complex of patterns acquired over many years. Unless one knows this and can recognise them, they cannot be changed or put to good purpose because, in spite of their mechanicalness, some are very useful if only to act as tools in particular situations.

In order to have a command over these psychological habits one has to have a stable will. Now, many people believe this is possible to acquire without help. Indeed, many believe they possess will already. This is an illusion. Free will belongs to those who know themselves to at least the degree of being able to separate ego from Self; and few even know there is a difference. Most people are dominated by physical and social considerations. They cannot and will not change their situation because their security is based on material possessions or on the good opinion of others. It takes a crisis or a great impulse of will to prise an individual out of the grasp of Malkhut or Yesod. Further, while a crisis may precipitate such a transformation, it often cannot be sustained without assistance from outside which is why many people fall back into their old ways or, worse, get lost by not looking for help.

In Kabbalah the help comes from a senior or tutor who acts as the temporary Self to the individual. For example, an exercise might be given at the end of a meeting and such a project will be carried out during the week. This could be to remember the face of each member of the group at ten o'clock in the morning, noon and three o'clock in the afternoon. The order is carried out obediently, not because the student wants the good favour of the instructor but because it will help to encourage self-development. By recalling the exercise at those times, no matter what is being done, you are not only learning how to command consciousness but increasing the capacity of the feeling triad's sensitivity. This will open the door to the triad of awakening above and so gain access to the higher levels of the Tree. Moreover, from such a practice the beginning of Love starts with one's companions in the Work. Further, receptivity will be enhanced and with it the ability to perceive one's own inner state which is the prerequisite of all operations. What is perhaps the most relevant element in this particular exercise is that a covenant with oneself, rather than one's instructor, is met by real commitment and this is the essence of obedience which arises out of real willingness.

Traditionally, the feeling triad is the one of devotion. Here, however, we have to understand that devotion is not just the obvious acts of prayer or meditation. In Kabbalah one is taught that devotion also means reliability in whatever one is given to carry out. This quality of character is crucial because it is usually the feeling triad that rebels when under pressure and, therefore, it is vital that it be obedient to the will. Obedience comes after long practice and many backslidings but perseverance develops stamina and power. When the feelings come under inner authority, prayer and meditation deepen to a degree undreamed of in the normal state of being.

In classical Kabbalah there is a practice called *Devekut*, that is 'cleavage unto God'. In this exercise there is a constant recollection of WHO is always with us, WHO knows us better than we know ourselves and from WHOM we may learn what real devotion is. To be in the *Gadlut* or greater state of consciousness is to strive to be alert in all of the three sub-triads. Alas, this is not easy because, at their centre, is the complex and subtle mind of ego which will precipitate action without consultation, divert the thinking processes on a whim and distort a feeling because of a prejudice. This Yesodic mind is the focus of a continuous flow of images and conversations. In order to master the phenomenon, we must comprehend the ego's nature. This requires another set of training exercises, for without knowing the ego's capacity to block even the Light gained from *Devekut* we can do no serious work.

17. Ego

In traditional Kabbalah the sefirah of Yesod, or the Foundation, has several symbols. One is the unilluminated mirror which reflects only that which is projected upon it unlike Tiferet, the illuminated mirror, which also shines as well as reflects. The lesser mirror of ego tells us that it has no active power but merely images whatever comes into its field. However, like an ordinary mirror, its image is remarkably convincing if you do not realise that it is just a reflection. Moreover, it should be noted that, like most looking-glasses, it has flaws that can present an imperfect picture. In some cases the image can be so distorted that the reality it is mirroring is totally unrecognisable. This often occurs when a person is under duress and panics. If the condition becomes chronic, then it may be seen as neurosis and, if permanent, as a state of madness. This is why the understanding and command of Yesod in any spiritual work is vital, for any major imbalance of the ego will be magnified and corrupt whatever is being reflected, no matter how spiritual.

Another traditional symbol for the yesodic ego is the Moon, with the Sun at the Tiferet of the Self. This echoes the idea behind the two kinds of mirror. If we examine the symbolism of the Moon we will learn much by analogue about the nature of the ego mind. Here we have the application of the 'as above, so below' principle so beloved by all esoteric traditions, for the same laws apply to the macrocosm of the universe as they do to the microcosm of a human being.

Like the Moon, the ego has a face that is always seen and a face that is not. This tells us that there is a certain fixity present that always turns towards or away from consciousness. Thus there is an unseen side to the ego about which most of us know little. The face that we are familiar with has, like the Moon, a definite geography or rather selenography. In us, this is what is called the personality or the mask we wear to the world. It is composed of mountains and valleys, craters and seas of habits and attitudes long frozen into a configuration, like the face of the Moon. In most people this is acquired in early life and remains unaltered until death. While many of the skills and ploys of

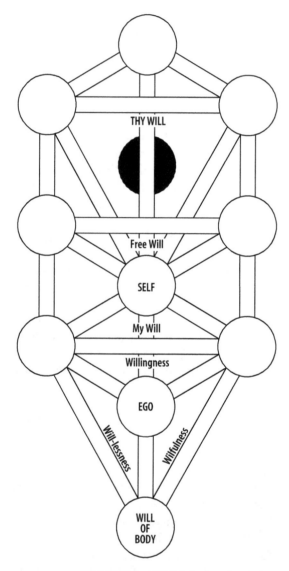

THY WILL

Free Will

SELF

My Will

Willingness

EGO

Will-lessness

Wilfulness

WILL
OF
BODY

FIGURE 20—STRUGGLE
The Kabbalist has to be on constant alert to that by which they are being ruled
and influenced. The body and its appetites have a enormous effect on our lives.
The ego, also, with its inclinations to be wilful or will-less, can dominate our
existence. It is only when we are 'willing' that the possibility of exerting free will
can occur. Then we have the choice to be Self-ish or serve a much higher purpose.
This battle goes on every day until we know exactly what we are required to do;
to live out our fate fully and perform our destiny. (Halevi, 20th century.)

the personality may be useful in negotiating ordinary life and striving in the professional and social scene, they are often useless and even dangerous to any in spiritual work because they can prevent, or even destroy, possibilities of inner growth. For example, so called good manners can stop the truth being spoken. In Kabbalah this could mean a lack of honesty between the student and tutor or between Yesod and Tiferet. Many people are too polite to themselves when considering unpalatable truths as bad taste or unacceptable.

In order to obviate such an occurrence, exercises are given out by an instructor to observe the nature and working of the Yesodic ego so as to identify its patterns and weaknesses. Such a project might be to take the symbol of the Moon and relate its phases to fluctuations in the ego. Thus, the new Moon might be seen as the stage when one begins to awaken in the morning. Here, a thin crescent of consciousness slowly emerges from the unseen side of the Moon where the inward looking dream face has been illuminated during the night. The first quarter could be regarded as a period of half-awareness when the concentration is not fully engaged whilst the full Moon could be seen as the state when the personality is totally projected outwards and everything is on the surface. The last quarter, and the degrees in between, might be considered as a phase of retreat or the beginning of introspection when the interest in outer things is waning. The dark Moon describes, in its lack of light, that the ego is either asleep or turned totally inwards in reflection or reverie. Observing all these phases in oneself, and others, will reveal much about the scope of the ego and its ability to alter its state, in contrast to the constancy of the Sun which always shines whatever condition clouds its face.

Taking the Lunar symbol further, in order to show how the technique of analogue is useful for exploration, one might be asked to consider the phenomenon of the eclipse. The Lunar eclipse, when the Earth's shadow passes over the Moon, could be seen as the body overshadowing the ego, either in illness or some physical activity that occludes its reflection; whilst the Solar eclipse, when the Moon stands between the Sun and the Earth, is quite identifiable as the ego preventing the light of the Self from reaching Malkhut and the World. To ponder one's findings, when applying this approach, will deepen the comprehension of Yesod and allow a more objective penetration when it comes to looking at the operation of one's own ego.

From what has been said, it will be seen that the ego has a distinct and complex character. It undergoes constant change, its degree of consciousness alters and focuses in a full circle of directions and it has an unseen side. Now, whilst the observable face might be very familiar, at least to others, the hidden side is not. Most of us recognise that we have thoughts and feelings and do actions that we do not show to the outer world but few realise the significance or power of these unrevealed aspects of our ego. Many of these hidden activities relate to our fears and hopes and, sometimes, to our fantasies. These, in most people, are largely unconscious and cause much trouble as they interfere with any possibility of perceiving reality, be it inner or outer. The Kabbalist cannot afford to allow such an intrusion into the flow of light from above or that which is coming in from below. It would thwart the pursuit of self-knowledge and the opportunity to be useful to the Work.

This is why many of the exercises in the early stages of kabbalistic discipline are concerned with studying and separating out habits and attitudes that are detrimental to progress. You are first of all taught, for example, to leave any egotistic elements like status, whether of inflation or deflation, outside the door of the study house. Later this rule applies to general life, in that you perform your worldly tasks in a state of continual detachment, because the ego will latch itself onto almost anything and claim it for its own. It will at times, moreover, not only try to interfere with ordinary situations but seek to control spiritual ones. It will, as control of it becomes serious and therefore a threat to its long-established autonomy, begin to resist any reduction of its ego-esteem. Indeed, at the critical point it will start to fight. At first this manifests as simple resistance but later, as a conflict develops, the ego turns from blind obstinacy to subtle cunning as it seeks to retain its authority by subterfuge or by feigning token assent. This process is continuous throughout life, for an undisciplined ego will seek to take advantage of any lapse in the Kabbalist's watchfulness.

The exercises concerned with mastering the ego are many. For instance, some are designed to use the body as a control factor. Heavy physical work, for example, can bring to the surface a violent protest from the ego which has an image of itself as being very spiritual and 'above' such toil. Another exercise might be to make ego act out of 'character' in a real life but contrived situation. Yet another project could be to expose the ego to others involved in the Work by speaking honestly about one's life and aspirations. Here the audience must not only be discerning but also merciful and interested in the truth. (This is the soul triad.) After a while, you soon know whether it is the ego or the Self speaking. Moreover, you also discover that even the ego has spiritual ambitions and fantasies.

Generally, the instructor acts as the Self in these exercises. Such a person must also be working on his or her ego because there is the dangerous phenomenon of projection when the student sees the tutor as an idealised Tiferet to his or her own Yesod. This situation can be a great temptation for both parties. A good tutor will watch out for the symptoms of projection and correct the imbalance. Obedience is not submission to your teacher but to the Teaching which represents a manifestation of the Truth. The cultivation of one's own Tiferet is the best way of putting Yesod in its proper place but this takes some time. Meanwhile, the different techniques discussed and practised based on the triads surrounding Yesod will begin to set its components into their correct acting, feeling and thinking parts. These methods will, over a period, make the particular nature of one's ego emerge as a distinct sub-personality. However, while much attention is devoted to the curtailing of Yesod's useless habits, one must also develop its considerable range of skills. We have already touched on the ego's capacity to deal with images, so let us now explore and develop this talent so that Yesod might be encouraged, like the body, to participate with willingness in the Work. In this way ego becomes co-operative and not disruptive. This is vital, for without Yesod's help very little can be accomplished; one is a blind artist whose visions can never be painted. Therefore, in the next chapter, we shall look at Yesod as the screen of consciousness.

18. Imagery

Judging by its position on the Tree of the psyche, Yesod is a complex sefirah. This complexity, as noted, is increased by the fact that the Daat of the body underlies it and connects it with the physical world. As such, the ego is the place where the impressions gathered by the senses and material generated by the psyche are cast into an intelligible image. This means that not only are the electrical impulses from the eyes, ears, nose, tongue and skin interpreted into recognisable signals, upon which action may be based, but so are feelings, thoughts and inner actions. The latter material is cast in a variety of forms from flashes to complex moods, single ideas to intricate metaphysical themes, simple reactions to detailed manoeuvres. All these, plus the occasional mystical experience with its strange symbols, are projected upon the screen of Yesod that day and night produces a continuous show of illuminations, delusions, dreams and realities.

The first exercise to be given is devoted to distinguishing what the body contributes. Here you are told to observe how we have a body image which is held by Yesod over our whole life. Anything that does not concur with it is registered, be it a scratch on the finger or the loss of a limb. Yesod knows, for example, by ache or bump, bruise or strange taste, that something is amiss in the same way as a good driver suspects all is not well by an unfamiliar vibration or noise in his vehicle. The interior image of the body is a good place to begin differentiating the various levels. For example, one can tell the difference between physical cardiac pain and emotional heartache, although they are often closely associated. After a series of exercises in identifying the differing qualities of the Worlds, like remembering a place and then seeing it in reality or reading a recipe and then following it, one should be able to move on to examine the anatomy of the psyche by means of Yesod's mirror.

Normally, the ego reflects only events in the lower psyche. That is whatever you are doing, thinking or feeling at that moment. These preoccupations are not difficult to spot and isolate. However, what is not so easy is to perceive the forces that underlie Yesod's activity.

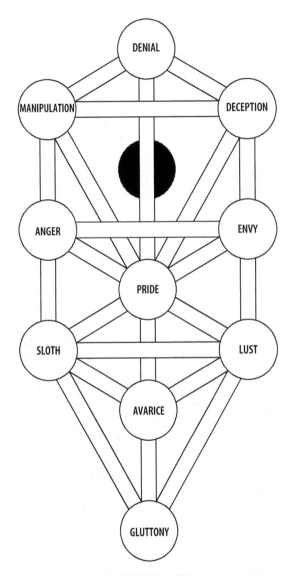

FIGURE 21—SIN

In Hebrew, 'sin' means 'to miss the mark'. Here are the seven deadly misdemeanours plus three more that relate to the Tree. The lower ones are easy to explain as they are the negative side of the qualities of the sefirot to which they relate. The three upper are about the abuse of power and the rejection of the Divine. These three are often found in a corrupt priesthood, government and even in schools of the soul that have been taken over by intelligent but evil people. (Halevi, 20th century.)

These factors may come in response to external stimulus, like a stolen kiss, where the reaction of frigidity might reveal physical repulsion, checked emotion or the power of concepts about love, timing or infidelity. There is also the possibility that the ego is being influenced by your personal devil or angel. This is an old fashioned way of saying that a constraint is coming from the level of the soul concerning your inner morality. Great skill and much experience are required to identify the reality of what is really happening. Many people are told again and again by their souls what to do or not to do in oblique and sometimes direct communications but they still do not recognise what level is speaking because they do not listen. The Kabbalist must take note of anything unusual, be it an external or internal signal, for it may be a directive from the Self to be on the alert for some crucial moment that is about to occur. What today are called synchronistic happenings that echo interior events were called omens in former times. To recognise such phenomena requires constant observation of the Yesodic processes of daily life.

After a period of watching, a picture begins to emerge of one's inner activity. Now the psyche, like the body, has many routine patterns but they are not so well defined because they belong to a subtler World than the body. However, because we know that the processes are based upon the Tree, we can at last perceive their general principles. One of the first things to be recognised is the fact that it is not easy to penetrate up the path between Yesod and Tiferet. This is because it emerges out of the hidden side of the ego—the back of the Moon which is largely unknown. By the constant collection of fragments of information the Kabbalist learns, by inference, what is this hidden aspect of the ego. Help can be given by your tutor or other students about this blind area but much trust has to be established between people before you take their view into serious account. The picture that is built up of your hidden or shadow-side has to be checked and rechecked before the pathway of integrity, between the ego and Self, is fully opened.

The traditional method of gaining access to the shadow and beyond is to interpret dreams that are memorable. Generally speaking, most dreams reflect the digestive processing of material being absorbed by the psyche but occasionally a dream will be so clear or potent as still to remain in the memory by morning. These are the ones to be examined. To analyse every dream is like having an x-ray of the intestines after every meal. Common sense will tell one what is remarkable because most dreams fade, as they should, once their essential substance has been extracted by the psyche. Those which remain are meant to be noted by the conscious aspect of the psyche and pondered, for their content requires special attention.

Dreams, according to Kabbalah, may be classified as normal psychological processing, as those concerned with individual development or prophetic vision. The first is related to the ego and the functional triads of the Tree, the second to the soul and the third to the triad of the Spirit. There is a fourth but that belongs to contact with the Divine and is, therefore, beyond the present discussion. Those dreams relating to the individual are usually highly dramatic and often disturbing. They will be an emotive mixture of symbolism and elements of the person's life. Very often, but not always, they will come at a crucial point in that person's development and indicate some decision or initiation. You should record and reflect upon these alone or with others who are skilled or objective about such things. Dreams of prophecy are rare but they also have a distinct quality. They likewise are strikingly lucid but, unlike the other dreams, are impersonal although they instill awe in their dreamer. These also should be noted for reflection and interpretation.

Traditionally, Joseph is related to the sefirah of Yesod. This is because he was a dreamer and an interpreter of dreams. Indeed, his coat of many colours represents the ego and his raising to be the Grand Vizier to Pharaoh symbolises the talented and disciplined Yesodic servant of the ruler of the self. To be able to interpret dreams requires both a gift and much knowledge. In Kabbalah an understanding of the Tree is a great aid, for one can examine a dream in the light of the sefirot and gather much more information from it. First the main elements of the dream are divided into their sefirotic qualities. Then the characters or symbols involved are related to archetypes associated with each sefirah. Thus, the severe or gentle factors may be seen as Gevurah and Hesed while the dark and powerful mother figure could be related to Binah. The trickster, in most dreams, belongs to Hod and the sensuous figure sometimes encountered, to Nezah. As the configuration of archetypes begins to reveal its loading and emphasis, so the levels and their relationships start to emerge. Blended with a well-informed background of the individual and a good understanding of their nature and problems, a useful kabbalistic interpretation can be given. However, such consultations should be used with discretion or a morbid preoccupation with one's psychological process can begin to unbalance the person, like a hypochondriac's obsession with the body. One must always work within the equilibrium of the Tree.

Normally, Yesod acts as the unconscious screen for both the body and psyche but, as we have already seen, it may also be consciously directed by imagination. This capacity is unique to a human being because of the gift of free will. Now the capacity to create images means that one can plan the future as well as remember the past. It also means that you can formulate images to be projected, as any artist, writer or musician knows. This ability may be applied, as we have seen, to kabbalistic work in creating a simple or elaborate ritual. It can also be used to penetrate beyond the veil of ego unconsciousness, that is, the line stretched between Hod and Nezah, and so glimpse the workings of the inner psyche or the upper Worlds. This, however, also requires much skill because the operation can be very disturbing to the uninformed person who has no real grasp of, or training to deal with, the forces involved. Here we enter the frontier zone of personal darkness beyond which few people go, except in dreams or in moments of heightened consciousness.

In Kabbalah, such an excursion can be undertaken in controlled conditions. These are in the company of a trusted and experienced tutor or group of good companions under strict spiritual discipline. The reason for this prudence is that this is the area where some people, on experiencing increasing sensitivity, become aware either of their own psychological defects or the presence of those who inhabit this twilight border between the two lower Worlds. This is the realm of Hecate and the Witch of Endor, sorcery and the creatures who cannot for the moment touch the Earth nor enter into Paradise. However, there is a way straight through this psychic forest that we tread each night in safety and this is the path between Yesod and Tiferet, whose name and practice give good safeguard. The traditional title of this path is *Zadek* or righteous integrity.

What follows is an exercise designed to walk the Zadek path using the mirror of Yesod both to create and reflect, in guided imagery, an insight into the Higher Worlds and the state of our souls. In this way we can see how it is done and what can be gained on the basis that the objective is self-knowledge. Here begins the art of using Yesod's imagery consciously.

19. Excursion

To have experience of the Higher Worlds is not unusual. It can happen in sleep or ordinary consciousness. But here it is spontaneous, a gift of Heaven. Under these conditions there is no personal control or capability, except to look and learn. What is shown is under Providential guidance, so that no exploration beyond what is presented is possible. Some people have these experiences when gravely ill, like the woman who, weary of life, yearned for death. She was taken up through the various levels of existence during a deep depression and shown the Throne of Heaven from which a Voice issued, commanding her to return to Earth and complete what she had been born for. The details of the event, with its cosmic landscapes and beings, was remarkably similar to the accounts set out in the early apocalyptic writings like the Book of Enoch, except that here the place was not the Judean Desert but a suburb of London. The implication is that the upper Worlds are an objective reality that people can recognise at any point in history, for they exist in a different order of time.

Another case of a glimpse into the higher Worlds was the man about to take a sip of whisky in a London pub. As he put the glass to his mouth, his surroundings faded and he saw before him a vast glittering wheel turning slowly in a black void of space. The wheel was composed of myriads of golden strands which he knew to be the lives and destinies of all the human race. Having had his obsessive question about rebirth answered, the sights and sounds of the pub returned and he stood for a long time without drinking, wondering whether he was going mad. Both the instances quoted were the result of inner crises and the response of Grace to a profound puzzlement. In the first case, the woman decided to return to life, remarried. The man, alas, could not cope with the situation confronting him and later killed himself. This illustrates the power of such experiences and why a gradual and disciplined approach is absolutely vital so as to be able to handle them. It is also the reason why drugs, which allow rapid access to the higher regions, are discouraged. One may see the wondrous sights of Heaven and Hell but few drug-takers can hold such an experience and

FIGURE 22 – EXPERIENCES
As the result of hard inner work or act of Grace, it is possible to go beyond the material level and enter the Higher Worlds. Here the subtle cosmic cycles are seen and their purpose revealed. Here the mystic, with his staff of knowledge and thick coat of protection, safely passes into the transpersonal realm without his mind being blown. This is due to a thorough training and idea of what to expect. Without such a discipline there will only be confusion, as the scale of such a vision can be overpowering. (Woodcut, 16th century.)

make sense of it. Many never want to intrude into the other worlds again, like Jack of the Beanstalk who encountered giants. He destroyed the beanstalk, thereby cutting himself off, because he was not ready for the experience of another reality.

To go on a conscious excursion into the next World requires a seasoned guide and a map. The map is provided by Jacob's Ladder which shows the various levels and frontiers to be crossed. The guide should be someone, preferably your tutor, who has been there before and knows the way both there and back and, more important, what to do in an emergency, as sometimes happens. This is why the study and practice of Kabbalah is limited to the mature and stable. In this exercise we are to go on a short flight to the ceiling of the physical world and just beyond. It will be a training run and a reconnaissance following a set flight-plan.

First, the student and his guide must be in a place where they will not be disturbed. Then they must make themselves at ease, so that the body will not distract the attention. In ancient times fasting and a short period of celibacy, followed by both physical and psychological ablution, made up the preparation for such an excursion. This meant a bath and entering into a state of devotion, purity and sincerity. In this case we wish to make only a limited journey, and so we ablute accordingly with a washing of the hands and face. Having prepared, the student, under the direction of his guide, comes into a state of attention and awaits instruction.

After the invocation of the Tree and permission from the Holy One that the operation be approved or aborted, according to Divine Will, the guide then takes the student through the first stages of becoming conscious of different levels. First the elemental levels are contacted within the body, then the vegetable and animal souls which are calmed and told to wait. Then the ego is attended to and instructed, so that it obeys the direction of the guide who gives out the following instructions with a pause in between each sentence to allow the images and the experiences to unite. The excursion follows roughly in this form. The guide says:

"You sense the chair you are seated upon—Feel the weight of your body—Become aware of the room—Close your eyes—Perceive your thoughts and feelings—Awaken—Differentiate between the ego mind and that which watches within—Hold that position—Now begin to ascend—First imagine yourself hovering above the house—Become a bird—Now climb higher, so as to see the neighbourhood—Go higher—Look out over the whole area—Observe the houses and streets—Watch the people go about their lives—Shift the scale—Perceive the town as a single organism—Catch the sense of its life—Is it at work or play?—Is it expanding or declining?—Climb higher and take note of what kind of bird you are—Look out over the country—See all the lines of communication between the towns—Become aware of the electronic signals in the air about you—Fly yet higher and note the state of your bird—Observe the coasts and frontiers of the land—Ascend further—View the whole continent—Recognise the geography and see the peoples who live there—Reflect on their different characters and histories—Climb higher and take in our hemisphere of the world—Observe the advance of day and night—Note the seasons above and below the Equator—Fly higher and perceive your own state—Look at the globe of the Earth and feel its life—Move out past the Moon—Go beyond the planets, one by one—Watch yourself—See the Sun's size diminish as you leave the Solar system—Hover amongst the constellations—Draw back from our galaxy—Hold your position in the silence of deep space and listen—Listen—Listen."

After a long pause the guide speaks again:

"Now return—Come back into the Milky Way—Move through the constellations—Enter the Solar system—Approach the Earth—Move by the Moon—Penetrate the atmosphere—Look down on the oceans—Descend through the clouds—Fly towards our country—Float over our town—Swoop down to this house—Hover for a moment and observe your bird before you become human and find yourself sitting in this room—Open your eyes and feel your body on the chair."

After a pause in which to recover, reflect for a while on the experience before any analysis. When the student and his guide are ready, the student should then debrief, like a pilot after a mission. He should give first a general account of the voyage and then the detailed examination can begin. During this, the guide should not suggest anything but just comment or ask questions. The debriefing should be divided between what was seen and heard in the universe and how the bird was experienced. The observation of what was picked up in this case is less important than the information gathered about the soul through the symbol of the bird. Its size, form and state would be very informative, both to the tutor and the student. A scruffy bird with a damaged wing or an over-weighted flyer indicate much, as would a creature with cunning claws or weak eyes. These discrepancies, seen as aspects of the psyche, can be interpreted and worked on so as to attain improvement.

From the foregoing, it can be seen how much could be gathered about your state and what it is like to leave the Earth, if only for a few moments. In longer and deeper excursions more could be learned, but these should not be attempted until there is a certain familiarity with working in this manner. The practice should not be done too frequently. Moreover, the journey should be varied over different ranges, so as to develop the power of projection. It is important not to overreach your capability but always to retain contact with the Earth. If a student loses it, the guide should order him back and even tap or shake (only if necessary) the student, should he not respond to verbal instruction. You should always begin and end with consciousness of the body and each journey should be completed by a descent of the Tree and a stamping of the feet, after giving thanks for what has been received. This both earths those present and reminds them that the objective is not the pursuit of occult phenomena but preparation and training for the service of God. This brings us to the counterbalance that must always be present in such work. Ascent towards Heaven must always be balanced by a deep contact with the Earth. Here is where tradition plays its part to bring about balance and so we will next examine the Tradition in relation to manifestation in the world.

20. Tradition

To retain contact with the World below is essential for several kabbalistic reasons. The first is that it keeps a solid balance which checks any inclination to drown in the psychological world or fly away into the realm of the Spirit. The second reason for maintaining a terrestrial contact is that it allows what has been received from above to be imparted to the Earth which is part of the process of conscious unification between the worlds.

The need to be well grounded is emphasised in kabbalistic work because when the focus of attention moves out of normal ego consciousness into the unknown, the individual can extend consciousness up Jacob's Ladder without danger of splitting the body and psyche. This sometimes happens with drug users, who force a separation, or in psychic experiments by the unprepared that isolate aspects of the being from external reality. Exploring the Higher Worlds is like visiting an unfamiliar city. After finding a place to live you first get to know your own house and then the surrounding streets. Having established what is home, the exploration then extends out to the adjoining districts. Later, the more distant areas of the city are explored until the general geography is known. After each excursion a return to home is vital, in order to rest and digest what has been seen. Over a period, you gain an insight into the life of the city; its high and low sections, its administrative zone, centres of art and science, work and play. Slowly all becomes familiar. Even the dangerous and criminal areas begin to fit into the layers of a complex infrastructure that goes to make up the character of the city. So it is when exploring the upper worlds and, like the situation in the city, you always return to home base with its anchor of security.

In most spiritual traditions this place of familiarity and safety is found in the customs and practices of formal religion. A tradition may be elaborate in form, a modified compromise or a simple set of beliefs. It can be orthodox or even heretical, depending on your point of view of what is important. What does matter is that the mode holds a spiritual significance for the practitioners of that rite. The truly

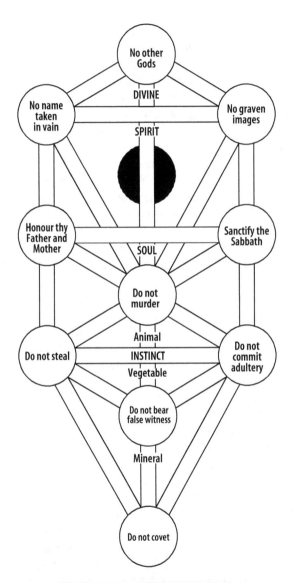

FIGURE 23—COMMANDMENTS
*These are the rules by which a Kabbalist lives. While the top three are simple,
the other seven are more subtle. To honour one's parents means the tradition into
which one was born while the Sabbath can mean a period every day for reflection
and prayer. Do not murder means not to destroy one's own possibilities and those
of others; while adultery and stealing can relate to mixing things that are
inappropriate and robbing others of their ideas and emotions. Finally, do not lie
to oneself or covet anything that is not yours. (Halevi, 20th century.)*

spiritual do not quarrel over which sect is correct. It is a sign of spiritual ignorance when the form is considered more important than the content of the Teaching. What should be taken into account, however, is whether the form of the tradition helps or hinders the devotee. Does it aid in the contact with the Higher Worlds or not?

Dark elements always hover near any spiritual work, like moths to a candle, because they wish to draw on its power. Therefore, the integrity of a tradition is crucial, for sacred ceremonies open a door from below into an inner holy space and structure that has been created, often over a long period, by the tradition. This invisible temple, which exists in the World of Formation, provides an approach to the Gate of the Spirit. It is called, in both Christian and Jewish Kabbalah, the *Malkhut ha Shamaim* or the Kingdom of Heaven; through its rites one may reach, by traversing the seven great palaces of Heaven, the Presence of the Divine.

Now the outer material form of the inner temple may be seen in terms of a great cathedral, a stone circle or an old synagogue. It may even manifest in a room set aside for such religious practice. The key to such a place is to be found in the form and dynamic of an orthodox liturgy or in a simple prayer repeated with deep sincerity. It does not matter what the mode is; what counts is the intention. A day's prayer in Jerusalem without real intent is worthless while a moment's full consciousness, as one says the Holy Name on a London bus, may bring knowledge of God. This, for the Kabbalist, Sufi or Christian mystic, is the aim. Buildings, books, liturgy and rites are secondary. This, however, does not invalidate traditional modes of worship; they have their purpose for the people who need a form for a guide. Without such religious customs and practices society would be barbaric and devoid of a social-religious focus and standards.

Throughout the ages there has always been this apparent split between the mystics and the orthodoxy of any religion, with the mystics usually accused of being antinomianist, that is, opposed to traditional law. This is quite untrue in most cases, as many Kabbalists, for example, have adapted Kabbalah to religious custom; some indeed added a deeper dimension to the existing liturgy and, although at the time there was a conservative resistance, today many of these additions are considered quite traditional. What is always forgotten is that every religion begins as a mystical revelation. It is usually when the Teaching has become priestcraft or spiritually dim that mystics have trouble, especially when they try to revive some atrophied practice that binds, instead of releasing, the soul of the congregation.

Taking an objective look at a tradition, one can see that it is divided into several recognisable levels. First comes the mineral in the church, synagogue or mosque building. This is the Malkhut. Then there is the congregation at Yesod. Into this the generations are born and die with marriage and funeral ceremonies celebrating the vegetable cycle of life. The animal element is present in the social activities and the sense of community with its elders giving the seal of tribal approval. The soul dimension is manifest in the commitment of circumcision and baptism and the vows made at Bar Mitzvah and confirmation. Beliefs spoken of on the Sabbath relate to the spiritual, each sect having its own view on the meaning of life. The universal aspects of the faith are seen in the annual cycle of festivals which celebrate the history of the tradition and the cosmic pattern of the year. Few Jews and Christians recognise their festivals as overlaying ancient spring or harvest rites. The deepest mysteries of religion are often only touched upon or hinted at during high Holy Days or moments in the Sabbath service. Those who wish to penetrate this veil must often seek elsewhere to find the door into the esoteric depths of their faith. However, this does not mean that they cannot participate or use the traditional mode of their religion to attain entry into the Promised Land.

With intelligent application a student may use the form most familiar to his or her culture to a greater or lesser degree. Some Kabbalists are ultra orthodox and fulfil as many of the six hundred and thirteen commandments as possible. Others are less strict and adhere to a modicum of precepts, whilst others keep the bare minimum but with complete integrity. As one rabbi observed, the greatest law is 'To love others as oneself.' If we realised WHO the Self was then this saying would take on its ultimate meaning of I AM THAT I AM. In this way we see again how intention is always the measure of a sacred action. Using this criterion one may participate in an existing service, design one's own rite or blend ancient and modern methods in order to rise up and relate to God. The middle way is followed in this book.

The traditional approach of maintaining a connection between one's place in time and space and the Divine is well worked out in a cycle of daily and annual rituals, devotions and contemplations. This working method is the most common, because it has been in existence for millennia and is well tried. Whilst tradition has the advantage of a vast backup of collective power and experience, it also has the disadvantage that it can drown the individual, as it imposes a social conformity which is often mistaken for spirituality. We see this in the manners and dress of extreme sects. The strange irony is that real spirituality always has the quality of true individuality despite concurrence of view, so that apparently widely divergent Buddhists and Kabbalists can discuss questions without essential disagreement because they are both in contact with the same cosmic world. This is rare for those encased in too much outer form and little inner comprehension of their tradition. The Spanish Inquisition demonstrated this well.

For the Kabbalist the use of tradition is influenced by temperament and background. Unless one has a strong reaction at this point, the wisest thing is to use those elements of one's upbringing that evoke the *Gadlut* or greater state. These may be rituals, prayers and symbols or ideas that draw upon the deep memory of one's roots, as well as personal experience. Use these forms to remember the Holy One in the morning, remind one of God during the day and bring the Divine into consciousness in the evening. Try to recall, in between these times, who one is and why one is here on Earth. Maintain this awareness of being incarnate day and night whilst constantly remembering that one is in the presence of God. Change the form of the recollection when it loses its freshness and gradually go deeper into those moments set aside for meditation. To repeat a Holy Name whenever one recalls God is slowly to realise what it means as one recalls the Source. In this way Adam reflects the Divine gaze as that moment unites with Eternity. This is the aim of every tradition with an esoteric heart.

21. Day

Having looked at the general cultural background of a tradition, let us examine how it might be used by a Kabbalist in his everyday life. Firstly an individual must recognise where he stands in relation to the world in which he lives. Most people are classified by physique, intelligence, social class and nation. To the world an individual is an amalgam of these labels, whether he accepts it or not. This means that a certain mode of conduct is expected. The prudent Kabbalist does not resist these expectations because he operates from a different level and can work within a social framework without being untrue. As one well-known Kabbalist said, 'Be in the world but not of it.' This requires not only spiritual maturity but great skill in mundane matters. For example, an individual may seem to be doing business when he is in fact testing an initiate for reliability. Only the perceptive would know the difference. Thus, one may perform the same outer actions as the conventional professional but have quite an opposite objective. Two people in the same office or workshop can serve very different Gods.

Taking a day as a model, the first moments after waking can be used to advantage. That peculiarly lucid state of consciousness between dreaming and waking reveals the presence of the Watcher of the Self as it observes the dreams fade and the body come into view. At such a moment prayers may be said or deep questions asked. Perhaps a problem posed the night before has received an answer or the day ahead needs deeper planning. Reflection on how to approach this or that situation is considered from the point of view of the Work and not personal gain. Action to be taken is seen in terms of interior consequence rather than an exterior solution, for the Kabbalist recognises that everything done on Earth influences the balance of the universe so that nothing is without its effect, no matter how small.

After carrying out whatever ablutions have been decided upon, the Kabbalist then sets aside a period for a morning ritual, devotion or contemplation. Some combine all three approaches. A ritual might consist of laying *Tefillin* in the orthodox Jewish way. In this, two boxes containing certain scriptures and inscribed with the initials of the Name of God are strapped onto the head and arm whilst praying. At the other extreme a Kabbalist may do no more than place a hat on his or her head to mark the moment whilst another might sit facing a certain direction for half an hour in silent meditation. One person might, in their devotion, repeat the Name of God over and over in an endless chant whilst another could be slowly saying each word of a prayer and weighing its meaning. Yet another might just contemplate the Sefirotic Tree or light a candle and consider why light is the symbol of Divinity. There are many possibilities and variations of the same intention.

After contact between above and below has been established, the Kabbalist then goes out into the world. Whether at home or away, in the market-place or factory, office or field, the intention to be conscious of God is ever present. For much of the time *Devekut*, or cleavage to the Divine, will be lost but it must be striven for nevertheless. In time a pattern will be set up in body and psyche that will help to retain the state and, indeed, providential reminders will be forthcoming after a while, both from this world and above, as the selected times of the day are approached. The suggested hours of 10 am, noon and 4pm could be used to recall your aim. Another set of reminders could be at particular junctions in your daily routine. A coffee break or a point in a journey could be utilised; so could an interval in a work process or recurring high mark of the day. Any time or place may be applied as a beacon. So can certain people, like the man who always passes you on the way to the station or the woman who brings in the mail. One 18th-century Kabbalist said, 'One should learn from the thief. He is ever watchful and takes every opportunity for gain. It is the same in the matters of the Spirit.'

The midday break should be used for inner as well as outer nourishment. Besides the exercises in conscious action and his emotional state in relating to others, the Kabbalist could contemplate the World at the daily zenith of the Sun. In the morning the body is in one state and in the evening another. At midday it responds to the life about it in a particular way which you can observe in order to pick up the full range of the body's capacity when the Sun is high. At the noon Nature is opened right out in response to the cosmic influx, before beginning to fade towards night. At such a time you can experience things about the World as at no other. It is the climax of outward expansion when the Sun is at its maximum point of radiation. At this moment the zenith of light stands in opposition to the darkness of midnight. Holding the consciousness through the moment of noon can reveal much about the nature of good and evil, cosmic cycles and the Divine reflected in the Sun.

The afternoon brings about the waning of the body and the waxing of the psyche. If the morning is concerned, as traditional Kabbalah suggests, with the active pillar, then the afternoon reveals the more reflective column that begins to look back on what has been done. The same techniques used in the morning are applied again but with different times and places to remind one of what the Work is about. When the daily round of a monastery is examined, it will be seen that the same criteria are applied. The various offices repeated every day perform a similar function but in a secluded and orthodox situation. Kabbalah, however, is not a withdrawn order; it operates right in the midst of life. This makes it more difficult as regards distractions but it also offers a unique variety of opportunities in which to act directly upon a situation. Thus, while you are reminded by routine of the cycle of creation, you can also be involved in the unusual events, no matter how small, that make up the drama of existence.

An evening routine may include a formal meditation. If there is not a group meeting, the time can be spent at private work or play. The latter, however, to the committed Kabbalist, is still an opportunity to study and practise. A game of badminton or chess can reveal some hidden animal traits in your character and a swimming session can be used to learn something about negotiating the watery world of the psyche. Social occasions are excellent times to observe the personality at work and, in the little battles between the ego and self, which seems to have the upper hand. Differences of opinion over small or grave matters can indicate wilfulness in oneself, as well as others, and the test of spiritual pride is always present when with people not involved with spiritual work. To remain inwardly awake at a party is not easy and many a serious student has made a fool of himself, although no one else except those on the Path would have noticed it.

At the end of the day comes the time for reflection. This may be done with others or alone. Many individuals may analyse what happened that day with partners or friends who judge everything according to ego but few relate it to a set of principles. Most people consider gain or loss in terms of cash or position, but the person under spiritual discipline sees everything from the viewpoint of inner success or failure. These assessments might be in the form of an intimate conversation with spiritual companions who do not judge but gently reflect what lessons might be learned. Originally, this was the point of confession, here used not just for penance but for constructive reflection. For example, an incident on that day might be a warning light or the indication of deep change. Good companions are more than helpful on the Way. They are vital as there are many pitfalls and diversions that you cannot see for yourself.

The final act of the day is the last session of ritual, prayer or contemplation. This again is a matter of personal choice. The minimum that is required is that it be based on the Tree, in that you rise up from Malkhut to Keter to acknowledge God and are grateful for what you have received that day. After this formality, the last moments before sleep can be used to distil the essence of what has been experienced. In this process, details of the day are pared away into a simple summary that is pondered upon, with its arising questions, until sleep overtakes the consciousness. These questions will be taken deep into the psyche and considered during the night, so that there may be an answer in the morning on awakening. This daily cycle should be repeated with periodic modifications. Over the years the accumulation and refinement of the experience gathered will bear profound fruit, for it produces what is called the Wine of Merit. Merit is the result of Work and this, in time, is matched by Grace.

22. Festivals

To complete this consideration of the mundane aspect of Kabbalah, let us look at the annual festivals. Now in all religions there is a yearly cycle of celebrations. These are usually based upon the ancient recognition that there are rhythms in the cosmos which rule our lives. The solstices and equinoxes are obvious examples of crucial turning points of the year and many Jewish and Christian high Holy Days are to be found to coincide with them. These mark not only the waxing and waning of natural processes but also the tides of spiritual forces. Ceremonies performed at such moments indicate a respect for these nodal points and seek to catch the cosmic rhythm manifesting at that time, as the celestial balance shifts from ebb to flow and back again.

The harvest festivals are clear instances of ancient rites adapted to Judaism and Christianity and so are the winter celebrations of Christmas and Hannukah. The former celebrates the coming into the world of a great Light, signified by the Star of Bethlehem, and the marking of the beginning of the New Testament; the latter, the rededication of the desecrated Temple after a period of desolation and spiritual darkness, with lights that increase in number over eight days. Both, in fact, come at the time of year when nature is at its nadir and the life principle is at its weakest, that is just at the point when the Sun is about to turn up again in its progression round the zodiac. This winter solstice is the period when the soul is least fettered by the flesh and can easily rise into the realm of the Spirit. On the daily model, it is like the state of inner freedom often experienced at midnight when the body is at its least active. Here we begin to· see how the Kabbalist might begin to view and use these annual celebrations as a mode of study and work.

If you consider each festival from its esoteric standpoint, its outer aspect is in the story and its associated rituals and its inner in symbolism and content. Thus, the celebrations of Easter and Passover that come at the same time of the year can take on a deeper significance than is generally realised. Both these festivals relate to Spring, to a renewal of life after Winter. Historically they coincide because the Last Supper

FIGURE 24—CELEBRATION

Here a Jewish family celebrates Passover. Each participant must consider that he is an Israelite about to leave the bondage of Egypt. While this was an historic event, the ceremony symbolises freeing oneself from being enslaved by the body's needs and the mind's conditioning in order to begin the long journey across the purifying desert of a psychological Sinai on the way to the Promised Land of the Spirit. Most festivals have this inner dimension which has been forgotten. (Passover plate, 19th century.)

was in fact the Pascal feast. To participate in either is to experience rebirth; one tradition seeing it as the resurrection of an individual, the other of a nation being reborn. Both in essence are saying the same thing as they speak of the promise of spiritual freedom after a period of physical bondage, as represented by Egypt and the taking of Jesus by the authorities. Viewed this way, one begins to perceive how those who designed these festivals tried to incorporate several levels into them.

A little reflection will reveal the same content and intention in either of the two stories. Both speak about preparation, trial, despair, doubt and the breakthrough experienced by anyone on the spiritual path. Both describe in detail the resistance of the world to anything new and the confrontation with the authorities of their time. Each celebration speaks of sacrifice and departure. Both Jew and Christian sense an anticipation of a new epoch, although few recognise what it really means. To the Kabbalist both festivals speak quite clearly about initiation and so to participate in an Easter or Passover service becomes, with perception, a deeply profound experience because it is more than just a celebration of what happened many centuries ago. It is what is occurring inwardly, in that very moment, that becomes significant.

The Kabbalist can relate to the whole annual round of Holy Days in this way as he or she moves through the rituals and prayers with a consciousness of their present reality. By this method the student can not only reflect upon his or her own spiritual situation but draw upon the vast collective experience held by the form of the festival. In this manner, it is possible to perceive the cosmic implication of the festival's function. You might for example, glimpse the juxtaposition of terrestrial and celestial forces and sense the state of mankind. You could, with sufficient perception, catch sight of the communal soul of that tradition and be shown its level of maturity. It is quite possible, for instance, to key into the life of the existing generation and see if it is waxing or waning or have an insight into the spiritual depth of individuals participating in the festival. This is the cosmic dimension.

As we can appreciate, there are many possibilities available whilst taking part in such activities. However, while you may draw from these great accumulators of spiritual power, you must also give back in return. Thus, the Kabbalist, in his public worship, tries to make an inner connection between Heaven and Earth. In this way, a channel is opened through which it is possible to bring down into the congregation present some of the spiritual substance accumulated over the centuries by the ceremony. If one is operating from Tiferet, then the flow will occur and, whilst no one else may notice it, the quality of the service will be raised, although some people might detect a slight change of atmosphere or a degree of purity present. They might even sense a certain severity, if it is needed, or a touch of loving-kindness should the service be too much on the Judgement side of the Tree. Whatever is required will, if the Kabbalist is in the correct state, be imparted from above.

The implication of this is that one may practise Kabbalah, which means 'to receive', in a public place. This is not only indeed so but is one of the main objectives of the Work, though it has to be done with tremendous discrimination and should not be attempted until the first stages of training are complete. However, it will be observed that descent of the spirit can occur quite spontaneously at baptisms, Bar Mitzvahs, weddings and funerals when a Kabbalist has become aware of an inner light beaming down upon those participating in the ceremony. If one is the fortunate agent of such Grace at that moment, then thanks should be given. Such events are not rare but they can only occur if the person is open, knows what is happening and can allow the transmission.

Returning again to the theme of festivals, it can be seen that much may be learnt from their essential content, provided one does not become lost in the detail. Every festival has its particular message and if studied and practised in the right way it will reveal many secrets embedded in it by its creators. Take, for example, the festival of All Saints in the autumn which celebrates the existence of those who have reached some degree of spirituality. This is quite different from All Souls who have not reached this level. Its purpose is the acknowledgement of an illustrious group of beings who may be seen as the Body of Christ or the House of Israel, the Blessed Ones or the Inner Council of Mankind according to the terms of your tradition. If one could be in the right state during a service dedicated to these great souls, then it might be possible to experience who and what they are. You might even be allowed to glimpse the world they live in and even become dimly aware of their task in the universe. During such a ceremony, contact might be made with your own particular inner teacher or at least with those in charge of your section. Thus, the festival is not just remembrance of their existence but a meeting place, in time, between us below and those above who are involved with the Work.

So the annual cycle of festivals is more than a round of traditional customs. They are the mark points of cosmic fluctuations within which rituals, devotion and contemplation are designed. For the Kabbalist they can also be a doorway into mystical experience as he uses the great physical, psychological and spiritual vehicles of these festivals to gain access to the Higher Worlds. Consider the millions of people round the world celebrating a New Year. Such a festival is quite a tangible construction whose approach and departure in time can be sensed like a great ship coming and then going. Festivals are massive temples in the World of Formation that are entered, at certain points of the year, by a mass of people, although they can be contemplated by a solitary mystic who may choose to go there at a less busy time. This leads us on to the notion that you may wander about and explore the inner Worlds at will, for perhaps by now you begin to perceive the reality of these subtler realms that permeate our fondly-imagined solid world. However, before proceeding further we must never forget to retain our contact with the mundane level of existence; for this reason it is good to adopt, as an anchor in life, some of the customs of our upbringing which keep us in touch with the Earth. For this reason, we will examine the seventh day or the Sabbath which marks the Malkhut of Creation when God rested and reflected on what had been done.

23. Sabbath

Resuming our progression up the Tree, let us blend the exoteric with the esoteric to perceive the bridge between the outer and inner aspects of a traditional celebration. The fourth commandment is that the Sabbath should be sanctified. This injunction comes between the commandments related to God and those related to human beings. It is indeed the point of interaction between the Divine and lower Worlds because it belongs to the first of what are called the seven lower sefirot of construction. In this arrangement it relates to Hesed or Loving-kindness and Mercy.

The Sabbath is a day of rest and reflection. On it, the committed Jew and Christian worship God in the three approaches of ritual, devotion and contemplation. The Kabbalist uses these same modes to enter the fourth condition, of mystical experience. In this way the orthodox form is used as a method by which one may enter the higher realms. In public worship, this is done by the various services held in the synagogue and church. However, very often the real level of these gatherings is usually not much higher than a social meeting with the spiritual element giving it an occasional touch of other-worldliness. For most people this is sufficient. To read from the scrolls of the Law, or to take communion, is often as much of a spiritual experience as most people want. To try to live by the precepts of tradition is also too much for many, for it is an enormous commitment that few can keep. The Kabbalist knows this from personal experience but strives, nevertheless, to meet the criteria of the Spirit although he may not be seen by the conventional as a good Jew or Christian.

Because of the difficult conditions found in church and synagogue, many mystics down the ages have held private Sabbath celebrations that run parallel to public worship. They may take place before or after the regular services in secluded rooms without the distractions of the usual places of gathering. Occasionally one reads of or hears about such a meeting of perhaps two or three people, although some Kabbalists prefer to celebrate the Sabbath in solitude. This does not mean that they are alone, by any means, because if they attain the

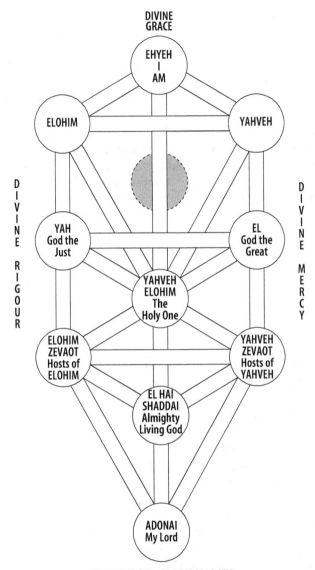

DIVINE
GRACE

EHYEH
I
AM

ELOHIM

YAHVEH

DIVINE RIGOUR

DIVINE MERCY

YAH
God the
Just

EL
God the
Great

YAHVEH
ELOHIM
The
Holy One

ELOHIM
ZEVAOT
Hosts of
ELOHIM

YAHVEH
ZEVAOT
Hosts of
YAHVEH

EL HAI
SHADDAI
Almighty
Living God

ADONAI
My Lord

FIGURE 25—HOLY NAMES
These may be used in meditation and contemplation, if it is remembered of Whom they speak. It was not forbidden to say them. The original injunction was that they must not be said in vain because at one time it was common to hear them used as a vulgar expletive, like 'Oh my God!' Spoken consciously, as a mantra, they give an insight to the particular sefirot to which they are related. The ultimate NAME is I AM THAT I AM. This is the SELF addressing the SELF. (Halevi, 20th century.)

inner levels of soul and Spirit they are connected inevitably with the beings operating on those planes. Here begins kabbalistic communication.

Let us imagine how such an individual might go about his Sabbath. Taking the bare essentials, we will follow a service through from its inception to its conclusion. Assuming that the normal ablutions have been carried out and the person is wearing fresh clothes, we would find him in a place especially dedicated to the purpose. This, as noted, could be a corner of a room where an altar has been erected which may consist of a pair of candlesticks or whatever symbol has significance to the worshipper. After a period of silence in which to bring the elemental body into equilibrium and the vegetable and animal soul under the will, the service is initiated by an invocation. This can be by the ascent of the Tree and the evocation of the Holy Names or by whatever formula awakens the person's being to the Higher Worlds. This could be followed by a deep and long silence.

The purpose of the silence is to bring into harmony all the disparate aspects of the psyche. Certain problems, for example, may be plaguing one. To set these aside takes a little time. Perhaps one is feeling in a particularly inappropriate mood or anticipating what is going to happen tomorrow. When these inner distractions have been reduced to the minimum, for they can never be totally eliminated, the Yesodic ego is given something to occupy its attention and draw it into the operation. This can be the repetition of a Divine Name, a prayer to move the heart or a kabbalistic idea to contemplate.

The sounding of a Holy Name such as 'the Living Almighty' is like a mantra. It should be spoken with great reverence with its reverberation penetrating throughout the body and psyche. It may be said aloud but only with the full awareness of Whom one is naming, respecting the commandment not to take the Lord's Name in vain or without consciousness. Indeed, we are told it gives great pleasure to the Divine to see the Name come into full manifestation, as it is the final part of the process of bringing Divinity into the physical world. It is the conscious realisation of I AM THAT I AM that enables Adam to help God to behold God.

The same can be said of any prayer touching the heart, like, 'Lord have mercy upon us'. Here, the love that is extended from above is returned from below by the devotee and thus there is a deeply emotional dialogue between creature and Creator. This analogy of lovers is common to many traditions, for it speaks of the profound interchange that can occur during devotion. To express love to God and know one is loved in return is to experience the greatest intimacy possible for, when people draw that close to the Divine, they are nearer to God than they are to themselves.

The act of contemplation can also stimulate a mystical experience. While pondering the verses on the death of Moses who was not allowed to enter the Promised Land, one might perceive how it is possible just to fall short of the mark. This could lead on to what might be impeding progress in one's own spiritual life, thence to a reflection upon a particular problem out of which arises a solution. Such an insight could remove the difficulty and allow a movement forward into a new space. This piercing of a veil can make us aware that Divinity is always present to aid us. Such an experience might last an instant but be recalled each time we read the passage which we had been contemplating that Sabbath.

The normal use of the Bible is traditional, the cycle of the scriptures being read in a weekly sequence. However, in Kabbalah, it may be applied in an unusual way, the portion to be examined depending on the Will of the Holy Spirit. After the invocation and a petition for guidance, the Kabbalist places himself in a deep state of receptivity, listening with great intent to what might be received from above. The Bible is then taken and opened at apparent random and the chapter presented read with infinite care. Often the content is directly relevant to the moment. Frequently, questions being posed at that time, such as 'Should I take such an action on a certain issue?' are answered and clarified by the text, either by the precise instruction of a verse or in the form of a parable that clearly relates to our situation. The lesson is then pondered so that further information may emerge out of what has been presented. Obviously, this mode of working requires enormous honesty to check any fantasy that may intrude to distort what has been given. If the reading is obscure at the time, then it should be held in the mind for the rest of the week until some event reveals its significance.

The final part of the Sabbath service is to return to silence after saying various prayers of praise or petition. These may be traditional or especially designed for that occasion. When they have been uttered, the Kabbalist then withdraws as deeply as possible into the Self and waits in a fully alert Tiferet before the door of Daat, the place of Knowledge. If nothing occurs this must be accepted. Should something happen the person may not know it has until the action is over, when he realises that he has been somewhere else other than where he is now. In this experience there is a moment of union, of knowing and of being known. It may be no more than a split second but it is quite distinctive and memorable, although nothing precise can be remembered of the moment. However, what is clear is that he was in touch with a Higher World.

Having completed the order of the service the Kabbalist then begins to return to the lower world of Action. This is accomplished by the acts of thanksgiving and descent of the Tree so as to bring consciousness down into the ego and body and so to the Earth. While such a Sabbath can be made more simple or elaborate, what must be remembered is that it will only be effective if the *Kavvanah* or intention is correct. No amount of ritual, prayer or contemplation will bring down the Holy Spirit if the person is not truly receptive; and this, it will be recalled, is the root meaning of the word Kabbalah. Having outlined some of the routine and cyclic exercises of the tradition, let us now examine a technique that can be used occasionally for gathering information from beyond the threshold of ordinary consciousness.

24. *Journey*

So far we have seen how an individual can use various methods to move from Malkhutian body consciousness up to the Tiferet of the self. We have been shown how this is done by private work and the use of public occasions. Most of what has been discussed has been preparation but now we may begin to perceive how everything is moving towards generating an inner vessel. This interior vehicle is strengthened by constant practice and study of Kabbalah. After a while, things that were previously not possible, like insights into the upper Worlds, begin to be received from above because there is now an instrument within the psyche by which one can examine what has, up to now, remained hidden.

The following method shows how this growing faculty may be developed and used in determining one's state or anything else that may be relevant that is within range of the study. The technique can be done within a group or practised in private. As before, it requires an experienced guide to lead the student and a place where he will not be disturbed. Let us assume that these conditions have been obtained, that the Tree has been evoked and permission from on High has been granted. After a pause to accustom the body and psyche to the situation, the guide then proceeds roughly in the following manner.

First the student is asked if he is in a state of readiness. This the student checks, observing, from the position of the inner Watcher of Tiferet, the routine processes of body and mind. On declaring readiness, the guide then asks the student to imagine himself standing up and going out of the room. This the student does by projecting, in imagination, what will be observed on leaving the room, and a position is taken up outside the house. The scene is then visualised in great detail as the prevailing conditions are examined and perceived by the extended senses. The voyager then moves on out of sensual range into pure imagination. Here memory of the locality is brought fully into action as consciousness shifts out of direct contact with the Malkhutian body and into strictly Yesodic imagery. The guide then instructs the student to leave the immediate area and travel out into the countryside.

This is done, the student still observing a recognisable landscape as he moves by memory along a familiar highway.

The student is then asked to turn off into a side lane and go to a wood that is quite unknown. Having entered it, he goes right into its depths where there is no sight or sound of the modern world. After a long pause to adjust and to appreciate the place, he is then asked to proceed to the very centre of the wood. Here there is a clearing where the traveller is to rest because it is late and growing dark. After a short sleep he is told to wake up. If he is sufficiently absorbed in the situation and responds to direction without being distracted, then consciousness has crossed the first threshold into his inner world and the next stage can proceed.

On awakening in the clearing, the traveller is told to find that it is quite dark. The stars can be seen above and the Moon is just rising. Nearby, there is a horse eating grass. The traveller observes that he is wearing different clothes. These might be of any style or period. It does not matter at this point. As dawn breaks, he mounts the horse and rides out of the wood and into the nearest town. Here, he discovers a city that is like no other ever seen. It is both strange and familiar. All the people in the streets look at the traveller with recognition. The traveller knows some of them well but most are only vaguely familiar or total strangers. As he rides along the streets and passes the various private and public buildings their condition is noted and a series of questions is asked to ascertain the state of the town, such as, 'Is it happy? If not, why not?' Moving on, the traveller leaves the town, although some of the inhabitants accompany him to the town's limit. The dress and manner of these followers should be noted.

After an eventful day's ride across grass, desert and marsh, the sea is reached. There on the beach the traveller is told to rest and sleep a deep sleep in which a strange dream occurs. This, like all unusual events, should be noted for analysis later. In the morning a boat is found riding at anchor just off shore. It is waiting for the traveller. He leaves the horse to grass and goes out to the boat but not before having a good look at it to see what kind of vessel it is, what condition it is in and to record its name. Once on board the crew appear. Mark each of them. Your life may depend on their skill. Walk round the decks and examine the boat from above and below. What does it carry for cargo? The guide should be by now no more than a voice.

Find the captain's cabin. Is he/she there? If so, what is she/he like? Note that the boat has now set sail. Go up on deck and watch the land slip away. Observe the state of the sea and how the boat is handled. At first all is calm but soon a squall comes up and then a full-blown gale. How do you react? How does the captain respond and the crew perform as all around the sea boils and lightning and heavy rain split and blur the sky? Observe everything. Note areas of stress and strength. Time passes. The storm begins to abate. The sky clears and the sea becomes calm. As the boat and crew recover equilibrium, record any damage. Land is seen. The captain directs the helmsman as the boat moves towards a port. The boat approaches the harbour but does not tie up. Instead, it lies just off shore whilst you look through a telescope the captain has given you. Gather what you can about this far country. It is another world. Note how the buildings are not like any others on Earth, nor are the people. Just as you begin to react to the nature of this strange land, the captain orders the boat to weigh anchor and return home.

The student, still deep in this guided imagination, is then brought back across the sea, taking note all the time of what is happening, until the home shore is reached. There the boat is left and the horse-ride back across the country to the town is re-experienced, noting if there are any differences in the landscape or the traveller. On reaching the town he observes any changes there, especially in the attitude of the townspeople. When the traveller returns to the wood, dusk is falling. As the Sun sets he dismounts and lies down to· rest. After a night's sleep, he awakens and realises that his original clothes have been restored. He then sets out for home, leaving the wood for the familiar countryside before returning to the house and room that the operation is taking place in. Here he is brought back into physical consciousness by coming down the Tree and stamping the feet. After a suitable pause, the debriefing can begin.

As should have been gathered, the journey relates to various levels with each stage and symbol containing much information about one's inner condition. The first shift occurs in the wood where one is lifted out of the physical realm by entering an unfamiliar clearing. The wood is the vegetable principle and the horse the animal soul. The sleep, night sky and Moon induce and evoke the experience of entering into the realm of Yesod and the unconscious. The journey out of the wood and into the town take one deeper into the psyche where the town and its inhabitants tell one much about the state of the psychological organism and the various sub-personalities that govern our inner life. The few townspeople, that is interested aspects, who follow one out are aids or hindrances to development whilst the cross-country ride is the inner terrain we have to traverse in order to reach the threshold of the deep emotional level, represented by the sea. Here the style of boat and its condition give us some idea of our capacity to move in that world and the crew the emotional complexes that make or mar the boat's performance. The captain, if there is one, can be seen as the inner guide whose way of dealing with the storm indicates what to expect when confronted with a crisis of the first order. The distant shore is the deepest part of the psyche that is rarely experienced, except in illumination. Here, the dream that might have revealed some insight while one was asleep on the sea-shore may be related to what was consciously seen of the strange port from the boat. All the information gathered about the people and buildings at this entrance to the unconscious should be considered as a glimpse into the higher levels of the psyche, which act as the frontier and veil to the hinterland of the World of the Spirit.

Much prudence must be exercised in the analysis of the data revealed in the imagery. At first one should simply note what occurred without comment. Later, in discussion, one may begin to perceive the various levels and differentiate between mundane imagining and real vision. This takes time and practice. One should consider each element of the account and relate it to what one actually knows about oneself or, if one is the guide, about the student, although there must be no interference with his conviction if he judges it to be the one thing and you another. People must teach themselves with the minimum of projection from the instructor. Further detail can be added by returning to certain points in the journey and re-creating the situation, so as to get a higher resolution of image to interpret from. After the debriefing has made some sort of sense, the student should then write out a report whilst it is still fresh and file it for further reference and reflection. The operation could be repeated from time to time and later, under strict self-discipline, may be done on his own.

The foregoing technique is an ancient one, illustrating how to exploit Yesod's capacity to act as the non-luminous mirror of the psyche. In this case the range has been extended a little beyond the extent of our first exercise. In skilled and intelligent hands it is a fine instrument and can be developed so as to be able to penetrate to all but the highest level of the psyche. However, it must be used sparingly, otherwise conscious imagination turns into uncontrolled fantasy which is far from the objective of Kabbalah. The line between the mystic visionary and the mad is not, as generally believed, very small. There is a wide gap defined by great discipline and a definite aim, ordered knowledge and self-command. The lunatic may see impressive images of truth but these are usually tainted or distorted by ego-oriented fantasies and dreams. The Kabbalist does not seek the grandiose but the essence of what is embodied in these visions. Therefore the student relates all that has been seen to the Tree and its laws. If one knows it well, then each element of the journey will identify itself quickly and many puzzling things will fall into place. To illustrate this point, let us explore one of the most important factors in our journey, so as to interpret it in greater detail. In the next chapter we will look at the captain as the symbol of the first stage of selfhood that brings one into contact with the Inner Teacher.

FIGURE 26—INNER TEACHER
*This figure can be seen as either the Self of the Kabbalist, that is the Tiferet of
the psyche, or what is called one's* maggid, *or guardian angel in some traditions.
The former is at the pivotal point of the mind, the head of the body Tree and the
bottom of the Tree of the Spirit. In some cases, a maggid is a discarnate tutor
for someone of special merit who has a mission to carry out on Earth.* (Woodcut
of Rabbi Akiba, 16th century.)

25. Captain

The notion of an inner teacher is not strange to Kabbalah. Many Kabbalists down the centuries have spoken of their *maggid* or celestial instructor. Sometimes the teacher has just been a voice, like the mentor of the great Safed Kabbalist, Joseph Karo, and sometimes they have been figures visible to the eye, like the maggid of the Gaon of Vilna who was once seen by two students through a window but not to be found with the rabbi when they entered his study. More often than not it is an inner instructor who directs the Kabbalist—when it is needed— and advises on matters that the Kabbalist cannot read about or have access to on Earth. Legends say that the greatest Kabbalists were taught by Elijah himself who is responsible for the spiritual direction of the Tradition. Other stories tell us that Elijah not only turns up in many disguises to aid those on the inner path but manifests as the *Khidr* or 'the Green One', in the Sufi tradition, where he performs the same role. According to folklore Elijah had neither father nor mother, like Melchizedek who initiated Abraham at the beginning of the tradition. All this suggest that other strange characters, like Hermes Trismegistus and Thoth, were none other than Enoch, the Initiated, the first fully realised human being, but in different forms.

For ordinary people the likelihood of being taught by the highest teacher is remote, although many just beginning spiritual work often want nothing less. This is due either to innocence or ambition. If it were to happen, then all the power and responsibility that goes with it would crush or explode the student. The spiritual cyclist, however skilful, is not ready to pilot the supersonic jets of Heaven, although many dream they can. This is a Yesodic illusion, as are many fantasies about instruction coming from the upper Worlds. That is why such communications must be tested and approached with prudence, by dealing with the phenomenon of inner signals in stages so that the student becomes familiar with what is happening and can deal with it.

The first stage is to learn how to discriminate between different levels. For example the voice of the body, which has a distinct character, must be distinguished from the voice of the ego which can adopt many disguises in order to get its way. Then one has to develop an ear for intruding intelligences that sometimes whisper or call from the sidelines. These can be either very crude or extremely subtle. They are to be recognised and then ignored. Also to be recognised are the various negative aspects of one's own psyche, like certain memories that warn or encourage or particular ideas that thrust and weedle their biased views into the consciousness. These may be from the distant past or a current opinion that can taint a real experience. The psyche has many such voices; some are obvious and others hardly noticeable and yet more powerful than can be imagined. The archetypal principles, for instance, that embody the sefirot are extremely potent. These, when out of balance, can often distort a truth. The Trickster of Hod is a prime example. This clever function can easily cloud the most lucid inner instruction by a brilliant quotation of something it has read but never understood. Many insights have been drowned in this way.

The most interesting archetype from the point of view of this chapter is the Inner Teacher who resides at the centre of the Tree at Tiferet. Called the Seat of Solomon, this sefirah is the focal point of many paths and triads. As the place of the self, it occupies the position of being the most directly informed focus in the psyche, for it perceives the Worlds below and has access to those above. It connects with nearly all the sefirot of the Tree and has direct contact with the individual and collective unconscious, as well as the soul and the Spirit. It is, therefore, the most qualified sefirah in terms of all round experience. As such it operates as the Inner Teacher.

In the guided inner journey of the last chapter the boat on the sea may be regarded as the vessel by which consciousness negotiates the volatile waters of the psyche. As we saw, the captain can be understood to be the one who knows the ways of the sea and how to handle the boat in difficult times. If we reflect on how the boat was managed during the storm, as well as all the finer points of seamanship throughout the voyage, we may catch a glimpse of the nature of our own Inner Teacher.

To develop this further, it is possible to go back, after invoking the Tree and asking permission, to look at the captain and his/her cabin in greater detail. One might, for example, scrutinise more carefully the captain's face for clues as to his/her order of intelligence. It may be a mask or wise old man or woman; or a countenance that does not belong to this world at all. The captain could turn out to be an experienced but drunken sailor which would suggest that perhaps there is more Grace than Judgement watching over us. In some cases there is no captain which might indicate that no direct relation with the self is apparent. Observation of the captain's uniform and its condition could be highly informative. A slapdash skipper would reveal much, as would an impeccable naval officer. One might find one has a clever pirate which suggests some liaison with the Lucifer principle. Such contacts are quite capable of influencing the captain of some people's ships at certain crisis points in their development. The story of Faust tells this tale.

As one can see, much can be learned from this exercise about the situation and state of the Self. Here it must be understood that the Self is made up of three components. The lowest is the Keter or Crown of the body. This level is very susceptible to self-glory, if there is great physical vitality. The second level is the psychological, whose subtle versatility is tested and tempted by powerful forces within and without the psyche until it can maintain a stability even in the gravest crisis. This is the aspect we are examining at the moment. The highest facet of the Self is the lowest part or Malkhut of the Spirit. Here is the true supervisor of the lower levels who slowly emerges into our experience as our mentor and friend.

The image of our captain tells us much about self image. It also gives us the opportunity to redress any imbalance we observe on board the ship. For example, suppose discipline amongst the crew is slipshod it is possible, by an act of conscious imagination, to alter the situation. This action will correct the discrepancy at the psychological level and it should follow, if the intention is genuine, that one's inner performance will improve. Here we are applying the tool of symbol in reverse. That is, instead of being receptive to what is being said the process is turned round in a conscious act which can affect the as-yet unconscious part of our psyche. This, of course, must only be done in self-evident cases of neglect or rebelliousness.

In the early stages of spiritual work very little is known about the workings of the psyche and, indeed, many avoid this area because it is too fraught with trouble, pain and conflict to be dealt with directly. Now, while an excessive preoccupation with one's psychological anatomy is as unhealthy as hypochondria, a certain amount of work has to be done. This is because there are, in all of us, certain imbalances due to genetics, environment, fate and karma. These problems cannot and should not be avoided because they contain vital lessons for our development. Conscious reflection on the ways of the psyche under skilled instruction is necessary and here the foregoing exercise is most useful. As time goes on, the unconscious becomes illuminated and converted into consciousness. This is done by relating one's life to both external and internal work. The workings of the psyche can be seen by introspective analysis or external conditions. Both reflect our problems and their solutions in our relationship to life and the Work. However, before you apply the technique described, you must know what you are about or more harm than good will be done. In order not to interfere with normal psychological processes, you should consult either your outer instructor for advice or contact the Inner Teacher, deep in the unconscious.

In order to be able to do this much practice must be carried out in the active imagination. Many sessions have to be experienced before beginning to form a clear idea about the various levels and aspects of the body and the psyche. As a precaution, while you should note everything that happens, you should not act on everything that is suggested unless its message makes sense or the truth of it is obvious. It is a mistake to be lured beyond one's capacity or attempt an impossible suggestion. Some people become over enthusiastic with their first inner instructions and imagine that they are in contact with the highest beings. It must be remembered that we are still working at a relatively low level and demonic elements like to interfere, especially when the person does not know friend from foe. Therefore, in the next exercise we will set out a ritual so as to avoid unwelcome intrusion and so go directly to our Inner Teacher. Even our captain could be a disguised member of the opposition, in the same way that some gurus are wolves in sheep's clothing.

26. Inner Teacher

In this exercise we intend to penetrate deeper. Therefore our preparations must be increasingly thorough. This does not imply that they should be elaborate but that the intention has more to it than just to explore the inner regions of our psyche or the upper Worlds. We have to have a specific reason. This means that our aim is to be more limited with greater focus of power. Here we begin to understand the dynamics of our consciousness for if we take the traditional symbol of light we can see how a narrower beam produces greater intensity and deeper penetration. Such a beam of consciousness can be obtained by giving the structure and dynamics of the exercise a tighter form.

The mode of generating such an inner laser beam is first of all to set out the aim of the operation. Up till now we have simply observed the inner realms and noted what we have seen. In this case we formulate a definite objective. Here it can be a question that has not been answered by the usual means. It might be about some metaphysical problem or something related to our lives. It could be about correct personal conduct or the solution to a current issue. It certainly has to be a question of some gravity. No trivial matter should be considered for not only will this bar access to the Inner Teacher but it will devalue the exercise for future use; and one of the objectives of the exercise is to build up a contact that can be used periodically for the rest of our lives.

Having formulated a question, we then proceed to prepare for the inner ascent. This is carried out in the suggested way of ablution and evocation of the Tree. Initially it is best done with a tutor or trusted companion under instruction. This is advisable because an inexperienced student could be panicked if led off course or faulted in procedure. The operation should take place in a dedicated space, so that no unwelcome visitors of any World are likely to interfere. By this time you should have some ceremonial symbol to wear during such sessions. As we have suggested, this could be anything from a complete traditional outfit to a simple object hung round the neck. This is a reminder to the body and lower psyche that you are about to enter another dimension. To add weight to the occasion, you can, by an act of imagination, don a ceremonial robe of your own design. This might be a cloak or some all-enveloping garment which evokes the three traditional sacred prerequisites of devotion, purity and sincerity. The colours could be purple and blue, according to the Book of Exodus, with red and white representing the lowest and highest Worlds.

The function of these interior robes, based on the priestly raiment, is to enclose and protect their wearer as well as act as the symbol of the higher bodies we all possess but of which we do not, as yet, have conscious knowledge. In most people these inner bodies are very under developed, so that only a vague sense of their presence is perceived. Here the garments are used to enhance the Kabbalist's awareness of these levels, so making for greater sensitivity. Like a physical equivalent, much thought and work must go into the design of such vestments. The more refined they are, the subtler the receptivity of the person who wears them because the creation and formation of these symbols affect the higher vehicles they represent.

Having dressed for the occasion you now make yourselves ready for the action. First you ask permission from the Most High; if this is given by the inner voice or a sign, the mission proceeds. You begin the ascent in total silence for a few moments. When the sense of a door being opened is experienced, you then approach the threshold of normal awareness. This position is held for a moment before stepping into the realm of conscious imagination. From here you start to ascend, going first to a place above where you are physically. After looking down on the landscape as if it were at the bottom of the sea, you gaze upward so as to perceive reality in a different way. In this state you convert the winds into watery currents, swirling about and rising and falling above and below. Ignoring anything that might appear to be nosing about in these depths, you rise up towards the light filtering down from the distant surface high above. Ascending by degrees you float up through the various levels of lessening density, looking neither to left nor right, although you might see out of the corner of the mind's eye all sorts of intriguing sights. Just below the surface you stop and float for a moment with it just above the head. You do not look back down into the depths but keep the gaze only on the veiled light beyond the waves. From here it can be seen more clearly than ever experienced in the World below.

On breaking the surface of the sea of Yezirah you take a deep breath of Beriatic air and see a landscape of quite another world. It is cosmic in appearance. As you swim ashore, vast mountains can be seen with one particularly tall peak in their midst, upon which a jewel of a city can be made out. Clambering up onto the shore, you rest a while to dry out your garments which takes no time in the fresh and clear atmosphere of the place. Before setting off inland, look back at the sea and see how moody it is. On the surface it looks calm but there is much turbulence deep down. You move on, away from the shore and begin to climb up the foothills of the great range. After picking a way over several ridges and along some valleys, you become aware of beings that watch your progress, although you may or may not see them. You do not bother to find out what they are because your attention is caught by the sight of a beautiful building on the crest of a high hill. It is clearly the home of some holy person because it emanates light and peace. You climb up to it by a path that has obviously been used by others and approach the place. You open the gate and enter, taking note of all that is to be seen in the garden as you come up to the door and knock.

After a moment's pause in which to make ready to meet your Inner Teacher, the door opens and there stands a being with deeply penetrating yet kindly eyes. You are greeted and invited in. Let nothing be missed, be on the maximum alert as you are led into an upper room. Before sitting down opposite your interior mentor, look around and take note of everything in the room. If asked a question, reply with courtesy but no fear. When the moment is right, ask the main question you have been holding. Listen for the answer. It will be given. If other questions arise, keep asking again and again until it is indicated that the conversation is over. Having received all that you can, ask what you can do in return. Take note of what is said and carry out whatever you have been instructed to do, there or elsewhere, when the time comes. At a certain moment the meeting will be clearly over. After paying respect to your spiritual superior, retire graciously after asking permission to visit again. This might or might not be granted. Take your leave at the door of the house and, after seeing it shut, start down the hill to the seashore.

On gaining the shore, reflect for a moment on what has happened and look towards the distant city on the mountain top. One day you may go there. Then turn your back on the scene and, with gaze fixed on the sky above, walk into the sea and allow the waves to break over your head. Begin to swim. Diving down and away from the surface, sink into the depths until you come to just above the bottom. Float there for a moment and sense the weight, pressure and flow of this ocean of the psyche. Again ignore whatever creatures might approach you, and convert the water back into air and the image of yourself hovering above the local landscape. Observe the sights and sounds of the neighbourhood, descend to the house and into the room where you are seated. Thank the Holy One for what was given and come down the Tree to Malkhut. Let the inner robes remain. They will dissolve of their own accord until they become a permanent feature of your interior world. Stamp your feet and enter life at the ordinary level. Relax and reflect.

During the debriefing note down all the questions asked and the answers given in a book especially devoted to the purpose. This must be done first. Then reflect on what was observed about the Teacher and the upper room. Do a drawing of the place adding, even if later, details missed while debriefing. Recall the books and symbols about the place, the robes worn and any other unusual features of the room or person. Some of these might be recognised or need to be researched so as to identify their meaning or connection with another time and place. These can be useful clues into one's own history, which leads us on to the next exercise of distant memory. But first we must tie up our present exercise by saying that if you are invited to return by the Teacher, then do not neglect to renew the contact because it is easily lost. After a series of such sessions, stretching over several years, you will eventually be able to go there almost directly and speak with your mentor.

27. Memories

In Kabbalah the concept of transmigration or reincarnation is accepted. Known in Hebrew as the process of *Gilgulim* or Wheels, it means the repeated turnings of rebirth. It is referred to in the *Zohar*, the great Kabbalistic classic of the Middle Ages, and frequently mentioned by Kabbalists in 16th century Palestine. The idea of recurring lives was dropped in later times as Kabbalah became regarded, by Western-educated Jews, as irrational and fell into disrepute. Nevertheless, whilst cultural patterns may change, the laws of the universe do not. Therefore we take into account the notion of a chain of lives in order to understand our present fate and what our spiritual work might be. This past can be explored by the imaginative technique under kabbalistic supervision and so give insights into our personal destiny.

All of us have memories. Indeed, one exercise is to recall our earliest moments of consciousness, so as to recapture the flavour of our Tiferet view of the world before the ego of Yesod was clouded over by education. These moments are a clue to our nature and the things to which we can relate. Some individuals, for example, connect with places and others with people while others are aware of small things and others the large. A collection of these memories can give a very clear picture of our fate and its development. It is the same when carrying out a similar exercise in terms of previous lives.

One often hears about people who feel that they lived in ancient Egypt or were certain great personages in history. This may be so but it is more likely that it is an identification or association based on a need to be different, especially in an area where nothing can be proved, and it carries a certain romantic charisma. If it were true, then more often than not the person will never speak of the matter because it is too precious a realisation to be worn as an ornament by the ego. As to the notion of memories of several former lives; this might be considered if one accepts that a soul can remember remarkable moments in the same way that one recalls certain days. Life for many individuals is a routine of seeking security, food and relationships against a background of general circumstances that, for most people,

FIGURE 27—PAST LIVES

Some people have an affinity with a specific country or period in history. This is sometimes due to a dim memory of having lived there in another life. Certain individuals have a quite sharp recollection of the place and period in great detail. Yet others have a strong desire to go to India, China or Spain to find out they know not what. This impulse may be due to an important event in an earlier life or the need to further their development. Spain was an important centre for Kabbalah in the Middle Ages and stirs the memory of many Kabbalists. (Toledo, 19th century engraving.)

does not become notable unless there is intense suffering, deep love or a glimpse of higher things which leave a trace in the psyche. These moments are the memories that people dimly recall when they visit certain old places or see historical objects. An individual who, for example, actually remembers the plan of a vanished town quite clearly is recalling a deeply etched memory that has not been erased by the post-mortem process of death. A long or dramatic life in that place has left its mark on the soul.

If we accept the teaching that the soul has passed through more than one body, we can see how those who were incarnated many millennia ago might have matured over many lives to become old souls, as against young ones who have only been on Earth a few times. These older souls, moreover, like the elders of any generation would become more pronounced in character and will, according to their inclination and development. Thus the wise and good may influence the inner lives of their contemporaries while the clever but evil old souls dominate external history. Younger souls, in contrast, are innocent and less marked in character and fate, as they grope their way through life. This tells us much about the composition and state of the world population. In earlier times the number of mature souls would be small although, we are told, on account of the primitive conditions on Earth, these were of especially high calibre, such as the prophets who chose to remain below rather than ascend to spiritual regions of existence. This might explain the remarkable level of esoteric knowledge to be found amid the wide ignorance and extensive violence of the ancient world, for there was as yet no middle management of the spiritually-oriented.

In order to find out how we might fit into this scheme, let us begin by reflecting on the memories behind our consciousness. This deep stratum is generally only accessible in moments of heightened consciousness or by seeing and being in a situation that seems strangely familiar. This can occur in certain fatal meetings. It is almost as if one was being reminded of some incident involving them but long ago. Sometimes very powerful emotions of fear or love are evoked in such encounters. These incidents should be noted and collected. When enough have been gathered together, a common quality will often emerge. Take, for example, people with whom we fall in love or have as constant friends. They will nearly all share the same characteristics. While this may be seen as the attraction to certain types, there is often a sense of mutual recognition that forms a deep connection in which some unfinished business is worked out over months or a lifetime. Here is the law of karma reminding one of previous relationships in another time and place.

As regards places, a book about some remote country can spark off a strange yearning or instant interest to find out more about the area and its history. Take the example of people who feel at home in particular cities and find they know their way round even though they have never been to them in that lifetime. While most people regard this phenomenon as just odd, the Kabbalist sees it as a window into a past life. However, if it is treated as no more than flicking through an album out of curiosity then it is of no real use. By this it is meant that the significance of these ancient memories is lost and an important aid to inner development wasted, because if one knew why one remembered them, then some vital clue about one's present life could be gained. Let us make an imaginary investigation into such an example so as to learn what we can about it.

Suppose a man had the experience of being profoundly moved as a boy by seeing a picture of Toledo, the old capital of Castile, in an encyclopedia. He does not know why, except that he knows that he must go there one day. Later as a student he visits the city and finds it strangely familiar. This perplexes him. He recalls the picture but this does not explain the sense of coming home. Some years afterwards he enters a Kabbalah group and is put through the following exercise aimed at opening up a door into his deep memory.

Led by his instructor he is asked, after the ritual of evoking the Tree, to go deep in memory and imagine a room. This he does, exploring with the mind's eye the floor, walls and furniture. He then goes on to describe what he can see, with remarkable clarity, outside the window. Fine details of what the streets are like emerge, so that gradually a picture is built up of a town that is obviously Toledo. Now while this could be ordinary memory, the period seen is not today but the 13th century, for the people in the streets are wearing medieval dress. Later in the visualisation he sees a group of Jews in deep meditation and study in a house in the Juderia. They are obviously Kabbalists. Subsequent research and another visit to the town reveals that it was indeed a kabbalistic centre at that time and that he, unknown until then, had Spanish Jewish ancestry. As he wanders about the narrow lanes of the ancient Jewish quarter he finds that he is conscious of specific Kabbalists who lived there. One name in particular recurs and this man's work relates to his own

FIGURE 28—RECOGNITION
On visiting the place to which one has a strong connection, the sense of familiarity
can be overwhelming. Memories of how it was centuries before can come flooding
back. One knows what is to be seen around the next corner and, in some cases,
a vision of long-dead people and particular individuals may be seen. This usually
occurs at a crucial turning point in spiritual development and confirms what
one's destiny might be. (Gate of the Sun, Toledo. Doré engraving, 19th century.)

view. This gives the student an extraordinary sense of being among companions.*

Such an insight not only relates the individual to his past but grants access to knowledge that no learned thesis on Spanish Kabbalah could provide. Thus a link with the chain of the tradition is established between the student and the group of souls with which he has been working over the centuries. The implication of this is enormous because it reveals the scale and depth of the Work which transcends physical time and space.

Naturally, everything seen in the visualisation must be checked as far as it can be to see that it is not romanticising. Often confirmation of the material received comes unexpectedly like a sketch, made during a session, of an unvisited city matching a photograph obtained later. Sometimes places are so well described that someone who knows the site will recognise it and confirm some pertinent detail.

Arising out of such sessions can come the identity of one's spiritual supervisor. This may be someone with whom one has worked in the past. Hints on his identity are sometimes indicated, in that a name persistently crops up in conversation, books, dreams and even a magazine. One must, of course, check that fantasy has not taken over before accepting anything as valid. If an identity does present itself then only facts, as yet unknown, can verify the credibility of the phenomenon. If these emerge within a short time, like finding out the place of birth of such a person by a series of coincidences, then it can be taken seriously. Even then, one must regard such identities with discrimination for there are beings in the invisible realms who like to mislead. Always consider any information given with great caution and act upon it only if it makes sense and fits into the larger scheme.

All the foregoing of course lends itself to delusion. This is why it has rarely been written about. Many people today are using the same technique of guided imagination in psychological work but, without the grand design, it can lead to much confusion. Therefore we speak here from the Kabbalist viewpoint, so as to make a clear distinction between different disciplines that use the same process. What is laid out in this chapter is a blend of the psychic and spiritual, held and checked by the practical, that is a combination of the three lower Worlds. This is made possible by evoking the Tree and asking permission of the Holy One. If the moment or the motivation is not

---

*This incident was in fact the author's experience.

right, then the operation is not permitted to proceed. The practice of this principle is essential in all kabbalistic work which takes one out of contact with the physical world. No one with neurotic or psychotic tendencies should be allowed to take part in these operations, as it will enhance their malady. That is why Kabbalah was restricted to the mature. We apply this balance by returning to look at daily life, so as to remain well grounded whilst still progressing up the Tree.

28. *Daily Life*

One of the most important kabbalistic exercises is to be aware all the time. This means to be constantly watchful, that is to be operating not from the ordinary consciousness of the Yesodic ego but from the Self of Tiferet. This is no easy matter, as distractions from within and without constantly draw the attention away from being in the Seat of Solomon. However you must persist, so that gradually such a degree of consciousness is maintained that nothing significant is missed in either the upper or lower Worlds. This practice is vital in that it enables you to perceive the reality of any situation and, perhaps, be of use in the transmission of higher influences to the Earth. However, before this can be done with any real effect you must be able to enter the state of *Gadlut* at will.

As we discussed earlier there are two basic states common to most of us; the *Katnut* or Yesodic consciousness and the *Gadlut* or greater condition. The latter is attained by Grace or deliberate effort to hold this position. It is done by incessant practice which alerts the Hod-Tiferet-Nezah triad of awakening. Here, the individual experiences a keenness of the senses and a lucidity of psychological awareness that can detect not only what is going on inside oneself but often in others. Such a condition should eventually become the norm in everyday life for the Kabbalist. This is essential because it allows a link between Heaven and Earth to be established within the individual which can be of use in the outer world.

The application of the awakened state is that one watches life without interfering in the normal Yesodic process unless necessary. From this point of view, many things can be seen that are normally unnoticed. For example, one's own and other's unconscious motivations become apparent and so do trends, such as community tension, that are often only recognised as dangerous when it is too late and there is a riot. Besides the utilitarian function of a higher degree of consciousness than the ego, much can be learnt about one's own unconscious character. If you take each day as a microcosm of your life, many things emerge to surprise, please and displease. For example, you will

FIGURE 29—LIFE
The everyday world does not change much in time and place. The same patterns of livelihood, relationships and achievement face everyone. Life is seen by Kabbalists as a workshop of the soul and spirit as well as a physical activity. When and wherever you are born, that is the best place to learn the lesson of your particular fate. Karma, or 'Measure for Measure' as it is called in Kabbalah, is the result of your performance in other lives. The art is to live as consciously as you can, observing and transforming your being in the midst of the hurly-burly of living. (London, Doré engraving, 19th century.)

observe certain parental attitudes that you acquired during early upbringing and how they colour and often distort your view of others. You may also note that there are particular ideas that dominate you without your knowledge, like not trusting, which may come from some long forgotten personal experience or some notion imbibed from your culture which inhibits social or racial intercourse. These are the more obvious things to detect. A little deeper observation carried out over some time will reveal many other unconscious attitudes that govern our lives. Indeed, we learn that there is a massive set of emotive and conceptual complexes that rules us without our knowledge.

The identification and modification of such unseen, deeply hidden attitudes, emotional responses and reflex actions is part of the process of self-perfection. Indeed, becoming acquainted with these unconscious aspects of one's nature is just as important as learning about the remote past or what the higher realms are like. In fact much of the Work will be to deal with this level as you operate within the pressures of the collective unconscious. Therefore the cleaning and polishing of the two mirrors of the ego and self is essential, so that they may reflect, without blemish or distortion, a true picture of the world and the light that shines down from above.

The daily exercise of direct contact with ordinary life is absolutely necessary because it completes the octave of the Tree that stretches from Keter the Crown to Malkhut the Kingdom. Without this link with the mundane nothing real can happen, for the flow is incomplete and any good impulse remains only in Yesodic imagination. Thus, one must be fully present at work and play, during serious and amusing moments, social occasions and whilst alone or even making love. There is no time when you should not be present, observing and reflecting on what is going on within and without. In this way you begin to realise that you are always being watched, if not by your mentor then that other deeper self which is always present, although you may forget it.

To live one's daily life like this is not easy. It doubles the burden of living. However, there are benefits far beyond the effort put in. Not only do you start to appreciate life more but you perceive the rhythms of existence. This gives you the knowledge of when to act, because you will recognise the right moment and not make effort when the tide is flowing the wrong way. It allows you to see the pattern of your life and know what is advantageous and what is detrimental. This is what the Chinese call 'Moving with the Tao'. In kabbalistic terms it means shifting with the balance of the Tree of Creation as it alternates its emphasis within the three pillars. At one point, for example, the stress of a situation might be on Severity and therefore great restraint may be required. At another stage the pillar of Mercy might be active, and so all effort is devoted to exploiting the process of expansion, while at another time the middle pillar of Clemency might be operational and so the individual waits to see which side is to become prominent before moving.

The foregoing principles can be applied to a personal or a general situation. There may be a time, for instance, when certain important decisions have to be made about leaving a job. If the conditions are seen from the Gadlut state, then the possibilities open or closed will become self-evident and one will respond accordingly. If the trend is Gevuric or curtailing, it should be acknowledged and accepted unless a confrontation is right and will achieve its objective. Here is real Judgement. On the other hand, it may be a period when Hesed brings abundance and one should make hay while the sun shines, before the opposite pillar reverses the tide. The Kabbalist may also observe current affairs in this way, identifying certain tendencies long before the media or economic and political commentators notice it. For example, often the most sensitive or intelligent members of a community recognise quite early on the dangers of a situation in a country. This happened in Germany when certain Jews left long before the Second World War. It is interesting to note that many Kabbalists left Spain some time before the great expulsion of 1492. They could not only see what was to happen but took precautions so as to preserve the tradition which we now inherit.

Self-observation in everyday life not only earths you but serves as the working method in the market place of the world. While private study and secluded group practice are important, much effort has to be made under the conditions of mundane reality. Here, there are no special concessions, no tutor to keep an eye on one, no sympathetic companions or carefully tailored conditions. It is as it is and this is how life, for most of us, has to be dealt with. If you cannot manage the ordinary problems of living, then Kabbalah is not for you. There has to be a good level of competence and a familiarity with things of this world or what is brought down from the higher realms will never come into manifestation. If you have not one real skill then you cannot transmit the teaching or communicate the essence of what Kabbalah is about. You must be effective in life, even if it is only some small ability that allows the expression of what you are working towards. You need not be the master of a profession because you can be an excellent servant. To know how to sweep the floor with consciousness, as one rabbi did while he contemplated the universe, is as valid as the captain of industry who had a small room in his tower block to which he retired for a period each day to meditate.

According to tradition, every Kabbalist should have a trade; that is, not only have a means of livelihood by which he earns his bread but a profession that is relevant to his nature and its development. Thus, being a gangster is not conducive to a spiritual life although, as noted, even a thief can teach a Kabbalist how to be observant. Right livelihood, as the Buddhists call it, is part of a Kabbalist's way of living. Preferably, it should be as close to the perfect as possible, so that the gifts given by the Almighty are used to the full. These are often not recognised for many years until the professional or social conditioning imposed on us has lost its force and we seek what we really want to do with our lives. This, however, can only come about after the early stages of self-development and the dominance of the ego and its ambitions or fears have been dealt with. That again is the reason why Kabbalah should only be seriously taken up in maturity when the true calibre of our being begins to emerge. This takes us up to the long term exercise of examining ourselves in relation to others and the world. Here, we begin to see how we may fit into and take part in the Work of Unification.

29. Fate

As consciousness increases so does the awareness of great and small, depth and height. This means that the Kabbalist not only observes the minutiae of every day but begins to discern the patterns in his or her life as a whole. This detection of the interconnectedness of everything must happen because all things are, indeed, linked at every level. It is seen in space, as the relationship between things in a given moment, and in time, in the unfolding of events, because every entity in existence moves in a rhythm that has been ebbing and flowing since the universe began. Clearly only those with a high degree of spiritual consciousness can perceive the cosmic pattern but it is possible for those even quite early into kabbalistic work to pick out the design of their own fate. This is done by an ordered reflection.

The first part of the process is to consider the present. Here, we look at our own state as impartially as possible, either alone or with the help of a trustworthy companion. This may be your own instructor, a good friend, or a skilled professional who might be the practitioner of one of the many arts devoted to self-study, from the ancient discipline of astrology to modern psychological analysis. In all cases the supervisor should possess a comprehension of the cosmic view which goes much deeper than just the personal. To probe only the psyche is to become immersed in an essentially fluid and ever-changing world and, without reference to a higher order, many people have been lost to reality, drowned by their dreams. Therefore it is vital that all assistance has the transpersonal dimension. Indeed, it is better to have a down-to-earth adviser than a brilliant theorist who is full of comment but has no experiential wisdom in their being.

The reflection of the present may be set out in diagrammatic form. First you contemplate your relationship with God. This is usually done during the daily meditation. Then you consider your relationship with yourself by focusing upon the state of the Spirit, the condition of the psyche and the health of the body. This will indicate the general situation as regards your interior being. After this comes the examination of your outer world.

FIGURE 30—BIRTH
The moment one is incarnated is crucial as it determines the general pattern of temperament and fate. The thesis is that the cosmos is an ordered progression and one is put in just the right time and place to fulfil one's lesson or mission. The ancient art of astrology, accepted by many rabbis such as Ibn Ezra, stated that a birth chart was an accurate picture of a person and his life. Free will, however, was a major factor in choosing to live one's full potential or drift with the cosmic tide of history. (Moment of a birth chart being drawn up, 16th century.)

The first thing taken into account is your relationship to your most intimate companion. Here will be seen the world's immediate reactions to what one is at the moment. A long and deep view of your partner's response will indicate either advance or retreat, growth or stagnation in the art of relationship. Many things unperceived about oneself will be reflected by your partner. Of course, you must take into account his/her psychological projections but, even so, your choice of partner indicates your own nature and inclinations. Thus we get a precise mirror of our fate, that all-inclusive pattern that reveals our mode of being. In the creative tensions of a close relationship, many aspects of our character are exposed and for this we must be grateful, even though it might be painful. To avoid such encounters and what is brought out in them is to miss one of life's most important working areas. Friendship, love affairs and marriage are designed by Providence to aid and increase development and many who retreat into safe solitude remain out of touch with their destiny. There are times to be alone but in excess and without contact with life one becomes ego-centred and prone to delusion.

The next level to examine is your family. This may or may not be blood relationship. As many have discovered, their circle of friends is often closer and more supportive than their own kith and kin. This group will reveal, by its various components, connections with the various aspects of oneself. The presence of an outwardly moody person amongst your intimates indicates an inner moodiness of everyone attached to them. A look at each character of your circle will tell much about who you are and where you are. The proverb about being judged by your friends is put to good use by the Kabbalist. Your position in the circle as the leader or follower, the joker or charmer, the fool or wise one is extremely informative. There is much to be learnt about your strengths or weaknesses, role and function from these reflections. Friends and even enemies acknowledge your talents and ask for their application or restriction, like jealousy of a good talker. These gifts are an indication of one's potential use to the Work, as well as our fatal path.

Our path through life is largely determined by our gifts and our capacity to use them in the environment in which we live. Reality is not concerned with illusion and you will be where you are because of what you have or have not done with them. Egotism, optimism or cynicism may blind you, and maybe others, about your capability but Providence knows better and sends opportunities for you to find out

154

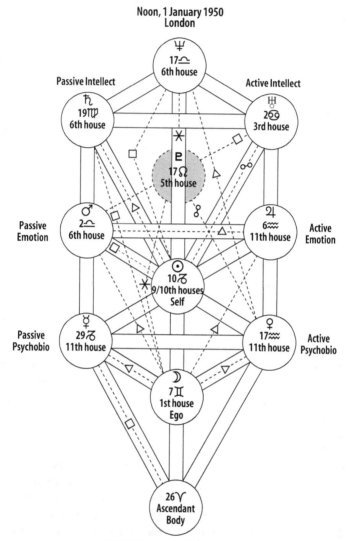

Noon, 1 January 1950
London

Passive Intellect   Active Intellect

Passive Emotion   Active Emotion

Passive Psychobio   Active Psychobio

FIGURE 31—HOROSCOPE

Here a birth chart is put on to the psychological Tree. This is because the Solar system is based upon the sefirot. Each celestial body is placed in a specific zodiacal position, according to calculations. So too is their place in a particular House or part of the sky at the moment of birth. The lines indicate the stresses and eases within the psyche. In this case, the person would be a blend of having a basically steady nature with a lively mind. However, a sub-factor is Mars in Libra afflicted by Uranus and the Sun. This would make them indecisive whereas the Moon trine Uranus would give them flashes of inspiration.(Halevi, 20th century.)

and explore what you might be. If you recognise your hour and meet it, you may come into your own. Many a person with delusions about what should be done if they were given a chance has failed to match the inevitable moment because their ideas were not based on anything but Yesodic dreams. A sense of reality is vital to the Kabbalist, otherwise nothing can be accomplished. Therefore, the criterion of what is feasible and what is not is related to every occasion that fate presents. Impeccable honesty about each opportunity and its possibilities is practised. In this way a less gifted person can be more effective than many more talented people who waste the limited number of opportunities given to accomplish certain things.

To establish a general picture of your life situation, there should be a session of reflection, preferably each week or at least once a month. In this way the past and its relationship to the future may be considered. To miss a session is to break the continuity and lose the gradual accumulation and cohesion of the picture of, say, recurring incidents which become seen as strands that are clearly trends in your fate. People who do not pause to reflect wonder why certain things always happen to them. They never look up in time to avert an avoidable disaster or to take advantage of an obvious opportunity. To be immersed in nothing but Yesodic concerns is to be out of touch with the Self and, therefore, with the real potential of one's life. Sometimes, the Self of Tiferet will indicate, by some unusual interior or exterior action, an oncoming event but very often we miss this signal and are caught by surprise. This is why periodic reflection is vital. It is learning how to watch over our fate and not allow ourselves just to be carried by circumstance. In this way we rise above being a victim, even though we may not be able to change the external pattern.

If we review our past from the standpoint of Tiferet, that is as honestly as we can, we should, at the age of around thirty, have some sense of who we are. We may not yet know what our particular work is but some indication of what kind of training we need should be apparent by then. By training is meant not the formal study at university or in the workshop but what the soul has to pass through in order to mature. Initially, this may have been a tough childhood, an easy youth or a difficult coming of age. Seen with the inner view, such periods may appear the opposite to the conventional view of life which is success-oriented. The sons and daughters of the privileged often have little experience of, or aptitude for, self-reliance whilst the socially deprived may know more about God than an archbishop. It is not unusual, for example, to find the rich to be mean and imprisoned by their possessions and the poor to be free and generous, in spite of their limited conditions. However, we speak here of people who are involved with some kind of spiritual work where mastery of intense difficulties brings about a deep strength and integrity. Many worldly-wise people are outwardly strong but quite amoral, which later precipitates an inner collapse in the face of changed external conditions. The Kabbalist should be able to handle the most difficult crisis fate provides.

To begin to piece together the pattern in your life is to start to see the laws of fate. For example, you begin to discern that certain events were inevitable, that the meeting or parting with this person was ordained and that a particular set of circumstances were simply unavoidable. After a time, there emerges the sense of some kind of plan and you suspect that the whole of your life is indeed supervised so that the maximum can be gained from every situation, good or bad. This, it would seem, is equally true for everyone, although most people are not conscious of the fact because they see only the surface of events. To realise the possibilities in each moment is one of life's great secrets, and when you begin to flow with the tides of descending creation and ascending evolution much unnecessary suffering is removed. For example, when you look back at events that no longer affect the immediate present, it can often be seen that much of the pain generated was caused by wilful resistance to the inevitable. Most of this comes from the ego which cannot see beyond its habits and convenience and this usually means those fantasies we have about ourselves. When we recognise our useful patterns, we can allow more useful tendencies to develop. These will help us for a time until they too become redundant. Thus, we utilise the forms we have been given to help mould our fate consciously. This means we may be able to influence the future.

However, more important than the future is how one performs in the present, both in the personal area and in relation to Kabbalah. Only what is done in the present can change the future, although not always in the way we imagine. To live out your fate consciously is to begin to know what your destiny might be. This means how your gifts may contribute to the operation of unifying the Worlds in mankind. Here we start to perceive the spiritual strand of our lives carried over perhaps centuries, even millennia. In order to have an insight into this cosmic stratum of being you must paradoxically maintain an alert watchfulness on the ever moving moment 'now', for it is the key to time. In this way, we may be shown how the pattern of our fate has led up to each moment to reveal that it is the only place we can be, even if it is in the midst of a major crisis. To the Kabbalist there are two orders of crises; those caused by faulty conduct which act as correctives and those that test integrity. Each fate contains at least one of these major trials. People engaged in the Work usually get more. Here is a part of the training for which most people are not prepared. Therefore the next chapter is devoted to the theme of trial.

158

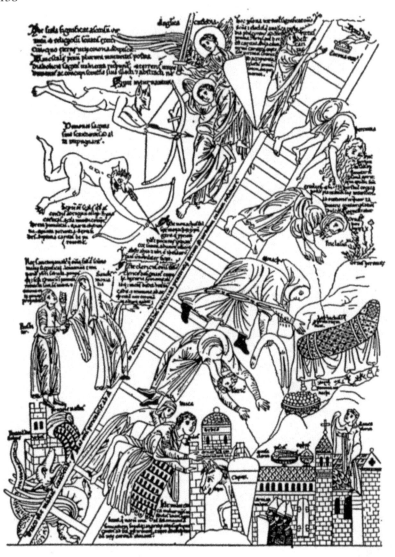

FIGURE 32—TEMPTATIONS
In this woodcut, even the saints and sages can fall off the Ladder of Self realisation.
Everyone has one weakness and this can be exploited by others or the Devil within.
This shadow side of human nature is preyed upon by the Lucific archetypes, such
as spiritual pride, or seduced by the other mortal sins. These are the trials to test
the integrity, for no-one is allowed beyond their capability in this sacred Work.
The fall, or regression, stops any corrupted person doing more damage.
(Medieval manuscript.)

30. Trials

All of us experience crisis. It is a part of life. We see this law in our personal lives and in the world about us. It applies to private and public events, to individuals and communities. It can also relate to mankind as a whole and, by speculative observation, probably to the individual planets and the whole Solar system. What then is a crisis? In Kabbalah it is when the flow of existence, at whatever level we are looking, reaches a stage when resistance matches progress. At such a time the pressure increases to a critical point where the flow is turned back or breaks through a barrier. Seen at extremes it may be regarded as a moment of passing inconvenience or a major disturbance to the status quo. Either way it makes life difficult, if not impossible. To the Kabbalist, there is always more than what appears on the surface. Crises are seen as effects, not causes and these, when examined in depth, often totally change the view of the occurrence.

The mechanism of a crisis is that when the Tree of a situation is out of balance, or is momentarily one of equilibrium, then the loading of that situation is about to be changed. Thus, for example, if a person is too severe then either more Severity is applied to create a reaction or Mercy is introduced to correct the imbalance. This usually precipitates a crisis, like a bad judgement which induces conscience that brings the person back towards the central column of Clemency. In an individual's life it can be excessive indulgence against a strict upbringing or, in a larger sphere, a revolution opposing oppression, both leading, in time, to greater personal and political maturity. On the vertical scale, crisis can occur when one level is in conflict with another. The most frequent in the individual is when the ego is about to relinquish its power to the Self. This is a major crisis that can result in either level holding ascendency for a period until the matter is settled in favour of evolution because, in the long run, the cosmic process will always win, even if it takes many lives. Lesser crises can occur within each sefirah or triad, so that we may witness or experience, for example, a Hodian crisis when the person realises that facts are not enough; or a passive emotional crisis when old fears seek to hold back an impulse to love without reservation, as they struggle with dynamic complexes in the triad of active emotion. The solution lies in equilibrium but this is often not seen until the episode is past.

There are minor and major crises. The minor are to be observed every day and, whilst these may be managed with relative ease, they should not be regarded as unimportant. If one reflects, it will be noted that major crises are often precipitated by a minor one. For example, on a large scale it only took one man to shoot another and his wife to start the First World War. Likewise, a casual remark can cause a quarrel or trigger a turning point in someone's life. The reason for this is that many small factors can build up to a major event. The persistent criticism that undermines a marriage is an example, so is an increasing unease which can make a person suddenly leave an outwardly pleasant but stale situation without anyone in it knowing why. We should take note of each crisis that presents itself and search for its root and where its conflict is directing us.

A major crisis is easy to identify. It is usually spectacular and will often be remembered as one of the most productive periods of our lives, although at the time we thought it hell. However, to some a crisis is a way of life. This can be a pathological way of gaining attention or a constant warning that they are not on target. For most of us, big crises come at turning points in our lives. They usually have a long build-up and often their foreshadow touches us, in indicative events, some time before they actually occur, like a rattle in a car engine before it breaks down. This is the use of reflection, so that we are not caught entirely unawares. Sometimes, because of such fore-knowledge, we can avoid a catastrophe although this is not always possible; but at least we can prepare the sea captain who battens the hatches for a storm. However, for the Kabbalist, the objective is not just to survive but to learn as much as possible from the experience, because very often these periods of disruption are when the most direct knowledge is gained about oneself and existence.

Seen from the cosmic point of view, the dimension alters and one begins to see such critical events as spiritual tests. Now, according to Tradition, Satan is the tester. Indeed, his name means just this. As one of the *Benai Elohim*, the Sons of God, it is his task to pressure the righteous and test their genuineness. We see this described in great detail in the Book of Job, when God allows Satan to try this remarkably fortunate man by taking everything from him and afflicting his soul. Throughout the book, Job complains to God that his punishment is unjust, as he has done nothing wrong. His friends, who do not understand what is happening, naturally assume he must have broken some law to come into such trouble. This issue, however, is not about karma or the law of retribution but about whether Job will crack under the strain and lose his integrity. The wager between God and the devil may seem, on the surface, odd and unfair but the contest between evil and good is vital to Creation because it makes Adam bear witness to the fact that mankind has free will, can rise above physical and psychological circumstances and still hold the Divine Light on the Earth. Satan failed with Job and all was restored to the man with yet more increase. However, the battle still goes on in each generation, as the Job in every evolving individual is tested almost to breaking point. If there is a break, then that is the person's own decision for Satan is not permitted to destroy the soul.

This is one of the reasons why people on the Way are often tried so severely. Once they have been proved they can be given much and bear the heavy load of spiritual Work. When one considers how few follow the Path beyond the honeymoon stage, then the weight of responsibility involved has to be carried by those capable of holding it. If a person in charge of training souls should fail, many will fall and that must not happen. Indeed, when such individuals have cracked, whole schools have become corrupt and many seekers lost for that lifetime. The vessel must be thoroughly tested before it is allowed to be filled with heavenly dew.

If a crisis is to be regarded as a test, then even the most unfortunate circumstances can be put to good use. This transforms the situation into a Kabbalistic exercise and changes its whole aspect. Thus, the break-up of a relationship can be seen as the working out of karma, whilst the coming together and confrontation of another couple may be regarded as a chance to develop Gevuric courage or Hesedic compassion in one or both of them. An on-going crisis in the family may become the workshop of several souls, as might a strike at work be the spur to an individual's realisation about the mass mind and how he or she is facing in the opposite direction. Every situation of tension has its creative element. Conflict and its resolution are normal in the process of evolution. Most plays and books are about the confrontation between good and evil. Great literature develops the issue in depth, like Tolstoy's *Resurrection* where a man struggles with his conscience. In the mass media the theme is the same; the baddies have their moment but, in the end, they must lose or evil will rule and cause anarchy in society and the universe. Here the archetypal confrontation between order and chaos in the cosmic drama is acted out in individual and collective consciousness.

The key to a safe passage through the great and small dramas of Creation is correct conduct. By this I do not mean conventional customs, which are often outmoded patterns of behaviour, but acting from true integrity. In the Bible it is spoken of as righteousness. A person who lives in this way is called a *Zadek* in Kabbalah. To be such an individual means that one moves according to conscience, that is, the way of the soul. This triad composed of Gevurah, Hesed and Tiferet gives the qualities of discernment, courage and love of the Good, Truth and Beauty. To think or dream about behaving according to these criteria is not enough. As one sage said, 'Anyone can be an angel if their feathers are not ruffled.' Therefore life, or fate to be more precise, creates situations in which one's integrity is both tested and deepened as a result. Such examinations are not always at our convenience because usually there are others also involved. These may be people who are consciously being put to the test or bystanders in the process of being woken up by the shock, because it is a fact that even the most dozy soul can become conscious when shaken by dramatic events. This is another function of crisis. Thus it is that all levels have an opportunity to be shaken out of exterior patterns that bind the interior habits which imprison the soul. If history had no drama there would be no civilisation, nor would we have the Great Ones who teach us how to meet the problems of being born, living and dying.

This discussion of crisis and trial leads on to the larger scale of Providence, which is the concern of the spiritual levels, as it watches over the world and supervises events below. Without a general plan in the universe, and an occasional adjustment to meet special situations, there would be disorder which is just what the devil thrives upon. Therefore, let us take a look at Providence so as to know a little more about the cosmic theatre in which we act out our parts.

31. Providence

According to kabbalistic Tradition, existence unfolds in the form of a grand design. First manifestation emerges from nothingness into a void which is then filled by the Will of God in the appearance of the sefirot which, in turn, organise themselves into the Tree of Life that contains all the principles of manifest existence. Out of this primal instrument of Divine government emerge the three lower Worlds of Creation, Formation and Action. These descend in an ordered impulse of consciousness, energy and matter to create, form and make the great Ladder of Jacob stretching between the first Keter of total unity to the fullness of multiplicity at the bottommost Malkhut. This graduated process has distinct levels of laws that increase the further they are from the highest Crown with each superior level ruling its inferior levels in the same way that man can direct and control the conditions of a garden in order to produce the finest plants. The level of celestial government is general, in that it deals with stars and planets, nature and species. However, in the case of mankind, Providence can be concerned with the particular but only when an individual raises him or herself above the law of the masses.

When the descending impulse of Creation reaches its limit at the elemental level of the most solid of metals, there is an upward turn that becomes a process of cosmic reflection, known to us as evolution. This movement begins the return journey to its source. At the present stage our Earth has completed the making and developing of the mineral, vegetable and animal kingdoms. The human race has only recently arrived on the planet. Here we see the meeting of the natural World of organised matter, energy and intelligence with the levels of soul and spirit. Thus each individual, as a cell of Adam Kadmon enwrapped in a physical body, has access to the Higher Worlds and contact with their Divine origin. This makes a human being the only creature in existence that can consciously span all the Worlds, as he or she grows in the experience of both visible and invisible realms. Such a uniqueness gives us access to Providence and *vice versa*, in that we may individually evolve with help from Providence which

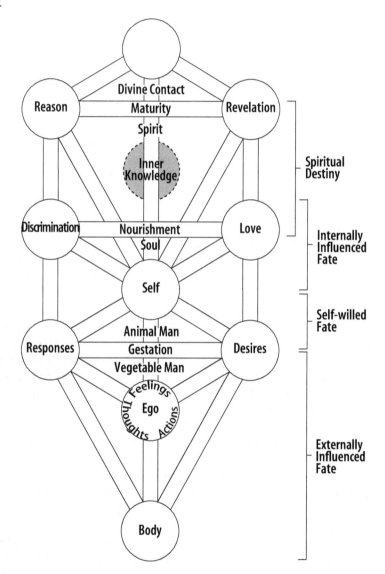

FIGURE 33—FATE AND DESTINY
Providence operates at several levels. The lowest is in the general fate of the
mass of humanity. Nature supplies most of their needs while animal level people,
the leaders, take advantage of the opportunities that history puts in their way.
Individuals working on their souls are given chances that others never notice to
develop inwardly so as to exploit their fate to its limit. The men and women of
destiny are those who understand and aid the process of human evolution.
(Halevi, 20th century.)

provides the best conditions for us, although we do not always appreciate it at the time. The supervision of Providence is a vast, subtle and complex operation. For most of us its workings are a mystery that give us just what we need, rather than what we want, at the right time. Its main aim, in accordance with the Will of Heaven, is to help mankind transform the World of Action and the Elements into a Paradise on Earth in which the Presence of the Holy One is known by every incarnate being.

Such a project cannot be completed quickly. It is a vast effort extending over many millennia, carried on by each generation of aspirants which is composed of people who have committed themselves to this Work of Unification. Paradoxically, to help in the process of unification often initially separates those on the Path from the rest of mankind because few understand what is involved. Moreover, many seekers of the Way do not know what its aim is to begin with, despite the fact that Providence tells them each day by its interaction with their lives. For most, such a realisation can only come about over many lives, as accumulated experience brings about insight by degrees and then real knowledge about the purpose of existence. Not everyone is sensitive or intelligent and many in pursuit of wisdom or happiness are still children in matters of the soul and spirit. Therefore, Providence designs special situations in which the person seeking Truth can find it, so that growth can occur and the next stage be prepared for. This phenomenon takes some time to recognise but, once it is, the aspirant flows with the movement of Heaven. Here we have a person who lives out fate consciously and uses it for self-development.

Fate is the pattern of one's life. It is the result of all that has gone before in other lives. It is designed by the laws of retribution which deal with both reward and punishment and the needs of the time in which the person has incarnated. Because of past actions certain relationships with others continue until the work together is complete. This means that each person has a set of fatal meetings arranged by Providence which cannot be avoided, although they may be discarded once the connection is made. This, however, does not mean that the business is finished. The meeting will recur, if not again in that lifetime, then in another until the issue is resolved. The Kabbalist, therefore, considers each relationship in this light. It might be that one encounter will suffice to complete something from a previous existence or it could take many years to work through a complex karma with another individual or group. The Kabbalist takes this factor into account in all relationships, whether intimate or distant, for they are part of his or her training to become aware of the inter-relatedness of the inner and outer worlds, because nothing is separate in the universe. Here is the underlay of Providence.

In the early days of life a child takes everything for granted. Parents supply food and comfort and, later, education and training is given by the community. It is the same on the spiritual path. At the beginning one is handed out all sorts of help. Books come one's way as if by accident. Coincidence brings certain people into contact who can direct one and answer some pertinent question. Situations occur as if by design, rather than the random laws in ordinary life. One meets someone, as if by accident in a remote place, or picks up a spiritual contact in the middle of the market place. It is as if one were being guided and given just what one needs at that moment. This is the hallmark of Providence.

The name Providence is just what it says. It provides with precision and capability because the cosmic level from which it operates can see the overall picture. Thus, two people can be directed towards each other from different sides of the world and at the right moment be made to meet in Times Square, New York City, or on a mountain between India and Persia where few people go. The Kabbalist is always on the lookout for such incidents because they not only form a part of the chain of connections but reveal how the Spirit works in the world. Contrary to a common view, esoteric operations are not always carried out behind locked doors. They are often performed in the market place of the public domain where no one notices them or sees them for what they really are. Usually it is only years later that some people begin to suspect that more happened than was seen or reported. The life of Joshua ben Miriam of Nazareth is a prime example of this. To most of the people in Judea he was an itinerant rabbi, one of many individuals who might have been their deliverer. The authorities saw him as a troublemaker and the possible focus of an uprising. Only a handful of people realised he was more than just a great teacher. It was only much later that it became apparent he was the Anointed One of his time. When Ibn Arabi, many centuries after, met the *Katub* of his Age, as the Sufis call the Messiah of the period, only he recognised the Katub. He was forbidden to tell the others with him who was present.

To meet the Messiah of one's time is not likely but one never knows. Perhaps more important is simply to be watchful and see what Providence puts your way. While you may grow to allow Providence to look after you, what is sometimes given, after the ease and encouragement of the early days, is not always what is expected. Indeed, it sometimes comes as a great shock to learn that even on the Path you have to earn your keep. This is not a metaphor of business but a cosmic law of paying a spiritual debt and of increasing your potential and profit, like the good servant in many parables. Thus, you are sometimes posted a problem 'out of the blue', which means out of the sky or Heaven. It might come in the form of someone looking for an entry into the Tradition. Here is where the Kabbalist pays off his account to his early helpers by adding a link in the chain of generations.

Sometimes the task allocated is not so easy or obvious. It might be a difficult relationship in which one partner watches over the other and helps him or her through a spiritual crisis that might last for years. When a certain Hassidic rabbi was asked why had Heaven given him such a shrew of a wife, he replied, 'So who else could cope with her?' Being good does not always bring a harmonious life. Many very conscientious people are pushed to their limit by the irresponsible who seek them out to balance off their own difficulties. This has the effect of testing out the depth of commitment to integrity and improving, by example, the state of the afflicted. One often finds spiritually-orientated people engaged in difficult, dangerous and even mad situations because that is where the light is most needed, although the choice to leave is there. Providence arranges these opportunities according to your capability. Here it is worth noting that the easy options are rarely the most profitable. However, it takes hindsight to appreciate this when the job is done.

After the Kabbalist has been involved in this type of activity for some years there emerges a set of skills that attracts certain situations. These are heaven-given gifts and indicate the nature of your life's work. Thus talents that are needed and well used, like those of a healer or artist, reveal what is your destiny. Destiny is the long chain of fates that makes up the aim of your reason for existence. Its distinct quality passes from life to life and may be detected, by the observant, in the unique quality that underlies an individual. Thus, the Kabbalist observes his or her performance in whatever task Providence puts their way, because in it is the clue to what they were called forth, created, formed and made for. If you come to see what you are and work within your gifts, then you know your place in the grand design and can happily serve the Holy One from any level. If this state is obtained then acceptance of whatever work is ordained grants a profound sense of purpose to the Kabbalist's life. This often means that many petty problems and ambitions are curtailed, leaving more energy available for the task in hand. However, before this is reached many stages have to be passed through, so that you arrive at such a conviction with the knowledge of experience and not just the theories and fantasies of innocence. In order to do this, we examine the next phase of development and the hazards to be mastered as the psychic faculties awaken, which they do after a sustained period of kabbalistic work.

32. Psychic Faculties

Over a period of time there begins to develop within the Kabbalist certain higher faculties. By these is meant that as the Yeziratic or psychological body develops with diligent work, so do the subtle organs and their sensibilities. Some people are born with these faculties which are regarded as psychic gifts. In the case of the Kabbalist they are the result of conscious work. In the discipline of magic such faculties are deliberately developed, so as to perceive and manipulate the laws of the Yeziratic world. In the case of low magic this power to command is all that is sought; but it is at a high price for, more often than not, such powers generate temptation, abuse and eventually psychological confusion with the more serious loss of access to the Worlds beyond, of the Spirit and Divine. High magic, like Kabbalah, seeks to be of service to God but practitioners of this superior occult art are very rare for integrity at just the psychological level is difficult to maintain. There has to be the spiritual dimension. This, however, does not mean that the Kabbalist is not put to the temptation of occult powers.

As the psychic senses begin to awaken, so the person becomes increasingly aware of the subtler levels of events nearby and, sometimes, from afar. You may, for example, become conscious of someone's innermost intention or pick up what is really going on behind an apparently ordinary conversation. There can be times when you become conscious of some person not related directly to your own life and not know why, until you hear that an event took place involving that individual in some spiritual situation. Some people find that they are informed about events far across the ocean or know beforehand that some important event is about to occur, whilst others have the ability to cast their consciousness into the past and find out what actually happened.

At first these faculties arise quite naturally out of the Work. Mostly they grow gradually but occasionally they blossom quite suddenly. To the unprepared this can be somewhat disturbing in that to become aware of the workings of other people's inner processes means that you have the capacity to influence, as well as be influenced, because

FIGURE 34—LEVELS

Mineral people are usually oblivious of everything except themselves. A drunk is an example. Vegetable persons are aware of their immediate environment but not much beyond their family or clan. Animal individuals have a degree of consciousness but use it to gain what they want. Human people, however, can perceive the psychological and spiritual dimensions. Great writers can, for instance, depict complex situations in a novel while prophets can perceive the history and future of nations. (16th century woodcut.)

the flow operates both ways. Many sensitive people, for example, can pick up tension within a household of conflict and come away from it agitated, although they themselves are not personally involved. This same gift of reception can be consciously reversed to transmit good feeling or understanding. But first you must take into account whether it is right to interfere. Here is the test of manipulation.

Let us take a hypothetical situation and draw some lessons from it. A Kabbalist goes out to dinner. During the meal he perceives that his host, the husband, is having an affair with one of the guests. He arrives at this conclusion by a series of insights that are presented to his Yesod in flashes. He may have picked up the interior communications between the two people or he might have glimpsed the subtle threads that stretch between them. These can be perceived by the psychic eye as links between the head, heart and pelvic regions. A closer look would determine whether the relationship was a passing encounter or something more serious. This is done by seeing which of the strands is the thickest and at which place their ends are situated. Thus, a head to head predominance would clearly be quite a different relationship from a strong pelvis to pelvis connection. As you can imagine, the possession of such information bears a certain responsibility and some temptation to those who wish to do good or ill.

Another example of this problem is when you see, with very precise vision, the solution to another's dilemma. You not only observe the game as an outsider but have an inner view of what brought the person to this point. It would be easy to speak and advise but this is not permitted without a clear indication that it is correct, for to interfere with another's karma may cause yet more trouble for him and a little for yourself. Thus, discretion is tested again and again, so as to prove that you can possess psychic faculties but must not misuse them. Occasionally the test is reversed and you have a responsibility to speak on the basis of inner knowledge. This exercise must be done with enormous tact, taking into account all the effects that might follow. Consider the Kabbalist at our dinner party. If he spoke to the hostess, who was a close friend, it could be a disaster. If he let the husband know he knew, he might be held responsible for the result and if he informed the third party—who knows what would happen? And yet, the Kabbalist was shown the situation for some reason. So it may be necessary to speak to the husband or prepare the wife to ride the shock; or just wait. It is a very difficult decision. Such psychic gifts carry their burden.

Whilst these phenomena may occur spontaneously by being stimulated in a dramatic situation, they can also be induced deliberately. For instance, the following technique can be applied after some practice but it requires firstly that the psychic centres are operational and secondly that one can interpret accurately what is shown, because not all the information that is received is reliable. It has to be soundly edited and converted into an intelligible form.

Supposing that you want to see what is your own inner state. After the recommended preparation of ritual and prayer, imagine that you are riding a horse on a long journey. You may find yourself crossing a particular landscape in certain weather conditions. From this image much can be deduced. First look at your clothes and the condition of the horse. Observe how you appear and examine the terrain. It will not always correspond to an outer situation. In tough times, for example, the ride could be up a steep mountain pass on an exhausted horse with sleet in your tired face and a cold wind biting into your worn-out coat. At another time you might find, when you flip this image up to take a reading, that you are riding a yearling through a beautiful summer meadow in fashionable cotton gear whilst on the horizon dark clouds are to be seen forewarning some trouble ahead of this present good period. This technique is particularly useful when the ordinary mind cannot see clearly what is happening below its habitual thoughts and feelings.

A further application of this method is to project an image, after considering a general question about a situation. What may be presented is, for example, a picture of a battle with the people involved playing out their roles as generals or soldiers on either side. A close examination of the image might reveal that someone is not what he appears. The obtrusive watcher in the outer situation might reveal himself as the real field marshal behind the nominal commander. In another case you might wish to know how an absent friend is and so, after reflecting on his or her face, you visualise them as a ship. Its situation will, if the vision is not fantasy, tell much about their circumstance. Here you must double check with known and hard facts.

The use of such methods is fraught with dangers. You can just be deceiving yourself or others; another responsibility. Therefore, whilst much information may be useful, it must not be acted upon until confirmation is received by external means or the image is repeated often enough not to be ignored. Even so, to act on insubstantial advice requires great discernment and prudence. This is not the work for the neurotic or psychotic. Such people often have visions which, though at the heart are correct, are usually distorted images that suit their own world picture. They have this faculty because their unbalanced mentality sometimes triggers this psychic function which feeds deranged images into their already ego-centred Yesods, leading to an inflated personal view. Everyone has these dark elements in them to a greater or lesser degree and therefore, even if you are convinced that you are right, you must check assiduously to see if any personal motivation has corrupted the essential modesty required for service.

The temptation to use these psychic skills improperly is a great test. You may justify their use by various reasons ranging from self-knowledge to helping others. While these objectives are valid, it is always the intention that must be watched. Spiritual vanity may allow the abuse of such gifts for what is believed to be the common good and, whilst a person might not think he is performing psychic manipulation, others may perceive magic being worked on themselves or others without their consent and this is not permitted, however good the reason might be. Many an individual in the early stages of spiritual work has tried to change a situation from the subtle level for the best of reasons and finished up forgetting what was the original aim. This is because it is very easy to drown in the watery World of Yezirah. One needs good connections, both in Heaven and on Earth, so as not to be washed away in the powerful currents of the psychic realm and out to sea.

Direct access to the World of Formation brings not only new sensibilities and powers but contact with those beings who live in that zone. During formal meditation and sleep we pass quite safely through these areas but, as one raises the conscious centre of gravity, so one encounters the inhabitants of the next world. Thus, the ability to discern and handle whatever entities might emerge out of one's own psyche or the lower levels of Yezirah must be cultivated so that we may safely approach and enter into the upper Worlds.

33. Entities

As you begin to penetrate beyond the line that stretches between Hod and Nezah you come into the lower unconscious, which is unconscious until you are aware of it. Then, like the stars that are not seen in the day but are nevertheless present, there emerge, as consciousness rises, the middle levels of the psyche with its various constellations of intellectual and emotional complexes. These psychological configurations hold and relate all the memories and ideas imbibed by personal experience or passed on through the collective unconscious of our background. They may be clusters of fears or loves or groups of positive or negative ideas that take on, at this level, a kind of life of their own, sometimes to become distinct and powerful entities within the psyche, like mini-archetypes.

Examples of such entities are the virgin and the whore in women and the tyrant and the victim in men. These sub-personalities, as they are sometimes called, are legion and are represented, in traditional Kabbalah, as angels and demons. We all know the imp in us that likes to be mischievous and the saint who seeks to be good. We also are acquainted with the Jekyll and Hyde as well as the fool who blunders occasionally into our lives. These are all parts of ourselves, created by our own experience and that which is present, like the ancestral parts of the brain, as the ancient archetypal intelligence of the human race. Thus, in addition to containing all biological evolution in our bodies with its mineral, plant and animal levels, we also have very primitive aspects of the psyche underlying the more sophisticated levels of the unconscious. Thus a highly educated, urbane man, in time of war or great fear, can become as violent as any savage because it is there to be aroused if it is not controlled. The reverse is equally true, in that the collective sage and saint is equally present to be awakened.

The arousing of these unconscious aspects normally does not occur except in especially cultivated or dramatic situations but, nevertheless, they are there and sometimes influence our ego consciousness without our knowledge. This is apparent in an unbalanced state like neurosis, where a person fears constant attack or believes themselves to be all-

FIGURE 35—PSYCHISM
While advanced stages of development awaken psychic powers, these must be used with great discretion. It is one thing to have a flash of insight into a situation but another deliberately to cultivate this faculty to gain some advantage—this is magic. When King Saul asked the witch of Endor to conjure up the dead prophet Samuel, he was not happy with the result. To encourage the discarnate to communicate can allow undesirable lost souls to enter our lives. (Raising the dead Samuel, Bank's Bible, 19th century.)

knowing. As we work towards heightened awareness, these entities emerge to help or hinder our progress towards healing and further evolution. This is why, in spiritual work, a very personal crisis sometimes occurs as split-off psychological aspects are exposed to the light of increased consciousness. In the case of those without a discipline or tutor, it occasionally results in a breakdown whilst among those working under supervision it can be no more than what has been called the 'Down' without the 'Break' because they are carried through this dark night of the soul by experienced support and inner knowledge.

Another set of internal psychological entities to be met are the archetypes. These are focused round the various sefirot. The old planetary gods associated with each sefirah give a clue to their nature. Thus, the Moon and Artemis are associated with Yesod, Mercury with Hod, Venus with Nezah, Apollo with Tiferet, Mars with Gevurah, Jupiter with Hesed, Pluto with Daat, Saturn with Binah, Uranus with Hokhmah and Neptune with Keter. Around these principles accrue both individual and collective material which manifests in dreams and drives that both illuminate and motivate the psyche. In cases of madness an archetype sometimes breaks free of the checks and balances of the other sefirot and takes possession of the person. We see this in the compulsive hero and the nymphomaniac who are dominated, respectively, by a split-off Gevurah and Nezah. When you enter the domain of these great beings, you must acknowledge their territory and power and tread most carefully. In ancient kabbalistic literature, they were seen as angels and demons with whom one negotiated a middle-pillar passage to the higher gates of Heaven.

Besides these internal entities there are those who do not inhabit our psychological body but draw near to it when they see a possibility of access or communication. These entities may be good, bad or indifferent. Some, for example, can be no more than curious, like dogs or cats that wish to see who has risen up from the physical world and into their time and space. These creatures range from stupid to highly intelligent. They have their place in existence and can be regarded as the flora and fauna of the lower Yeziratic world. One treats them as one would animals and plants when out in the wild. Some are harmless and some otherwise. Fortunately, the psyche has an inbuilt sensitivity to danger if something sinister is provoked but this usually only occurs if one's intention is tainted, as like is drawn to like. Here is the reason why sorcery or dealings with the lower spirits are forbidden in the Bible as is uninvited communication with the dead.

The logic behind such an injunction is that most people are frightened by the unknown and this is a healthy reaction. One does not go into the jungle without a guide or a great deal of preparation. To encounter the dead of this level is to contact people who have not yet become used to the idea that they no longer have a body and this suggests that they have very little inner development. As such they will grasp at any opportunity to attach themselves to the living, which is a very unpleasant experience for the incarnate as they feel the intrusion of someone else's will into their mind. Many people have been deeply disturbed by such a phenomenon when playing with calling up the deceased. There is a kabbalistic procedure to contact those great spirits who no longer live on the Earth but these operations are directed to a level well above the lower Yeziratic stratum. Generally speaking, the dead are best left alone. They will come of their own accord in a dream or a voice if there is something important to communicate.

If such an unpleasant encounter does occur (and it can if all the precautions are not taken such as ablution, setting up the Tree and asking permission) then centre in Tiferet at the solar plexus and go directly in consciousness up to Keter, above the head, and pray for protection or straight down to Malkhut and stamp the feet so as to earth as quickly as possible. Do the same thing if it happens to someone else and take them out to walk in the fresh air, preferably into a garden or where there is an abundance of nature.

Along with all the creatures who inhabit this level of existence are those intelligences that wander about looking for trouble and those who patrol the zone to police it for that very reason. Sometimes, during a kabbalistic practice, some of the villains will seek to disrupt the operation. It may be out of sheer devilment or a serious attempt to destroy the Work and discourage the participants. This usually occurs when a new group or inexperienced individual is setting up a channel to hold the flow of energies between the upper and lower Worlds. Subtle diversions, such as strange inner noises, are used to interfere with the process of making a vessel. These distractions should be ignored and the opposing force blessed so that its energy is converted and incorporated within the operation, for evil dissolves when met by love. Actual voices are a more difficult matter because they are not always obviously the Opposition. Sometimes they will sound very like helpers who come to aid the Work but, after a time, something odd will be detected in their advice and directions. Experience will reveal how there is always a flaw in their recommendations or a perversity in their objectives. The remedy is to treat them with respect and ask them to withdraw in the Name of the Divine. If they do not, then terminate the operation and start again after a suitable time has elapsed, like another day.

This is how many students first contact evil directly. In most human beings there is a mixture of good and bad, with good predominating in the majority. In the non-physical Worlds, the difference between the two is more marked because the composition of a creature has a finer and less complex being. By this is meant that the essence of things becomes more apparent. We see this law very clearly in spiritual work, in that people become more transparently what they are, if one has eyes to see. The immoral man or woman who has developed the psyche but gone to the devil is decidedly evil. As Shakespeare said, 'Lilies that fester smell far worse than weeds'. From here on we must be yet more watchful because the opposition, as well as the Companions of the Light, has a keen interest in our development. To gain the allegiance of a developed soul is a great prize to either side. Therefore there begins, as the soul awakens to Self-consciousness, a battle around the person's life which accounts for the many unusual events that take place on an individual's spiritual path.

To become Self-conscious is to raise the focus of awareness into the triad of the soul. This means that one becomes directly involved with the great struggle between order and chaos that has gone on since Creation began. At this level, which is the ante-room to the first Heaven, an inexperienced person can be easily blocked or cast down as the angels and demons within and without struggle to influence us. Ultimately, we have the final word because here is the place where we exercise the gift of free will that was given to all human beings. To operate consciously in the field of the soul means one has much psychological power and this can be used as we alone choose. Thus no one else can be held responsible for our actions, although there will be those who seek to use our power for their own ends. This is where the issue of ethics arises for, unlike man-made laws that can change with newly elected governments, spiritual ethics remain constant because they are based upon Eternal laws. Their purpose is to protect and guide the individual on the Path at every level.

34. Integrity

The soul triad on the Tree is composed of Tiferet-Beauty and the Self, Gevurah-Judgement and Hesed-Mercy. It is the triad of deep emotion and the bridge between the upper and lower faces of the psychological Tree. This means it has access to the worlds of Action and the Spirit, that is the physical level of the particular and the cosmic dimension of Creation. It is a focus and vessel for receiving and imparting material from above to below and *vice versa*. As such it is a crucial triad and one that carries great responsibility. Normally, the soul operates as an unconscious organ of the psyche but, as the Kabbalist begins to work so it becomes, at first, alert and then awakened into consciousness. This brings a number of gifts but also many problems.

Most people experience the soul as a tinge of conscience, a moment of deep insight or as a dim presence behind their daily thoughts, feelings and actions. Occasionally, direct access to the soul will be experienced when in love or during a crisis, perhaps while observing an emotionally moving scene or in a decisive point in some drama. Besides its qualities of truth, discernment and loving-kindness, it is also the seat of free will. By this is meant that while the ego cannot but react according to habit and the Spirit be too remote to be controlled by the will, the soul can be and is affected by the way we choose to live our lives as individuals. This is the area of free will which can follow the good or incline towards evil because we can as wilfully abuse the Laws of Creation as accept and flow with them. The privilege of choice makes for much tension within a human being.

To illustrate by analogue; when an adolescent realises that he is no longer a child and can physically match his parents and teachers, he begins to disobey their rules in order to prove his individuality. This, of course, is an illusion because all people of this age go through a rebellious phase before recognising, after a number of disasters, that power means responsibility. It is the same on the path of inner growth when an individual becomes aware that he can use the gifts of the soul for selfish or selfless purposes. Strange as it may seem, you are not

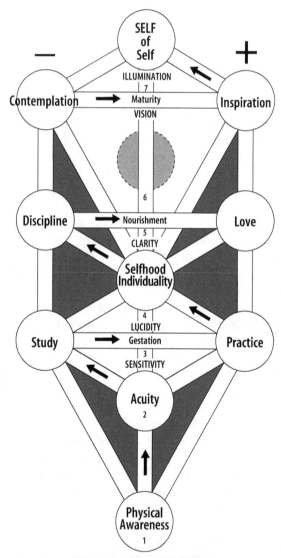

FIGURE 36—SEVEN STEPS

As study and practice of kabbalistic principles are integrated, so the level of consciousness rises. Each step raises the centre of gravity of perception. First, one becomes physically alert, then acutely aware of social situations. Then comes psychic ability, followed by lucid insight. The stage of clarity gives access to one's own and other souls. Vision brings a transpersonal view and, in illumination, one glimpses what great prophets see. To be enlightened means one knows what all these stages are for. (Halevi, 20th century.)

prevented from making use of your new powers, although a teacher or Providence will point out the unpleasant consequences that result from any actions contrary to the laws of existence. Like adolescents, some people ignore such advice and quite ruthlessly explore their capacity to exploit situations that often make others suffer. For a time nothing seems to happen and they begin to believe that they are immune from cosmic reaction, often ignoring a warning, comment or incident that hints at what could happen if they do not stop. What they fail to understand is that they are being given time to reconsider what they are doing and to realise that they may jeopardise what they have acquired. God is merciful.

Usually there are three stages of warning given out by retribution before things become critical. The first is often a gentle tap to draw to the attention that something is off the mark. If there is a positive response you can correct your course with little or no payment beyond remorse. The second stage is frequently in the form of a small accident or significant incident that jolts the conscience. This is sometimes enough to indicate that something must be done to retrieve the situation. If this is ignored then a major event, like an illness or series of disasters, brings your evil momentum to an abrupt halt. The scale of such events will range according to the degree of self-will and the influence the person has. They might be anything from losing a job or partner to madness and even death. The more evolved the person, the greater the responsibility and the response of providential justice whose task it is to limit evil before it does too much damage to the souls of others and the Work. Not a few people who have perverted knowledge and powers acquired on the Path have lost all they had. As a once-great occultist who sought fame and found disgrace remarked at the end of his lost life, 'I wonder what it was all about?' He had forgotten the aim of his Tradition and served the god of his own ego.

To avoid such tragic calamities there have always been systems of ethics given out by spiritual traditions. The Jew has the Ten Commandments, the Christian the Lord's Prayer and the Buddhist the Eightfold Path. In essence they are always the same. At first sight they appear to relate to ordinary life situations but, if we look closer, we will see that they apply to the Higher Worlds also. Thus, for example, you do not murder another's soul which is quite possible for someone with occult power. Nor do you steal or commit adultery at this level, meaning that you do not take for yourself that which belongs to God or improperly mix those elements that should not be related, like black magic. Neither do you bear false witness, because this cuts one off from the truth, or covet another's spiritual properties. These ethics are designed not only to give guidelines through the highly volatile World of the Psyche but to safeguard against the intrusion of evil.

In the line 'Deliver us from evil' from the prayer of Joshua ben Miriam of Nazareth is the implication that you will be faced by such an encounter. Now this prayer was given to people already on the Way, that means who were already operating at the soul level. Thus, they were of interest to and approached by those demonic elements that seek to disrupt the Work. This is clearly demonstrated by the betrayal of Judas, perhaps the cleverest of the disciples, whom the text says the devil entered, although an esoteric view of the relationship between Jesus and this apparently evil student is that Judas consciously took on the responsibility of the betrayal because no one else would carry out the necessary role. Ethics are spiritual conduct especially under adverse conditions. Thus a person on the Path is tested by Satan to see if his being is sound and his faith true. This occasionally involves some strange situations in which a person must sometimes act out the reverse of a commonly understood code, as many mystics have done.

The approach of real evil usually only occurs when the soul is awakened to its potential of free will. Prior to this, most of us behave according to our code of upbringing or acquired reflex actions, as any intense course of self-observation will reveal. However, when you are in a situation in which you can actually influence events by your inner knowledge, then a conflict can arise between what you would like and what you ought to do. To complicate things further as a test, the issue is often projected onto the external situation or people by the shadow side of our psyche which can block out the light of honesty with subtle ploys like blame and justification. This is the work of our interior Satan. In matters of the Spirit, the higher Lucific element offers apparently well-considered advice that can be disarmingly convincing, like knowing best, if one does not check it against a simple spiritual truth such as not interfering in another's life. Here is where the Ten Commandments and the Eightfold Path act as a bastion against the Luciferic distortion of reality which is witnessed in so many brilliant but deviant teachings about spiritual matters which do not free but imprison the soul. Many people mistake psychic charisma for the spirit. Real spirituality is simple and its essential principles are designed to support and protect. True ethics are self-evident truths that need no detailed explanation because they speak directly to the soul in any situation, no matter how complex it may seem on the surface. Conscience knows what is true and false. The soul possesses this capacity as a gift unless it is seduced by evil. Kabbalistic ethics are concerned with inner morality but they also relate to conduct in the world. Thus your integrity becomes a living expression of the root meaning of the word 'integration' between that which is below and above, within and without.

The practice of integrity is vital to a spiritual tradition for it not only safeguards the individual but the Work. Over the last few centuries kabbalistic ideas have been stolen and adulterated by those who only sought magical powers, with the result that an image of dangerous hotchpotch has overlaid the real purpose of Kabbalah. Because of this, tradition has fallen into disrepute amongst Jews who see it as a degenerate form of occultism. Thus, by the 19th century the reputation of Kabbalah had fallen from high respect during its most original period in Medieval times to a superstitious repetition of magical formulae. This happened because the Work was not protected in the right way. It is not secrecy that guards the tradition but correct conduct and, if this is not present, then people do not find the door to the inner path which is their birthright. The lack of real spirituality today amongst clergy has made many Jews and Christians turn to the Eastern religions for their esoteric instruction. This is sad because they have within their own Western traditions all the higher knowledge and methods they need for the development of the Occidental psyche and spirituality.

Not all ignorance and immorality is to be found in the outer world. There are those on the fringe of the Work who are referred to, as noted, as 'Wolves in sheep's clothing!' They can be people of relatively high inner development who have all the appearance of being on the Path but have, in fact, left its narrow way. Many such gurus gather around them students who seek similar powers themselves; those who come are under the spell of other-worldliness or those looking for real knowledge. The characteristics of such dark teachers are their preoccupation with superiority, exclusivity, their own mastery, absolute obedience and with keeping up the mystery. If their position is ever doubted then there is inevitably a crisis in which they apply psychic and social pressure. Their word is law. They are usually fiercely supported without question by those dependent on them.

Sometimes it takes much experience to separate the genuine teacher from the false because the latter often possess fragments of Truth. One test is the level of ethics applied. A sound but strict instructor will acknowledge a student's right to disagree and allow him to depart with goodwill and perhaps a recommendation to another school. A false instructor will assert that his is the only way and seek to discredit any other tradition. This clearly is not the esoteric view which recognises that all truly spiritual ways lead to God. Often such a leader is the idol of his students and stands in the way of their progress. Sometimes it is 'the teaching' that is held up to be the sole mode of enlightenment. This is another Luciferic device to lead inexperienced aspirants into a gilded cage. Such 'teachings' cause psychological blindness and spiritual pride. One hallmark of this kind of school is the lack of humility and personal conscience. Often there is a strange collective sterility and conformity about the manner, dress and lives of the teacher and students. The converse is a real company of seekers in the presence of intelligent direction, love, discipline and integrity which allows for group and individual progress. Here we have the qualities of the soul and the mark of Companions of the Light.

35. *Companions*

When going on a long, arduous and dangerous journey it is always wise to have good companions. However, such people are not easily found. Normally, we feel that our closest relationships are with our blood family and in ordinary life this is true for most people. Certainly up until recent times, even members of a family who did not get on personally still retained a strong relationship. The social and economic revolutions of the twentieth century have changed much of this pattern in the Western world and so people do not always remain in their families or even the social groups in which they were brought up. Many, because of education, opportunity and travel, leave what was in effect their village, be it in the countryside or in the city, never to return except on visits to the old home. This is particularly true of those of the post-1960 generations who wandered throughout the world looking for a spiritual alternative to the materialistic solution that has brought much physical comfort but with it many social and psychological problems.

Seen on a large scale, mankind is on the move. It has, in the more economically advanced countries, tried both the extremes of a political ideal as a way of life and found them wanting. Young and not so young Americans, for example, are no longer convinced that the possession of wealth brings happiness and nor do the deeper thinking Russians believe that the Soviet system is the answer to life's dilemmas; hence the dissident movement. After a long search, many sensitive and intelligent people give up because they find no alternative to the rat race and immerse themselves in passing the time in many games that range from the infantile to the various sophisticated forms of amusement that avoid the obscure thoughts of ageing and death.

A few seekers still keep looking. They follow different trails trying to find the rainbow's end. They read of it in books, of which there are now legion, and they hear about it through hearsay but rarely do they make direct contact with anyone who is actually working on the spiritual path. There are many who believe they are walking the Way but it is soon clear from the style they live their lives that this is not so and that their driving motivation is ego. This can manifest in personal power or the need to be special, the wish to be led or the desire for the unusual. It can even be fashionable to be seen in spiritual work as it was with many like the 'Flower Children' and guru movements of the 1960s and 1970s. The residue of this period is still with us in that many people who are no longer young and idealistic are now deeply enmeshed in the realities of life. Most have families and pursue professions and many have forgotten the promise of that epoch of awakening. A few, however, still yearn for the inner life, even though they have lost faith in charismatic leaders and suspect that many so-called spiritual organisations are either power- or money-oriented. This creates a profound loneliness and sometimes a deep despair.

If one does contact a true tradition, it is usually the result of much work and the fact that Providence will respond and help the genuine seeker. A book turning up at a critical moment, an apparently chance meeting or the realisation that a certain acquaintance has an esoteric connection brings a sense of surprise and wonder. Such moments are momentous because they can only happen when the individual is ready. At any other time the book would not be seen, the meeting missed and the casual hint by the old friend go unnoticed. However, when the person is awake enough to spot and take up the lead, many new things begin to happen.

After the initial stages of confusion and conflict, as you extract yourself from your old life which sometimes means separating yourself psychologically, if not physically, from your family and friends, you enter into a companionship of the spirit. This does not mean that you reject your relatives or cut off from old friendships, although this does occasionally happen, but that you form a completely new set of relationships with yourself as the intermediary between your various worlds. This echoes the actual situation at a higher level. The effect, if properly carried out and not used as an excuse to escape worldly responsibility, is to act as a mediator between Earth and Heaven to help raise the level of the society or circle in which you live as you impart, often unseen, the spirit you have received from what are sometimes called the Companions of the Light.

The notion of the *Havarim* or Companions is an ancient one and is recognised in every tradition. In Kabbalah they have been called by various names down the centuries. At one time such groups were called 'Those who Know;' at another 'The Wise-Hearted;' at another

FIGURE 37—COMPANIONS
A school of the soul is like a desert caravan. There are many hazards on such a
journey and one needs people around who can be trusted. There are many who
join the caravan for fun or out of curiosity. They usually drop out as the difficulties
of development mount. Only those who stay the course, are proved to be reliable
and are a real support can be called the Companions of the Light. These become
closer than friends and family. (A rabbinic school, 16th century woodcut.)

'Masters of Service'. They have been named 'The Ones of Understanding' and 'Those who Reap the Field'. This last title perhaps gives us a clear picture of their aim in that they work in the world, even though their orientation is heavenward. However, before one enters fully into such a company there are several stages.

The first is the probationary period. This may last a few weeks or many years, depending on the commitment and quality of the work done by the individual. This is monitored by the next level whose members are not yet initiates but who are deeply involved in the Work. What constitutes an initiate has often been debated but the truth of the matter is that when a person is prepared to devote the whole of life unconditionally to the Work, he can be considered an initiate. No part-time Kabbalist exists. It must come first. Everything is centred round the Work. Personal and public crises may come and go but the Work must be continued. Nothing can take precedence over it. This has been said by many spiritual masters and not a few have died for the sake of the Work. It is a hard line of demarcation but humanity has benefited from such commitments, as the life's work and death of both Jesus and Socrates bear witness. Such constancy is vital to hold the chain of a tradition and keep the flow between the upper and lower Worlds. When going on a long, arduous and dangerous journey it is reassuring to have such reliable companions. One's life may depend on them at some time.

The companionship of the Spirit begins with the first contact of someone on the Way. From here, it develops into a deep friendship that no ordinary link or relationship can match. For example, people may not see each other for years and yet they will talk, when they meet, as if they had parted only yesterday because the level upon which they communicate does not belong to ordinary time. Over the years such relationships develop to a point that there has to be no immediate contact. Indeed, some grow deeper in distance. Gradually, there emerges a network of companions who are not only good company but act as mutual watchers over the progress of oneself, other individuals and groups. United, several such people can form not only a greater vessel of receptivity to the Higher Worlds but also act as a bastion against any onslaughts from evil, at either the physical or subtler levels. Such support is occasionally vital in certain crises.

Usually a group is centred round a tutor or teacher. The first focus is the most common because a tutor is often a senior student who just transmits the theory of the tradition and shows how to carry out its practices. A teacher is another matter. This is an advanced person who actually has the power to make a living connection for the group between those below and those above. The rest of the group is usually divided into beginners, who are learning how to learn, those who are translating the study into reality, those who are aware of what is involved, those who know but have not yet committed themselves fully and those who have formed an interior core within the main group. Thus, there is an internal hierarchy that has the possibility of every rung of the ladder of spiritual evolution from the probationer to the Messiah, if one were fortunate enough to be in the right place at the right time. There are, of course, the sub-divisions of personal resonance and things shared. Thus, the usual social and professional affinities generate fellowship, love affairs and even marriage although, like all human activities, such relationships can create the usual complications. These, however, should be handled by the Kabbalist with a deeper understanding and be put to use for self-development and service to the Work.

The presence of a group of companions is vital in spiritual work because it brings a sense of scale and balance. Many an individual has been saved from slipping off the Path by the check rope of their companions. To be alone is sad enough but to climb the Holy Mountain without a guide, or at least a friend, is to tempt trouble. Therefore, you learn to cherish your spiritual companions, even though you may sometimes be in conflict with them—which occasionally happens, for even groups have their crises as they undergo changes from time to time. Here, we begin to consider the wider and deeper implications of our study for, while we will not deal in detail with the work of a school (that is another book), we will go on to look at the next stage of contacting the Companions of the Light in the upper Worlds, who gather round and watch over any serious enterprise that is being carried out below on Earth. This will give us an insight into the connection and continuity of the kabbalistic tradition through time and space.

36. Upper Room

A kabbalistic meeting is a place where a working group comes together
to discuss or practise Kabbalah. It usually occurs in a space especially
prepared for the occasion. This may be no more than the slight alteration
of a domestic room to make it into a sacred spot, or a special chamber,
specifically designed for the purpose, that is used for nothing else.
There is no general rule, except there be a focus of attention upon
either an altar or a symbol of the tradition. The chair of the tutor is
secondary and must never be more than that. Seen in Tree terms, the
tutor sits at Tiferet with the point of aim at Keter, the Crown of the
group Tree. In this way there is no identification with even a teacher
as anything more than a place of interconnection, because each student
must make his or her own interior communication to the Crown.

The form of the meeting, like the setting, can be varied. This
depends on the time and place and the conditions prevailing. In one
period there may be no more than a brief format, in another time and
place a complex ritual to meet the needs and possibilities of the age.
For example, the service in the Temple of Jerusalem was highly formal
with prayers, music and sacrifices while the meetings in the small
apartment rooms of Gerona in medieval Spain were probably more
like university seminars. Some meetings in 16th-century Galilee
closely resembled a seance.

Every age has its particular work to do and every group its own
peculiar task. Thus, no two groups are ever the same although they
may be branches of the same line. However, there are certain things
they do share. The first is the reason why they gather together. If they
are not convened in order to serve God, they are not kabbalistic
groups. Anything less reduces them to low magic or worse, if they
seek only to exploit the forces they invoke. Another thing that is
shared is the high degree of honesty that is to be expected. This
level of integrity should be the norm; indeed, any deception will
automatically separate an individual from the group. This does not
have to be implemented by anyone but occurs spontaneously according
to inner laws. Without openness nothing can flow up or down or

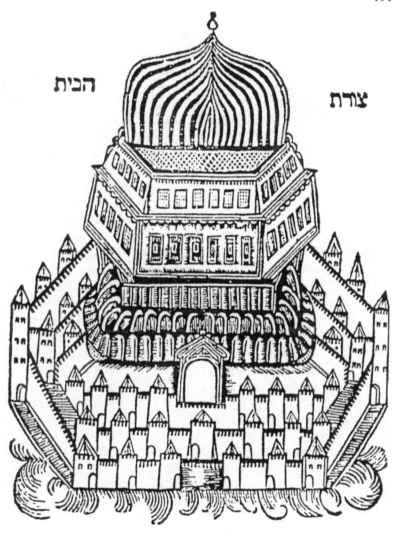

הבית

צורת

FIGURE 38—INNER SPACE

While a group may gather in a magnificent temple, a stone circle, a Masonic Lodge or a priest's home, the 'upper room' is not of the Earth. It is a place where those below meet each other and, at the level of the soul, their discarnate Teacher. Some people perceive their inner space as a hermitage, others a spiritual college or monastery. It depends upon the tradition of the school. Here the inner Temple was seen in the form of the Dome of the Rock in Jerusalem. (Image of the Dome of the Rock in Jerusalem, 17th century.)

between the members. This does not mean discretion cannot be exercised; that is quite different, although it requires maturity and some conscious development to discern and practise the difference.

Many groups meet once a week. This is a natural rhythm. Some members might contact each other on other days but that is according to necessity and inclination. Once a month a group might meet just to meditate or perform some ceremony that cannot be carried out during an ordinary workshop meeting. What is about to be described can be executed during a weekly occasion. Let it be a model that can be adapted to local conditions.

Let us assume that a group meeting has started off with a silent coming together. After this comes the evocation of the Tree and the Names of God. By the time the petition for the Holy Presence to manifest during the meeting has been asked for, everyone should have moved out of the ego state into the consciousness of the self. After a moment's pause in silence, the working session can begin with a discussion of the current exercise. Let us assume that the week's study has been the detection of help from above that often goes unnoticed. One person might speak about being directed out of his usual way in order to meet, by apparent accident, an old friend in need. Another may tell the story of how she was aware of a softening hand on her shoulder while writing a particularly severe letter—it was not sent. Yet another might describe how he came into possession of a much needed book which was out of print. A secondhand copy had been found in a junk shop where he had been looking for a mirror. A discussion could develop out of these examples and slowly, as other incidents are collected, a pattern begins to emerge. It might seem that in many cases a specific need is met or a certain danger warded off. All the events pivot upon a moment in time when the juxtaposition of spiritual, psychological and physical conditions are adjusted to achieve a definite effect. Out of this come many questions. These are collected and collated until they are formulated into a concise set of enquiries. The group is now ready to approach the Companions in the upper room.

Tradition has it that whenever two or more are gathered together in the name of the Holy Spirit, then there will be a corresponding gathering above to listen and assist those below. Sometimes members of a group who are in a higher state actually hear and see these beings quite spontaneously. In this operation, an attempt consciously to perceive them will be made. Drawing everyone in the room into full attention, the leader then proceeds to raise the communal level. This is done by taking the group into an awareness of the body, up through the preoccupation of the ego and into consciousness of the self. Then, working in concert, they hover above the roof of the house before rising up into a high and Holy Place of meeting. There each person is asked to visualise all those present in a domed chamber with a hole in the ceiling. After this scene is established, everyone is requested to look around with his mind's eye and see who else is there besides those they are acquainted with.

Many people discover that there are persons present that they do not know sitting next to them and then again sometimes they catch the face or voice of their spiritual teacher who greets them with a characteristic remark. While this phenomenon is interesting in itself, of greater importance is the discussion going on between the individuals at the centre of the circle. They sit directly under the aperture in the ceiling, through which can be seen the firmament of stars. A light percolates down into the room to illuminate the inner group who conduct a discussion on the questions posed. The group just listens. In Kabbalah the inner circle is sometimes called 'Members of the Academy on High'. The particular rank of those involved in the discussion, however, would depend on the calibre of the group.

After listening to the various reflections, which usually develop from what has been talked about below, the upper meeting is thrown open for questions. Here, the earthly tutor invites each person to ask his questions and others that might arise. A period of silence is observed to allow the answers to be given, although not everyone in the group below will receive a reply. People can lose the contact. When the process is complete and the heightened consciousness can no longer be held, the tutor will sense that it is time to close the session. After thanking the Companions above for their help, the tutor then slowly brings the group down by stages to the house and back into the room. All present stamp their feet to earth themselves after opening their eyes.

When everyone has fully re-entered his body, observations are called for by the tutor. Different people report on the answers they received. These are silently pondered for a few minutes before any discussion should begin. The analysis should generate more questions which lead to the development of the theme that is being explored. In some cases an enormous amount of material, say, about the nature of the soul, may have been received and this is shared with those who could not see or hear so clearly. Indeed, there may be some present who did not even get off the ground and sat in frustrated silence wondering if the others were just fantasising. This situation can happen for many reasons. A person may not be physically well, under psychological duress; he may not yet have learnt the technique of letting go of sensual experience or he may have been blocked from ascending because he was not in a suitable state. After the group has explored the experience to its full, new conclusions may emerge. Occasionally, if the company is in a particularly good state, they may return to the upper chamber and have a second and deeper session with their normally unseen instructors. This exercise must not, however, be carried out too often lest it lose its potency by over-familiarity.

At the end of the meeting the Tree is descended, finishing with an appropriate prayer or text.

After the candles have been blown out and the various duties, such as who will buy the next week's bread and wine, who will write up the evening's notes and who will make the coffee and wash up, have been dealt with, the formal meeting is dissolved. From this point on, until all go home, the talk can be personal so as to allow individuals to enter the earthly world and relate socially. This is carried out whilst still retaining the inner mood of the meeting which will be taken afterwards into ordinary life. Thus, each person always keeps an inner connection with the other members of the group and the Companions of the upper room.

This exercise, like the others described, is one of many used in Kabbalah. Obviously such operations must be executed with great care, with checks made on those who participate in them to make sure they can cope with such experiences. An epileptic fit, for example, can be triggered by such a high intake of energy. Generally speaking, people are only allowed to take part in these excursions when there is adequate precaution below and protection from above. This is one of the tutor's responsibilities, besides watching over individual development, co-ordinating the group and acting as liaison officer between the Worlds. In the next chapter we examine the long-term effect of this kind of work.

37. Chariot

Over a period of time the cumulative effect of kabbalistic work brings about a transformation within a group. One of the products of this change is the formation of a vehicle that can carry consciousness out of the ordinary state and into realms that are beyond the capability of most individuals. This is because the processes of inner development that co-ordinate the aspects of the psyche in the individual also form a collective organism within the group. This subtle chariot, as it was called, is a Yeziratic vehicle that can bring back something of the Higher Worlds as well as take people there. Let us look at its structure and dynamics so as to perceive its nature and substance.

Taking the group as the material and model of the chariot we can see, for example, how its Malkhut or physical base is established by meeting in the same place at the same time. Over the years the fabric of the house used for study and practice becomes saturated with the kabbalistic actions, emotions and thoughts generated and experienced there. It also builds up a reservoir of psychological energy that forms a detectable field in the room. This strengthens each time a meeting or operation is carried out and thus the chamber begins to become a vessel for the fine residue of the upper Worlds, which gradually accumulates and creates the distinct atmosphere of a sanctuary. This phenomenon will deepen over time to produce a remarkable effect in that whoever enters the room will be, unless he is sick or spiritually dead, inwardly lifted by a concentrated presence of Spirit such as sacred places have. Hence, the elemental structure is refined to such a degree that it is no longer just an ordinary room but a physical connection to the levels above.

The Yesod of the chariot is made up by the ordinary ego level of the group. After a time group members, like any other collection of people, will begin to relate. At first there will be individual connections; then associations through shared interests. Later, as deeper personal and spiritual relationships develop, the group will slowly divide itself into the doers, feelers and thinkers. Moreover, within these three sub-triads, there will be those who always tend to take the initiative and

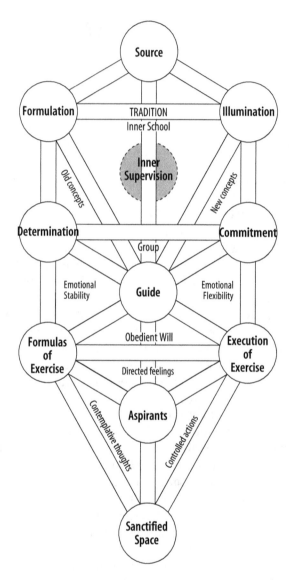

FIGURE 39—ORDER

Every esoteric school must have all the elements shown in this Tree. The level of discipline has to be very high and yet be both stable and flexible to allow inner growth. Tried and tested concepts should be retained but new ideas allowed in as times change. The life of a school may stretch over two generations or exist for centuries. All of the great world religions were born out of a great teacher and a small group. (Halevi, 20th century.)

those who will hold back, making up the extrovert and introvert division of the lower face of the group chariot. As the organism begins to emerge, the phenomenon of group identification will appear as each member integrates with the others in memory when they are not together. In time this will generate a comradeship such as is found on board a ship; and this analogue is not so far removed, if one considers a group as an ark floating on the waters of life.

As the lower face of the chariot Tree is slowly riveted together by shared experience to form the central Yesod of the company, so there begins the emergence of the different levels. The first is quite easily recognised when a stranger comes to a meeting. Initially, there is the tribal sense of the outsider, even though the much welcomed person might be from another group or spiritual discipline. This reveals the Yesodic image of the group and its particular character and limitations. Without guidance this collective ego could become an exclusive sect or clique. A kabbalistic group is expected to avoid this pitfall and raise a quite natural communal feeling up to the level of spirituality. This is done by applying the group consciousness to reflective observation about itself and its performance regarding the Work. This is not a mutual therapy but a process in which everything discussed is related to the principles of the Tree. Thus there is built up an objective working method and trust that holds the personal tendencies of all the individual egos in obedience to principles. Under this discipline, the Yesod of the group becomes a stable foundation and reflection of whatever might be going on collectively.

The gradual education of the group's Yesod by the techniques of ritual, devotion and contemplation produces, with diligent effort, a highly sensitive instrument which registers every action, feeling and thought in the group, so that the doer begins to comprehend the thinker and the feeler the thinker and doer and *vice versa*. This creates possibilities denied to the individual on his own, for it grants insight into other types of experience and enables even the newest student a glimpse of what it is like further along the path and what qualities might be needed. A group Yesod, moreover, facilitates a greater resolution of what is seen in the Worlds above and below. Its wider image, like that of a great telescope, gives a larger view than that of which most, if not all, members of the group are capable.

The next level to be developed is that which lies beyond the threshold defined by Hodian theory and Nezahian practice. It grants access to a higher level of consciousness than the ordinary mind. This is often noted, in that people who come to the group in a depressed state or with some mundane preoccupation, are usually elevated out of it. Indeed, some soon realise after a meeting has begun that they were just immersed in ego problems. The level of awakening is the weekly meeting itself and is the place where most of the members should be, at least once, during the session. Alas, many oscillate between Yesod and Tiferet, so that when the majority are below the Hod-Nezah line the level of the group is noticeably low. This is usually the point when the tutor introduces some stimulus to bring the group back into the triad of awakening again, that is Hod, Nezah and Tiferet.

At any given moment, a member of the group may be in one of three distinct levels. For example, a person's attention may be absent as they consider some worldly problem. Such a state almost excludes them from the group because they are there only physically. The second condition is to be so Yesodically involved in discussion that one is quite unaware of what is actually happening. This can only be observed by those in an awakened state who are really present and in touch with whatever is flowing down from above. The fourth level of the soul constitutes what is called the 'time-body' of the group. By this is meant the subtle organism that has evolved over the years which joins all its members, past and present, near and absent, in a union of love, discipline and truth; that is the three sefirot of the soul triad. This organism is the delicate chariot-cum-vessel a group can make, form and create for itself by conscious effort to collect, fuse and integrate their Work into a tangible form. Here is the group's upper room where it may meet with and welcome its Inner Teacher, as well as contact others who are absent or dead.

In kabbalistic terms, the soul level is the gateway into the Higher Worlds because it is not attached to the physical realm except by its connection with the place where the three lower Worlds meet. This triad is the *Merkabah* or vehicle in which all that has been acquired by the group is held in Yeziratic form ready for use each week. Such a chariot can exist for decades, even though a group may have long dispersed. Indeed, when a group that has not met for some years is reconvened, it usually finds that nothing has changed, despite their physical ageing, and that all can enter the collective chariot as before and make use of its facilities. Of course, in time such vehicles, like their physical counterparts, do become redundant so that over the centuries the form that was applicable during, say, the eleventh century is no longer as efficient as a new model. That is why Kabbalah periodically changes its mode of presentation, as in the 1200s when the Babylonian system was remodelled in Gerona to meet the crisis between faith and reason in Spain and France. Every culture and epoch has its own problems and solutions.

The development of such vehicles is essential, not only for a group but also for the Tradition because through them the Teaching is passed on. By this I mean that actual experience of the Higher Worlds transforms theory and practice into reality. Thus, there can be moments when everyone present at a meeting is lifted up and enters a higher state. This is possible because they are carried by the momentum of the group's chariot. Many novices have perceived for themselves, if only for an instant, the cosmic insights that they have read about. This can only happen within the safety of a group with its disciplined structure and support. One such example was when a group, which was composed of newcomers as well as senior students, was shown a shaft of golden light falling vertically through a ceiling from a great height out of a deep blue vault of sky and into a small crowded room to leave an indelible impression of the existence of Grace. At another time a probationer, not given to visions, saw a great eagle floating high over the meeting place. This is a symbol of the Holy Spirit. While on another evening some members of a group became suddenly aware of other beings in the room who were watching over the meeting as if from another dimension.

The development of the inner vehicle of a kabbalistic group requires great effort on everyone's part. For instance, each member can act as a changing element within the meeting and take up various roles in the structure and dynamics of its Tree. Sometimes, one can actually perceive who are the pillars and which triads or sefirot are being occupied or acted out by those present. Occasionally, the whole working scheme can come into view and one can know at what level the group is, at that moment, as it holds a position according to its centre of spiritual gravity. If a group can develop and maintain a high degree of conscious interaction, then even more can be given and received from above. This kind of work requires a commitment in which no member ever falls below the level of the soul triad during a meeting. Such a standard can only be achieved after many years when each individual has developed within him or herself a stable and receptive personal vehicle to act as a conscious instrument between the Worlds. This is the theme of our next chapter.

FIGURE 40—ASCENT
In some traditions it is believed that a soul incarnates through the forms of
minerals, vegetables and animals before becoming human. This is a misunder-
standing of the process of development. No one is reborn as rat, thorn or rock
because they have regressed. These are symbols about the state of a soul. All
humans have their origins in the Divine Adam and have the four Worlds within
their being. No stone, flower or mammal has such an inner anatomy. (Lully's
steps up to the Heavenly Jerusalem, medieval woodcut.)

38. Instrument

We have seen how a group develops and integrates its various levels; so it is with an individual. The chief difference, however, is that the group works on a different scale and operates from a less refined base to begin with. Like the group, an individual seeks to become a vessel that can receive and impart what is brought into its range. This is contingent on how far and deep the person is prepared to go in Kabbalah. Everyone has his limits, although there are some whose ambition exceeds their capacity at a given time. To develop the higher levels before the lower, and so skip in-between stages, is to court disaster. Every step must be filled before the influence of the Higher Worlds can be transmitted consistently. Indeed, to maintain a constant link between Heaven and Earth without a graduated connection would burn one out. Only those who have made, formed and created these inner bridges can carry a heavy spiritual charge for any period of time. To try is to strain those connections that have been made and so impair the levels that are operational. This is the warning of the tragic Talmudic story of the four rabbis who entered the Higher Worlds. One died, one went mad and one lost faith. Only the last returned safely.

In order to proceed with a degree of security, all the theories and practices given must be carefully learnt and carried out over a long period under wise supervision. In time the seven lower halls, as they are traditionally called, are systematically entered and a balanced position is established in each. This process follows the ascent up the Tree of the psyche and, though you may touch and even have a tentative hold on one level, there will be many moments when you have to drop level so as to correct a function or dissolve some habit that has crept in to distort a lower triad. A watch over the whole inner Tree has to be constantly maintained, so that a balanced progression in the refinement of the inner chariot can continue safely. When a certain degree of development has been obtained, there begins the connection and building of the next chariot of the spiritual body. However, before this can occur certain stages must be passed through.

We have seen how an increased physical awareness reveals the four elements at work in our bodies and how, through their intelligence, we may become conscious of the elemental world about us. We may also, through this elemental connection, gain access to our organic bodies and so receive insights into the mechanical, organic, chemical and electronic realms that operate beneath our skin. Observations of these levels are of immense use because, by analogy, we can ascertain the nature and state of our psychological functions. The ability to switch Worlds by conscious will is a vital skill in the Work and much effort should be devoted to shifting levels between body and psyche. In time we should be able to pinpoint and relate parallel levels in each body, like the organs reflecting feelings and *vice versa* or the ego working off the habits programmed by the autonomous nervous system.

The next stage is to integrate the ego and its adjacent triads of thinking, feeling and action. If well trained, then Yesod will function like a first class manager watching over the various functions and balancing them with great skill. The Yesodic ego shares the same point of cognition with the body's Daat or Knowledge and so co-operation between these two will be valuable practice for the similar but higher communication between the Daat of the psyche and the Yesod of the Spirit. The third level is that of the feeling triad which doubles as the place of willingness. Here a high degree of sensitivity enables the psyche's functions to operate and so help in the general co-ordination of the lower face of the psyche which is completed by the fourth level of awakening. When all the triads involved are within the range of an alert ego, then their combined power fuses into a concerted capability, of which ordinary fragmented consciousness knows nothing except in a crisis or a moment of Grace. The lucidity associated with this state of Gadlut alertness should become the norm for the Kabbalist. Buddhists call it mindfulness.

The extending range of interior awareness brings into the light of the self at Tiferet all the triads of emotional and intellectual complexes. These psychological aggregates of memories, reactions and stimuli, after a period of Work, become increasingly interrelated instead of being randomly triggered and associated by circumstance. As such they operate more like a well-organised company than a rabble. This allows for the accomplishment of things impossible to the undisciplined psyche. Interior or exterior problems can be handled with greater ease because the resources that can deal with them are not only more readily available but can also work with increased power. Thus, like an integrated group of people, the psyche develops its capacity to act and be receptive in the wider range made available by the improved communication between its normally divided parts. Some call this state 'being together'.

The soul triad which hovers above the centre of the Tree becomes, with the increased integration of the surrounding triads, more directly involved with everyday life instead of just being an unconscious conscience. It can actively participate in the lower face by working through the self of Tiferet. This means it can transmit what it has received at its level and inform the Yesodic ego. An example of this is when a man picks up that something is wrong in a situation. If it is correct, he can generate conscience in others by the presence of soul consciousness without interfering in the process that is going on. In this way he may create conditions for self-realisation without anyone but those on the same level knowing. In some cases people just start behaving decently because the person is near them. For obvious reasons this exercise can only be executed properly by someone who has no personal desire for power. It will be remembered that the soul triad is the place of testing and temptation.

The sixth level of the psychological chariot is the triad of the Spirit. This cannot be fully developed without passing through an awareness and integration of all the lower levels. Its unconscious presence is sometimes perceived in children and simple people. To possess a conscious spirituality is quite another matter. To operate at this level requires that person voluntarily to submit to the deepest kind of Work. However, this signifies more than just effort. It means that the ego is quiescent so that all that is personal no longer matters. This does not, in Kabbalah, suggest that the self is without will but that one does what one is told in obedience, although to whom or what is important. In this tradition only God's Will counts; the rest is but advice. When a true spiritual submission is made then the dark glass of Daat, the sefirah of Knowledge, begins to clear and the way to the Divine opens. Such a breakthrough can come because of long or intense work or through an act of Grace. Its quality is cosmic, in that the soul is seen set against a celestial background rather than in an earthly context. One begins to shift Worlds and so the Daat of psychological Knowledge becomes the spiritual Yesod of Creation. The man who suddenly saw all the lives of the people in a supermarket as patterns was perceiving through this level.

This conversion of state in the sixth hall is the prelude to the seventh which completes the psychological organism. Here, we are told, one comes in direct contact with the Divine Presence as one touches the Keter of Formation, the Tiferet of Creation and the Malkhut of Emanation. At this point, where the three upper Worlds meet, another transformation occurs as the whole of the psychological Tree becomes not only integrated but suffused with Divine Light and the Wind of the Spirit. In such a state the psychological organism becomes unified and so no longer split in sections by its functions and levels. Like a perfectly healthy physical body it can, in this state, carry out unearthly manoeuvres such as exploring history or observing distant places. However, while these powers and others come with the maturity of the psychological body, their prime purpose is to be agents between the upper and lower Worlds, so as to serve events in either. Clearly the possession of such a vehicle demands the highest integrity of the individual but then that is what is meant by the word. If this is lost then the unity of being is broken and a shattering occurs, often with tragic consequences. This is a crucial point of development, for here is where Lucifer especially seeks to tempt people to fall, like himself, from Grace. Thus, the greater the height, the more the individual is tested so as to prove that he or she is able to use their gifts responsibly.

As we have seen, the development of the psychological organism is a long and arduous matter. It may take many lifetimes to accomplish completion although it is possible in one, if the commitment is there and it serves Providence's purpose. For most of us who slowly plod up on the Way, it is the gradual acquisition of an instrument that is of enormous potential. A fully developed psyche can fly higher than any rocket and penetrate deeper into the nether regions than any bore hole. Its range extends beyond the most powerful microscope and largest telescope. In vision, it can wander around the solar system and perceive, through imagination, the smallest processes in matter. However, of greater importance is the fact that it is possible to enter Paradise or even Heaven while still on the Earth. Mystics have known and exploited this reality over the centuries, and not a few Kabbalists have experienced during life what most of mankind glimpses only at the moments of birth and death.

Such a possibility is open to anyone who works along a path of self-development but few, unfortunately, know what they see or hear when these moments of vision occur as the dark glass brightens just enough to allow a flash of the upper Worlds. It is one thing to visit a higher realm and another to realise what has been revealed, as many students discover when they read the writings of the mystics or go there themselves. The visionary must also possess knowledge.

39. *Vision*

In order to understand visions we must first be clear about illusions, so as to be able to tell the difference. As a general definition, it could be said that illusions are subjective projections of our own or of others while visions are objective and are impressions of things that exist in their own right. A simple example of this would be an imaginary anxiety that something bad has happened to someone, only to find it was a projection of our own anger or fear, as against the sense that something odd has occurred at home and later to discover that it has been burnt down. The latter is only too real in concrete terms while the former may be no more than a fantasy.

Another characteristic of illusion is that it often has no order, in that whilst it may have its own kind of pattern, it has no relation to what is really going on or connection with any kind of integrated reality. By this is meant that it does not fit into the general scheme of Creation, except as one of the elements of chaos or separation that seek to make a universe of their own, at the centre of which lies the ego of the maker. Many people live out their lives in this manner. Taken to its extreme come insanity and criminality because there is no relationship to the laws of reality or society. When penetrating into the depths of our own psyches or into the lower heights of the universe, encounters with these elements in ourselves and those beings who live on these levels are to be expected. Therefore, one must check what is experienced against the criterion of 'Does it take one closer to or further away from the Presence of God?'

In Kabbalah, order is implicit and this is a sign that whatever is seen is part of the general plan of Creation. Thus, whatever is shown should fall into the recognisable scheme of the Tree and its various divisions. It is taught that there are seven levels in everything that exists, even visions. These are usually divided into the literal, allegorical, metaphysical and mystical at the earthly level; and the soul, spiritual and Divine at the heavenly level. Seen practically, these levels represent different ranges of cognition, so that any event has the possibility of being a key to illumination. A vision is a situation

FIGURE 41—VISION
While the prophet Ezekiel sat by the River Cheber in Babylon, the higher Worlds opened up to him. How could he describe the indescribable, except through the symbolism of a vast chariot with a Throne set within it, upon which sat the fiery figure of Adam Kadmon. Anyone who has had a mystical experience has the problem of transmitting what they see. This can be done by allegory, metaphysics, mathematics, poetry or visual imagery. (Ezekiel's vision, Bear's Bible 16th century.)

where the emphasis is centred in the celestial rather than the terrestrial realm.

The reason why the Bible is so remarkable is because much of its material contains all seven levels. For example, the story of the fall of Jericho before Joshua and the Israelites illustrates many principles. First, let us consider the background. Now the Children of Israel, that is the as-yet unintegrated aspects of the psyche under the Spirit represented by Israel, have escaped the bondage of Egypt, that is slavery to the body, and crossed the wilderness. This desert represents a stage only too well-known as the purging of useless aspects of the psyche. During this period all but two of those who originally left Egypt died. That is, all the old habits have gone and a new generation, born out of the time in the wilderness, has arisen, led by the only original and constant psychological element that was fit to enter the Promised Land. This is symbolised by Joshua (the name means 'Deliverer') who takes the freeborn Israelites across the river Jordan which marks, like the crossing of the Red Sea, a major breakthrough into another dimension. Here, the situation may be seen as the entering into the zone between the psyche and the Spirit where many of the old collective concepts, represented by the Canaanites, have to be destroyed by Israel. This process, begun with the conquest of Jericho by help from above, came to be called the Wars of the Lord that were to clean out the land and make it Holy, for it had become degenerate since Jacob had left there.

Thus, we have in Joshua, chapter VI, the falling wall episode which may be seen literally as history or allegorically as a symbol of the first confrontation with a corrupt set of ideas, represented by the city, and metaphysically as a description of an esoteric approach to a psycho-spiritual problem with detailed instructions. This process involved circling the town six times, once each day, in silence and then seven times on the last day with the mass shouting of the host backing the blasts of the priestly trumpets. At this point the walls of Jericho collapsed and the army entered to destroy everything that lived in the town. Seen as a complex of concepts, this event may be considered as an account of the defence system around some redundant beliefs dissolving, whilst at the level of the soul the direction that 'the people shall ascend up, every man straight before him' speaks of the rising up and occupation of the vacated complex. This is verified by a moral test in the injunction that no one should take the treasure found for himself, lest he be accursed by it, but that it should be consecrated unto the Lord. That is, the spiritual wealth that Jericho did possess should be purified and rededicated to the Divine. A minor incident in this chapter, the saving of Rahab the prostitute and her family who had earlier helped the Israelite spies, is typical of the fine detail to be observed in scripture and visions, for they imply much to be pondered on besides the main story.

Strangely enough, when reading more directly visionary literature, like the Books of Enoch and the Merkabah texts, we find the material less easy to understand. This is because it is not earthed as are the scriptures, which are designed to blend mystical principles with historic events so that untrained people could sense that there is a relationship between the upper and lower Worlds. In the case of the Hekalot literature of old Judea and the Babylonian rabbinical schools, accounts of heavenly journeys were only for private circulation. This was because the mystical side of Judaism could easily be misunderstood. It was therefore restricted to the most learned or pious. Indeed, to speak openly about, for example, the three aspects of Divinity, could be seen as heretical in an essentially monotheistic religion. Thus, much of the material was made deliberately obscure in order to confuse anyone but those who had a foot on the ladder of vision.

Records tell us that the ancient rabbis would form groups in which a master would go into a deep meditation after all the procedures of ablution and preparation had been completed. As he rose from level to level, he would report back what he saw which would be noted down to be discussed later. Sometimes, a question would be asked through the master, if he had not lost contact with the incarnate level. Indeed, once a teacher was brought back by being touched by a piece of soiled cloth, so as to get an important observation clarified. For obvious reasons such exercises were carried out under strict supervision and certainly no one who was unqualified to be present was allowed into such a session.

The reason that such things can be written about now is that what was exclusive knowledge then is now general esoteric information. For example, you can go into any good bookshop on comparative religion and purchase texts that have been kept secret for centuries. Unfortunately, many of the ancient techniques of ascension have been adopted by people who do not understand the full implication of what is being done and thus avoid the responsibility of what goes with these processes. Therefore, books have to be written in order to give some idea of what is involved when these methods are used. To recapitulate:

before going on such a journey, there must be a solid background of discipline, theory and practice and a reliable instructor, as well as good company on hand. It is vital that an aspirant realises that there are great dangers in this Work but, if a correct and diligent path is followed, then these obstacles become useful tests of inner development. In the book of Enoch there are varied and detailed descriptions of the heavens and their inhabitants. These accounts were naturally influenced by the culture in which the visionary lived. Here we have the blend of the subjective and the objective inasmuch as the world of Creation has no form, being primarily a realm of pure essence. However, in order to be able to perceive that World, it is necessary to clothe these patterns of force and archangelic entities in an intelligible image for the psyche. Thus, the consciousness of the visionary uses what is already available in the memory which has an enormous bank of personal and collective imagery to draw upon. This is why each age and every mystic has a slightly different version of the upper Worlds. What is essential remains the same, if we can discern what lies beyond the face of the description. In the technique that follows, the process is reversed, in that an ascension journey is set out in a series of images which the student can enter, be guided up and through the various levels until he perceives, behind the scenes evoked, the reality they represent. There will be moments and places when illusion may intrude but these can be quickly identified after some practice. The method used is a reliable one because it does not allow the mystic to wander but holds the attention to the path like, as one rabbi said, 'A ladder in the midst of one's house by which one may ascend to and descend from Heaven'.

40. Chariot Rider

After the appropriate preparations have been completed, the Tree erected and permission and blessing requested from the Most High, the chariot rider moves from the state of being acutely aware of the body and the mood of the ordinary mind, into the position of hovering above the place where the operation is being carried out. From there the earthly terrain is surveyed as if from a great height, in ascending in imagination, until the world below, as previously suggested, looks like the bottom of a great ocean. At this point the scene is transformed so that the rider shifts Worlds from the level of elements and action into the watery realm of Formation or the purely psychological World.

Continuing to rise, looking neither to left nor right, the ascent takes the rider to the top of the waters from where the light filters down into the depths from which the rider is emerging. As the surface of the great sea is broken, the vision expands to that level where a deep blue sky containing a myriad of stars shimmers overhead. Looking up from the turbulent waves, a sense of the universe is experienced with extraordinary clarity and, as the rider swims ashore, the impression of cosmic power touches the face in the form of a great but gentle wind.

On gaining the shore the rider walks upon sand that is not of the Earth, for each grain is an exquisite pearl of perfect symmetry and purity. Nor is the landscape like the terrestrial World for the rocks are composed of the clearest refined crystal. The forms of the flora to be seen are also quite unlike any earthly foliage, their colours are deeper, yet more subtle, and the texture and design of each plant quite different although strangely familiar. It is as if the plants were the archetypal essence of each species, in that their appearance is a continuous cycle of manifestation from seed to fruit so that one perceives, in their ever repeating patterns, a whole season in every moment. The same could be said of whatever creatures come into the view of the rider. They also are continuous in their composition, having not only the life span of their species played out in each instant but the greater rhythm of evolution unfolding its manifestation. These creatures, like the plants,

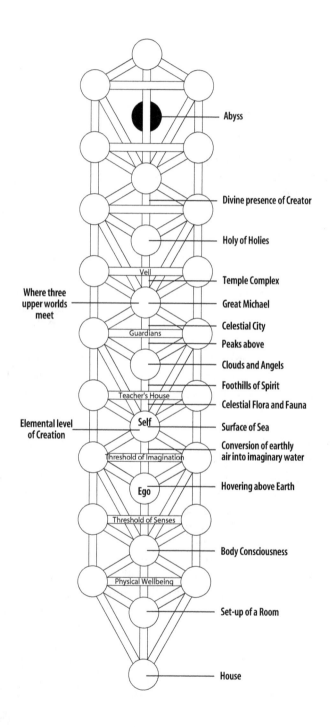

Abyss

Divine presence of Creator

Holy of Holies

Veil

Temple Complex

Where three
upper worlds
meet

Great Michael

Celestial City

Guardians

Peaks above

Clouds and Angels

Foothills of Spirit

Teacher's House

Celestial Flora and Fauna

Self

Surface of Sea

Elemental level
of Creation

Threshold of Imagination

Conversion of earthly
air into imaginary water

Ego

Hovering above Earth

Threshold of Senses

Body Consciousness

Physical Wellbeing

Set-up of a Room

House

are cosmic in scale so that the rider perceives only a fraction of their archangelic function.

Moving on, the rider, as in previous journeys, climbs the foothills of the huge mountain range that towers above the ocean. Far away on the horizon, the Holy City glitters on the crest of the tallest mountain. This distant goal has been observed each time the rider has ascended to the Beriatic shore. It is glimpsed through a gap in the high cloud that cloaks the peaks of the range. The rider notes how the clouds always part at this point, if only for a moment, to reveal the City. The rider can just make out the shimmering walls and towers before the cloud closes again. This act of Grace is encouraging for the City is where the rider hopes to go if permission is granted.

The rider proceeds up a by now well-known path. Taking care over dangerous crevices and ignoring the voices that call from gulleys to draw him aside, the rider eventually reaches the high hill upon which the Inner Teacher lives. As the gate is approached the Teacher is seen at the window waiting. The beloved and wise face smiles and nods. The door is reached and opened. The Teacher extends hands in a loving welcome. After taking some refreshment in the Teacher's study, the rider is asked to make ready. While the rider waits, he reflects upon that which is done and that which is yet to come. The front door has been left ajar, so there is still the opportunity for turning back.

Beckoning the rider to an inner room the Teacher, dressed for travel, stands before an altar and asks for safe passage to and from where they are about to go. If no omen or event occurs to deter them from departing, the Teacher then takes a staff and leads the way out of the back door of the house and up the mountain.

The first part of the journey is easy but, as height is gained, so it becomes more difficult to breathe. As the climb becomes more steep and dangerous so the Teacher's stamina and skill becomes more apparent while the rider becomes weary and unsure and has to be helped. When they have mounted the lesser peaks they look down to see an extraordinary sight; for the world below is now perceived floating

FIGURE 42 (Left)—INTERIOR JOURNEY
In this example the Kabbalist uses the art of imagination to go beyond the physical and enter the Higher Realms. This is possible because consciousness is very flexible and can use the psyche as a chariot or vehicle whereby it can ascend. The mind is filled with archetypal images, usually only seen in dreams but, in this case, directed by consciousness up the central column, through all the stages needed to gain access to the Heavenly City that exists where the three upper Worlds meet. (Halevi, 20th century.)

like a vast galaxy in space with endless depth in all directions. Turning back, the rider sees that the Teacher has gone on and is about to enter the cloudy mass that hovers overhead. The Teacher awaits the rider and then, stretching out the staff, instructs him to hold on to it no matter what happens. Going before the rider, the Teacher takes him into the cloud. The rider loses sight of the figure in front and becomes fearful as all about thunder and lightning crackle and split the misty darkness. Enormous creatures fly round them. The wind of their great wings almost tears the staff from the rider's grasp. It is only the gentle upward pull of the Teacher that enables the rider to go on through this awesome zone.

When the Teacher and rider emerge from the top of the cloud, the Celestial City is seen in all its glory. Its walls and towers sparkle like a frozen fountain that emanates light at every angle. As the couple draw near to the gates, great figures of mist with swords of fire step forward and demand identification. The Teacher speaks a Holy Name and the beings withdraw to allow them to enter the gates. The rider follows the Teacher along one of the great avenues that radiate out from the centre of the city. The streets are full of beings that are human and yet far more refined and perfect than those seen on Earth. Their faces and bodies are translucent and their eyes luminous with a profound intelligence. They are all conscious of who and what they are all the time. The awe-filled rider observes everything and takes note.

On reaching the focus of all the roads the rider sees that the Teacher has brought them to a vast Temple. It is a magnificent building constructed of variegated lights. Its substance is not of the world they are moving in. They approach its outer court and enter to be met by a company of radiant entities whose faces are strangely familiar to the rider. Famous and revered names and titles come into consciousness but the rider is not given time to identify anyone, for the second and inner court is opened to the Teacher, the rider following. They come to the sanctuary area of the Temple. There a huge angelic being stands in scintillating armour with a fierce sword of fire. The Teacher bows and presents the rider. Great Michael, Captain of Hosts, Priest of the Heavenly Jerusalem acknowledges them and the great Temple door opens into the sanctuary. The Teacher takes the rider to the entrance and indicates that he should go on alone. The rider hesitates to enter the sanctuary but his name is called and he enters and sees the Holy of Holies. It is an indescribable building of beauty, simplicity and pure light. A veil is drawn across its face. Nothing can be perceived, except an utter silence and stillness. After a moment's Grace, in which a profound sense of the Presence of the Divine is experienced, the rider's name is called again but from behind. Walking backwards, he withdraws from the sanctuary and into the inner court where the Teacher awaits. From there, the Teacher gently leads the awestruck rider out of the Temple complex. They pass once more along the great avenue thronged with shining beings to the City gates as the rider slowly enters the relative universe again. After a pause in which to reorient, they depart from the Holy City and descend into the cloud below. Having passed through this hazardous zone they come out onto the lower slopes of the mountain and make their own way down to the home of the Teacher. Here they rest and reflect on what has happened with questions and comments noted down for later consultation. The rider then takes leave of the Teacher and follows the solitary path back to the shore. Before re-entering the Sea of Yezirah there is a glance towards the Celestial City which may be revealed through the clouds. The rider then walks into the waves, quickly sinking down into its swirling depths. Holding firm against the current he approaches the bottom of the ocean and converts, by imagination, the psychological waters into terrestrial air so that he ends the journey hovering over the house where his body is. On entering the room he fuses the psyche into the elemental vehicle and terminates the operation with a prayer of thanksgiving. Coming down the Tree, the exercise is earthed by a stamping of the feet, so that the mundane is touched and connection with the physical senses re-established. After a pause the debriefing should begin and a report be written up. Later, notes should be added if any forgotten detail has not yet been included. Such personal visions should only be discussed with *Ha yode 'im*, or 'those who know' as the old chariot riders used to be called.

41. Interpretation

In order to gain a deeper comprehension of our journey to the inner Jerusalem, let us look at the exercise described in the last chapter from the point of view of kabbalistic theory and interpretation. In this way, we may begin to differentiate between the levels and their qualities.

Starting at the body, at the Malkhut or Kingdom of the psyche, we began with the first stage of the seven lower halls. Here, we became aware of the four elements before rising to the second stage of the ego to perceive the lower psyche's mood. We then shifted from the level of the ordinary sensual mind into that of the imagination, that is, we converted the Daat of the body into the Yesod of the psyche. From here, we rose out of the body up through the willing triad into the awakened state from where we viewed the world below our gaze, as if from a great height. This level is the Keter or Crown of the World of Action and Elements which is to be perceived in its physical form as the earth, the sea and the atmosphere with the light of the Sun as fire. Here we transformed the Keter of the physical world into the Tiferet of the psychological or the World of Forms.

At such a moment our normal view of the universe is changed; for example, we perceive how the physical World is much denser. Indeed, this is so much so that the atmosphere through which we are ascending is easily converted to a watery consistency, as we switch our frame of reference. Thus, by altering our state and scale, we no longer fly but swim because we ourselves have become sufficiently light to float in the fluidic World of Yezirah. As we break the surface of the atmospheric ocean we enter another dimension. Here we experience the upper levels of the World of Formation which present themselves in symbolic form as the mountains, sea, sky, and fire of another plane. If we examine the substance and dynamics of these higher elements, they will be seen to be of quite a different order to their earthly counterparts. At this point we stand where the three lower Worlds meet, that is the Keter of Asiyyah, the Tiferet of Yezirah and the Malkhut of Beriah, although we may not as yet be able to perceive all of them or be able to differentiate one from another. This takes time and much practice.

FIGURE 43–HEAVENLY JERUSALEM
This is where the most advanced human souls reside in-between incarnations.
The Messiah, or the person who holds this post at the moment, while still living
on Earth can visit the Holy City whenever required to confer with the Watchers
over humanity. This is done during a deep meditation in which an ascent puts him
or her at this place where the three upper Worlds meet. Above, as can be seen
symbolised by Light, is the higher part of the World of Spirit where the Great
Holy Council of Self-realised spirits and Metatron, alias Enoch, have their home.
(Doré's Bible Illustrations, 19th century.)

On gaining the shore our rider then saw some flora and fauna. These revealed both the pattern and dynamics that lie behind the plants and animals we see manifest in the physical World. Here we witness how the creative energy of Heaven unfolds in a multiplicity of forms to reveal the total cycle of each entity as it is seen in Paradise. We also glimpse what the Garden of Eden might be like. Every possible colour, texture and line can be observed in an ever changing scene. Everything is in motion as its potential is momentarily realised in the ebbs and flows of Yezirah. It is only on Earth that the cyclic forces and shapes are held in substance and decelerated in their rhythms to concur with the slower and gradual evolutionary process going on at the cutting edge of the universe in fully manifest matter.

Moving on, the rider then climbed the foothills to the mountain range. These represent the climb up to the place of the Inner Teacher and mark a separation from the physical realm but not before one is accosted by both friendly and hostile inhabitants of the intermediate zone. Safe in the House of the Soul, we meet and greet our mentor whilst still holding the providential sight of the Heavenly City in the heart. This is the objective of our journey, but first we must prepare to pass through the Daat-veil of the Spirit, the layer of cloud, before reaching the place where the three upper Worlds meet. While resting in the room of Self-consciousness, we pause and reflect a while. If we make use of the time the Teacher is preparing for the journey, we can look about us at the things in the room and learn something about our souls. The way the chamber is arranged and its state will tell us much. Some people find it simple, others complex. Yet others see it as very old or new whilst some are surprised to discover it ordinary, primitive or exotic. Each of these images reflect our inner world. The garb of the Teacher is extremely informative. Some mentors wear oriental clothes whilst others occult or religious raiment. This outfit is usually matched to the archetypal image associated with the self at the Tiferet of the psychological Tree. In one individual it might be a wise old person, in another a soldier or nun or even just a non-visible being. The relationship between the rider and the Teacher is very revealing as there are the various degrees of the child-parent-peer interconnections. Sometimes, for example, the face of the Teacher is often an older or younger version of oneself although it may be, at other times, someone quite different, a separate entity, if contact with one's own Tiferet is not yet established.

The inner chamber of the Teacher's home is the place where

permission and entrance into the next World is gained. This is the *Malkhut Ha Shamaim*, the Kingdom of Heaven, which opens the door into the sixth stage that lies behind the triad of the soul. Here the rider and Teacher begin the steep climb up through the spiritual peaks and into the cloudy levels where the creative and chaotic forces work amidst the cosmic weather system of the universe. Here we see the difference between the individual level of the soul, as represented by the intimacy of the Teacher's house, and the vast and transpersonal dimensions of the great mountains and their airy inhabitants who cannot be seen but only sensed as they thunder by amid the clouds. The tenacious connection of the staff between the rider and mentor in the mist is the axis of conscious attention that holds one to the path through that Daat-veiled zone. On emerging from the cloud, the seventh triad of the Yeziratic Crown, Wisdom and Understanding is reached. This is marked by the calmness of the fine air and the light emanating from the Celestial City which represents the Keter of the Psyche, the Tiferet of the Spirit and the Malkhut of the Divine. The Heavenly Jerusalem is within sight, although again its approach is not without risk for it is well protected for our own sakes.

The beings to be encountered before the City gates are the guardians of these higher thresholds and may be seen, according to one's level, as archetypes within the psyche or objective creatures protecting one from being burnt by the light of Divinity. If entrance is not granted, then one is not ready for the moment to be experienced in the Holy Temple. In the case of our vision, passage is made possible under the aegis of the Inner Teacher. Thus we enter by proxy and so glimpse symbolically the interior of the Celestial City and its inhabitants. The sights to be seen there may be only the projections of imagination but what the images portray can reveal something about the Higher Worlds. Take, for example, the layout of the avenues and the Temple. Their geometry is loaded with meaning and a great source of information for the contemplative. The construction of the Temple out of pure light, however faintly perceived, usually creates a deep awe, as the rider realises that this is the entrance to the Divine World of Emanation. Such a moment is not the stuff of dreams but of vision and leaves a deep impression upon the psyche.

After passing through the outer and inner courts, which represent the Yeziratic Keter and the Beriatic Tiferet, the sanctuary is entered, that is the Malkhut of Azilut. Here great Michael, whose name means 'Like unto God', presides as the guardian and High Priest in the

Heavenly Jerusalem. Beyond is the veil before the Holy of Holies that leads into the Divine Presence of the Creator. This is the deepest part of oneself that is accessible by vision. To go further is only possible to those who have the prerequisite of Holiness, for it involves leaving the body and this is obviously highly dangerous for the unevolved. Therefore, the veil is not drawn and we are called back by name to symbolise our limited individuality in relation to the Absolute of the Holy One. The return from the Temple to join the Teacher is to begin the descent. Here we come down from the highest level of the seven lesser halls which correspond to the fourth stage of the Spirit and the first of the Divine. Working primarily from the Yeziratic side of the experience, we catch only a flavour of these Higher Worlds in the forms presented to us but, at this phase of development, this might be more than enough.

To summarise, we left the physical World at the Self and climbed up through the psyche to the mid-point of the Spirit where we touched Eternity. Thus, on the way down, we will note a decrease of light, a loss of energy and an increase in density. What appeared before as brilliant will now seem, by contrast, dull. This is because as we descend from the City and into the clouds of the cosmos, we pass out of the serene influence of Divinity and are caught up in the great drama of manifestation in time and space. These events engulf us in the processes of becoming. We are no longer with the immortals. When we emerge out of the base of the cloud and look back, we hear the rushing of cosmic winds. This awareness can be retained even after we come down to Earth when we recognise the buffeting of Providence. The return to the home of the Teacher and our departure to the lower depths should by now be a not too infrequent venture.

Set out on Jacob's Ladder, this brief analysis will show how to place the main elements of an inner journey. Once the levels have been established, subtle refinements will emerge, on reflection, to fill in the gaps. After some practice the operation will be seen as a continuum with the details of the ascent and descent describing the interpenetration of the various levels as each phase merges into the other, according to the laws of the extended Tree. Thus if we observe closely enough, we may see how, for example, reality changes according to the level in which we centre our consciousness, as one does when shifting from a personal to an objective understanding of fate. The greater the precision of discernment, the finer the appreciation of the different Worlds, and so one becomes a better instrument to receive and impart the exchange of influences. In the next chapter we will attempt a deeper penetration but from another point of view, so as to experience, perhaps with Grace, the seven great halls of the Spirit.

42. Meditation

Up to this point we have used techniques related to the physical and psychological Worlds. These have the advantage of having substance and form to guide us on our inner journeys. What is about to be described takes the process much further, in that the Kabbalist begins to penetrate the dark glass of Daat or Knowledge where there are none of the familiar steps found in the lower World. However, because each World is based upon the same model, some notion of the spiritual realm is possible, as we theoretically climb Jacob's Ladder from the first Heaven, at the place of the Self, to the seventh Heaven in the process of meditation.

To attain such a height and depth requires either long and diligent work or an act of Grace. It cannot be obtained easily, because to exist at this altitude of the Spirit requires, as said, some kind of interior vehicle. This can only be evolved over time, although some people may incarnate with a highly developed spiritual chariot because of work done in a previous life. To possess such a refined spiritual body means that the lower half of the Beriatic organism of a person has evolved and become sufficiently stable for the paths between the Beriatic Hod and Nezah to emerge and convert the Yeziratic Daat into the Yesod of the Spirit. When this has happened, the person is said to have established a Foundation in the World of Creation.

Let us assume that our Kabbalist has worked for many years upon the body and psyche and that the balance and maturity of these two organisms is such that the spiritual body has evolved to some degree. If this is the case then it is possible for the Kabbalist to begin the practice of deep meditation. By this is meant something quite different from what has been discussed up till now. Meditation in this context means to experience directly the levels of the Heavens, to rise through the seven states of the Spirit and to come into the Divine Presence, not by the agency of an image but in intimate contact.

The procedure is begun like all other operations, although by now the Kabbalist should be able to reach an awareness of the Self, at the centre of the psychological Tree, by just remembering who he is and

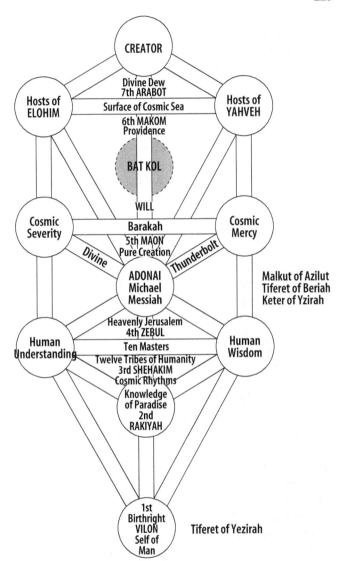

FIGURE 44—SEVEN UPPER HALLS
The lowest level in this Tree of the Spirit is the Vilon *or Veil where the three lower*
Worlds meet. It is needed to protect the undeveloped Self. To go beyond would
require a high degree of psychological balance and spiritual knowledge. There
is the story of four rabbis who entered the Halls of Heaven. One died, one went
mad and the third denied his experience as real. Only the fourth, Rabbi Akiba,
who had been well prepared, returned enlightened. This parable was a warning
to the over-ambitious. (Halevi, 20th century.)

why he is on the Earth. Indeed, the preparation should be a simple act of conscious intensification of the Gadlut state which is mindful of his inner and outer situation. However, meditation is a special occasion and so space and time is set aside for its practice. It should be begun in the usual way by deliberately bringing the body and psyche into a receptive condition.

Having reached the place of the Self, a shift should be made in which consciousness is moved from the Crown of the body and the centre sefirah of the psyche, to the Kingdom of the Spirit, that is the Malkhut of Beriah. This is the Gate of Heaven which is traditionally called the *Vilon*, or Veil. Here the stage of Devotion is entered. This means that all the power of the soul triad is concentrated into an emotional amalgam of Truth, Mercy and Justice to make the person aware of both their vices and their virtues. These are impartially reviewed and considered. All imbalances are corrected, if possible, by conscious acknowledgement and scrupulous honesty mitigated by generosity. This allows progress but holds the soul to account. When an equilibrium has been attained the Veil may then be drawn back to reveal the second Heaven which is called the Chamber of Purity. Here repentance can occur which cleanses the soul. This gives the consciousness a lucidity which may precipitate the window of the Spirit being opened through the Daat-Yesod conjunction that joins Yezirah and Beriah.

The state of purity can be described as like the clean freshness of mountain air with the scale of wide vision to match. This is where all spiritual traditions meet and no conflict over outer forms can occur. Such an objectivity leads on into the third Heaven of Sincerity. This virtue is rooted in the Beriatic sefirot of Hod, Nezah and Yesod and so constitutes the theory, practice and image of spiritual work in its true sense. Here a person operates from deep within, having the equivalent of willingness at the cosmic level. Thus, they will do whatever Providence requires, be it to live, work or even die for the sake of the Holy One. Few people can hold this level of spiritual action although many touch this plane of maturity, as it is traditionally called, in deep meditation. The dynamic calm that pulsates from this triad is the prerequisite for entering the next level.

As the meditator enters the spiritual triad of awareness it is said that they are 'with God', that is they are at the Crown of the psyche and in direct contact with Divinity in the Heavenly Jerusalem. They have come into the equivalent of the Temple complex or where the three upper Worlds meet. Here consciousness of God is no longer a remote reflection of Light but a direct coming into the radiance of Azilut. Some people actually perceive the rays of Emanation coming down into a deep inner space but this is only a psychological image of something that has no form. The shift into the meeting place of the three upper Worlds constitutes a major change in the person. In many cases, because the range of consciousness is still small, all contact with the Earth is lost. Moreover, the awareness of the psyche is diminished as individuality is reduced to a dot within cosmic space. However, the speck of 'I' responds to the Divine Presence, as the limited self within each of us experiences the SELF of the Unlimited. This takes the meditator out of the psyche and into the equivalent of the soul triad of the Spirit, that is universal Truth, Justice and Mercy. Here, we are told, we move into the triad of Holiness which means to experience a wholeness and healing of our beings. There it is possible, it is said, to perceive all we have ever been, even as the Buddha saw all his past lives in a cosmic moment.

From the place of Holiness one comes before the Azilutic sefirah of the Living Almighty and experiences the power of Divinity. This level, we are told, is where the great Archangels of the Face chorus the praises of the Holy One. Some people, we are told, actually hear their voices and even join in the universal choir that hovers in this vast Place of Sanctification, as it is called. Clearly no words can describe the ecstacy undergone in such a state and we can only guess that to touch this level is to know what it is to be blessed. People who reach this level usually say nothing about it although the shining of their faces often reveals where they have been. This extraordinary light sometimes remains for a while before fading, unless it is renewed by constant return to that level. The incident of Moses coming down the mountain with a blinding countenance is an example.

Penetration of the seventh Heaven is a rare occurrence as a conscious action, although it is said that each person at some point in his life has a flash of what it is like to be in the Presence of YAHVEH ELOHIM, the Lord God, Creator of the Universe, at the Crown of Creation. Such an experience can be obtained, according to Kabbalah, by inwardly repeating this Holy combination of Divine Names in a state of deep consciousness. This means it must only be done if a person fully realises whose Name he is calling. To reach the highest Heaven is to be at the heart of the Divine and therefore mutual Love is the key to this meeting with the Holy One. Indeed it will be noted that as each step is taken, so one is met by Divine encouragement. Some say it is like being welcomed by a beloved. The Song of Solomon describe well the yearning and union.

Anyone who comes into the *Arabot*, as the seventh Heaven is called, enters the place beyond which lies the Great Abyss. By this is meant the point where total union occurs from where no one returns because they have become one with the Godhead. Thus, unless one's work is done, there is no stepping into the highest place of Knowledge before the Three Great White Heads of the Holy Tree, for to go higher would be to meet God Face to Face and so realise the highest Name I AM THAT I AM. This can only be done when the destiny of an individual has been completed or Grace allows such a return. The seventh Heaven is the greatest height one can reach in the World of the Spirit. There, at the limit of the universe, a deep meditator must choose to go on or turn back to fulfil the Work for which they were called forth, created, formed and made.

To reach these depths in meditation requires total commitment. Moreover, one may wait perhaps for many years before achieving such a level while others might reach there by Grace in an afternoon. There is no guarantee of what can happen. Each individual has a different timing. Meanwhile, what is important is to retain what has been received during meditation, whether it be an insight into some small problem or the afterglow of the Divine Light. Some people attain the higher levels by constant persistence, others by great but short bursts of sustained effort, whilst yet others, who do little work, achieve great results because they move at the right moment and go easily through the eye of the needle at Tiferet. A useful way of seeing the process is to imagine a hollow shaft running through all the Worlds. Because of the ever-changing conditions, both within and without, the shaft is rarely in perfect alignment although occasional conditions, created by Providence, sometimes allow, like the hole in the clouds, a person to pass right up the shaft, if only for an instant. The objective is to align the axis of the shaft within ourselves and so be ready to ascend or experience the Divine Light shining down, without impediment, through all our being. Such a possibility must be prepared for during each meditation, although it may not happen very often. When it does, it is not easily forgotten, for then one knows that what seemed so far away is in fact so near that it is difficult to distinguish between I and Thou. This brings us to the moment when the relationship between mine and Thine becomes a reality and a responsibility.

43. Self

It is the aim of all mystics to know the Holy One. In Kabbalah this is a primal objective. Such an experience often places the mystic apart from the main orthodox body of opinion and custom because, having tasted the reality of the Divine, he finds it difficult to be encumbered by ritual actions, devotional forms or, indeed, even metaphysical ideas. However, while consciousness of God is possible without these modes, few mystics dispense with them because they are necessary to help comprehend and express the experience to themselves and others in their tradition. This is why Kabbalah operates within the context of Judaism, although the degree of identification with time-honoured practices varies according to period, place and individual inclination. This fact may be difficult for the conventionally-minded to accept but one must differentiate between following ancient custom for its own sake and worshipping God.

The life and work of the Kabbalist set out in this book can be practised deep within the orthodoxy or on the margin between the religious way and the method of occultism, both of which are part of the traditional Judaism as the line of *Baal Shemie*, or Masters of the Names, well illustrates. At the present time there are thousands of seekers of esoteric knowledge who hover somewhere between two apparent extremes. The difference, however, is only in the matter of method, provided the aim is the same. Thus, the unorthodox Kabbalist can have the same spiritual experience as the Hassidic rabbi because they share the same objectives as the mystics of Christianity, Islam and all the other great religious traditions. It cannot be any other way or the Universal Teaching found everywhere makes no sense and we have every reason to believe this is not so.

There can be only one pivot to every true and complete Teaching, one focus to all rituals, devotions and contemplations. There is only one reality that the mystic can contact and that is the Absolute. Now, the Name of God is known in every language spoken by the human race. It may be this and it may be that or it might not be anything that can be named. The Holy One is and is not, is remote and yet at the heart of all. This is the mystery of God.

228

FIGURE 45—SELF OF THE SELF
Every human has been called forth, created, formed and made in the image of
God, symbolised by Adam Kadmon. This primordial figure of Light, the fiery man
on Ezekiel's Throne, is portrayed here in the Hebrew Holy Name, YHVH, written
in vertical mode. Each individual is a cell of consciousness from some part of this
Divine being and will eventually return at the end of time when it is SELF- real-
ised. (Calligraphy by Halevi, 20th century.)

When the Kabbalist touches and is touched by the Divine, then it is said that he is known by name. The meaning of this is profound when you consider that a name is the acknowledgement of a particular being by themselves or others. To possess a name is to become individual, to be quite separate from others who might be quite similar to oneself. And yet this is another mystery; in this very uniqueness is an intimate solitude that can only be known by that self. This self is a spark of Divine consciousness. It is in this state of isolation because it was divided out from Adam Kadmon so that it might experience separation from the Divine and so be able to look back at its own reflection. Thus each self is a photon of Divine Light removed from its normal habitat in the World of Emanation and embodied in the lower Worlds of Creation, Formation and Action. When an individual comes to know and be known by the Holy One, then something Divine begins to manifest and this dissolves the sense of isolation that many people feel but know not why. To be known by name is the prelude to acquaintanceship, then love and eventually union.

The human self is an atom of Divinity. It is a miniature image containing in its nature the dynamics, structure and consciousness of the Divine SELF that permeates all Existence. Thus, as an individual becomes increasingly aware of the mirrored relationship between the macrocosm and the microcosm, so a human atom's consciousness expands above and below, without and within. In this way, the Divine starts to see ITSELF in ITSELF. This process of acquaintanceship is the beginning of a long and complex courtship that extends over all the Days of Creation. Gradually every level of Existence is involved and every creature takes part in the process that leads up to the Holy Marriage of God beholding God. However, as said, only mankind, wherever it appears in the universe, can encompass the totality of what is involved and even then only a few human beings at a time can climb the ladder of consciousness and file through the one place where each person realises Whose image they are.

Fortunately, such moments are not as rare as imagined for, when sufficient consciousness has been accumulated, the Divine can manifest in the most unusual settings. For instance, it has not been unknown for Divine consciousness to become present in the consciousness of an individual sitting in a room or walking down the street. There are many cases of this type of experience. Those nearby the person may not be aware of what is going on but this is because they are not conscious enough to perceive what is Self-evident. The word 'Self-evident' is used because in such an instant only the SELF can be aware of ITSELF and vice versa. This is the ultimate moment of reflection as I AM THAT I AM beholds I AM THAT I AM within the confines of the flesh, soul and spirit. Such a moment is a turning point in anyone's life. After that nothing can be seen in the same way any more.

In Kabbalah the term *Devekut,* meaning 'to cleave unto', is used to describe a state of inward holding and communion with the Divine. This condition is not reserved just for the Sabbath or for the daily cycle of ritual but is sought and performed in every moment of the day. In some traditions it is called 'to be in constant recollection'. Others call it 'Self-remembering' but we have to remind ourselves Who it is remembering WHO. Such a realisation can change our whole relationship to life and the world at large for we begin to perceive that the consciousness that looks out of and into our being is the same as that which looks down at us from the frontier of the universe and up from the edge of the atomic world. There is nowhere where God is not and yet, as the ancient rabbis noted, God is not the world which is but a reflection.

The mystery of the Immanence and Transcendence of God has puzzled many for centuries but for those who have experienced the *Shekhinah* or the Divine Presence there is no problem. I AM THAT I AM is also that which has no Name and is therefore in Kabbalah called both EN SOF, which means 'without End' and EN, which means 'Nothing'. As all these Names are but forms, they themselves are no more than ciphers for human intelligence to grasp. However, when a person moves beyond the range of the senses, the sensitivity of the psyche and the scope of the spirit, then the 'I' of the self encounters the THOU of the Holy One.

When this relationship between the Creator and the creature becomes apparent there emerges, between what is in manifestation and that which is beyond, a profound dialogue which is continuous, as long as consciousness is sought. From this conversation is established a connection that many mystics have spoken of, if only by hint, for not a few have been persecuted by the orthodox of their religion who do not know what it means to have such an experience. This is because direct experience is always a threat to a priesthood that has no real spiritual connection and is concerned only with preserving the social form of a tradition and its own status.

Generally speaking Kabbalists never speak of these matters to anyone except those who know and even then such conversations are limited, because it is not possible to describe the indescribable. It has been said that the Holy One enjoys good company and especially yearns for intercourse with human beings who are the only creatures capable of perceiving the grand design of Existence. This is because they can extend their being both below and above the level they are born into which gives them a special place and particular access to the Divine. As yet, most of the human race is insufficiently evolved to be able to recognise this possibility and therefore those who have reached the stage where they recognise their potential bear a considerable burden. They must not only seek to communicate with the Divine and assist in the unfolding of the Cosmic Plan but teach those who follow, as well as aid the millions of people who as yet do not even suspect what the universe is all about.

According to another kabbalistic tradition, the Shekhinah is in exile. This goes back to the fall of Adam and Eve who descended from a state of Grace in the Garden of Yezirah and put on coats of flesh which we acquire on being born. The Lord-God having compassion upon us, tradition says, came with mankind into exile in order to be a comfort to those who realise they are imprisoned in matter. However, the aim behind this act of Divine Love was also to assist these sparks of Adam embedded in the elemental world and help them return to what they were, even before the Garden of Eden. Thus, as an individual comes into the awareness that he or she is not alone, so a hidden radiance awakens and seeks to unite with Itself. This concealed Light illuminates everything about it, although only those with a degree of SELF-awareness may detect it. The effect of this consciousness of SELF upon the Earth is crucial because there is only a small amount of such knowledge at present on the planet. The implication of this is vast, because it reveals not only the starting point of the Earth's spiritual evolution but the reason for the third of the four journeys through Existence. Thus, having made contact with the Crown of Creation, an evolving human being must turn back down Jacob's Ladder in order to impart what has been received. This is vital for the universe for without everyone's consciousness parts of Existence will remain dark and unknown to Adam Kadmon. The Work of Unification is the concern of the Companions of the Light, whatever their earthly tradition might be. In this Labour of Love there is no differentiation, even as there is no difference between the SELF in one human being and another. All is One, say the mystics, and the One is in All.

44. Universe

When a Kabbalist looks at the world, nothing is seen as separate. The universe is one piece, like the body; it is an interlocked system of levels and aspects that make up a whole. Further, the Kabbalist perceives that the invisible part of Existence is the greater component and that this unseen dimension governs what happens in its denser and more physical realms. This is quite the reverse of how most people see the world. Modern science tends to examine the end of the chain of causes and assumes, for example, that the chemical processes in the brain determine the quality of the mind that uses it. Indeed for centuries, since the ancient world picture of a ladder of being was destroyed by the Age of Reason, the Western world has perceived the universe as a vast machine composed of elements and patterns with no explanation such as how it all might be designed by pure consciousness.

It is only in the last few decades that the notion that there is a remarkable order behind existence has re-emerged. The most advanced scientist now admits the chances of anything organising itself spontaneously into a monkey or a galaxy is very remote and that clearly, by the way the mathematics of the universe have been worked out, there is a distinct suspicion that there is a remarkable intelligence behind it. Of course, all mystical traditions have known this fact since such Work began and there are many systems in the various lines from Vedanta to Kabbalah which describe how the world began and how it will end. While this is a fascinating study in itself, perhaps more important to the mystic of today is what the situation is now.

The Kabbalist, belonging to a tradition that takes into account all the Worlds, sees the universe as several interacting levels. For example, one looks at a landscape. Let us take the view of Jerusalem from the Mount of Olives. On the face of it, it appears to be like many other Sun-bleached Middle Eastern cities. There are the hills and the buildings, the crowds and the markets, the communities and the holy places. Many artists and photographers have caught the image of it and yet, if we probe below the surface, we may perceive worlds within worlds.

Beginning at the bottom of Jacob's Ladder, the Kabbalist becomes aware of the elemental strata of the city. It is built on limestone that was formed by water millions of years ago on an ocean bed. It has moved since then from its flat, layered configuration into folds, then hills which still continue to move and shudder in the occasional earthquake. The element of water flows continually through it as rain and snow, mist and frost, to percolate and wear away its substance. Likewise, air moves over its hills and through its streets and houses, to raise dust and blow odours away as well as give breath to all the creatures that live there. Fire comes with the Sun, Moon, planets and stars to illuminate and warm every nook and cranny and so feed and nourish the living rock as well as plants, animals and human beings. These four elements interplay as rhythms in the seasons making the city cold, wet, dry and hot. Jerusalem has an elemental life that was begun with the first brick, grew with each new building, put out roots and leaves with its roads and walls, bore flowers in its palaces and fruit within its temples; all to decay and die when the final trace of the city has gone as the last brick returns to dust.

The plant and animal levels may be observed at a glance but there is more to them than may be seen in the olives and palms, the donkeys and goats that live in the city. A vast number of different species have bred and died in a great flow of life that passed through the fabric of the place. Every tree, bush, scrub and plant has its place in a long forest that has stretched through time to decorate, drop fruit, feed and shade Jerusalem. Above, below and among the ancient stones a whole world of insects, birds and animals live out their existence in exactly the same way as they did when Solomon ruled. Only human beings change and this we can see as our eyes wander over the many examples of architecture left by succeeding holders of the site.

As we enter the world of mankind there is a shift in dimension. Faint traces in the soil of the hill of Ophel reveal the work of long vanished Canaanites, as do fragments of the walls of King David's city. Houses and fortifications, now but ruins, speak of the Herodian epoch and a classic column at a street corner of the Roman period. A monk in ancient habit reminds one of Byzantium and the Dome of the Rock of the Arab conquest. The medieval church of St. Anne indicates the presence of the Crusaders and the scratched crosses in the walls the visit of pilgrims from all over Christendom. Mameluk and Ottoman Turk occupation of the city is revealed in the style of walls and windows while the brief British mandate is perceived in a cast-

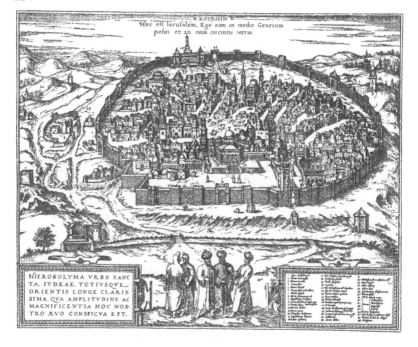

FIGURE 46—OLD CITY

Jerusalem has been in existence for over three thousand years. It contains many historic layers and every level of humanity. At its heart, on Mount Moriah beneath the Dome of the Rock where Solomon's Temple once stood, is the Eben Shatiah, *the place, it is said, where the material universe began. It was here that Abraham nearly sacrificed Isaac and where Mohammed rose up into the Heavens. To walk its streets is an important experience.* (16th century engraving.)

iron postbox. Throughout all these occupations by various conquerors, the Jewish population has retained a continuous foothold in its capital despite periodic massacres and exiles. This natural and historical aspect of the city is the lower face of the Tree of Jerusalem.

If we shift our perception once more to that of the mid part of the Yeziratic Tree, we shall see how Jerusalem is also a city of the soul. It began at the time of King David when it became the political and the religious centre of the nation. Later, exiles in ancient Babylon saw it as the Earthly focus of their spiritual home. This notion was developed after the destruction of the Second Temple and retained by Jews in the Roman and Persian Empires, the Moslem world and medieval Europe as a powerful symbol of identity. It is still held as such by Jews wherever they are. This Holy City has existed in the minds of people who have never seen it for over two millennia and, if one can see with the inner eye, it is possible to perceive a subtle structure within the fabric of the decay and restoration of present-day Jerusalem. This same charismatic city exists for Christians and Moslems, although they see their own versions of it. This is because each Faith has its own Yeziratic form with symbols and values that none of the others recognise. Indeed, even within the same tradition such divisions occur. The Armenian monk does not see the same Jerusalem as the Catholic, nor is the orthodox rabbi aware that his view of the city is quite unlike that of a Jewish tourist. Jerusalem contains many faces, each dependent on the beliefs and projections of the beholder. This is the level of the psyche or the World of Formation.

At the level of the Spirit, where there is no form, all who can operate here would perceive quite another Jerusalem. They would see it as a vortex of spiritual power into which the energy of millions of hearts and minds is focused. These currents would arise from all over the world, ebbing and flowing as the Sabbaths of Islam, Judaism and Christianity come and go each week. They would also perceive the permanent canopy of a spirituality built up over centuries of worship that hovers like a crown above the city. Such a field force of Beriatic energy acts as a great lens to catch and direct the celestial dew that falls continuously from the upper Worlds. This cleansing Grace enhances the city and makes it a holy place despite all the conflict that has occurred there, so that all that come to it sense something sacred which is greater than a nation and wider than a civilisation. It is to millions the spiritual Malkhut of the World.

To those with yet deeper vision, the Temple Mount, with its golden domed mosque set out upon the site of the Holy of Holies, has a sacred Presence. This is the trace of the Divine Light that once occupied that Place for tradition says that the Shekhinah departed from the Temple just before it was destroyed. The afterglow of the Light may be seen as a reminder of the Eternal, in contrast to the drama of the city's history. Many souls have borne witness to the Divine dimension in Jerusalem. The memory of saints, sages, prophets and Anointed Ones is still strongly felt, even though the sites of their tombs and memorials have long been replaced or decorated beyond recognition. To those aware of this level these holy human spirits are all one company, irrespective of their religion. Each carried in his or her own time a consciousness of Divinity as they strove to manifest Light amid the frequent bouts of darkness of ignorance and barbarity that possessed the city. Some were hidden and some were directly caught up in the battle between good and evil. Others were solitary and yet others deeply involved with society when religion became equated with political power. Jerusalem is a microcosm of the world and the mirror of mankind. Every human level is to be seen in its streets, from the most indolent mineral, hungry vegetable and assertive animal kind of person to those who are on various degrees of the spiritual path.

As we can see, it is possible to perceive the whole of Jacob's Ladder in Jerusalem. However, we cannot all be there and so the Kabbalist seeks to apply the same criteria to wherever he or she might be. Such an application of knowledge requires constant practice so that the vision does not fade but is continually enhanced as what is revealed is transformed into an expansion of being. In this way a quite ordinary street becomes the venue of the miraculous as things emerge about people and places in the eye of a conscious beholder. In such a moment, space and time become a kaleidoscope as the height, depth and scale of everything merges to form a vision of what has been, is now and will be. This is the insight of prophecy so often written about in kabbalistic literature. The possession of prophecy is one of the gifts of the Spirit. However, the responsibility that goes with it is not just to perceive the state of the universe and predict trends but actually to help those living in it to adjust to each situation as Creation moves on its way towards perfection. This is the carrying out of the Work at all levels.

45. Work

It is not enough to be able to see all the levels of Existence, although this would be an asset, but also to work within them. Despite its reputation of being concerned with the higher realms of the universe, Kabbalah has always been an essentially Earth-related tradition. Indeed, Kabbalah has been divided into a speculative and a practical aspect, the latter sometimes being associated with magic. This is a misunderstanding of what the Work is really about. In its original and purest form theurgy, to give it its more respectable name, was the art and science of adjusting situations from the higher realms so as to allow a process to proceed, or to create conditions wherein a situation could develop that would aid Creation at large, or an individual to evolve, and so serve God. To manipulate forces for private gain or set up relationships between elements that are out of the normative order was considered improper and, indeed, no more than bad magic. Fortunately, only those with real knowledge of such principles could perform these acts. Those dealing with natural magic were called shamans and sorcerers while those concerned with the psyche were known as magicians. Priests and high priests dealt with the Spirit. In Kabbalah, such individuals were known as *Baal Shem* although they might be at any of the levels.

Baal Shem means 'Master of the Name'. By this title was meant that a person had the ability to call upon supernatural powers. This skill enabled the practitioner to rearrange the higher flow of forms and forces in order to accomplish some purpose on Earth, according to their own will. Here is another dimension to the commandment 'Thou shalt not use My Name in vain', that is, for personal reasons. The most well-known individual to bear this title was the Baal Shem Tov, which means the 'Master of the Good Name', that is, he performed such acts only under obedience to the Divine. The Baal Shem Tov lived in 18th-century Poland where the most important miracle he performed was to heal and revitalise a deeply shattered Jewish community and give many thousands of despairing people back their faith in God, after one of the most tragic massacres of their history. This is an example of the Work of Unification on a large scale. Out of this apparently unlearned man came a major religious movement that is still very alive today. This could only occur because the Baal Shem Tov was able to bridge the Worlds and act as a channel for the Divine Radiance, so that Light could reach the mass level which had been isolated from the general stream of life by the grim shells of persecution, depression and poverty. From that time forth the simple and hard life of the Jewish peasant was converted into joy by everyday action being seen as a mode of worship and illumination of ignorance. Out of this came a completely new subculture of religious affirmation. The demonic grip of cynicism had been reversed and a whole community saved from going under in a loss of faith. Only the miraculous, working through a 'Master of the Name', could have obtained this result.

A miracle is when the laws of a higher World supersede those of a lower World. Thus, for example, human intelligence can override nature and men fly to the Moon and back. In Kabbalah the principle is simply taken further in that events are influenced from a higher and generally unrecognised dimension. Thus prophetic foresight will stimulate preparations many years ahead of the time when something is needed, like the building of the Ark for the preservation of the Teaching. In a more practical way, action taken at a higher level can open the door to possibilities denied by the usual mechanics of a situation which often repeat old patterns. An example of this is when the psychological climate of a district is altered by the spiritual charging of the atmosphere by a community of meditators. People in the vicinity start to sense a certain calm in that part of the town. Less crime occurs for instance. Sometimes it takes a long period to build up such a force field and at others times it might be achieved in a short while. This is due to the ebb and flow of Creation. Timing is one of the most crucial factors of the Work.

To understand when and when not to act is vital in Kabbalah. In order to be able to do this one has either to know the situation deeply or be able to sense when to move. Some people have an intuitive knack of knowing the moment. These we call lucky in petty matters. In the issues of history they are seen as symbols of an epoch like Napoleon or Hitler, who caught the tidal flow of their time but did not recognise its ebb and therefore were destroyed along with millions of others who followed or were caught in their wake. The Kabbalist cannot afford to make mistakes in matters of the Spirit, as did Shabbetai Zvi,

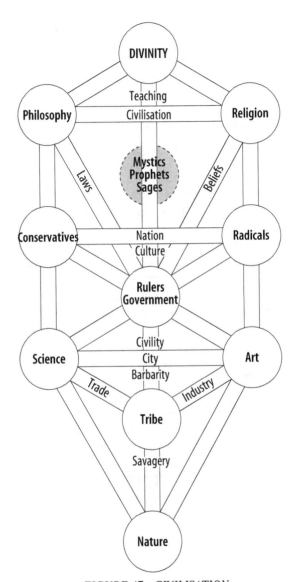

FIGURE 47—CIVILISATION
Human evolution manifests itself through the development of individuals and
communities. Here set out is the rise from savagery through tribalism to the city
which forms the basis of nations. High culture, however, comes from above
through the teachings of mystics, prophets and philosophers. They create the
conditions for a civil society in which every talent can flourish. Without religion,
law and artistic and scientific factors, the world would remain in a primitive
state with no possibility of development. (Halevi, 20th century.)

the 17th-century mystic, who with thousands believed he was the Messiah, until he was discredited at the crucial moment and so bitterly disillusioned his followers. Therefore, prior to any kabbalistic operation one contemplates all aspects of a situation before taking action, if any. This is done according to a familiar set of criteria.

Any event may be set out on the Tree because it must have its various levels in order to exist. Thus a situation has the interaction of the pillars and upper and lower faces, as well as the reactions of the different triads and sefirot that compose it. For example, if an event is waxing, then the right hand pillar is particularly active with all the processes of repetition (Nezah), expansion (Hesed) and inspiration (Hokhmah) in the initiative. If the opposite is true, then the process is the reverse. From this follows the principle of oscillation, as the Tree moves in a continually adjusting rhythm to the forces and forms at play within it. By this method the discerning Kabbalist can decide that it is not wise to move against the tide but wait for the flow to turn and place an impulse in the ebb that will bear fruit when the active phase begins again. Such operations can modify a process so as to accelerate or even stop it in its tracks, if required, as with the heroin taker whose addiction was neutralised by deep prayer which is more powerful than bodily desire. Here we see the upper face overruling the lower face, the Spirit commanding the flesh. Many of the Baal Shem Tov's miracles were of this order.

On a larger scale, the timing of miraculous events is often extraordinary in that several things happen simultaneously. This is because Providence works towards a moment where all the pillars, sefirot and triads of a situation are in near-perfect equilibrium. At such a moment the miraculous occurs apparently spontaneously in the birth of a remarkable person or an impulse that has an effect for many centuries. The Kabbalist watches for such moments on the lesser scale of his or her own life so that action can be taken in some local matter that could affect the future of a project related to the Work. This might be organising a lecture or the finding of a place for a group to meet.

FIGURE 48 (Right)—HIERARCHY
It is inevitable that, over time, those who work upon their souls and spirits will rise to a higher state than most on this Ladder. This can be achieved quickly by intense effort or, more slowly and surely, over many lives. The vast majority of people now on Earth are young souls; their leaders, in whatever field, are a little older. The more experienced elders are the lesser teachers. The most advanced Teachers do not often hold worldly positions. The Messiah of the time is usually hidden for his own protection. (Halevi, 20th century.)

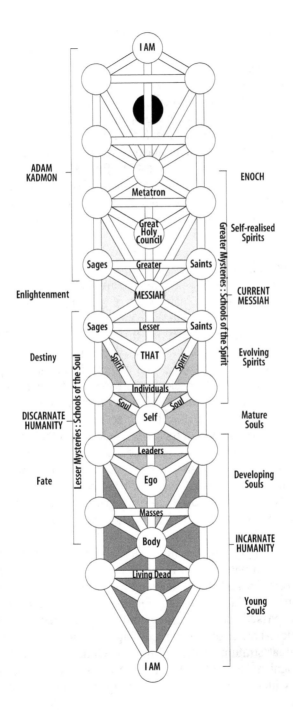

This is the day-to-day task of the Kabbalist. Larger operations, like the creation of a school of Kabbalah, require sustained effort over many years. During this time the long-term aim can be lost and the spiritual line broken due to missing critical moments. Modifications have to be made if a living esoteric tradition is to regenerate itself over the ages. An example of this is the operation that is designed to meet the need of both spiritual and secular communities, like the rule of St. Benedict upon which most monastic orders are based. These early monasteries spread out over Western Europe, bringing light and civilisation into the areas that had become barbaric after the fall of the Roman Empire. Whilst we do not live in such obviously difficult times there is still much work to be done in the world where materialism is rampant and the old forms of religion have lost much of their spirituality. Nearly every esoteric tradition has now come out into the open to meet this situation.

To provide a place where people who are seeking out a spiritual life can be taught may be the main work of a kabbalistic school. Many individuals wander about amid the conflict and confusion of ordinary existence with desperate questions that no one outside real spiritual work can answer. The priest and the rabbi will more often than not give a learned response rather than a reply from inner experience. This is not enough for the seeker who wishes to know the truth. It is vital to hear it from the mouth of someone who knows for him or herself. When the seeker makes a connection with a tradition it is the duty of the school to nourish their soul and cherish their spirit. This is done by the good company and genuine teaching given out by a reliable instructor. Thus everyone in the Work has the responsibility to look out for such people and bring them in, after they have proved that they are seriously committed to the spiritual path. In this way the line is continued from generation to generation and the knowledge of the Higher Worlds is transmitted down the ages.

Looking on a yet larger scale, a kabbalistic school is but part of a network spread around the world which not only operates in the present but forms part of a vast chain stretching back through time. As the living manifestation of Kabbalah, all Kabbalists hold to the covenant that has been passed down from Abraham who received it from Melchizedek. This tradition of receiving and imparting has created a deep spiritual stratum in the cultures of Christendom and Islam as well as Judaism. It is also the esoteric basis of the Western occult tradition which ranges from the early masons to the modern

Rosicrucians. Because of their common root, all these lines are joined in the Work although their areas of operation may be far apart. Thus communication between schools and respect for each other's way is essential to the unification process that is surging forward at the moment.

The impulse to unite and co-operate with other genuine spiritual traditions is not to be confined to those of the Melchizedek tradition but also extends to those whose Way originates in the Far East, the Far West and the southern hemisphere. If these paths come from and lead back to the same Divine Source, they are our spiritual kindred. The process of unification, however, does not mean a uniformity of mode, as past missionary movements have sought by conversion and Inquisition, but the realisation that the Divine takes pleasure in all the manifestations of the Work which may be seen like different flowers in a field. Indeed, we are led to believe that it is only in the upper realms, where form is no longer relevant, that religions lose their identity as people move closer to unity.

The Work goes on all the time and at every level. It is carried out here below by the living and simultaneously above by the Celestial Council of the Spirit. These great Beings direct the operation according to their rank and watch over mankind as it moves between the mass unconscious unfoldment of evolution and the conscious development of individuals as they take up their places in the awakened part of humanity. To realise what is being done for us is not enough. We must be deeply grateful to those who have gone before and help those in the next generation who will take our place. These in turn will aid the ones who will follow them. This is the way the Work of Unification is carried on. It is our privilege and obligation to perform it.

46. *Completion*

The Work of the Kabbalist begins and ends with the highest Name of God, I AM THAT I AM. In this Divine Name is the sum of everything that has been, is, and shall be. It defines all Existence from the coming in to the outgoing of Being. By this most Holy title the universe emerges from No-thingness into the full manifestation of matter and returns in the reflection of the Name to the One Who holds everything in Existence by the Will to be.

On the level of the individual this same Name has its profoundest meaning in that as the self becomes conscious of the SELF so the Name comes into realisation in the depths as well as the heights of Existence. Thus, the macrocosm and the microcosm meet in the individual who is a cell of Adam Kadmon. Seen from the viewpoint of our position, an incarnate human being is placed exactly midway between the Crown of Crowns and the Kingdom of Kingdoms. Thus a person centred in the Tiferet of the psyche is also at the place of Beauty on the Great Line of sefirot that runs down from the top to the bottom of Jacob's Ladder. Here, at the position where the three lower Worlds meet, a human being can hold a consciousness that has a contact with the middle face of the Five Gardens, as they are sometimes called, that span the extended Tree. This middle face has the sefirah of the Holy Spirit at its centre and the place where the three upper Worlds meet at its top. Thus, whoever holds their consciousness here has access to all the Worlds.

So far we have outlined the journey down from the Divine Adam in a state of innocence and the climb back up in the process of experience. We have also given a glimpse of how, after some training, one may become a vehicle to receive and impart what flows down from Heaven. While all this is important, the greatest effort eventually is, as stated, to be able to join all the Worlds within one's being so as to act as a liaison between the various levels. This means that one may also lift what is below to the attention of that above as well as convey the Heavenly influx consciously to a specific place below. The implication of this is enormous, for it brings up the possibility of intercession.

Intercession is the work of indirectly helping a situation. This may bring assistance from above or below. Such work requires an impeccable motive and the certainty that it is right to intervene. In this way it is possible at least to ease a situation or perhaps, at best, raise it from the mundane to the sublime and so effect a profound change, like a spontaneous healing. Most of these operations are appropriate when there is a situation that is clearly beyond the personal scope of the Kabbalist but, nevertheless, needs attention because circumstance has indicated that something should be done. It is then that the procedure of intercession is applied.

Intercession is when the Kabbalist presents a problem, such as the difficulty of another person, to the Higher Worlds so that something may perhaps be done about it from that level. This is permitted, in that Providence often brings about the circumstances so that others involved may witness or experience the intervention of Heaven. In the case of the person for whom the intercession is being made, it can be manifested in a miraculous moment or a graduated resolution as the mundane situation is eased from the Worlds above. This might take the form of some money turning up, or of someone going away which gives a respite that may be used to free or dissolve some old pattern and so allow everybody to move on. For the Kabbalist such an exercise will also be of benefit, if only to improve the contact points between Heaven and Earth as well as expand the range of possibility available at that stage of spiritual development. This is because such operations increase the scope of consciousness and refine the vehicles of body, psyche and spirit, so that they become more like the sacred robes of Aaron, the High Priest.

The symbolism of Aaron's raiment, described in such detail in Exodus, reveals what ideal an individual must slowly work towards when making these 'inner garments' by conscious effort. To hold this aim is a continuous process which begins with bringing the physical body into good health and goes on to organise and develop the psyche and spirit, which correspond to the chequered and blue vestments worn by Aaron. The golden ephod he had over the other garments represents the Divine factor with the golden plate on the turban engraved with the Name of God as the ultimate Crown. The making of these interior layers, however, was not enough in itself. There had to be, as described in Exodus, a ceremonial dedication before a priest could carry out his duties. It is the same for the Kabbalist. While formal ceremonies are performed, it is more often than not that Providence

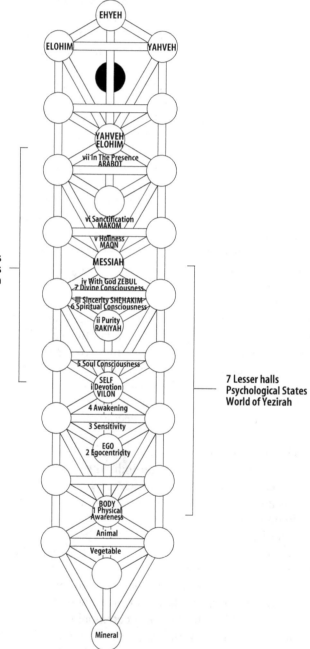

EHYEH

ELOHIM

YAHVEH

YAHVEH
ELOHIM

vii In The Presence
ARABOT

vi Sanctification
MAKOM

v Holiness
MAON

MESSIAH

iv With God ZEBUL
7 Divine Consciousness

iii Sincerity SHEHAKIM
6 Spiritual Consciousness

ii Purity
RAKIYAH

5 Soul Consciousness

SELF
i Devotion
VILON

4 Awakening

3 Sensitivity

EGO
2 Egocentricity

BODY
1 Physical
Awareness

Animal

Vegetable

Mineral

vii Greater Halls
Spiritual States
World of Beriah

7 Lesser halls
Psychological States
World of Yezirah

sets up an initiation procedure in real life situations which tests, checks and confirms one's degree of development at each stage to make sure one is ready. As each inner garment is put on, so there can be no return to the values and ways of ordinary life, although one may well be in the midst of it.

To be a true Kabbalist is to be responsible for what one does. This means that whilst one operates under obedience, nevertheless free will still operates. This can allow evil to have access for there is the possibility of temptation and corruption at every level. Thus, without seeking it, one is in the middle of the battle between demons and angels who represent the forces of order and chaos that struggle within the vast travail of Creation. To stand on the great axis of consciousness that stretches between the top and bottom of Existence is not easy because any mistake could be crucial, not only to oneself and others below but also for the beings of the upper Worlds.

The actions of a person at any level of spirituality are no less effective in the Heavens than they are on Earth. This is because the power focused in such an individual is greater on being grounded in the World of Action than any ethereal creature which is limited to its own level. The potency of human will is more than we ever imagine because we, unlike animals and angels who dwell below and above, are potentially universal creatures. No other entity has this capacity for unity for only the species of mankind is made in the complete Image of the Divine. All other beings are facets of this Image, that is, they can only operate within a limited context so that, however powerful or skilful they may be at one level, they are ineffective or cannot function at another. As one rabbi said, 'Consider a shark out of its element or an angel confronted with a machine. Neither would know what to do.' All other creatures, we are told, are incomplete aspects of Adam Kadmon. Every non-human type of life, above and below, is modelled on a particular attribute of the Divine Image. Thus each creature is a highly specialised faculty, with this animal expressing the nose and that one the sight, whilst different angels reflect such

FIGURE 49 (Left)—PATH
This is the great journey all will take after descending from Adam Kadmon to the Treasure House of Souls before being incarnated. This is the first journey. The second journey starts by ascending through the process of reincarnation and development. The third journey is when the individual has learned enough to be able to instruct others. The fourth and final journey is when, at the end of Time, all will return to the level of Adam Kadmon, prior to a reunion with the Absolute. (Halevi, 20th century.)

principles as memory or death. Only a human being has all the aspects of Adam Kadmon and the ability to experience them. However, perhaps the most important possession given to mankind is free will, which is unique to us alone.

The gift of free will is greatly misunderstood for while most people believe they have it they seldom use it, preferring to be carried by habit and circumstance until fate confronts them with choice. When the option of true individuality is taken up, there is an awakening of the soul which allows people not only to act independently but to be responsible for their own lives. If they come under spiritual discipline, then greater responsibilities are acquired. At the midpoint of development everyone stands upon the pivot of the inner and outer Worlds. This is the kabbalistic meaning of 'A righteous man is the foundation of the universe'. To be in this position opens up the implication of the Biblical expression, 'The Son of Man', for here is where the relationship between the individual and Adam Kadmon starts to operate.

Between the place of the self, where the three lower Worlds meet, and the place where the three upper Worlds meet is the sefirah of the Holy Spirit. From here the Sacred Voice instructs the self and brings it up to that mysterious position on the Ladder where the Messiah or the Anointed One resides at the place where the psyche, the Spirit and the Divine can mingle. Much has been said over the centuries about this enigmatic personage. I will repeat what I have learned; and that is that this being is the one perfect human incarnation of any moment in time. Thus, whilst the role is constant, the person filling it may change from instant to instant, as individuals on Earth reach this flowering of embodied realisation. As such they hold this role only as long as is needed so that whoever fills this position may complete their Earthly destiny. While most of these Anointed ones are unknown they are, nevertheless, the connection between all the Worlds and the Divine. Thus, according to this understanding there is a Messiah for every moment and generation. There always has been, is, and shall be as long as Mankind exists.

Beyond the Son of Man, who is at this point the Way, the Truth and the Light, lies the radiance of the Living Almighty Who sits above the Great Heavenly Council that governs the universe. Hence the perfected individual ascends on the penultimate stage of the fourth and last journey, to stand among the Holy Spirits of the Face before entering into the Presence of YAHVEH-ELOHIM at the Keter of Creation.

Here, we are told, the Divine atom that has been separated from Adam Kadmon since leaving the World of Emanation speaks the highest Holy Name I AM THAT I AM in the full consciousness of its meaning. This act begins the final process of becoming united with the ONE at the Crown of Crowns. In this union the last vestige of separation dissolves and individuality disappears into the Divine Abyss of Holy Bliss, before passing out of all Existence and into God.

Until that time we on Earth must carry out the task assigned to us, living out each day as a witness to the Name of Names. In this way we fulfil our fate and so move another link in the chain of our destiny. When our task is finished, then we too shall return with the realisation of where we have come from, who we are and where we are going. When this is done the Work of the Kabbalist will be complete.

ADONAI ECHAD: THE LORD IS ONE

Glossary of Terms

Arabot:	Seventh Heaven
Asiyyah:	World of Making. Elemental and natural world.
Ayin:	The No-Thing-ness of God.
Azilut:	World of Emanation; the sefirotic realm and Glory. Adam Kadmon.
Barakah:	Blessing or Grace.
Beriah:	World of Creation and Pure Spirit. World of Archangels.
Binah:	Sefirah of Understanding. Sometimes called Reason.
Daat:	Sefirah of Knowledge.
Devekut:	Communion.
En Sof:	The Infinite or Endless. A Title of God.
Gadlut:	The major conscious state.
Gevurah:	Sefirah of Judgement.
Gilgulim:	Cycle of rebirth. Transmigration of souls.
Hesed:	Sefirah of Mercy.
Hod:	Sefirah of Reverberation, Resounding Splendour.
Hokhmah:	Sefirah of Wisdom and Revelation.
Katnut:	The lesser conscious state.
Kavvanah:	Prayer with conscious intent; plural Kavvanot or special prayers.
Kellippot:	World of Shells and demons.
Keter:	Sefirah of the Crown.
Malkhut:	Sefirah of the Kingdom.
Merkabah:	The Chariot of Yezirah.
Nefesh:	Animal or vital Soul.
Neshamah:	Human Soul.
Nezah:	Sefirah of Eternity.
Ruah:	Spirit.
Sefirah:	Containers, Lights and Attributes of God; plural Sefirot.
Shekhinah:	Indwelling Presence of God in Malkhut of Azilut.
Shemittah:	Great cosmic cycle.

Teshuvah:	Repentance, redemption and conversion.
Talmud:	Recorded commentaries on the Bible and Oral Tradition.
Tiferet:	Sefirah of Beauty.
Yesod:	Sefirah of Foundation.
Yezirah:	World of Formation. Psychological and angelic World.
Zadek:	A just man.
Zelem:	Image.
Zimzum:	Principle of Divine contraction before Universe comes into being.

Index